Pretext for Mass Murder

NEW PERSPECTIVES IN
SOUTHEAST ASIAN STUDIES

Pretext for Mass Murder

The September 30th Movement and Suharto's Coup d'État in Indonesia

John Roosa

THE UNIVERSITY OF WISCONSIN PRESS

This book was published with the support of
the Center for Southeast Asian Studies and
the Anonymous Fund for the Humanities of
the University of Wisconsin-Madison.

The University of Wisconsin Press
1930 Monroe Street
Madison, Wisconsin 53711

www.wisc.edu/wisconsinpress/

3 Henrietta Street
London WC2E 8LU, England

1   3   5   4   2

Printed in the United States of America

Library of Congress Cataloging-in-Publication Data
Roosa, John.
Pretext for mass murder : the September 30th Movement
and Suharto's Coup d'état in Indonesia / John Roosa.
p.   cm. — (New perspectives in Southeast Asian studies)
Includes bibliographical references and index.
ISBN 0-299-22030-3 (cloth: alk. paper)
ISBN 0-299-22034-6 (pbk.: alk. paper)
1. Gerakan Tigapuluh September.
2. Indonesia — History — Coup d'état, 1965.
3. Partai Komunis Indonesia.
4. Indonesia — Politics and government — 1950-1966.
I. Title.   II. Title: September 30th Movement
and Suharto's Coup d'état in Indonesia.   III. Series.
DS644.32.R66   2006
959.803´6 — dc22   2006010196

To my parents

Table of Contents

	List of Illustrations	ix
	Acknowledgments	xi
	Introduction	3
1	The Incoherence of the Facts	34
2	Interpretations of the Movement	61
3	The Supardjo Document	82
4	Sjam and the Special Bureau	117
5	Aidit, the PKI, and the Movement	139
6	Suharto, the Indonesian Army, and the United States	176
7	Assembling a New Narrative	202

Appendixes

1 Some Factors That Influenced the Defeat of "the September 30th Movement" as Viewed from a Military Perspective (1966), by Brigadier General Supardjo   227

2 The Testimony of Sjam (1967)   245

Notes   261

Bibliography   305

Index   319

List of Illustrations

Maps

1 Jakarta, 1965   2
2 Merdeka Square   36
3 Halim Air Force Base and Lubang Buaya   43

Photographs and Cartoons

1 Sacred Pancasila Monument   8
2 Detail of Sacred Pancasila Monument bas-relief   9
3 Museum of PKI Treason   11
4 Detail of Sacred Pancasila Monument bas-relief   23
5 Supardjo and Ibu Supardjo, ca. 1962   87
6 Cartoon commemorating the twentieth anniversary of
   the nation   169
7 Cartoon supporting the September 30th Movement   171
8 Cartoon: "This week's film"   172
9 Anti-PKI cartoon   199

Tables and Figures

1 Army General Staff   37
2 Military and Civilian Personnel in the September 30th
   Movement   46
3 Organizational Structure of the PKI   147

Acknowledgments

I began writing about the September 30th Movement while a Rocke-
feller Foundation postdoctoral fellow at the Institute of International
Studies at the University of California–Berkeley, as part of its Commu-
nities in Contention Program in 2001–2002. I am grateful to the institute's director, Michael Watts, for providing such a lively environment
for learning. Joseph Nevins was the reader of the first formulations of
my argument. His ruthless criticisms over lunches in the cafes of Berkeley helped me realize that the brief journal article that I intended to
write about the September 30th Movement was insufficient to deal with
its complexities. His comments on later drafts greatly helped me to
think about the presentation of the argument. For their varied forms
of assistance in the Bay Area, I thank Iain Boal, Nancy Peluso, Silvia
Tiwon, Jeff Hadler, Hala Nassar, Mizue Aizeki, and Mary Letterii.

An audience at the Center for Southeast Asian Studies at the University of Wisconsin–Madison in late 2001 heard an early, unrefined
version of the argument in this book. I thank those who attended the
talk for their thoughtful comments. I thank Alfred McCoy, who taught
me years ago how to study militaries and coups d'état, for inviting me to
give the talk and encouraging me to write this book.

After putting aside the manuscript for two years so that I could finish my work relating to the experiences of the victims of the 1965–66
mass violence in Indonesia, I returned to it in early 2004 while at the
University of British Columbia. I thank my colleagues in the history
department, Steven Lee for commenting on a draft of the entire book
and Erik Kwakkel for help with Dutch terms. I thank Brad Simpson of
the University of Maryland, who shared his expertise on U.S. government records pertaining to Indonesia, and David Webster, a recent
Ph.D. graduate of the University of British Columbia, who shared his
expertise on Canadian government records.

I am deeply indebted to two anonymous reviewers who were gener-
ous in their praise even after spending what must have been many hours
correcting the inordinate number of errors in the manuscript and arguing against some of its claims. I hope their patience in writing such

xi

detailed, critical commentaries has been rewarded with the revisions they will find here.

Since early 2000, I have been researching the events of 1965–66 with a group of Indonesian scholars associated with Jaringan Kerja Budaya in Jakarta. This book has grown out of our joint research and our establishment of the Indonesian Institute of Social History. Extending a thank you to the following people would be inappropriate since this book is partly their own: Hilmar Farid, Agung Putri, Razif, Muhammad Fauzi, Rinto Tri Hasworo, Andre Liem, Grace Leksana, Th. J. Erlijna, Yayan Wiludiharto, Alit Ambara, B. I. Purwantari, and Pitono Adhi. The masters of the menagerie at Garuda—Dolorosa Sinaga and Arjuna Hutagalung—have provided office space for our research and open green space in the middle of a crowded megalopolis for our relaxation. Johan Abe and Mariatun have been of unstinting assistance.

My companion for the past twelve years, Ayu Ratih, has guided my writing on Indonesian history while ensuring that history writing is only one part of an active life inextricably bound up with the lives of many other people. I have been fortunate in being so close to a paragon of a warm-hearted, critical engagement with the world.

Pretext for Mass Murder

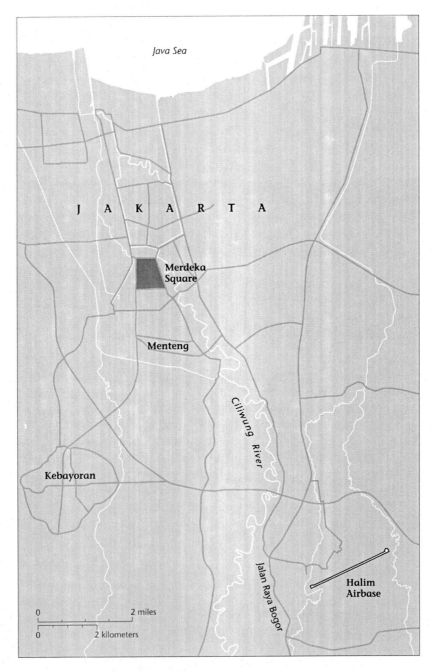

Java Sea

J A K A R T A

Merdeka
Square

Menteng

Ciliwung River

Kebayoran

Jalan Raya Bogor

Halim
Airbase

0   2 miles

0   2 kilometers

Map 1. Jakarta, 1965.

Introduction

The truth about the usurpation must not be made apparent; it came about originally without reason and has become reasonable. We must see that it is regarded as authentic and eternal, and its origins must be hidden if we do not want it soon to end.

Blaise Pascal, *Pensées* (1670)

For historians who have tried to make sense of the course of modern Indonesian history, a matter of some frustration is that the most enigmatic episode happens to be one of the most significant. In the early morning hours of October 1, 1965, the commander of the army, Lieutenant General Achmad Yani, and five generals on his staff were kidnapped from their homes in Jakarta and trucked to a desolate grove south of the city. The abductors killed Yani and two other generals in the course of capturing them. Back at the grove sometime later that morning, the abductors executed the three remaining generals and dumped all six corpses down a well. A lieutenant, grabbed by mistake from the home of a seventh general, suffered the same watery subterranean end. The people behind these killings also seized the national radio station that morning and identified themselves over the air as troops loyal to President Sukarno.[1] Their stated aim was to protect the president from a clique of right-wing army generals who were plotting a coup d'état. The abductors revealed the name of their leader, Lieutenant Colonel Untung, commander of an army battalion responsible for guarding the president, and the name of their group: the September 30th Movement (referred to hereafter as "the movement"). In a show of force hundreds of the movement's soldiers occupied the central square of the capital city. Later in the afternoon and during the evening of October 1, as if responding to a signal from Jakarta, troops in the province of Central Java kidnapped five of their commanding officers.

Part of the difficulty in understanding the movement lies in its defeat, which occurred before most Indonesians knew it existed. It collapsed just as suddenly as it had erupted. In the absence of Yani, Major

3

General Suharto took command of the army during the morning of October 1 and launched a counterattack that evening. The movement's troops abandoned the radio station and the central square only twelve hours after occupying them. All the rebel troops were either captured or sent fleeing from Jakarta by the morning of October 2. In Central Java the movement did not last beyond October 3. It evaporated before its members could clearly explain its aims to the public. The movement's leaders did not even have the chance to hold a press conference and pose for photographers.

Despite its brief lifespan, the movement had epochal effects. It marked the beginning of the end of Sukarno's presidency and the rise to power of Suharto. At the time Sukarno had been the single most important national leader for more than two decades, from the time he and a fellow nationalist, Mohammad Hatta, had proclaimed Indonesia's independence in 1945. Sukarno had been the nation-state's only president. With his charisma, eloquence, and passionate patriotism, he remained widely popular amid all the postindependence political turmoil and economic mismanagement. By 1965 his hold on the presidency was unrivaled. It is testimony to his popularity that both the movement and Major General Suharto justified their actions as means to defend him. Neither side dared appear disloyal to the president.

Suharto used the movement as a pretext for delegitimizing Sukarno and catapulting himself into the presidency. Suharto's incremental takeover of state power, what can be called a creeping coup d'état, was disguised as an effort to prevent a coup. If for President Sukarno the movement's action was a "ripple in the wide ocean of the [Indonesian national] Revolution," a minor affair that could be quietly resolved without any major shake-up in the power structure, for Suharto it was a tsunami of treason and evil, revealing something profoundly wrong with Sukarno's state.[2] Suharto accused the Communist Party of Indonesia (PKI) of masterminding the movement and then orchestrated the extermination of people affiliated with the party. Suharto's military rounded up more than a million and a half people. All were accused of being involved in the movement.[3] In one of the worst bloodbaths of the twentieth century, hundreds of thousands of individuals were massacred by the army and army-affiliated militias, largely in Central Java, East Java, and Bali, from late 1965 to mid 1966.[4] In the atmosphere of a national emergency Suharto gradually usurped Sukarno's authority and established himself as the de facto president (with the power to dismiss and appoint ministers) by March 1966. The movement, as the starting point of a concatenation of events leading to mass killings and a thirty-two-year dictatorship, is one of those momentous events in Indonesian history, on par with the shifts of state power that bracket it on either end: Sukarno and Hatta's declaration of independence on August 17, 1945, and Suharto's resignation on May 21, 1998.

For historians the movement has remained a mystery. The Suharto regime's official version—an attempted coup d'état by the PKI—has been unconvincing. It has been difficult to believe that a political party, consisting entirely of civilians, could command a military operation. How could civilians order military personnel to carry out their bidding? How could a well-organized party with a reputation for discipline plot such an amateurish action? Why would a communist party guided by Leninist principles of revolution be willing to plot a putsch by military troops? Why would a party that was growing in strength in aboveground politics opt for a conspiratorial action? The motivation seems absent. On the other hand, it has been difficult to believe that the movement was, as its first radio announcement claimed, "wholly internal to the army" since some PKI civilians collaborated with the military officers ostensibly leading the movement. Ever since those first few days of October 1965 the question of the mastermind has been an ongoing controversy. Did the military officers act on their own, as they claimed, and then invite, even dupe, certain PKI personnel to assist them? Or did the PKI use the military officers as instruments for its designs, as Suharto claimed? Or was there some sort of modus vivendi between the officers and the PKI?

A debate has also arisen regarding Suharto's connections to the movement. Circumstantial evidence suggests that those who designed the movement expected Suharto's support at the very least; they did not include him on the list of generals to be kidnapped and did not station troops outside his headquarters. Two officers in the movement's leadership were personal friends of his. One, Colonel Abdul Latief, claimed that he informed Suharto about the movement beforehand and gained his tacit consent. Was Suharto indeed informed beforehand? What information did the movement provide him? What was his response to this information? Did he promise support or did he go even further and help design the movement's operations? Did he deviously double-cross the movement so that he could rise to power?

Until now the only primary documents left by the movement have been the four statements broadcast over the state radio in the morning and early afternoon of October 1. These statements represented the movement's public face and naturally did not reveal its behind-the-scenes organizing and underlying intentions. After their capture the core organizers revealed little. Their testimonies at tribunals known as Extraordinary Military Courts (Mahkamah Militer Luar Biasa, abbreviated as Mahmillub) reflected the desperate exigency of refuting the charges against them rather than explaining in detail how and why the movement was organized. The accused, understandably enough, resorted to silences, lies, half-truths, and evasions to protect themselves and their colleagues or to shift blame onto other people. The prosecutors and judges were not concerned about resolving the many contradictions in their testimonies; the trials were not intended to get at the truth of the event. They were show trials. Not a single person brought before the Mahmillub was acquitted. Of the movement's five core leaders, all but one were convicted of treason, sentenced to death, and executed by firing squad, thus removing any chance that they might later emerge with new, more detailed and accurate accounts of their actions.[5]

The one member of the core group spared the firing squad, Colonel Abdul Latief, declined to explain the movement in detail. When he was finally put on trial in 1978, after years in solitary confinement, he did not use the occasion to clarify how the movement had been organized. His defense plea became famous and widely circulated for one explosive revelation: he had informed Suharto of the action beforehand. The significance of that revelation has overshadowed Latief's failure to say anything about the movement itself. Most of his defense plea was devoted to either relatively minor quibbling about the testimony of the witnesses or autobiographical information meant to establish his credentials as a patriotic soldier. After 1978 Latief neither departed from his defense plea nor elaborated on its claims. Even after his release from prison in 1998, he did not reveal any new information.[6]

The movement has presented historians with an unsolvable mystery. The limited evidence that exists is largely unreliable. The army fabricated much of it while whipping up an anti-PKI campaign in the months after the movement, such as stories of PKI followers' dancing naked while torturing and mutilating the generals.[7] Publications sponsored by the Suharto regime relied on interrogation reports of prisoners, at least some of whom were tortured or threatened with torture. Many surviving victims of the military's terror have been too fearful to speak openly and honestly. Both the defeated (participants in the movement) and the victors (Suharto's officers) have not left trustworthy accounts.

Nearly all the personal testimonies and written records from late 1965 onward seem intended to misdirect, obfuscate, or deceive.

Because the movement and its suppression were actions clandestinely plotted by military officers, intelligence operatives, and double agents, a historian's usual sources of information—newspapers, magazines, government records, and pamphlets—are of little help. Merle Ricklefs writes in his textbook on Indonesian history that the "intricacies of the political scene" in 1965 and the "suspect nature of much of the evidence" make firm conclusions about the movement nearly impossible.[8] His fellow Australian historians, Robert Cribb and Colin Brown, note that the "precise course of events" is "shrouded in uncertainty." Around the time of the movement "rumor, half-truth and deliberate misinformation filled the air."[9] Most historians of Indonesia who have attempted to solve the mystery have admitted a lack of confidence in their proposed solutions.

The movement is a murder mystery whose solution has profound implications for Indonesia's national history. The stakes involved in the "mastermind controversy" are high. The Suharto regime justified its murderous repression of the PKI by insisting that the party had initiated and organized the movement. Although the actions on October 1 were little more than small-scale, localized mutinies by army troops and demonstrations by civilians, the Suharto regime rendered them as the start of a massive, ruthless offensive by the PKI against all non-Communist forces. The movement was supposedly the Communist Party's opening salvo for a social revolt. In constructing a legitimating ideology for his dictatorship, Suharto presented himself as the savior of the nation for defeating the movement. His regime incessantly drilled the event into the minds of the populace by every method of state propaganda: textbooks, monuments, street names, films, museums, commemorative rituals, and national holidays. The Suharto regime justified its existence by placing the movement at the center of its historical narrative and depicting the PKI as ineffably evil. The claim that the PKI organized the movement was, for the Suharto regime, not any ordinary fact; it was *the* supreme fact of history from which the very legitimacy of the regime was derived.

Under Suharto anticommunism became the state religion, complete with sacred sites, rituals, and dates. Suharto's officers turned the site of the murder of the seven army officers in Jakarta on October 1, 1965, Lubang Buaya (Crocodile Hole), into hallowed ground. The regime

1. Sacred Pancasila Monument, Lubang Buaya, Jakarta. Photo credit: John Roosa

erected a monument with seven lifesize bronze statues of the deceased officers, all standing in postures of pride and defiance. On the wall behind the statues was placed a massive sculpture of the spread-eagled Garuda, the mythical bird that Indonesia has adopted as its national symbol.

Across the monument at eye level the regime installed a long bronze bas-relief similar to the ninth-century friezes at the Buddhist pagoda Borobudur in Central Java. When visitors walk the length of the bas-relief from left to right, they view the anti-Communists' version of Indonesia's postcolonial history. From the Madiun revolt in 1948 to the September 30th Movement in 1965, the PKI appears to act as an instigator of chaos. The bas-relief presents a classic fable in which the hero (Suharto) defeats the evil villain (the PKI) and saves the nation from misrule. The scene in the very center of the bas-relief is of women garlanded with flowers and dancing naked around a man stuffing an officer's corpse down a well. These psychological warfare fabrications, full of powerful images of sex and violence, were cast in metal and

2. Detail of bas-relief on the Sacred Pancasila Monument. Female members of the Communist Party dance naked while male Communists murder army officers and dump their corpses down the Crocodile Hole. Photo credit: John Roosa

acquired the status of indubitable fact. In front of the bas-relief is inscribed the slogan "Be vigilant and self-aware so that an event like this never happens again."

The edifice, opened in 1969, was named the Sacred Pancasila Monument (Monumen Pancasila Sakti).[10] During the reign of Suharto, Pancasila, the five principles of Indonesian nationalism first enunciated by Sukarno in 1945, was elevated into the official state ideology.[11] Pancasila was imagined to be the sacred covenant of the nation and Lubang Buaya the site of its most horrific violation. Thus the monument purified the space of this violation and turned the deceased army officers into saintly martyrs. As sacred space, the monument became the site for the staging of the regime's most important rituals. Every five years all members of the parliament gathered at the monument before starting their first session to take an oath of loyalty to Pancasila. Every year on September 30 Suharto and his top officials held a ceremony at the monument to mark their abiding commitment to Pancasila.[12] Also on September 30 all television stations were required to broadcast a film commissioned by the government, *The Treason of the September 30th Movement/PKI* (1984). This painfully long four-hour film about the kidnapping and killing of the seven army officers in Jakarta became mandatory annual viewing for schoolchildren. The film began with lengthy shots of the monument accompanied by somber, foreboding drumbeats. Lubang Buaya was imprinted on the public consciousness as the place where the PKI had committed a great evil.

Next to the monument the regime built the Museum of PKI Treason (Museum Pengkhianatan PKI) in 1990. Nearly all the museum's forty-two dioramas, whose windows were placed low enough for viewing by schoolchildren on field trips, depict episodes of the PKI's alleged brutality from 1945 to 1965. What visitors learn from the museum is a simple morality lesson: the PKI was, from the moment of independence onward, antinational, antireligion, aggressive, bloodthirsty, and sadistic.[13] The museum offers no edification about communism as an ideology opposed to private property and capitalism; it offers no history of the PKI's contribution to the nationalist struggle against Dutch colonialism or of the party's nonviolent organizing of workers and peasants.[14] The scenes of violence are designed to impress upon the visitor the impossibility of the PKI's being tolerated within the national community.

For the Suharto regime October 1, 1965, revealed the truth of the PKI's traitorous, antinational character. It discredited Sukarno's

3. Museum of PKI Treason, Lubang Buaya, Jakarta. Photo credit: John Roosa

much-touted principle of Nasakom—the acronym signifying the trinity of nationalism, religion, and communism—that had legitimated the PKI as an essential component of Indonesian politics. The movement seemed to mark an "immanent break" with "instituted knowledges," to use the language of the French philosopher Alain Badiou, and "induced" subjects who would be faithful to its truth. As Badiou puts it, "To be faithful to an event is to move within the situation that this event has supplemented, by thinking . . . [of] the situation according to the 'event.'"[15] The Suharto regime presented itself as a vehicle by which Indonesians could remain faithful to the truth of the event of October 1, 1965. The truth revealed by that event was that the PKI was evil and irremediably treacherous. The Suharto regime would seem to be a kind of "truth process" if truth is defined in the way that Badiou defines it, as "a real process of a fidelity to an event"—all the officials of the state had to pledge loyalty to Pancasila and swear that they (and their relatives) were free of any association with the PKI and the movement. However, if one uses Badiou's framework to think about the movement, one finds that the movement was not "an event" in the Badiou-ian sense since it was partially fabricated ex post facto. The Suharto regime, with its psychological warfare operations, lied about the manner in which the six generals were killed (inventing stories of torture and mutilation) and the identity of the agents responsible (alleging that every member of the PKI was guilty). The movement was not like the Indonesian revolution of 1945–49, which had been the "truth-event" for Sukarno. That revolution was open and public. Millions of people participated in it (as guerrillas, couriers, nurses, financial contributors, etc.). In destroying the racist principles on which the Dutch colonial state was based, the revolution stood for universal principles of human liberation.[16] The movement, however, was a quick, small-scale, largely covert event of which the general public had little direct knowledge. Only the Suharto regime claimed to have the ability to discern the truth of the event. The regime was thus faithful to a nonevent, to a fantasy of its own making. "Fidelity to a simulacrum," Badiou writes, "mimics an actual truth process" yet reverses the universal aspirations of a genuine "truth-event." It recognizes only a particular set of people (e.g., non-Communists) as partaking of the truth of the event and produces "war and massacre" in the effort to eliminate all those thereby excluded.[17]

To the very end of the Suharto regime in 1998, Indonesian government and military officials invoked the specter of the PKI in response to any disturbance or sign of dissent. The key phrase in the regime's discourse was "the latent danger of communism."[18] Invisible agents of Formless Organizations (Organisasi Tanpa Bentuk) were constantly lurking about, ready to sabotage economic development and political order. The unfinished eradication of the PKI was, in a very real sense, the raison d'être of the Suharto regime. The original legal act under which the regime ruled Indonesia for more than thirty years was Sukarno's presidential order of October 3, 1965, authorizing Suharto to "restore order." That was an emergency order. But for Suharto the emergency never ended. The military operation established at that time, Kopkamtib (Komando Operasi Pemulihan Keamanan dan Ketertiban, Operations Command to Restore Order and Security), remained in force until the end of Suharto's regime (with a name change to Bakorstanas in 1988); it allowed military personnel to function outside and above the law in the name of ending the emergency.[19] Suharto's takeover of power accorded with the dictum of the political theorist Carl Schmitt: "The sovereign is he who decides on the exception."[20] For Suharto the movement was the exception, the break in the normal legal order that required extralegal powers to suppress; it was not just "a ripple in the wide ocean of the Indonesian Revolution" as the nominal sovereign, Sukarno, claimed.[21] Schmitt's theory, however, needs qualification to handle those cases when the sovereign decides that "the exception" should become the rule.[22] Suharto decided that the exception of October 1965 was permanent. His regime sustained the "latent threat of communism" and kept Indonesia in a constant state of emergency. As the anthropologist Ariel Heryanto has remarked, communism never died in Suharto's Indonesia.[23] The regime could not allow communism to die because it defined itself in dialectical relation with it or, to put it more precisely, the simulacrum of it.

The Movement and the United States

The movement was a significant event and not just for Indonesia. The U.S. ambassador to Indonesia in 1965, Marshall Green, opined that the movement was one of the most dangerous moments for the United States during the cold war. He interpreted it as an "attempted communist coup" that, if successful, could have turned Indonesia into a Communist state aligned with the Soviet Union and/or China. In a 1997 television interview he stated, "I think this [the movement] was a momentous event in world affairs, and I don't think that the press and the public has ever seen it that way. And I don't think I'm saying this simply because I was there at the time: I think it was true—that here was what is now the fourth largest nation in the world . . . it was about to go communist, and almost did."[24]

Suharto's attack on the Communists and usurpation of the presidency resulted in a complete reversal of U.S. fortunes in the country. Almost overnight the Indonesian government went from being a fierce voice for cold war neutrality and anti-imperialism to a quiet, compliant partner of the U.S. world order. Before the movement the U.S. embassy had sent home nearly all its personnel and shut down consulates outside Jakarta because of militant PKI-led demonstrations. President Sukarno seemed to be winking his approval of these demonstrations by failing to order sufficient police protection for the consulates. If the attacks on U.S. government facilities were not worrisome enough, workers were seizing plantations and oil wells owned by U.S. companies, and the Indonesian government was threatening to nationalize them. Some U.S. government officials were contemplating a complete rupture of diplomatic relations. It appeared that Washington might have to write off

Indonesia and consider it part of the Communist world. A high-level intelligence report prepared in early September 1965 argued that "Sukarno's Indonesia already acts in important respects like a Communist state and is more openly hostile to the U.S. than most Communist nations." The report predicted that the Indonesian government would become completely dominated by the PKI within two to three years.[25]

The loss of Indonesia would have been a very large loss for the United States, much costlier than the loss of Indochina. In postwar U.S. foreign policy Indonesia was considered the largest domino in Southeast Asia, not merely because of its demographic weight (the fifth-largest population in the world) and geographical expanse (an archipelago stretching more than three thousand miles from east to west) but also because of its abundance of natural resources. It was a particularly important source for oil, tin, and rubber. With greater investment it stood to become an even larger producer of raw materials, including gold, silver, and nickel. As the historian Gabriel Kolko has argued, the United States in the early 1950s "assigned Indonesia to Japan's economic sphere of influence"; Indonesia's oil, minerals, metals, and plantation crops would fuel the industrialization of Japan. The "primary concern" of the United States was "the security of Japan, whose access to the islands' vast resources it believed crucial to keep it safely in the U.S. camp."[26] Kolko's assessment is based on the National Security Council's 1952 policy statement titled "United States Objectives and Courses of Action with Respect to Southeast Asia." Policy makers of the Truman administration viewed the region in terms of its natural resources: "Southeast Asia, especially Malaya and Indonesia, is the principal world source of natural rubber and tin, and a producer of petroleum and other strategically important commodities." The loss of the region to the Communists (or, for that matter, to any local force that wished to restrict the exports of those natural resources) would put a strain on Japan's industrialization and would "make it extremely difficult to prevent Japan's eventual accommodation to Communism."[27] The Eisenhower administration issued a similar policy statement on Southeast Asia two years later, repeating the language of the earlier memorandum nearly word for word.[28]

Washington regarded the prospect of the Indonesian government's coming under the control of Communists as a doomsday. Holding the line against communism in Indochina was to some extent motivated by a desire to protect Indonesia. By the logic of the domino theory, the relatively nonstrategic countries of Indochina would have to be secured against communism so that the more important countries of Southeast

Asia could be isolated from its influence. In a 1965 speech Richard Nixon justified the bombing of North Vietnam as a means to safeguard Indonesia's "immense mineral potential."[29] Two years later he called Indonesia "by far the greatest prize in the Southeast Asian area"; it had "the region's richest hoard of natural resources."[30] The ground troops that started to arrive in Vietnam in March 1965 would be superfluous if the Communists won a victory in a much larger, more strategic country. A PKI takeover in Indonesia would render the intervention in Vietnam futile. U.S. troops were busy fighting at the gate while the enemy was already inside, about to occupy the palace and raid the storehouses.

In the weeks before the outbreak of the movement, policy makers in Washington were reminding themselves that the war in Vietnam should not distract their attention from the equally dire situation in Indonesia. A small group of State Department officials, meeting with Undersecretary of State George Ball in late August 1965, affirmed that Indonesia was at least as important as all of Indochina. The group also affirmed that a left-wing takeover there was imminent. According to one official who was present, William Bundy, the group believed that such a takeover would have "immense pincer effects on the position of non-communist countries of Southeast Asia."[31]

With the wisdom of hindsight Robert McNamara, the secretary of defense under presidents John F. Kennedy and Lyndon B. Johnson, has argued that the United States should have downscaled its involvement in Indochina after Suharto's annihilation of Communists in Indonesia. Once the major Southeast Asian domino was safely in the hands of the Indonesian army, U.S. policy makers should have realized that Vietnam was not as crucial as it had first seemed. The "permanent setback" of the PKI in Indonesia, he now acknowledges, "substantially reduced America's real stake in Vietnam."[32] Although McNamara, in a memorandum of 1967, cited the PKI's destruction as a reason to halt U.S. escalation of the war, he did not push for a thorough-going policy reevaluation.[33] The war had come to acquire a logic of its own, divorced from the domino theory. Despite his grasp of the implications of the Indonesian events, McNamara remained locked into a mind-set that demanded either a victory in the Vietnam War or a method of disengagement that preserved the prestige of the U.S. government. The policy makers failed to appreciate after 1965 that "fewer dominoes now existed, and they seemed much less likely to fall."[34]

While preoccupied with Indochina in 1965, Washington was nothing short of joyous as Suharto's army defeated the movement and rampaged against the Communists. Sukarno's neutrality in the cold war and the PKI's growing power within the country were ended in one fell swoop. Suharto's army did what the U.S. puppet state in South Vietnam could not accomplish despite its millions of aid dollars and thousands of U.S. troops: it finished off its country's Communist movement. Within ten days of the outbreak of the movement, the *New York Times* reporter Max Frankel already had noted that the mood in Washington had brightened; his article was headlined "U.S. Is Heartened by Red Setback in Indonesia Coup." He observed that there was "hope where only two weeks ago there was despair about the fifth most populous nation on earth, whose 103 million inhabitants on 4,000 islands possess vast but untapped resources and occupy one of the most strategic positions in Southeast Asia."[35]

As reports of the massacres arrived during the months that followed, the hope in Washington only grew. By June 1966 a leading editorial writer for the *New York Times,* James Reston, had called the "savage transformation" in Indonesia "a gleam of light in Asia."[36] A *Time* magazine cover story called Suharto's ascent "the West's best news for years in Asia."[37] Deputy Undersecretary of State Alexis Johnson believed that the "reversal of the Communist tide in the great country of Indonesia" was "an event that will probably rank along with the Vietnamese war as perhaps the most historic turning point of Asia in this decade."[38] As Noam Chomsky and Edward Herman have noted, the massacres in Indonesia represented a "benign bloodbath" and a "constructive terror" because they served U.S. foreign policy interests. While Washington adduced every human rights violation in the Soviet bloc as evidence of the iniquity of the cold war enemy, it ignored, justified, or even abetted atrocities committed by governments allied with the United States.[39]

Rethinking the Movement

The movement was thus a trigger for several events: the annihilation of the Communist Party, the army's takeover of state power, and a sharp shift in the strategic position of the United States in Southeast Asia. I was aware of this importance when I began field research in Indonesia in early 2000, yet I did not intend to write about the movement because I considered it an impenetrable mystery about which nothing new could be written. The Suharto regime's version was obviously suspect, if not entirely fraudulent, but the paucity of evidence made it difficult to counterpose an alternative version. Without any new information about the movement, one could only rehash the well-known meager set of facts and add to the already excessive amount of speculation. My research in oral history focused on the aftermath of the movement. I was concerned with the experiences of the survivors of the mass killings and arrests.[40] The movement itself appeared to be the equivalent of the John F. Kennedy assassination in U.S. history—a topic fit for those with a penchant for conspiracy theories or "deep politics."[41]

I first became convinced that something new could be said about the movement when I came across a document written by the late brigadier general M. A. Supardjo. According to the movement's radio announcements on the morning of October 1, 1965, he was one of four deputy commanders under Lieutenant Colonel Untung. I had been intrigued with Supardjo because he represented one of the many anomalies of the movement: perhaps for the first time in the history of mutinies and coups, a general played second fiddle to a colonel. Why was Lieutenant Colonel Untung the commander and Brigadier General Supardjo the deputy commander? I had, by chance, met one of Supardjo's sons at the house of a former political prisoner. I talked to the son on that occasion, and at several subsequent meetings, about how his mother and eight siblings survived their post-1965 impoverishment and stigmatization. Out of curiosity, I went to the military's archive in Jakarta to read Supardjo's statements at his military tribunal in 1967 and the evidence presented against him. There I found, near the end of the last volume of the tribunal's records, in a section marked "Items of Evidence," an analysis that he had written about the movement's failure. At first I thought that the document was a fake or that it was somehow unusable. In my reading of the scholarly literature on the movement, I did not recall its ever being mentioned. If it was authentic, surely someone would have written about it before. But, as I studied the text, I could not imagine its being anything other than what it appeared to be: Supardjo's candidly written postmortem analysis. I discovered later that General A. H. Nasution (the one general who had managed to escape the movement's morning raids) had included an excerpt from it in his multivolume autobiography.[42] Nasution did not comment on the excerpt. All these years scholars have simply overlooked the document.[43] The full document first appeared in print in 2004 (after I had completed the first draft of this book). Victor Fic included a translation of it in his book published in India.[44] The long neglect of the document has been unfortunate. Written by the person closest to the core organizers during the day of the action, it is the most revealing primary source about the movement.

Supardjo wrote it sometime in 1966 while he was still in hiding. He was not captured until January 12, 1967. It was meant to be read by people connected with the movement so that they could learn from their mistakes. As an internal document, it is more reliable than the testimonies that the participants gave before interrogators and military tribunals.

My interest in the movement grew when I met, again unexpectedly, another former military officer named on the radio as a deputy commander of the movement, Heru Atmodjo. He had been a lieutenant colonel in the air force. Atmodjo had accompanied Supardjo for much of the day of October 1, 1965, and was imprisoned with him in 1967–68. Atmodjo confirmed the authenticity of the Supardjo document. Supardjo had once given him a copy to read in prison.[45] (As Atmodjo explained, documents were routinely smuggled in and out of prison through sympathetic guards.) Atmodjo also confirmed many of the claims that Supardjo had made. I spoke with Atmodjo on numerous occasions during the course of three years and conducted four recorded interviews with him.

After reading the Supardjo document and conversing with Heru Atmodjo, I decided that a fresh analysis of the movement was needed. I began a more purposeful and systematic gathering of information. Given the nature of the topic, I had to think like a detective (as historians must on occasion). I located one former high-level member of the PKI who had extensive knowledge of the party's Special Bureau, a clandestine organization that had played a significant role in the movement. He had never spoken to any journalist or historian about his experiences. He spoke to me on the condition that I not reveal his name or any information that might identify him. He is an old man leading a quiet life in a small town and does not want to become embroiled in the controversy. I refer to him throughout the book by the pseudonym of Hasan.[46]

My colleagues and I in Indonesia interviewed four rank-and-file participants in the movement, four former high-level PKI leaders, and several other individuals who had some knowledge of the movement. One former PKI leader whom I interviewed handed me a copy of an analysis of the movement written by a friend of his, the late Siauw Giok Tjhan.[47] Before October 1965 Siauw was the leader of Baperki, a large organization of Chinese Indonesians supportive of President Sukarno.[48] Siauw, who was imprisoned for twelve years, based his analysis on his discussions and interviews with his fellow political prisoners. His analysis represents the collective wisdom among the political prisoners about the movement.

Following Suharto's downfall in May 1998, many writers took advantage of the greater press freedom to publish accounts critical of the official version of the events of 1965. The former first deputy prime minister under Sukarno, Soebandrio, imprisoned for most of Suharto's reign, published his analysis of the movement in 2001.[49] The former commander of the air force, Omar Dani, gave interviews to the press and assisted a team of writers in compiling his biography that same year.[50] In 2002 a team of writers unofficially representing the air force officer corps published a detailed account of the events at Halim Air Force Base.[51] This spate of new publications also helped to persuade me that a new, more comprehensive analysis of the movement was needed.

While Suharto's victims were publishing their accounts, the U.S. government released a volume of declassified documents pertaining to the events in Indonesia in 1965–66. The volume largely consists of the memorandums of Johnson administration officials and the cable traffic between the U.S. embassy in Jakarta and the State Department in Washington, D.C. For reasons that it did not make explicit, the State Department immediately withdrew the volume after releasing it. The withdrawal was futile because some copies had already been sent to libraries. It was also counterproductive (for the State Department) because the scent of controversy piqued public curiosity. The entire text is now available on the Web site of a Washington, D.C., research institute.[52]

I also came across two important documents in an archive in Amsterdam. Two former PKI Politburo members, Muhammad Munir and Iskandar Subekti, wrote analyses of the movement that have not been used by historians before.

Using the bits and pieces of information that I have gathered from these various sources, I have tried to determine who organized the movement, what they hoped to achieve by the specific actions they took, and why they failed so miserably. The analysis presented in this book is necessarily complicated since the tale has many twists and turns. Different individuals joined the movement with different motivations and expectations, and they possessed different levels of knowledge about the plan. As with many covert operations involving such a wide array of people and institutions, there were mistaken assumptions, miscommunications, and self-deceptions.

This book can be considered an exercise in what Robert Darnton has called "incident analysis" since it focuses on a single dramatic event and poses the typical questions of this genre: "How can we know what actually happened? What delineates fact from fiction? Where is truth to be found among competing interpretations?"[53] Darnton notes that the authors dealing with atrocities and massacres tend to sift through written documents and oral narratives to understand "what actually happened": the identity of the perpetrators, the number of fatalities, the precise chronology of events, and so on. Confronted with refractory and partial evidence, a historian is tempted to adopt the strategy of Akira Kurosawa's famous 1950 film *Rashomon* (based on the short story by Ryunosuke Akutagawa). Four individuals provide four different narrations of the same crime. The story ends without a determination as to which narration is true. One of the characters trying to figure out who was responsible for the crime tells his equally perplexed friend at the end, "Well, don't worry about it. It isn't as though men were reasonable."[54] Such a conclusion is unproblematic for a fictional story. It is difficult, however, to tell societies that "want to know the truth about the traumas of the past" that they should resign themselves to the ideas that truth is relative, the past is inscrutable, and humans are irrational.[55] Although I eschew a *Rashomon*-like ending, neither do I resort to a Sherlock Holmes- or Hercule Poirot-style ending. No one points a confident, accusing finger at the culprit, and the entire mystery of the movement is not neatly resolved. Much remains unknown or uncertain. One must grant that there may well have been still-unidentified individuals who played crucial behind-the-scenes roles. To borrow from Donald Rumsfeld's unfairly maligned epistemological comments, there must be a great many "unknown unknowns," that is, things we do not know that we do not know.[56] The ending of this book aspires only to bring us a bit further through the labyrinth, mark some dead ends, and point to the most promising paths for further research.[57]

Presentation of the Argument

This book begins with a chapter describing the movement's actions and statements of October 1, 1965, and its defeat at the hands of Major General Suharto. This chapter introduces the reader to all the oddities of the movement, the reasons why historians have viewed it as a puzzle. Its actions lacked an underlying rationale, worked at cross-purposes, and achieved very little. The radio pronouncements were inconsistent and bore little correspondence to the actions. When considered as a whole, the movement appears as a strange, irrational creature. A pattern fails to emerge even after one chronicles the events about which there is general agreement—what we can posit as facts. The movement is not classifiable as a mutiny by military troops, an attempted coup d'état, or a social rebellion. I have not written the first chapter in narrative form precisely because the events lack the coherence of plot and character required of narrative. The point is to highlight the messy anomalies of the movement, the obstacles to a smooth, straightforward narration.

The second chapter recapitulates the various ways that these anomalies have been interpreted and made to cohere into a narrative of events. The Suharto regime, with little subtlety, imposed a simple-minded narrative that rendered the PKI into a villainous puppet master that was controlling every aspect of the movement. A number of foreign scholars, more concerned with procedures of evidence and logic than state propagandists, have pointed out the weaknesses in the regime's version and have proposed alternative story lines. These scholars have claimed either that the role of the military officers involved in the movement was greater than that of the PKI or that Suharto himself was implicated in the operation.

Chapters 3 to 6 examine the new primary source material: the Supardjo document, my oral interviews with Hasan and others, internal PKI documents, recently published memoirs, and declassified U.S. government documents. I analyze each set of characters in turn: the military officers in the movement, Sjam and his Special Bureau, the PKI leader D. N. Aidit and his fellow PKI leaders, Suharto and his fellow army officers, and the U.S. government. These chapters, as reviews of the available evidence, progress according to the logic of a detective's investigation. Only in the final chapter do I construct a narrative that moves chronologically and aims to resolve many of the event's anomalies that I describe in the first chapter.

The Movement as a Pretext

In the social memory of Indonesia as shaped by the Suharto regime, the movement was an atrocity so evil that mass violence against anyone associated with it has appeared justifiable, even honorable. There was supposedly a direct cause-and-effect relationship: the repression of the PKI was a necessary response to the threat posed by the movement. Indeed, it is common in Indonesian political discourse to conflate the movement and the subsequent mass violence as if both constituted a single event; Indonesians use one term, the *September 30th Movement,* to refer to both. From the start of Suharto's offensive against the PKI, however, something has appeared amiss with this tight association between the two events. President Sukarno routinely protested in late 1965 and early 1966 that the army was "burning down the house to kill a rat."[58] The anti-PKI campaign was out of all proportion to its ostensible cause. By itself the movement was a relatively small-scale affair in Jakarta and Central Java that was finished by October 3 at the very latest. Altogether, the movement killed twelve people.[59] Suharto exaggerated its magnitude until it assumed the shape of an ongoing, nationwide conspiracy to commit mass murder. All the millions of people associated with the PKI, even illiterate peasants in remote villages, were presented as murderers collectively responsible for the movement. Every person detained by the military was accused of being "directly or indirectly involved in the September 30th Movement," to quote from the standard form given to each political prisoner upon his or her release. (Note the flexible term *indirectly*.) Two Indonesian specialists at Cornell University, Benedict Anderson and Ruth McVey, observed in early 1966 that Suharto's army began the anti-Communist campaign well after the movement had collapsed and presented no signs of re-emerging. Between the moment that the movement ended and the moment that the army's campaign of mass arrests began, *"three weeks elapsed in which no violence or trace of civil war occurred, even according to the Army itself."* The authors argued that the movement and the subsequent anti-Communist campaign "form *quite separate* political phenomena" (emphases in original).[60]

The violence of late 1965 and early 1966 should be considered the founding moment of a new regime rather than a natural response to the movement. Suharto and other high army officers used the movement as a pretext for imposing an army dictatorship on the country. They needed to create a national emergency and a sense of total chaos if they were to overturn an entire generation of nationalists and extinguish the popular ideals of President Sukarno. They knew that they were going against mainstream opinion.[61] Suharto was a relative nobody, a bland functionary who was maneuvering to displace the charismatic leader of the nation. Suharto and others in the army leadership knew they would face massive opposition if the army launched a direct, undisguised coup d'état against Sukarno. Instead of attacking the palace first, Suharto attacked the society with a thunderclap of violence and then, treading over a fearful, confused populace, effortlessly entered the palace.

Suharto, not surprisingly, disclaimed responsibility for the mass violence of 1965–66—perpetrators rarely take public credit for their crimes.[62] In official accounts the "destruction of the PKI" (*penumpasan*

4. Detail of bas-relief on the Sacred Pancasila Monument. Suharto ends the chaos, creates order, and restores women to submissiveness and domesticity. Photo credit: John Roosa

PKI) appears to have been accomplished through bloodless, administrative measures; suspects were arrested, interrogated to determine their guilt or innocence, classified into three categories (A, B, and C) according to their degree of involvement in the movement, and then imprisoned. The official accounts do not mention mass deaths.[63] In his memoir Suharto writes that his strategy was to "pursue, purge, and destroy."[64] He does not inform the reader that anyone died in the process. The state-sponsored film about the movement does not portray the mass arrests and killings. The bas-relief on the monument, in its final panel, shows Lieutenant Colonel Untung on trial in military court, as if cool-headed legal proceedings were the military's only form of response to the movement. No memorials were erected at the Sacred Pancasila Monument for the hundreds of thousands of victims. On the very rare occasions when Suharto mentioned the violence, he explained it as something originating from conflicts within civil society. He provided a brief, one-sentence causal analysis of the killings in a 1971 speech:

"Thousands fell victim in the provinces because the people acted on their own, and because of nasty prejudices between social groups that had been nurtured for years by very narrow political practices."[65] The army supposedly played no role in organizing the killings; the people did it on their own for reasons unrelated to the military's operation for crushing the movement.

Suharto's cryptic etiology of the killings is not idiosyncratic. Many Indonesians, even those otherwise critical of state propaganda, believe that the killings represented spontaneous violence from below, a wild vigilante justice that accompanied the military's admirably restrained and well-organized efforts to suppress the PKI's revolt. Lacking a sense of events in regions of the country other than their own, people who witnessed a military-organized massacre might well believe that it was anomalous. The absence of public discussion and careful study of the killings has created great uncertainty about the general pattern. When searching for answers, educated Indonesians have tended to fall back on their ingrained prejudices concerning the volatility of the masses. Middle-class Indonesians have often told me that the killings resulted from a preexisting antagonism between the PKI and other political parties. PKI members, through their militancy and cruelty, had supposedly made themselves so hated in the years before 1965 that their rivals jumped at the chance to slaughter them. The killings just seem to have happened without any one particular person or institution's being responsible. As Robert Cribb has remarked, the killings "have been treated as if they fall into an anomalous category of 'accidental' mass death."[66]

Indonesian newspapers did not report the killings. The army closed down most newspapers during the first week of October 1965 and began censoring the small number it allowed to continue publishing. The army itself published several. One searches in vain through the newspapers from late 1965 to late 1966 for even a mention of the massacres. The papers carried stories about the nonviolent methods by which the PKI was suppressed: the dismissals of alleged PKI supporters from various government bodies (such as the news agency Antara), disbanding of PKI-affiliated organizations, and student demonstrations demanding that the government ban the PKI. Newspaper editors no doubt knew about the massacres—horrific stories circulated widely by word of mouth—but they declined to publish any news about them. Instead, they filled their papers with the fictional stories of the army's psychological warfare specialists, stories that depicted the PKI as the single perpetrator of violence in the society. Even independent papers, such as *Kompas*, which later became Indonesia's newspaper of record during the Suharto years, were complicit in the army's campaign to whip up an anti-PKI hysteria.

The army kept foreign journalists on a tight leash, barring many from entering the country after October 1965 and keeping the few who managed to stay or slip through confined to Jakarta. Most of the reporting from the journalists staying in Jakarta concerned the high-level political maneuvers of President Sukarno, General Nasution, and other government officials. Polite army spokesmen assured the reporters that whatever killings were occurring represented the uncontrollable wrath of the people, not an army-organized slaughter. From the stories filtering into Jakarta, journalists guessed that the figure Sukarno announced in January 1966 for the number of dead, eighty-seven thousand, was far too low. But they were unable to begin in-depth reporting on the massacres until the army eased restrictions in March 1966. The scale of the killing became clearer as journalists traveled outside the capital. The first to conduct an investigation, Stanley Karnow of the *Washington Post*, estimated after a two week-tour through Java and Bali that half a million people had been killed. Seth King of the *New York Times* suggested in May 1966 that 300,000 dead was a moderate estimate. His *Times* colleague Seymour Topping investigated the killings a few months later and concluded that the total deaths could be even more than half a million.[67]

All three foreign correspondents reported that army personnel and anti-Communist civilian militias were committing the murders and often committing them in systematic, secretive ways. King noted that foreigners in Jakarta did not witness any violence. They noticed only that the army raided houses at night, herded suspected PKI supporters into trucks, and then drove them out of the city before dawn. King heard from one person who happened to hitch a ride in an army truck that about five thousand Jakartans abducted from their homes were detained in a prison on the city's outskirts where they were slowly starving to death. (King did not mention the thousands more starving in prisons inside Jakarta.) Karnow described one massacre in the town of Salatiga in Central Java: "At each building, an army captain read names from a list, advising them of their guilt 'in the name of the law,' though no trial was ever held. Eventually filled with 60 prisoners and piloted by a platoon of troops, the trucks drove six miles through a dark landscape of rice fields and rubber estates to a barren spot near the village of Djelok.

The neighborhood peasants had been ordered by their headman to dig a large pit the day before. The prisoners, lined up at the edge of the pit, were shot down in a matter of minutes. Some may have been buried alive." From stories such as this one, Karnow concluded that the army was organizing an ongoing, systematic slaughter in Central Java.[68]

Topping also concluded that the army was summarily executing people in Central Java but noted that the pattern of the violence was different in East Java and Bali. In those provinces the army usually incited civilians to kill instead of ordering its own personnel to do the dirty work. The army generated a climate of fear by telling people in the towns and villages that the PKI was about to go on a wild killing spree: the Communists were digging mass graves, compiling black lists of people to be executed, and stockpiling special instruments to gouge out eyeballs. Topping noted that most experienced observers of Indonesia treated these stories as mere fabrications: "There is no substantial evidence that the Communists had large supplies of weapons or were planning a mass nationwide uprising to seize total power in the near future."[69] Topping added that the army's disavowals of any responsibility for the killings were not contradicted by just his own brief investigations but also by the private statements of one of Suharto's top commanders. Major General Sumitro, the commander for the East Java division, told Topping in an interview that Suharto had issued a detailed order in November 1965 calling for the destruction of the PKI. Sumitro and his staff visited all the district army commands in East Java in December to ensure that the order was understood. Topping quoted Sumitro as admitting that "most local commanders did their utmost to kill as many cadres as possible."[70]

By mid-1966 the two main U.S. newspapers had informed the public that the Indonesian army under Major General Suharto was largely responsible for the mass murder of about half a million people and that many of the murders had been cold-blooded executions of selected detainees. Yet this information did not deter the U.S. government from warmly welcoming Suharto as the new ruler of Indonesia. Not a single official of the Johnson administration expressed outrage at the Indonesian army's gross human rights violations. Robert Kennedy deplored the silence while delivering a speech in New York City in January 1966: "We have spoken out against inhuman slaughters perpetrated by the Nazis and the Communists. But will we speak out also against the inhuman slaughter in Indonesia, where over 100,000 alleged Communists have been not perpetrators, but victims?"[71] The answer to his question, of course, turned out to be no. After all, the U.S. government helped Suharto come to power. The joy at his overthrow of Sukarno and destruction of the PKI outweighed any humanitarian considerations.

Such priorities are apparent in *Time* magazine's cover story on Suharto in July 1966. It correctly noted that the "army was responsible for much of the killing" and acknowledged that the killing "took more lives than the U.S. has lost in all wars in this century." Not shying away from gory details, the article mentioned that some suspected Communists were beheaded and some corpses dumped in the rivers. But then the article praised Suharto's new army-dominated regime for being "strictly constitutional." Suharto was quoted as saying, "Indonesia is a state based on law not on mere power."[72] Because the bloodbath was constructive in terms of U.S. foreign policy interests, *Time* could describe the perpetrators in a wholly positive light, even when this resulted in bizarre juxtapositions of decapitated heads and constitutional procedure.

Outrage at the killings was muted not just because the perpetrators were anti-Communists. Many media reports downplayed the responsibility of the army for the killings and highlighted the role of civilians. The Orientalist stereotypes about Indonesians as primitive, backward, and violent came to the fore, swamping the factual reporting about army-organized cold-blooded executions. Foreigners were led to believe that the mass killing represented a sudden, irrational, vengeful outburst of a volatile people outraged by the PKI's years of aggressive behavior. Even without detailed investigations, journalists felt confident that their presuppositions about the so-called Oriental character justified reaching definitive conclusions. At the *New York Times* the headline on one of C. L. Sulzberger's editorials read "When a Nation Runs Amok." For him, the killings were hardly surprising since they occurred in "violent Asia, where life is cheap." The bloodshed only confirmed his belief that Indonesians possessed a "strange Malay streak, that inner frenzied blood-lust which has given to other languages one of their few Malay words: *amok.*"[73]

Similarly, Don Moser's report for *Life* magazine consisted of little more than vulgar clichés about premodern and exotic Indonesians: "Nowhere but on these weird and lovely islands . . . could affairs have erupted so unpredictably, so violently, tinged not only with fanaticism but with blood-lust and something like witchcraft." The violence did not even involve the army; it came entirely from the people. The "frenzied" slaughter on Bali was "an orgy of cruelty." Everywhere was a "mass hysteria."[74] Robert Shaplen's lengthier articles in the *New Yorker* repeated the same story line about a spontaneous revolt against the PKI. Indonesians were simply primitive people whom one could hardly blame for human rights violations when they were not civilized enough to be considered mature humans. The repression of the PKI "turned into a wild and indiscriminate outpouring of vengeance based on personal feuds and on mass hysteria among people who were emotionally and psychologically ready to run amok."[75] It was unfair for what he called "the rest of the 'rational' world" to expect the Indonesians to feel that they had done anything wrong because "the Indonesians were able to explain the bloodbath, at least to their own satisfaction, in ancient terms of catharsis and the eradication of evil."[76] While resurrecting old colonial myths about the tradition-bound, mystical "natives," Shaplen uncritically retailed the Indonesian army's own version of the events of 1965–66.

Some scholars of Indonesia have remained loyal to this narrative of the slaughter as a spontaneous, vengeful reprisal against the PKI.[77] On the basis of his visits to a small town in East Java in the 1970s and 1980s, the anthropologist Clifford Geertz argued that townspeople remembered the killings as a "broken piece of history, evoked, on occasion, as an example of what politics brings."[78] In his famous essay on the cockfight in Bali, Geertz notes in passing that the violence of the cockfight shows that the massacres on an island with a world-famous reputation for social harmony were "less like a contradiction to the laws of nature"; the cockfight supposedly sublimated the society's usual tendencies toward violence.[79] Theodore Friend, a historian of Southeast Asia, asserts with great confidence that the killings represented a "vast popular irruption [*sic*]"; they began "spontaneously" without military direction and involved a violence that was "face to face" and "strangely intimate."[80]

It is remarkable that the anti-PKI violence, such a large-scale event, has been so badly misunderstood. No doubt, the participation by both military personnel and civilians in committing the killings has blurred the issue of responsibility. Nonetheless, from what little is already known, it is clear that the military bears the largest share of responsibility and the killings represented bureaucratic, planned violence more than popular, spontaneous violence. By inventing false stories about the movement and strictly controlling the media, the Suharto clique of officers created a sense among civilians that the PKI was on the warpath. If the military's propaganda specialists had not provided such deliberate provocations, the populace would not have believed that the PKI was a mortal threat because the party was passive in the aftermath of the movement.[81] The military worked hard to whip up popular anger against the PKI from early October 1965 onward. Suharto's propaganda specialists invented an acronym for the movement that associated it with the Nazis' secret police. The acronym, Gestapu, only loosely corresponded to the Indonesian words comprising the term September 30 Movement (*Gerakan Tiga Puluh September*).[82] The newspapers and radio broadcasts were full of falsities about the so-called Gestapu: the PKI had been stockpiling weapons from China, digging mass graves, compiling lists of individuals to murder, collecting special instruments for gouging out eyes, and so on.[83] The military demonized and dehumanized millions of people by setting up a chain of associations: the movement *equals* the PKI *equals* every person associated with the PKI *equals* absolute evil.

This propaganda by itself, however, was not enough to provoke civilians into committing violence. The propaganda was a necessary factor but not a sufficient one. The timing of the violence in the different provinces indicates that the arrival of the army's Special Forces (RPKAD) functioned as the trigger. I noted Anderson and McVey's observation about Central Java earlier. The violence did not begin there until the Special Forces arrived in the province's capital, Semarang, on October 17 and then fanned out into the smaller towns and villages in the days that followed.[84] It was fortunate for West Java that the Special Forces skipped over it in their haste to move into Central Java, a PKI stronghold; relatively few killings occurred in West Java despite a preexisting bitter conflict there between PKI and anti-PKI organizations.[85]

The case of Bali is revealing, especially since those who adhere to the "spontaneous violence" thesis invariably point to Bali as proof. They allege the Balinese went on a frenzied killing spree until Special Forces troops arrived in early December 1965 to stop them.[86] This argument misrepresents the actual chronology of events. Before the Special Forces troops arrived on December 7, no major killings occurred in Bali.[87] The months of October and November were tense. Anti-Communist mobs attacked and burned down the houses of PKI members. Some party members were arrested; some sought protection from the police. But no large-scale massacres occurred before December 7. All the PKI leaders in Bali were still alive when the Special Forces arrived.[88] The Special Forces themselves organized and carried out the execution of Bali's PKI leaders on December 16, 1965, in the village of Kapal.[89] Witnesses were numerous because the Special Forces had invited anti-Communist politicians in southern Bali to watch.[90] This massacre of about thirty men, including I Gde Puger, a wealthy businessman who was a financial backer of the party but not a party member, reveals that the military was encouraging civilians to kill people affiliated with the Communist Party. Given that the Special Forces initiated the killings, one has to assume that it received orders to do so from Suharto himself. The coordination between Suharto and the Special Forces was tight: he visited Bali the day after the paratroopers landed.[91]

The civilians who participated in the killings, whether in Central Java, East Java, Bali, or elsewhere, were usually members of militias who had received training from the military (either before or after October 1), along with weapons, vehicles, and assurances of impunity. They were not just ordinary civilians who acted independently from the military. While the precise dynamic of the interaction between the military and the militias varied from region to region, overall the military played the dominant role. Robert Cribb has noted that the militias did not usually last much beyond 1966; many "seem to have vanished as soon as their bloody work was done," unlike, for instance, the "autonomous militias which had emerged after 1945 to fight for independence against the Dutch" and had become a problem for the military's monopolization of armed force in the 1950s.[92] The military has routinely manufactured militias since 1965 to retain plausible deniability while committing violence against unarmed civilians.[93] There is no reason to believe the situation was very different during the 1965–66 violence itself.

A point that has often gone unnoticed is that these killings were from the start meant to be forgotten. In his book *Silencing the Past,* Michel-Ralph Trouillot notes that people "participate in history both as actors and as narrators."[94] The agents of history are simultaneously narrators of their own actions. The narrative intended by the agent may well be tied up with the action itself. In the case of the terror of 1965–66, army officers wanted the narrative of their terror to be, like their victims, nonexistent. They did not narrate their terror campaign at the time. As Trouillot notes, "Professional historians alone do not set the narrative framework into which their stories fit. Most often, someone else has already entered the scene and set the cycle of silences."[95] Suharto conceived of the killings yet ensured that he could not be proved to be the author. While the killings were occurring, he did not mention them, yet he lauded the abstract process of destroying the PKI "down to its roots."[96] His method of simultaneously concealing and praising the killings was similar to that of the perpetrators of the Rwandan genocide: "Verbally attack the victims, deny—even in the face of the clearest evidence—that any physical violence is taking place or has taken place and fudge the responsibility issue so that, although there are victims, the killers' identities remain vague and undefined, almost merging into non-existence. When talking to your supporters never claim any 'credit' for what you are actually doing but hint at the great benefits derived from the nameless thing which has been done, sharing complicity in the unspoken secret with your audience."[97]

The conclusion that I have drawn from the existing literature and from interviews with survivors, perpetrators, and witnesses is that the killings were in many cases executions of detainees. Contrary to common belief, frenzied violence by villagers was not the norm. Suharto's army usually opted for mysterious disappearances rather than exemplary public executions. The army and its militias tended to commit large-scale massacres in secret: they took captives out of prison at night, trucked them to remote locations, executed them, and then buried the corpses in unmarked mass graves or threw them into rivers.[98]

When compared with the mass killings, the movement itself appears as a minor affair. I have titled this book *A Pretext for Mass Murder* to emphasize that the real significance of the movement lies in its relationship to the event that followed it. The movement is a significant event only because Suharto and his fellow army officers decided in early October 1965 to make it significant: they fetishized the movement, that is, they assigned greater significance to the movement than it actually had. They used the movement as a pretext to legitimize their already-planned moves against the PKI and President Sukarno. Perhaps the military personnel and civilians responsible for that terror have spoken incessantly about the movement to prevent discussion of their own crimes. Perhaps they have exaggerated the evil character of the movement and the PKI to assuage their consciences. When they have acknowledged the mass killings, they have presented the movement as *the cause* of the killings, as if the deaths of hundreds of thousands and the detention of more than a million people were inevitable, proportionate, and natural responses. This has been a blaming-the-victim narrative writ large.[99]

As a pretext, the movement is analogous to the Reichstag fire that served as Hitler's excuse for a crackdown on the German Communist Party in early 1933. The Berlin police determined that the fire inside the main chamber of the German Parliament was set by a lone Dutch radical who had entered the city only ten days earlier.[100] But even before he learned of the police findings, Hitler decided that the arson was the start of a nationwide uprising by the Communist Party. Within hours of the fire set on the morning of February 27, the police began rounding up Communists. Nazi leaders claimed that the arsonist had been seen with Communist leaders before entering the building and that the party was planning to burn down more buildings, poison public kitchens, kidnap wives and children of government officials, and sabotage the electrical system and the railways. Hitler told his cabinet the day after the fire: "The psychologically correct moment for the confrontation has now arrived. There is no purpose in waiting any longer for it."[101] Tens of thousands of Communist Party members were arrested in the weeks that followed and were detained in the Nazis' first concentration camps, such as Dachau. The Reichstag fire was a convenient pretext to justify a crackdown that the virulently anti-Communist Nazis had already planned. The manufactured crisis atmosphere allowed them to pass a law that suspended many articles of the constitution and thereby deprived all Germans of civil rights.

The similarities between the movement and the Reichstag fire are numerous: the predetermined decision to attack the Communist Party, the propaganda exaggerating the dangers that the party posed, the mass detentions in concentration camps, the artificial emergency used as a moment to seize dictatorial powers. Yet the analogy is not exact. In the case of the movement, the head of the PKI was somehow involved (Aidit was at Halim Air Force Base) and some PKI personnel were participants. The Indonesian Communist Party cannot be entirely acquitted of any connection with the movement in the way that the German Communist Party can be acquitted of the Reichstag fire. Still, whatever connection the PKI had was insufficient by itself to justify violence against everyone associated with it.

Suharto accomplished his takeover of state power behind a smokescreen of legal procedures. He disguised his creeping coup as a Sukarno-endorsed, scrupulously constitutional effort to prevent a coup by the PKI. Suharto retained Sukarno as a figurehead president until March 1967, a year and a half after he had already lost effective power. Sukarno issued verbal protests, but his words had little power when the army was in control of the media from the first week of October 1965. He even lost the battle about what to call the event. To stop the media from pejoratively referring to the movement as *Gestapu*, he suggested at a cabinet meeting on October 9, 1965, that the event be called Gestok, an acronym for "the October 1 Movement" (*Gerakan Satu Oktober*).[102] The army-controlled media ignored him and persisted with *Gestapu*.

Although Sukarno realized that the army was gradually eroding his power, the president refrained from venturing a serious challenge. His reasons for playing the role that Suharto had scripted for him remain little understood. Going by Sukarno's public speeches, it appears that he was primarily worried about the dismemberment of Indonesia by what he called "imperial, colonial, and neocolonial" powers, a collection of foes he referred to by the acronym *nekolim*.[103] Sukarno feared that if he attempted to mobilize his supporters against Suharto, he would touch off an uncontrollable civil war from which the *nekolim* would benefit. In the ensuing chaos the country could wind up divided into smaller countries, with the United States, Britain, the Netherlands, and other governments carving out their own spheres of influence. Obsessed with the unity of the country, Sukarno seems to have believed that a bloodletting, no matter how loathsome, was preferable to the dissolution of Indonesia as a nation-state and the return to foreign rule. He chose to appease Suharto, allow his own authority to be eroded, and ultimately exit the palace without a fight.[104]

Even in this post-Suharto era most Indonesians do not understand the process by which he came to power. He is reviled today for his stupendous corruption and greed but not for misrepresenting the movement and organizing a pogrom. The bloody origins of his power rarely come under critical scrutiny. Most champions of the anti-Suharto reform movement (e.g., Megawati Soekarnoputri and Amien Rais) nurtured their political careers during the Suharto years and still cling to the official myths about 1965. The Sacred Pancasila Monument still stands unchanged. The official annual ceremony there is still held, albeit without the same pomp as before.[105] The post-Suharto parliament has maintained the laws forbidding public discourse about Marxism-Leninism and the participation of ex-political prisoners (and their children and grandchildren) in political parties.[106] The makers of a film about Soe Hok Gie, a youth active in the anti-PKI and anti-Sukarno demonstrations (and who later regretted his actions), had to request police permission in 2004–5 to use the PKI's hammer-and-sickle flags as props and had to agree to turn the flags over to the police for burning once the shooting was finished.[107] The Suharto regime constructed a distinct fantasy world, elements of which, especially those pertaining to the events of 1965, are proving remarkably persistent as seemingly eternal truths of the Indonesian nation. A reexamination of the regime's moment of birth, Suharto's original unreasonable usurpation (to use Pascal's terms), is long overdue.

1

The Incoherence of the Facts

> If any section of history has been painted gray on gray, it is this. Men and events appear as reverse Schlemihls, as shadows that have lost their bodies.
>
> Karl Marx, *The Eighteenth Brumaire of Louis Bonaparte* (1852)

The Morning of October 1

The September 30th Movement first made itself known by a broadcast over the national radio station on the morning of October 1, 1965. Troops loyal to the movement occupied the station and forced the announcer to read a typed document for the broadcast. Those tuning in to their radios at about 7:15 A.M. heard a ten-minute announcement that seemed to be a simple news report. Instead of writing the statement in the first person, the organizers of the movement wrote it in the third person, as though a journalist had composed it. The message twice mentioned a "statement obtained from Lieutenant Colonel Untung, the Commander of the September 30th Movement," implying this radio report was quoting from another document. This feigned third-person voice lent a more re-assuring air to the message. It seemed as if the radio reporters were still on the job and that gun-wielding troops had not burst in and interrupted their normal broadcasting. In this way, the movement's first statement did not appear to have been issued by the movement itself but rather by the radio station's news service. It was the beginning of a long series of discrepancies between appearance and reality.[1]

The only member of the movement whose name was announced in this first message was that of Lieutenant Colonel Untung. He was identified as a battalion commander of the presidential guard who wished to prevent a "counterrevolutionary coup" by a group known as the Council of Generals (Dewan Jenderal). These unnamed generals "harbored evil designs against the Republic of Indonesia and President Sukarno" and planned to "conduct a show of force on Armed Forces Day, October 5." In acting against their superior officers, the troops within the movement appeared to be motivated by a higher loyalty, that to President Sukarno, the supreme commander of the armed forces.

The message noted that the movement had already arrested "a number of generals" and would soon take wider action. There would be "actions throughout Indonesia against agents and sympathizers of the Council of Generals in the regions." The people who were to carry out such actions went unnamed. Something called an "Indonesian Revolution Council" (Dewan Revolusi) would be established in Jakarta and would exercise some sort of executive power. All "political parties, mass organizations, newspapers, and periodicals" would have to "declare their loyalty" to the Indonesian Revolution Council if they were to be allowed to continue functioning. Lower-level revolution councils would be established at each rung of the government's administrative hierarchy, from the province down to the village. The announcement promised that details about the revolution councils would be forthcoming in a later decree.

In addition to taking over the radio station and forcing the newscaster to read the statement, the movement's troops also occupied Merdeka Square, the city's main square, which was in front of the radio station.[2] Along the four sides of this expansive grass field stood many of the nation's most important centers of power: the presidential palace, army headquarters, ministry of defense, army reserves headquarters (Kostrad), and the U.S. embassy. In the middle of the field stood the 137-meter-high monument to the national struggle for independence. To the extent that the sprawling archipelago of Indonesia had a locus of political power, Merdeka Square was it. Most of the roughly one thousand soldiers in this square were from two army battalions: Battalion 454 from Central Java, and Battalion 530 from East Java. These troops were stationed on the north side of the square in front of the palace, on the west side in front of the radio station, and on the south side near the telecommunications building, which they also occupied and shut down. The telephone network in Jakarta was put out of operation.

By positioning themselves in this central square, one section of the movement's troops had made themselves visible. Much less visible was

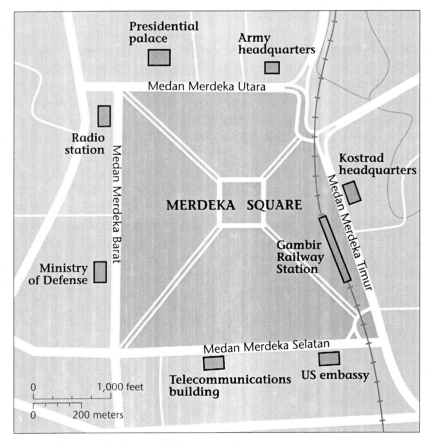

Map 2. Merdeka Square.

another contingent that was operating from Lubang Buaya, an unin-habited grove of rubber trees seven miles south of Merdeka Square. At the time of the first radio broadcast these troops had already carried out their assignment under the cover of darkness. They had congregated at Lubang Buaya during the night of September 30 and had received or-ders to kidnap seven generals thought to be members of the Council of Generals. The troops were divided into seven teams, and each team was ordered to seize a general from his home and bring him back to Lubang Buaya. The various teams boarded trucks at about 3:15 A.M. and rumbled off for the thirty- to forty-five-minute drive into the city. Most teams headed for the neighborhood of Menteng, where high-ranking govern-ment officials lived. The targets were General A. H. Nasution, the min-ister of defense; Lieutenant General Achmad Yani, the commander of

Table 1. Army General Staff as of October 1, 1965

Commander of the Army
Lt. Gen. Yani

Deputies	Assistants
1. Maj. Gen. Mursid	1. *Maj. Gen. Parman*
2. *Maj. Gen. Suprapto*	2. Maj. Gen. Gintings
3. *Maj. Gen. Harjono*	3. Maj. Gen. Pranoto
	4. *Brig. Gen. Panjaitan*
Auditor General	5. Maj. Gen. Sokowati
1. *Brig. Gen. Soetojo*	6. Brig. Gen. Sudjono
	7. Brig. Gen. Alamsjah

Source: Notosusanto and Saleh, *The Coup Attempt,* appendix B.
Note: Generals whose names appear in italics were abducted and killed by the Movement.

the army; and five generals on Yani's staff: Major General S. Parman, Major General Mas Tirtodarmo Haryono, Major General R. Suprapto, Brigadier General Soetojo Siswomihardjo, and Brigadier General Donald Ishak Panjaitan.

The troops moved through the deserted streets and descended upon sleeping houses. Six teams grabbed their targets and returned to Lubang Buaya. The seventh team, the one assigned to kidnap the most important target, General Nasution, returned with his adjutant. In the confusion of the raid the troops shot Nasution's five-year-old daughter and a security guard stationed in front of the house next door (the home of the second deputy prime minister, Johannes Leimena). Nasution was able to jump over the back wall of his compound and hide in the home of a neighbor, the Iraqi ambassador. Despite the commotion in Menteng caused by the sound of gunfire, the seven kidnapping teams were able to quickly return to Lubang Buaya without being identified or followed. By 5:30 A.M. at the latest, the movement had six generals and a lieutenant in its custody in a relatively remote and little known corner of Jakarta.[3]

Meanwhile, the movement's leaders gathered at Halim Air Force Base just north of Lubang Buaya. A courier informed them that the abducted officers had arrived. With the kidnapping operation completed, the leaders dispatched three officers—Brigadier General M. A. Supardjo, Captain Sukirno of Battalion 454, and Major Bambang Supeno of Battalion 530—to the palace to meet with President Sukarno. Supardjo, a commander of combat forces in Kalimantan along the border with Malaysia, had arrived in Jakarta only three days earlier (September

28). Sukirno and Supeno commanded the battalions stationed in Merdeka Square. Around 6 A.M. the trio boarded a jeep and headed north toward the presidential palace. With them were two other men: an air force officer, Lieutenant Colonel Heru Atmodjo, and a soldier serving as the driver.

When Supardjo and his colleagues arrived at the palace, the guards at the front entrance told them that President Sukarno was not inside. It is not clear what the three would have done had he been present.[4] At his trial in 1967 Supardjo stated that he wanted to inform Sukarno of the movement and ask him to take action against the Council of Generals.[5] The plan may have been to bring the abducted generals to the palace and demand that the president validate their arrest and order them to stand trial for treason. Or perhaps it was to take Sukarno to Halim to meet the generals there. In its first message, broadcast at about 7:15 A.M., the movement had claimed that President Sukarno was "safe under its protection." The intention must have been to provide that protection either at the palace or at Halim.

While Supardjo and the two battalion commanders were waiting for him, Sukarno was being driven back to the palace from the house of his third wife, Dewi, where he had spent the night.[6] The acting commander of the palace guard, Colonel H. Maulwi Saelan, contacted Sukarno's bodyguards by radio and asked them to avoid the palace because many unknown troops were stationed in front of it. Saelan radioed from the house of Sukarno's fourth wife, Harjati, in the neighborhood of Grogol. He had gone there earlier in search of Sukarno. On the advice of Saelan the president and his escorts headed for Harjati's house. They arrived there at about 7 A.M.[7]

The movement's inability to put Sukarno "under its protection" is strange, given that the job of its supposed commander, Lieutenant Colonel Untung, was to know the president's location. Untung commanded a battalion of the palace guard. On the night of September 30 he had been part of the security detail for Sukarno when he spoke at the National Conference of Technicians at Jakarta's Senayan stadium until about 11 P.M. Even as Untung moved over to Halim Air Force Base after the conference, he could have easily kept track of Sukarno's whereabouts by contacting other officers in the presidential guard. The task of guarding the palace at night rotated among four units; each of the four services—the army, navy, air force, and police—had a detachment seconded to the palace. On that particular night it was the turn of the army, meaning Untung and his subordinates. They should have known by about midnight that the president was not spending the night at the palace. Untung, like Saelan, certainly would have known from experience that the president often slept at the homes of his wives. With the collective knowledge of the about sixty army soldiers of the presidential guard in the movement, how could Untung not manage to keep track of Sukarno? This is an oddity that has rarely received notice: a high-ranking officer in the presidential guard, leading an action to safeguard the president, did not know his location when such knowledge was a crucial element of the plan.[8] As it was, the movement worked at cross-purposes: it placed troops in front of an empty palace at about 4 A.M., prompting Sukarno to avoid the palace and thereby ending any hope that Supardjo's mission would succeed.

Supardjo and the two battalion commanders loitered at the palace entrance. They had no means of contacting the movement's core leaders back at Halim to inform them of Sukarno's absence. They waited. In the meantime the air force officer who had accompanied them in the jeep from Halim, Lieutenant Colonel Heru Atmodjo, decided to go look for the commander of the air force, Vice Marshal Omar Dani. Air Force headquarters was not far from the palace. Atmodjo drove the jeep there and must have arrived sometime before 7:15 because he recalls that he heard the movement's first announcement over the radio there. His fellow officers at headquarters told him that Dani was at Halim air base. Atmodjo then drove the jeep back to Halim and found Dani at the main office. Atmodjo arrived between 8 and 8:30 A.M., and he reported what he had just witnessed: Supardjo had gone to the palace but had failed to find the president.[9]

Shortly before Atmodjo found him, Dani had received a telephone call from a member of Sukarno's staff, Lieutenant Colonel Soeparto, who said that the president would be leaving Harjati's house for Halim Air Force Base.[10] The president's airplane was always on standby at Halim in case he needed to leave the city in a hurry. Sukarno thought it best, at that moment of uncertainty, to be close to the airplane. As Sukarno emphasized in his later public statements, he went to Halim on his own initiative, as standard operating procedure during a crisis, without having any contact with the movement beforehand. When he and his aides decided that Halim would be the safest place, they did not know that the movement's leaders were based there.[11]

When Omar Dani heard that Sukarno would be arriving at Halim, the vice marshal ordered Atmodjo to use an air force helicopter to quickly retrieve Supardjo from the palace. Dani wanted to ensure that the representative of these rebel troops had a chance to speak with the president. Atmodjo returned to Halim with Supardjo in tow at roughly 9 A.M. and escorted Supardjo to the air base's main office. Supardjo conferred with Dani there while Atmodjo waited outside. After the two men emerged from the office, Atmodjo drove Supardjo over to the on-base residence of Sergeant Anis Sujatno, which was being used as the movement's hideout. Supardjo had directions to the house. Atmodjo claims that he did not know its location beforehand. They meandered through the streets of the air base by jeep until they found the house where the core leaders of the movement were gathered. A little while later Atmodjo drove Supardjo back to the office of the air base commander. There Supardjo was finally able to meet Sukarno, who had arrived in the meantime. Sukarno appears to have arrived in Halim sometime between 9 and 9:30 A.M.[12]

By the time Supardjo and Sukarno met face to face in the Halim commander's office at about 10 A.M., all six kidnapped army generals probably had been killed. Supardjo might have known this from the discussions he had just held with the movement's core leaders. Sukarno must have suspected that at least some of the generals had been killed. Reports were circulating by word of mouth that two generals, Yani and Panjaitan, were probably dead. Their neighbors had heard gunfire and later found blood on the floors. It is likely that Yani and Panjaitan died instantly in their homes from gunshot wounds. Another general, Haryono, probably also died in his home of a deep stab wound in the abdomen that his abductors inflicted with a bayonet. The other three generals (Parman, Suprapto, and Soetojo) and the lieutenant taken by mistake from Nasution's house (Pierre Tendean) survived their abduction, only to be killed at Lubang Buaya. A contingent of the movement's troops shot each of the four officers multiple times. To hide their victims and cover their tracks, the troops dumped all seven corpses down a thirty-six-foot well and then covered the well with rocks, dirt, and leaves.[13] Precisely who killed the officers still is not known. The Suharto regime's story—that the seven officers were tortured and mutilated by crowds of ecstatic PKI supporters, while women from Gerwani (the Indonesian Women's Movement) danced naked—was an absurd fabrication by psychological warfare experts.

In all, the movement's participants carried out four operations that morning in Jakarta. They seized the radio station and broadcast their first statement; occupied Merdeka Square, including the telecommunications building; covertly kidnapped and killed six generals and one lieutenant; and dispatched three officers to the presidential palace, one of whom, Brigadier General Supardjo, was able to meet the president back at Halim Air Force Base.

Composition of the Forces

The leadership of the movement consisted of five men. Three were military officers: Lieutenant Colonel Untung of the presidential guard, Colonel Abdul Latief of the Jakarta army garrison (Kodam Jaya), and Major Soejono of the Halim air base guard. The two civilians were Sjam and Pono, who were from a clandestine organization, the Special Bureau, which was run by the chairman of the Communist Party, D. N. Aidit. These five men had met numerous times during the previous weeks and had discussed the plan for the operation.[14]

They ranged in age from their late thirties to their midforties. Untung, stocky and thick necked, looked like a stereotype of a soldier. He had a brief moment of fame in 1962 when he commanded guerrilla forces attacking Dutch troops in West Papua (the western half of the island that also contains Papua New Guinea). From that operation he gained a medal, a promotion from major to lieutenant colonel, and a reputation for bravery. His slightly younger but higher-ranking coconspirator Latief had a distinguished military career from his days as a youth fighting the Dutch army in Central Java. Having passed officer training courses and proven himself in combat, Latief had attained a sensitive posting: he was the commander of an entire brigade of infantry troops (about two thousand men) in the capital city. He carried himself with the imperious, confident attitude of a colonel conscious of the need to earn the respect of his subordinates. At Halim air base on October 1 Untung and Latief were hosted by Soejono, who commanded the air force troops at the base. Wiry and high-strung, the major issued blunt orders to his subordinates as he arranged the hideouts, meals, and jeeps for the movement leaders. Sjam and Pono, as civilians, were the odd men at the air base. Sjam, who had gone by the name of Kamaruzaman when he was young, was a descendant of Arab traders who had settled on the north coast of Java. Pono was also from the north coast of Java but was of Javanese ancestry, as his full name, Supono Marsudidjojo, suggested. Heru Atmodjo recalls that when he first saw the two men that day at Halim, he suspected immediately that they were not military men: they slouched, put their feet on the chairs, and chain smoked. They lacked physical training and military discipline.[15] The two men, however, had years of experience in covertly contacting military personnel and disguising their identities.

On the morning of October 1, beginning at about 2 A.M., the five sat had together in a building just off the northwest corner of Halim. The building housed the office of the air force's aerial survey division, Penas (*Pemetaan Nasional*). For reasons that have never been explained, at about 9 A.M. the five shifted from this hideout to Sergeant Sujatno's small house, which was in a residential section of Halim. This was the house to which Supardjo had headed after he returned from his unsuccessful mission to meet President Sukarno at the palace. The five stayed at this house throughout the day and night of October 1. Although Untung was identified on national radio that morning as the leader of the movement, he spent the day invisible to the public and even to his own troops. In fact, the movement's leaders had no means of communicating with their troops in Lubang Buaya and Merdeka Square except by personal courier. They did not have walkie-talkies or two-way radio sets. The movement itself had shut down the telephone system when its troops occupied the telecommunications building. (Even if the phone system had been functioning, it is not likely that a sergeant's humble house on the air base would have had a telephone line.) Supardjo's shuttling by jeep between this hideout and the Halim commander's office attests to their lack of communication devices.

The leadership was in contact all that day with the PKI chairman, Aidit, who was also present at Halim Air Force Base. Aidit was staying at a different house within another residential compound on the base. Accompanying him were his personal assistant, Kusno; another PKI leader, Iskandar Subekti; and a Special Bureau member, Bono (who also went by the name Walujo).[16] The five core leaders sat at one hideout (Sujatno's house) while Aidit and his group of assistants were about a half-mile away at another hideout (the house of Sergeant Suwadi). To communicate with each other the two groups had a personal courier drive a jeep between the two hideouts carrying documents. At times one or two of the core leaders would drive over to Aidit's hideout and confer directly with him. Heru Atmodjo recalls that Sjam and Soejono occasionally consulted Aidit.[17]

The movement's five core leaders remained in Sergeant Sujatno's inconspicuous house throughout the day of October 1. They did not as a group show themselves to President Sukarno, the person they were supposedly protecting. Supardjo met the president on their behalf. Why Aidit and his assistants remained in a separate house, instead of joining

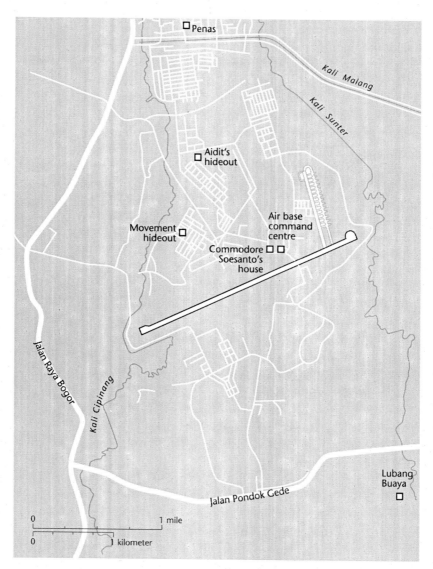

Map 3. Halim Air Force Base and Lubang Buaya. Source: Based upon map in Katoppo, *Menyingkap Kabut Halim 1965,* 314–15.

the five men of Untung's group, is unclear. Perhaps it was to ensure that if they were attacked, they would not be arrested together. Or perhaps it was to ensure that few people would see that Aidit was involved with the core group of plotters. Or perhaps it was to keep each group ignorant of the other group's decision-making process. The movement's organizers must have had some reason for keeping the two groups a half-mile apart, although it is difficult to fathom that reason now. The communication between the two groups would have been much easier and quicker if they had all stayed in the same hideout. Even their decision to hole up inside the residential quarters of Halim remains inscrutable. It would have made more sense for them to occupy a military command center where they could take advantage of radio communications for coordinating their disparate troop units.

Although the leaders of the movement were based at Halim, there is no evidence that they were working with anyone in the air force besides Major Soejono. All the facilities that they used in and around Halim — Penas, Lubang Buaya, two houses, air force weapons, and trucks — could have been provided solely by Soejono. The commander of Halim, Colonel Wisnoe Djajengminardo, and the commander of the air force, Vice Marshal Omar Dani, do not appear to have been consulted beforehand.

According to Omar Dani and Heru Atmodjo, they became mixed up in the movement as outside observers, not as participants. The accounts of both men are in agreement on the course of events. On the afternoon of September 30 Soejono had told Atmodjo, an air force intelligence officer who specialized in aerial reconnaissance, about an action against anti-Sukarno army generals. This was news to Atmodjo, who reported the information to Dani at about 4 P.M. that day. Dani ordered him to find out more about the plot and report back that night. At about 10 P.M. Atmodjo returned to air force headquarters and met with a group of senior air force officers to report what else he had learned from Soejono.[18] One significant detail was that Supardjo was a participant. Dani ordered Atmodjo to find Supardjo, who was Dani's immediate subordinate in the multiservice command (Komando Mandala Siaga, or Mandala Vigilance Command, called Kolaga) for the Confrontation against Malaysia.[19] Supardjo had met with Dani on September 29 to discuss Kolaga affairs. He might have told Dani that an action against the Council of Generals was in the works.

As Dani had ordered, Atmodjo sought out Soejono to determine how he could find Supardjo. Soejono told Atmodjo to go to the Aerial Survey Office at about five the next morning. After Atmodjo arrived and explained that he was on orders from Dani, Supardjo invited him to go along to the palace. Without any planning or coordination, Atmodjo became Supardjo's companion for the rest of the day.[20] Even if Atmodjo was more deeply implicated in the movement than he admits today, his actions on October 1 appear to have been limited to helping Supardjo move around the city and Halim air base.

While neither Atmodjo nor Dani can be considered among the leaders of the movement, they (and most senior air force officers) were sympathetic to it on the morning of October 1. Atmodjo recalls that he cheered when he heard the first radio announcement that morning.[21] He and his fellow officers thought the movement was a purge of the army's right-wing officers who had been sabotaging President Sukarno's policies. Dani drafted a public statement, an "Order of the Day," at 9:30 A.M. that hailed the movement as an effort to "secure and safeguard the Revolution and the Great Leader of the Revolution [Sukarno] against CIA subversion." It appears that Dani thought that the movement was nothing more than an internal army action, one that was still entirely loyal to Sukarno.[22]

The troops used in the morning's operations were largely derived from the units commanded by the three military officers within the core leadership: Untung, Latief, and Soejono. The movement's personnel included one company from the presidential guard under Untung, two platoons from the Jakarta army garrison under Latief, and a battalion of air force troops under Soejono. In addition, there were ten companies—five each—from Battalions 454 and 530. The troops from these two battalions had arrived in Jakarta only days earlier to take part in the Armed Forces Day parade on October 5. They formed the main body of troops that occupied Merdeka Square. Also among the movement's forces were small contingents from a paratroop command south of Jakarta and from the military police.[23]

Besides these various military troops, about two thousand members of the PKI or PKI-affiliated organizations also participated in the morning's operations.[24] These civilians were mostly members of the youth organization Pemuda Rakjat who had received a brief military training course at Halim air base for several weeks over the previous months. Major Soejono had organized their training. The young civilians were scattered among the forces that kidnapped the generals and occupied the buildings on Merdeka Square. Some were armed but most were not.

There is no reliable figure for the total number of military and civilian personnel who participated. Table 2 represents a synthesis of data from various sources. Although the figures might be inaccurate, they at least give a rough sense of the movement's strength.

The number of soldiers involved in the movement was minuscule compared with the total number of troops in the city. In terms of military strength, the movement was certainly not imposing enough to deter rival forces from attacking it. The army's command for Jakarta, called Kodam

Table 2. Military and Civilian Personnel Participating in the September 30th Movement

Personnel Participating	Number of Men
MILITARY PERSONNEL	
Two platoons of Brigade 1, Kodam Jaya, Jakarta	60
One company of Battalion 1, Cakrabirawa	60
Five companies of Battalion 454, Diponegoro	500
Five companies of Battalion 530, Brawijaya	500
One air force battalion, Halim air base guard (PPP)	1,000
Contingents and individuals from other military units	
(military police, paracommandos)	50
Total military personnel	2,130
CIVILIANS	
Civilians from PKI and PKI-affiliated organizations	2,000
Total personnel	4,130

Sources: *"Gerakan 30 September" Dihadapan Mahmillub, Perkara Untung,* 9, 40; Notosusanto and Saleh, *Tragedi Nasional,* 231; Saelan, *Dari Revolusi '45,* 91.

Jaya, had about sixty thousand soldiers, thirty times the total number of military personnel involved in the movement.[25] Colonel Latief commanded a brigade of Kodam Jaya that consisted of about two thousand soldiers, yet only two of its platoons participated in the movement. The size of the movement's potential opposition becomes even larger if one counts the tens of thousands of additional soldiers stationed near Jakarta. The Special Forces (RPKAD) were located just south of the city, and the Kodam covering West Java was located in the city of Bandung, about a seven-hour drive away. Compared with all these troops in and around the city, the movement's forces were remarkably few.

Note that the movement's troops did not deploy as troops typically do for a coup d'état. They did not position themselves to defend against any rival troops. If the aim was a coup d'état, they should have surrounded or occupied the headquarters of Kodam Jaya and the headquarters for Kostrad and positioned detachments near the main concentrations of army barracks. They also should have set up checkpoints on the roads leading into Jakarta to prevent outside troops from entering the city. They did none of these things.

The movement lacked the equipment that was almost de rigueur for coup plotters in the latter half of the twentieth century: tanks. The movement's entire strength consisted of foot soldiers with rifles. And it made no effort to disable the tanks held by troops potentially hostile to the movement. When the commander of Kodam Jaya heard about the raids on the houses of the generals, he ordered several tank companies to patrol the city streets.[26] Thus, within hours of the start of the movement, the city was already coming under the control of armored troops who were not part of the movement.

Given the small number of troops involved, their ineffectual deployment, and the absence of tanks, the movement does not appear to have been designed to seize state power. It would appear, going by the actions of the movement that morning, that it was designed as a kind of mutiny of junior officers against a group of senior officers.

Public Statements in the Afternoon

After taking over the radio station and broadcasting its first statement, the movement did not issue another statement for about five hours. The movement was remarkably taciturn just when it needed to rally public opinion behind it. The second statement, broadcast around noon, fulfilled the promise of the first by providing details about the Indonesian Revolution Council. The "entire authority of the State" had, the statement declared, fallen "into the hands of the Indonesian Revolution Council." The powers assumed by the national council were total: it "will constitute the source of all authority in the Republic of Indonesia," pending a general election to choose representatives to the parliament. (The timing of the election was left unspecified.) Subsidiary revolution councils were to be formed at the provincial, district, subdistrict, and village levels. Each council would function as "the highest authority in the region that it covers." Decree no. 1 declared that President Sukarno's cabinet of ministers had been "decommissioned," and that the Indonesian Revolution Council would make all future appointments of ministers.

Although the movement's first radio announcement had justified the suppression of the Council of Generals as a means to protect President Sukarno, the second statement usurped his authority and did not even mention Sukarno. By proclaiming the leaders of the movement as the leaders of a council that held the entire power of the state, the second statement showed that what had appeared in the morning to be an internal army putsch was more like a coup d'état.

This second statement also listed the names of the deputy commanders under Lieutenant Colonel Untung: "Brig. Gen. Supardjo,

Flight Lieutenant Colonel Heru, Navy Colonel Sunardi, and Adjunct Senior Police Commissioner Anwas." This list shows an effort to have each of the four military service branches (the army, air force, navy, and police) represented and to hide the identities of the real leaders of the movement who were working with Untung, namely, Colonel Latief, Major Soejono, Sjam, and Pono.

The selection of the deputies seems inexplicable. Of the four, only Supardjo and Atmodjo were connected in some way to the movement. And it was odd that Supardjo, a brigadier general, was under Untung, a lieutenant colonel. Another oddity is that Atmodjo was identified only by his first name, Heru, which is a very common Javanese name. Many Indonesians use only one name (Untung and Suharto, for example). But Heru is usually not used as a single name. Heru Atmodjo was known by his full name. The use of just Heru in the statement suggests the movement organizers were unfamiliar with him. The other two deputy commanders, Sunardi and Anwas, had not attended any of the planning meetings, were not at Halim air base on October 1, had not been informed about the movement beforehand, and took no action on behalf of the movement.[27]

It is not clear who, if anyone, signed Decree no. 1 concerning the formation of the Indonesian Revolution Council. There exists neither the original document nor a photograph of it. Untung claimed at his trial that he, Supardjo, and Atmodjo signed it.[28] Atmodjo, as a witness at the same trial, admitted to having signed it.[29] However, Atmodjo now states that he never signed it and never even saw the text before it was broadcast. He claims that his admission at Untung's trial was a capitulation to the demands of the prosecutors. He hoped that the court, in recognition of his cooperation, would give him a lighter sentence when his trial came up.[30] Supardjo, at his Mahmillub trial, disowned the radio announcement about the Indonesian Revolution Council. He claimed that he had not agreed with the idea of the council and had refused to sign the document.[31] Without the original document of the decree, it is impossible to know who actually signed it. Given that Sunardi and Anwas certainly were not signatories, there is no compelling reason to believe that the other two men named as deputy commanders (Supardjo and Atmodjo) signed it.

The movement's third statement, which was broadcast between 1 and 2 P.M., was titled "Decision no. 1."[32] (It is hard to fathom now what the writer[s] of these statements thought the difference was between a decree and a decision.) This third statement listed the forty-five members of the Indonesian Revolution Council, including Untung and his four deputy commanders. (The number 45 must have chosen to symbolize 1945, the year of Indonesia's proclamation of independence.) The members represented a fairly wide spectrum of political opinion: Muslim politicians, midlevel Communist Party figures, journalists, women, and youth leaders. The group best represented, with eighteen seats, was the military. Some military officers on the list were known anti-Communists, such as Brigadier General Amir Mahmud. And it included the names of two relatively unknown officers who were later revealed to be in the leadership of the movement: Colonel Latief and Major Soejono. The leader of the movement in Central Java, Colonel Suherman, also appeared on the list. The movement gave no explanation of the principle that guided its choices for council membership. Except for those few individuals directly involved in the movement, none of the people appointed to the council appear to have been contacted beforehand and invited to join.

Immediately after providing this listing of the Indonesian Revolution Council members, the radio station broadcast the movement's fourth statement, titled "Decision no. 2." It declared that, since the commander of the movement was a lieutenant colonel, no military officer could hold a higher rank. All ranks above Untung's were proclaimed to be invalid. In one stroke the system of military ranks was transformed so that Untung's rank became the highest rank. Those officers holding a higher rank were eligible to obtain the rank of lieutenant colonel if they submitted in writing a statement of loyalty to the Indonesian Revolution Council. Meanwhile, all lower-ranking soldiers who supported the movement would be promoted one rank.

These two "decisions" were issued under the name of Lieutenant Colonel Untung and signed by him. The military published photographs of the original documents of Decisions 1 and 2.[33] The photographs reveal that only Untung signed them. Perhaps the distinction between a decree and a decision resided in name of the issuer: the former was issued under the names of the commander and the deputy commanders, whereas the latter was issued only under the name of the commander.

The four statements issued by the movement constituted the sum total of the movement's presentation to the Indonesian public.[34] Taken together, the statements revealed very little about the nature of the movement. Most noticeably, they provided no justification for the decommissioning of the cabinet and the establishment of an entirely new form of government. The statements did not spell out any ideological disagreement with Sukarno's existing government. All the principles that the movement explicitly vowed to uphold were those that Sukarno had either advocated or invented, namely, the Constitution of 1945, a foreign policy opposed to colonialism and neocolonialism, Pancasila, Message of the People's Suffering, and Panca Azimat Revolusi.[35] The movement called for the creation of provincial and district-level revolution councils and even specified the number of members that would sit on such councils. But it did not explain how the members were to be selected and what authority the councils had in relation to existing state institutions, except to say that the councils had "all power." The movement expressed adherence to the Indonesian constitution and then proceeded to create an entirely novel, ill-defined institution that would supersede those institutions provided by the constitution.

The public face of the movement was inconsistent (its statements claimed that the troops wanted to both protect and depose Sukarno), bizarre (lieutenant colonel was declared to be the highest rank), and vague (the distinctive ideals of the movement were not specified). What is even more confusing is that the public face accorded very little with reality: Sukarno was not under the movement's "protection"; two of the four deputy commanders had nothing to do with the movement; four of the real leaders (Sjam, Pono, Latief, Soejono) were not mentioned as leaders; and the generals who had been "arrested" actually had been murdered and their corpses concealed. The four statements broadcast over the radio were not necessarily written by the men whose names appeared on them. Because Aidit was also at Halim, he could have had a hand in composing them. Untung and the two vice commanders of the movement present at Halim (Supardjo and Atmodjo) may not have written Decree no. 1. Even Untung may not have written decisions 1 and 2, although he signed both documents.

Sukarno and Supardjo's Discussions

For President Sukarno the face of the movement on October 1 was Brigadier General Supardjo's. The president did not meet the five core leaders of the movement while he was at Halim. Because of the morning's radio broadcast the only other person he definitely knew to be involved was Lieutenant Colonel Untung. Similarly, Sukarno did not meet Aidit and was perhaps never told that Aidit was on the grounds of the air base. Given that the only person from the movement whom Sukarno met was

Supardjo, the president likely would have concluded in the morning that the movement was indeed what it claimed to be in the first radio broadcast: an action purely internal to the army and designed to purge right-wing officers and defend his presidency. And recall that the movement initially intended to have the two battalion commanders, Captain Sukirno and Major Bambang Supeno, meet with Sukarno as well. But only Supardjo was brought back to Halim by helicopter. As it turned out, Supardjo became the ambassador of the movement.

Sukarno and Supardjo first met at around 10 A.M. in the office of the Halim Air Force Base commander, Colonel Wisnoe Djajengminardo. At that time Sukarno knew that Yani had been kidnapped. Since it was also reported to him that shots had been fired at Yani's house and blood had been found there, Sukarno probably presumed that Yani had been killed. Thus the president knew that Supardjo was representing a movement that, in all likelihood, had just murdered his army commander.

Sukarno must have been confused to see a brigadier general coming to meet him on behalf of a lieutenant colonel. Untung mentioned at his trial that Sukarno asked Supardjo, "Why is Untung the leader?" Although Untung had no direct knowledge of the discussion—whatever he knew was based on what Supardjo told him—Sukarno probably did ask such a question. Supardjo's response, again according to Untung, was unenlightening: "He was the one we thought appropriate."[36]

The only first-person accounts of their discussions in the morning have been provided by Supardjo (at his trial in 1967) and Vice Marshal Omar Dani, who was present during their first conversation. The accounts of Supardjo and Dani are very brief and clearly do not convey the details of what must have been delicate and fairly lengthy discussions. Sukarno himself never offered an account.

At his Mahmillub trial Supardjo testified that Sukarno did not react with great alarm to the news of the generals' kidnapping. The president did not accuse the movement of being criminal, treasonous, or counter-revolutionary. Supardjo reported that Sukarno retained his equanimity and said something to the effect that "this kind of thing will happen in a revolution." Sukarno was nevertheless anxious lest the incident touch off an uncontrollable civil war between the left-wing and right-wing forces in the military. He asked Supardjo to call off the movement while he attempted to find a political resolution. Supardjo testified: "I was asked to sit closer to him. He said that if this continues the war could become wider and then the neocolonial powers would benefit. So he asked me: 'Do you have the capacity or not to call off the September

30th Movement?' At that point I replied that 'Yes, I have the capacity.'
So he patted me on the shoulder and said jokingly, 'Alright, but look
out—if you can't stop it I'm going to have your head.'"[37]

According to Omar Dani, Sukarno refused Supardjo's request to
come out in support of the movement and then demanded that Supardjo call off the movement. In the words of Dani's biographers,

> He [Supardjo] reported in person to the president that he had,
> with his comrades, taken action against some high officers in the
> army. The junior officers in the army and the lower-ranking sol-
> diers were not content with the attitude, behavior, and indiffer-
> ence of the generals toward their subordinates. When asked by
> Sukarno whether he had any proof [of the existence of the
> Council of Generals], Supardjo affirmed that he had and could
> get it at the army headquarters if so ordered. Sukarno ordered
> him to get it, but because he [Supardjo] disappeared on October
> 2, he could not present that evidence to Sukarno. The president
> ordered Supardjo to stop the movement and avoid bloodshed.
> The president also refused Supardjo's request to support the
> movement. Once his request was rejected by Sukarno, Supardjo
> immediately left the airbase's Command Headquarters. His face
> appeared a bit confused, tired, sleepy, and disappointed.[38]

This account of Dani's confirms Supardjo's claim that Sukarno demanded the cancellation of the movement. Sukarno neither supported
nor opposed the movement. On the one hand, he did not issue a statement in support of it (as Dani had already done) or privately encourage
it to continue. On the other hand, he did not view it as a mortal danger
to himself or his presidency. That he stayed at Halim, the very site he
knew to be the center of the movement's leadership, suggests that he
viewed Supardjo and Untung as officers loyal to him. Sukarno appears
not to have been panicked by the morning's events. Between 11:30 A.M.
and noon, after speaking with Supardjo in the air base command center,
Sukarno shifted to the relatively spacious nearby home of Commodore
Soesanto and spent some time napping.

Not only did Sukarno remain at Halim, he summoned his leading
advisers there. One of his three deputy prime ministers, the only one
then in Jakarta, Leimena, arrived in Halim sometime in the late morning or early afternoon, as did the commander of the navy, the commander of the police, the head of the palace guard, and the attorney
general. These men spent the afternoon and evening with Sukarno.[39]

These ministers witnessed some of the later discussions between Supardjo and Sukarno. They provided some comments to journalists afterward and brief testimonies as witnesses in court trials but have not, to my knowledge, written detailed accounts of the exchanges between the two men.

Supardjo met Sukarno for the second time after Supardjo returned from his discussions with the movement's core leadership. In all Supardjo conversed with Sukarno on about four or five separate occasions throughout the day. Only the first conversation took place in the Halim commander's office. The later conversations took place in the house of Commodore Soesanto. His house was chosen for the president because it was the best appointed on the base.[40] Supardjo shuttled back and forth between Sergeant Sujatno's house, where Untung, Sjam, and the others were hiding out, and Soesanto's house, where Sukarno and his ministers sat.[41]

The main topic of Sukarno and Supardjo's discussions in the early afternoon, around 12:00 to 1:30 P.M., was the choice of a temporary replacement for Yani as commander of the army. Sukarno was certainly not hostile to the movement since he was asking its advice on a key appointment. Supardjo claims in his analysis that the movement's leaders recommended the names of three army generals.[42] The movement was supportive of Major General U. Rukman, interregional commander for eastern Indonesia; Major General Pranoto Reksosamodra, an assistant on Yani's general staff who is usually referred to only by his first name; and Major General Basuki Rachmat, the commander of the East Java division.[43]

The decision about Yani's replacement was entirely Sukarno's. The movement did not dictate terms to the president. The officer whom Sukarno ultimately chose was Pranoto, a member of Yani's staff who had not been kidnapped. Sukarno signed an order at 1:30 P.M. appointing Pranoto as the temporary caretaker of the army and sent couriers to summon him to Halim. Meanwhile, the movement, for unknown reasons, did not broadcast Sukarno's order over the radio.

In their discussions Supardjo implicitly recognized Sukarno's authority as president. He neither threatened Sukarno with physical harm, attempted to kidnap him, forced him to approve of the movement, nor insisted that he make certain decisions. Supardjo, by all accounts, played the role of the subordinate officer. It is thus odd that at roughly the same time as these discussions at Halim (noon to 2 P.M., the radio station aired a statement that implicitly deposed Sukarno as president. At

Halim the person speaking to Sukarno on behalf of the movement continued to treat him as if he was the president. On the radio waves, however, the movement proclaimed that it had unilaterally decommissioned Sukarno's cabinet.

Sukarno either heard the movement's announcements or was informed of their contents. He was not pleased. At a cabinet meeting in early November 1965 he referred to the movement's demand when he responded to student demonstrators, who had been organized by the army and were demanding that Sukarno decommission his cabinet: "Are you crazy, thinking that I will decommission my own cabinet? Yeah, that's what I said when I was confronted by the 'Revolution Council.' At that time here I sharply said, 'Are you crazy?'"[44] Sukarno had already decided not to support the movement by the time the council was announced over the radio. But hearing that his cabinet was being decommissioned must have hardened his opposition to it.

Actions in Central Java

The only significant military actions in support of the movement occurred in the province of Central Java and the region of Yogyakarta.[45] The rebellion was extensive in these two locations.[46] Junior officers mutinied against the highest-ranking officer in the province, Brigadier General Suryasumpeno, and three district army commanders. In Semarang, the capital of Central Java, a colonel on Suryasumpeno's staff occupied the radio station with a group of rebel troops and proclaimed himself to be the new commander at about 1 P.M. He was Colonel Suherman, the provincial chief of army intelligence.

In Yogyakarta Major Muljono led the rebel troops in raiding the home of their commander, Colonel Katamso. They abducted him and his chief of staff, Lieutenant Colonel Sugijono, who happened to be at the house when the rebels arrived. They brought these two officers to a small town just north of Yogyakarta and confined them in the barracks of an army battalion. Later, they killed these two officers.

The military officers behind the movement in Yogyakarta, unlike their counterparts in Semarang, worked in coordination with local civilians. A crowd came out into the streets of the city in support of the movement. Major Muljono, as an officer in charge of civil defense affairs, already had close connections with civilian organizations such as those of the PKI. As soldiers spirited away Colonel Katamso, youths in various PKI-affiliated organizations surrounded the Yogyakarta sultan's palace, the seat of civilian authority. They also took over the city's radio station and began broadcasting statements in favor of the movement around 8 P.M.

Similar events transpired in the province's second-largest city, Solo. A junior officer led the movement. Left-wing civilian organizations issued statements of support of the movement, although there do not appear to have been any street actions as in Yogyakarta. The rebel leader in Solo, Major Iskandar, proclaimed himself head of the Solo Revolution Council and ordered soldiers loyal to him to arrest his commanding officer, Lieutenant Colonel Ezy Suharto, chief of staff of Solo's Korem (Komando Resort Militer, the Resort Military Command), Captain Parman, and another officer, Lieutenant Colonel Ashari. The major called for representatives of all political parties to gather under his auspices for a meeting to establish a revolution council for the city. The mayor of Solo, Utomo Ramelan, a member of the PKI, issued a statement supporting the movement.

In another city in Central Java, Salatiga, rebel army officers acted without any civilian support. Lieutenant Colonel Idris, the chief of staff of the Korem in Salatiga, mobilized troops against his commanding officer, Colonel Sukardi, and the other key army officer in the city, Lieutenant Colonel Sugiman. No civilians issued statements of support or participated in demonstrations. The mayor of Salatiga, Bakri Wahab, belonged to the PKI, but he did not publicly express support for the movement.

Thus in Central Java on the night of October 1, midranking officers seized control of the provincial command in Semarang and abducted the district commanders of three key cities. Only in Yogyakarta did civilians take to the street in support of the movement, and only in Solo did civilian politicians issue statements of support. Only in Yogyakarta were officers killed. The actions taken in the name of the movement in Central Java formed no distinct pattern.

The movement appears to have been in contact with army officers in other provinces. Supardjo noted in his postmortem analysis that the movement had sent couriers to a variety of provinces. While officers in other provinces may have known about the movement and contemplated taking some sort of action, they remained passive.[47] Central Java and Yogyakarta were the only territories outside Jakarta where the movement manifested itself.

Suharto's Attack on the Movement

Back in Jakarta, a senior army general who had not been targeted for kidnapping was Major General Suharto, commander of the army's Strategic Reserve, known as Kostrad. The troops occupying Merdeka Square (Battalions 454 and 530) had not been instructed to blockade Kostrad headquarters or otherwise neutralize it. The troops occupied the north, west, and south sides of the square and left empty the east side, where the Kostrad building stood. Suharto's officers moved freely in and out of the building during the day as they organized an attack on the movement. One of the great oddities of the October 1 events is that the movement's enemies operated from a building that stood directly in front of most of the movement's troops.

The movement may have decided not to neutralize Kostrad head-quarters because it was not a major military installation in Jakarta. Un-like the Jakarta regional command (Kodam Jaya), Kostrad had no troops permanently barracked in or around the city. Kostrad's reservists were always on loan from the regional commands (the Kodams). Kostrad called up battalions for temporary service within specific combat operations.[48] Nevertheless, Kostrad was of great strategic value in that it was headed by Suharto, who temporarily served as army commander whenever Yani traveled abroad. If rebel troops wanted to control Jakarta, they would have had to ensure that Suharto, who was first in line for Yani's position, was in no position to rally the troops for a counterattack. Suharto had been appointed Kostrad commander in May 1963 and thus had more than two years of experience in dealing with the military's top officers in Jakarta.

According to his own account, Suharto learned of the shootings and abductions from neighbors while still at his residence in Menteng. He arrived at Kostrad between 6:30 and 7 A.M. Assuming that Yani had been killed, Suharto appointed himself interim army commander. The key officer controlling the largest number of troops in Jakarta, Umar Wirahadikusumah, reported to Suharto at about 8 A.M. and put himself under Suharto's command.[49] The surviving generals of the army's general staff held an emergency meeting at about the same time and de-cided to appoint Suharto as the temporary commander. According to one member of the staff, Major General Pranoto, whom Sukarno later appointed commander, "the meeting decided to ask Major General Su-harto to be ready to fill the vacuum in the leadership of the army. By special courier, the decision of the meeting was conveyed to Major

General Suharto at Kostrad headquarters."[50] Throughout the day a large number of officers gathered at Kostrad as it became known that it was the center of the military's antimovement forces. Nasution arrived there sometime in the evening.[51]

Suharto's first action in countering the movement was to demand the surrender of the two battalions in Merdeka Square. The commanders, Captain Sukirno and Major Supeno, were inside the palace grounds (having accompanied Supardjo from Halim earlier in the morning). Kostrad officers contacted the deputy commanders still outside in the field with the troops. The deputy commanders did as they were told: they reported to Suharto inside the Kostrad building. Upon meeting them, Suharto informed them that he viewed the movement as a coup attempt and threatened to attack if their troops did not surrender to him by 6 P.M.

Yet another oddity of the movement is that those two battalions— 454 from Central Java and 530 from East Java—had been summoned to Jakarta by Suharto himself. In his first public explanation of the day's events, a speech on October 15, Suharto acknowledged that the battalions belonged to Kostrad.[52] They had been brought to Jakarta along with a third battalion, 328 from West Java, to participate in the Armed Forces Day parade scheduled for October 5. Suharto inspected the three battalions on the morning of September 30, 1965, on the field where they camped. In the 1980s copies of the original Kostrad orders to the three battalions came to light—they had been signed by Suharto.[53]

While they were based in Merdeka Square, neither of the two battalion commanders had any contact with the movement leaders at Halim. They pondered how to respond to Suharto's threat on their own, without consulting Untung, Sjam, and the others. One battalion, 530, abandoned its position and surrendered to Kostrad sometime in the early afternoon. Captain Sukirno of 454 was able to prevent his troops from defecting but felt unable to remain at Merdeka Square without the other battalion. He ordered all his troops to board trucks and head back to Halim later in the afternoon.[54]

Suharto managed to clear Merdeka Square of soldiers without firing a shot: one battalion surrendered, the other fled. Suharto's troops encountered no resistance in taking the radio station at about 6 P.M.[55] At the telecommunications building Suharto's troops came upon some of the movement's civilian volunteers. Because the volunteers were thoroughly confused about what they were supposed to be doing, and unsure whether the troops were friend or foe, they offered little resistance. They were quickly overpowered and taken away.[56] By evening the movement had no more forces left inside the city. The remnants of its forces had returned to Lubang Buaya. Suharto was in control of Jakarta. Between 7 and 8:30 P.M. he had the radio station broadcast a message that he had taped earlier that afternoon. The sound of his voice on the air marked the symbolic end of the movement.

To take the radio station, Merdeka Square, and the telecommunications building, Suharto used troops from the Special Forces that had been brought in from their base in Cijantung, a small town just south of Jakarta. He also used the one Kostrad battalion that did not join the movement, Battalion 328 of West Java, and portions of Battalion 530 that had defected only hours earlier. It is curious that Suharto did not avail himself of the troops of the Jakarta garrison (Kodam Jaya) that were under Wirahadikusumah's command. Suharto used only troops under his direct command, even to the point of preferring troops that had participated in the movement.

With Merdeka Square clear, Suharto turned his attention toward Halim, which he knew to be the base of the movement. Various couriers and officers had come to Kostrad from Halim earlier in the afternoon and reported that Supardjo (whose position as deputy commander had been announced over the radio) was conferring with Sukarno there. To isolate the movement at Halim Air Force Base, Suharto refused to allow any army officers to go there, even those summoned by the president.

As I have already noted, Sukarno had appointed Pranoto as army commander at 1:30 P.M. and ordered him to come to Halim. Sukarno was not aware that Pranoto and the rest of Yani's surviving staff had already agreed to Suharto's serving as commander. Suharto refused to allow Pranoto to leave army headquarters and meet with Sukarno. In a brief retrospective account Pranoto recalled, "I had already clearly put myself under the tactical command of Major General Suharto, so I could not directly go and meet the president without authorization from Suharto as the interim commander. Because of the summons from the president's emissaries, I kept requesting that authorization. But Suharto always forbade me to go to the president with the excuse that he did not want to risk the possibility of losing another general when the situation was still so chaotic."[57]

Because Sukarno was the commander-in-chief of the armed forces, Suharto's refusal to follow his order on the Pranoto appointment amounted to insubordination. Sukarno had already determined that it was safe for Pranoto to come to Halim. Thus Suharto had no justification, within military protocol, to second-guess Sukarno's judgment. Suharto defied his commander and implemented his own strategy. While Sukarno was negotiating with the movement leaders at Halim and persuading them to call off the action, Suharto was busy plotting a military assault on them.

Suharto began giving orders to the president. Through couriers he told Sukarno at about 8 P.M. to leave Halim to avoid becoming a casualty in the upcoming combat. Suharto declared that his troops would attack the air base and clear out all the forces of the movement. Apparently seeing that it was futile to order Suharto to call off the attack, Sukarno discussed with his advisers how best to flee Halim. He finally decided to travel by car to the Bogor palace south of Jakarta where he usually spent his weekends. He arrived there at about 10 P.M.

With Sukarno out of the way, Suharto's only remaining obstacle was the air force. He received word that the air force officers at Halim would resist an assault on the air base and were contemplating a bombing or strafing run over Kostrad headquarters. Suharto and his staff abandoned their headquarters and reestablished themselves near Senayan stadium.[58] As it turned out, the aerial attack never materialized. The threat of one, however, delayed Suharto's preparations by a number of hours.

Special Forces troops massed along the southern border of Halim air base in the early morning hours of October 2. They momentarily skirmished with the troops of the Central Java battalion who happened to be grouped along the same road. After abandoning Merdeka Square during the afternoon of the previous day, Battalion 454 had moved down to Halim but had found the gates of the air base closed to it. Forbidden to enter Halim, they had spent the night loitering on the road that ran between the air base and Lubang Buaya. This was the road that Special Forces troops entered around dawn on October 2. An air force officer, Commodore Dewanto, was able to intervene and prevent a full-scale battle between the Special Forces and Battalion 454 troops. A rough truce was negotiated that called for Battalion 454 to withdraw from the area and for the Special Forces troops to enter the air base. The Special Forces commander, Colonel Sarwo Edhie, met senior air force officers at the air base headquarters. He assured himself that Sukarno had indeed left and that Halim no longer posed a threat to the army. The air force was not going to launch an aerial attack, as Kostrad had feared during the night.[59]

Sometime during the morning of October 2 the movement's core leaders abandoned their hideout at Halim and moved south into Lubang Buaya. There they discussed the situation with Battalion 454 officers and with PKI members who had joined the movement. Ultimately, all the movement's forces disbanded and headed off in different directions. The arrival of the Special Forces troops apparently prompted their flight. Sjam, Latief, and Supardjo made their way into the city center. Untung and soldiers of the palace guard sneaked away on a train headed for Central Java. Aidit and Omar Dani had already been flown out of the city during the night (Aidit to Yogyakarta, Dani to East Java). The movement was finished in Jakarta. Within another day it would be finished in Central Java.

2

Interpretations of the Movement

We make sense of action when there is a coherence between the actions of the agent and the meaning of his situation for him. We find his action puzzling until we find such a coherence. . . . This coherence in no way implies that the action is rational; the meaning of a situation for an agent may be full of confusion and contradiction; but the adequate depiction of this contradiction makes sense of it.

Charles Taylor, *Philosophy and the Human Sciences* (1971)

A question mark has hung over just about every aspect of the September 30th Movement. Why would a movement that announced itself to the public on October 1 name itself after the previous day? Why would a movement that proclaimed itself to be a purely internal army action also decide to decommission President Sukarno's cabinet and form a new government based on "revolution councils"? Why would a movement that claimed it was an effort to prevent a coup against President Sukarno not explicitly declare that he would remain president within this new government? Why would a movement that wanted to change the government not deploy troops to seize control of the city according to the classic procedures of the coup d'état? Why did the movement not kidnap Major General Suharto or prepare to counter the troops under his command? The movement appears to have been a tangled, incoherent mess.

Over the years many people have tried to discern what the movement's underlying logic might have been. One has to presume that the perpetrators were not schizophrenic, idiotic, or suicidal. They must have had particular goals in mind and must have designed their actions and statements as reasonably effective means for achieving those goals. They may have misread the political situation and miscalculated their own abilities, but they could not have gone forward with the movement without a plan that made sense to them.

There have been four primary methods for resolving the oddities of the movement and imposing some coherence upon it. The Indonesian army's interpretation, from the early days of October until today, has been that the movement was a plot by the PKI *as an institution* to seize state power. Far from being just a mutiny or a coup, the movement was the start of a full-scale social revolt against all non-Communist forces. The Cornell scholars Anderson and McVey proposed an alternative reading of the movement in their analysis of January 1966. They affirmed the movement's own representation as an internal army putsch by junior officers. A third method, that of the political scientist Harold Crouch, has been to argue that the movement was essentially the work of discontented military officers but that the PKI played a large supporting role. The fourth method, pioneered by the Dutch sociologist W. F. Wertheim, is the hypothesis that Suharto and other anti-Communist army generals organized the movement through double agents (Sjam especially) in order to provide a pretext for attacking the PKI and overthrowing Sukarno. Let me review in detail each of these four approaches.[1]

The Movement as an Attempted Coup d'État by the PKI

In his memoir Suharto claims that he guessed that the PKI was the mastermind of the movement when he heard the first radio announcement on the morning of October 1: "There and then I had a sense of foreboding. I knew who Untung was. He was very close to the PKI and a keen disciple of Alimin, the PKI boss."[2] Suharto's assistant for intelligence at Kostrad, the army reserve, was Yoga Sugama, who claims in his memoir (written in the third person by writers he hired) that he was convinced that the movement was led by the PKI even before Suharto thought so: "Yoga was the first one in Kostrad to be certain that the kidnapping of the army generals at the end of September 1965 [*sic*] was committed by PKI elements. Some officers appeared doubtful about his conclusion because there was not yet any evidence on October 1 to support it." Sugama supposedly told the doubters, "This is definitely the work of the PKI. We only have to find the evidence." He boasts that he was the one who convinced Suharto of the PKI's culpability, who turned Suharto's sense of foreboding into an unshakeable conviction.[3] Sugama's account suggests that Kostrad brass identified the mastermind before receiving any definitive proof. The conclusion came before the evidence.

Suharto did not immediately accuse the PKI of being responsible for the movement. Instead, officers under him mobilized various anti-PKI political leaders to do that. Only one day after the outbreak of the movement, an anti-Communist general, Brigadier General Sucipto, formed an ostensibly civilian organization called the Action Front for Crushing the September 30th Movement. After meeting in private, the group's leaders held their first press conference on October 4. They included men such as Subchan Z. E. of the Muslim organization Nahdatul Ulama, who had long been working with anti-PKI army officers.[4] Given their earlier collaboration, they were able to organize themselves quickly.

On Armed Forces Day, October 5, instead of holding the scheduled military parades with troops marching lockstep and showing off the latest weaponry, the army held a large-scale funeral procession for the seven slain officers. The same day the army released a quickly composed 130-page book that chronicled the events of October 1 and accused the PKI of being the mastermind.[5] It appears that October 5 was the day the army leadership decided to begin an offensive against the PKI. According to a CIA dispatch from Jakarta, the top army generals met on that day and agreed to "implement plans to crush the PKI."[6] Under Suharto's direction the army quickly mobilized crowds of civilians and spread anti-PKI propaganda in the press (which was wholly under the control of the army by the end of the first week of October). One sensational story described how PKI members tortured, mutilated, and castrated the captured generals. As newspapers and radio stations began running alarmist stories about the PKI, army-instigated crowds went on a murderous rampage. They burned down the PKI national headquarters in Jakarta on October 8 and attacked the offices of virtually every other organization connected with the party. The homes of PKI leaders in Jakarta were either torched or confiscated.[7]

Even at the height of the brutal repression in late 1965 and early 1966, the public had no evidence that the PKI had masterminded the movement. Citizens had no compelling reason to distrust Untung's proclamation that the movement was "solely a movement within the army corps" (*Gerakan 30 September adalah gerakan semata-mata dalam tubuh Angkatan Darat)* or the PKI Politburo's statement on October 6 affirming that the movement was "an internal problem of the army and the Indonesian Communist Party does not involve itself in it."[8] True, Untung seemed an unlikely leader of such an ambitious intervention into national politics. He had a reputation for being a simple-minded, brave soldier, not a clever schemer with enough self-confidence to organize such an action. Untung's character by itself suggested that there were forces involved in the movement beyond some patriotic soldiers who disliked their commanding officers. But that suspicion was not enough to conclude that the PKI was the hidden hand behind Untung.

The PKI had obviously supported the movement, as evidenced by the October 2 editorial in its newspaper, *Harian Rakjat,* endorsing the movement as patriotic and revolutionary. But this editorial did not prove that the PKI led the movement, especially since it stated that the movement was an "internal army affair." Likewise, the participation in the action by hundreds of members of the PKI's youth wing (Pemuda Rakjat) did not prove the party's leadership of the movement. There was no reason to believe that its role was anything more than what party leaders, such as Njono, later claimed it to be: auxiliary manpower for an internal army putsch. The proposal by some PKI leaders in districts outside Jakarta to establish local revolution councils, in accordance with Lieutenant Colonel Untung's first decree, again showed only that the party was firmly in support of the action, not that it was at the helm. Aidit's presence at Halim Air Force Base did not necessarily prove that he was anything but an approving spectator or adviser.[9]

The army's Information Department issued a series of three books from October to December 1965 that were intended to prove that the PKI had masterminded *(mendalangi)* the movement. The evidence adduced in these publications was either insubstantial, circumstantial, or unreliable. The key evidence was the admission by both Untung (who was captured in Central Java on October 13) and Latief (captured October 11 in Jakarta) that they were stooges of the PKI.[10] The army cited the interrogation reports of the two officers. It is unlikely that either officer had sincerely and voluntarily confessed to serving the interests of the PKI. I have a copy of Latief's interrogation report (dated October 25, 1965), and it does indeed have him admitting to following the orders of the PKI. However, he claimed in his 1978 defense plea that he was suffering from an infected bayonet wound in his leg and barely conscious at the time.[11] In any decent court of law or court of history, testimony extracted under duress and torture is inadmissible. At their later trials both Untung and Latief contradicted their interrogation reports and insisted that they, as military officers, had led the movement. The PKI, they claimed, was invited to join only as an auxiliary force.[12]

Given that Suharto's interpretation was imposed by force of arms and not by force of argument, it does not have much to recommend it. The army never proved its case. One has to be suspicious when the case is partly based on black propaganda and torture-induced testimonies. The confessions of two PKI leaders, Njono and Aidit, printed in the army press in late 1965, were transparent fakes.[13] Likewise, the highly publicized story about the movement's female participants' torturing and castrating the seven captured officers in Lubang Buaya turned out to be a fabrication, presumably by psychological warfare specialists.[14] Despite the steady stream of propaganda for more than thirty years, Suharto's army never proved that the PKI had masterminded the movement.

In targeting the PKI as the "puppet master" of the movement, Suharto's army could not explain one basic fact: the movement had been carried out by military personnel, namely, Lieutenant Colonel Untung and his troops of the presidential guard, Colonel Latief and his troops of the Jakarta garrison, Major Soejono and his troops of Halim Air Force Base, Captain Sukirno and his troops of Battalion 454 from Central Java, and Major Supeno and his troops of Battalion 530 from East Java. Likewise, in Central Java the movement's forces mainly consisted of army officers, not party activists. Again, there was no evidence of the dominant presence of the PKI. Whatever the precise involvement of certain party members, they appeared at that time to be peripheral to an action undertaken by military personnel. The Suharto regime's version could be correct only if one assumed that the army officers involved had subordinated themselves to the PKI and been willing to carry out the party's orders like robots.[15] Benedict Anderson and Ruth McVey were justified in arguing in their "preliminary analysis" of January 1966 that the PKI was not the mastermind. Up to that time, there was no solid evidence for that claim in the press reports and army's statements. It made more sense to explain the movement as an internal army putsch.

The issue of the PKI's involvement became more complicated soon after Anderson and McVey finished their report. At the trials of Njono and Untung in February and March 1966, the names of two PKI members—Sjam and Pono—were mentioned as members of the core group of plotters. Untung testified that Sjam and Pono were representatives of Aidit, who had assisted the movement but had not directed it.[16] Their role, Untung claimed, was insignificant; they were present simply to ensure that the "PKI would provide support with its masses."[17] He and the other military officers wanted auxiliary manpower to assist their action so they turned to the PKI, which could provide thousands of youths who had recently received a short military training course at Halim air base. Untung, however, undercut his own version of events by stating that Sjam's assistance included the drafting of the movement's first decree concerning the formation of the revolution councils.[18] Another of the core leaders, Major Soejono of the air force, testifying as a witness at Njono's trial, implicated Sjam and Pono even further in the movement. He claimed that Sjam was the leader of the movement's plotters: "He was a person who held the determining voice in the meetings."[19] Because Soejono mentioned that Sjam was also known by the alias Sugito, many observers assumed that Sjam, a person they had never heard of before, must be a pseudonym for *Tjugito*, an aboveground member of the PKI's Central Committee and one of the forty-five people named to the Indonesian Revolution Council.[20] Pono's identity was similarly uncertain. These revelations about Sjam and Pono introduced a new wrinkle in the story. Were Untung and Soejono telling the truth? Who were these two men? What position did they have in the PKI? What was their role in the movement?

Initially, the army's story line presented Sjam and Pono as nothing more than faceless functionaries in the PKI machine. They were presumed to be Aidit's subordinates, carrying out his orders. But the army did not explain how these two men could organize a group of military officers and lead the movement. The American journalist John Hughes, writing in early 1967, mentioned them in passing as the PKI's representatives to the movement.[21] The official story line substantially changed, however, after the former Politburo member Soejono Pradigdo betrayed his erstwhile comrades after his arrest in December 1966. The army began using his interrogation report (the text of which was not made public) as the basis for the claim that the PKI had maintained a clandestine organization called the Special Bureau (Biro Chusus) to infiltrate the military and cultivate party sympathizers among the officers. Sjam was said to be the head of this Special Bureau and Pono his assistant. Although the names of Sjam and Pono had come up at Mahmillub trials in 1966, the term *Special Bureau* had not.[22] The army used this information from Pradigdo to add a new twist to its story line: the PKI had organized the movement through Sjam and Pono's Special Bureau. One flaw in the previous story line—the absence of a medium between the party and the military officers—became rectified by the addition of the Special Bureau. Taking this information into account, an army-employed historian, Nugroho Notosusanto, and a Mahmillub prosecutor, Ismail Saleh, supplied a new narrative for the Suharto regime with their book *The Coup Attempt of the "September 30th Movement"* (first published in April 1967).[23]

The arrest of Sjam in March 1967, apparently a result of Pradigdo's betrayal of the location of the party's hideouts, allowed the army to publicize more information about the Special Bureau. As a witness at a trial in 1967 and as the accused at his own trial in 1968, Sjam was surprisingly loquacious. According to his testimony, Aidit had ordered him to carry out the movement. Sjam explained that some members of the Politburo and the Central Committee were aware of the existence of the Special Bureau but knew nothing of its operations; it remained outside the formal structure of the party and functioned exclusively under the command of Aidit. It was this underground party organization, he claimed, that persuaded various military officers to participate in the movement. All subsequent books sponsored by the government, such as the 1994 white book, based much of their narrative on Sjam's testimony.[24]

The government's version was, in two fundamental respects, an unwarranted extrapolation from Sjam's testimony. Whereas Sjam had claimed that only Aidit had ordered the Special Bureau to organize the movement, the army claimed that the broadest organ of the party's leadership, the Central Committee, made the decision.[25] Whereas Sjam had described the movement as a purge of the right-wing generals working for neocolonial powers, the army described it as an attempted coup d'état. Because the army had already banned the PKI by 1967, murdered many of its supporters, and held hundreds of thousands as political prisoners, it had to argue that the entire organization of the party, from top to bottom, was complicit. The army had to target the Central Committee as the movement's brain. In order to justify the severity of the repression, it had to present the action as a coup that threatened the entire structure of the government.

The CIA's 1968 report followed the Suharto regime's line that the PKI, through the Special Bureau, conceptualized and implemented the movement. As in Notosusanto and Saleh's book, the primary sources were the transcripts of the interrogations of the movement's leaders. The report failed to note that some of the movement leaders rejected the validity of those transcripts at their trials and claimed that they had been threatened with violence if they refused to sign them.[26] The CIA acknowledged that the answers may have been coerced but persisted in basing most of its narrative upon them. The report included an appendix that justified its reliance upon these sources. The author of the report, later revealed to be Helen-Louise Hunter, a CIA agent specializing in communism in Asia, argued that the interrogation reports were reliable because of the "striking similarity in the stories told by Untung, Latief, Soejono, and Supardjo." Such a similarity, to the extent that there was one, could be explained just as well by the interrogators' forcing them to agree to the army's own story line.[27] The CIA's methodology was irremediably flawed: one cannot rely on the statements of captives of a military that routinely practiced torture, especially when that military was committed from October 2 on to framing the PKI as the mastermind (or "finding the evidence," as Yoga Sugama wrote). One might as well write the history of European witchcraft by treating the confessions before the Inquisition as truthful.

The Suharto regime's interpretation of the movement had its takers in the United States beyond the halls of Langley, Virginia. For strongly anti-Communist writers, the level of proof required was not very high when they assumed that the movement was the predictable manifestation of the Communists' violent quest to seize state power. They held what Anderson and McVey parodied as a monster image of the PKI, as if the party had been "driven by an overweening ambition and a congenital need to express itself in violence."[28] The prolific political scientist Justus M. van der Kroef wrote a series of articles in the late 1960s and early 1970s pinning full blame for the movement on the PKI. Supposedly, the party had been building up its strength in 1965, going on the offensive, and plotting a coup d'état. The movement was, in his eyes, a natural and predictable consequence of the party's determined drive for power.[29] In a similar vein a political scientist with close connections to the Indonesian military, Guy Pauker, wrote a report for the Rand Corporation that presented the culpability of the PKI as an established truth.[30] Writing for a wider public, the journalist Arnold Brackman penned two accounts of the 1965 events that recycled the standard line of the Suharto regime.[31] An examination of Notosusanto and Saleh's book and these publications from van der Kroef, Pauker, and Brackman reveals the same tainted evidence packaged in different ways. Ultimately, the only proof that the PKI directed the movement was the army's say-so.

One obtrusive flaw in the Suharto regime's post-1967 narrative about the Special Bureau was that it largely relied upon the testimony of someone who acknowledged that he had made deception his profession.

Sjam was an unknown person. He had never been an aboveground leader of the PKI. He was claiming that he was so trusted by Aidit that he was put in charge of a complex, high-stakes operation to eliminate the army's top commanders. Sjam's behavior and style of speech on display in the courtroom did not suggest that he was a powerful party leader. If he had risen to such a sensitive and high position in the party, why did he so casually spill the party's secrets at the Mahmillub trials? Why was his language not more like that of other party leaders, such as Sudisman, the sole survivor of the Politburo's Working Committee?[32] Sudisman's statements at his trial in July 1967 were full of a defiant determination and an unshakeable belief in the power of the party and the proletariat. Sjam, in his capitulation before the army's court, seemed to be a poor excuse for someone who was supposed to become the equivalent of a KGB head if the party had ever successfully taken state power. His story about a clandestine network of party operatives' infiltrating the military was greeted, understandably, with great suspicion by many observers. Again, Benedict Anderson and Ruth McVey were justified, when writing in 1978, to cast doubt on the veracity of Sjam's testimony and suggest that he may well have been a double agent who was working more for the army than for Aidit and the PKI.[33] In a more recent article Anderson has again affirmed that Sjam's identity cannot be determined with any certainty: "Was he an army spy in the ranks of the Communists? Or a Communist spy inside the military? Or a spy for a third party? Or all three simultaneously?"[34]

It is undeniable that some leaders and members of the PKI were involved in some way or another in the movement. Sudisman admitted as much at his trial (a point to which I will return in chapter 5). The open question is precisely how they were involved. Which individuals and organs of the party participated? What was their understanding of the movement? What were their motivations? What was their relationship to the military officers in the movement? By blaming the PKI as a whole, down to village-level members of PKI front organizations who had no connection with the movement, the Suharto regime never brought its case against the PKI above the level of a crude witchhunt. If the army had been serious about compiling evidence about the PKI's involvement, it would not have summarily executed four of the five top leaders of the party. D. N. Aidit, precisely the person whom the army claimed was the mastermind, was executed in a secret location in Central Java on November 22, 1965, soon after his capture.[35]

The Movement as a Mutiny of Junior Officers

In the final months of 1965, when the movement remained a mystery to everyone except those who trusted military propaganda, Anderson and McVey assembled an analysis of the event by reading through a great variety of Indonesian newspapers. As I noted earlier, they found no evidence of the PKI's serving as the mastermind. The party had not mobilized its masses to support the movement. While it expressed support for the movement in its newspaper, *Harian Rakjat*, it did not throw its full weight behind the movement to ensure its success: "No one came out on the streets of Jakarta, and there was no visible coordination of activities either in the city or throughout the nation," Anderson and McVey noted.[36] The *Harian Rakjat* editorial on October 2, representing the party's official line, implicitly instructed members to do nothing because it stated that the movement was an internal army affair. To believe that the PKI organized the movement and then did nothing to prevent its going down to defeat, one would have to believe that the PKI was astoundingly self-destructive. Whatever the PKI's shortcomings, it was hard to believe, as Anderson and McVey wrote, that the party leadership would have "tied a rope around its neck and then waited to be hoisted from the nearest lamp post."[37] They noted that the PKI did not appear to have had a motivation for staging a coup d'état because the party "had been doing very well by the peaceful road" under President Sukarno.[38] W. F. Wertheim agreed with Anderson and McVey on this point: "Since 1951 the strategy of the PKI had been based on legality and parliamentary struggle and under the Sukarno regime this strategy had by all appearances been rather beneficial to the party, which makes the whole idea of a sudden shift of strategy towards violence highly improbable."[39]

Since the movement was a military operation involving very few civilians, Anderson and McVey believed that it must have emerged from within the military. They noticed that most of the movement's leaders were either former or current officers of the army's Diponegoro division, which covered Central Java. Latief was a Diponegoro officer who had been transferred to Jakarta in 1962. Untung had been the commander of Battalion 454 in Central Java before his posting to the presidential guard in early 1965. He had been very close to Colonel Suherman, the movement's main leader in Central Java, when they were serving in Battalion 454 together. Suherman had been the commander of 454 before Untung. That, of course, was same battalion that participated in the movement on October 1 by occupying Merdeka Square. It was striking that the only part of the country outside Jakarta where the movement was active was in Central Java.

Anderson and McVey viewed the movement as a kind of mutiny within the army by Central Javanese junior officers repelled by the decadent lifestyles and pro-Western political orientation of the high command in Jakarta. Such officers deemed the general staff under Yani guilty of "succumbing to the corruptions of Jakarta elite society, neglecting their former subordinates (General Yani and several others had been former Diponegoro officers), and consistently opposing and thwarting President Sukarno's external and internal policies."[40] Anderson and McVey contended that the movement was an attempt to shift the army in a more populist direction. They pointed to the movement's first statement, which had declared that "power-mad generals and officers who have neglected the lot of their subordinates, lived luxuriously and decadently atop the soldiers' accumulated sufferings, humiliated women, and squandered government revenues must be kicked out of the army and given appropriate punishments."

According to Anderson and McVey, the network of Central Javanese officers wanted to purge the army of such corrupt and politically conservative generals and allow Sukarno greater freedom to carry out his policies. To build up their forces these Central Javanese officers invited certain men of the air force and the PKI into the operation while they maintained control of its direction. The officers wanted the PKI to provide not only additional personnel for the operation but political backing once the action was over. Thus, instead of being the mastermind, the PKI was the dupe of these officers; the party had been "bamboozled" into involving itself in an action that it did not fully understand.[41] Since the PKI leaders thought they were playing only bit parts in someone else's drama, they did not take the action seriously and did not imagine that they would be blamed if the movement failed.

Anderson and McVey's thesis is vulnerable on a number of points. Is the Central Javanese background of the officers enough to explain how they bonded as a group? While some conspirators had been in the Diponegoro division (Latief, Suherman, Untung), others had not. Soejono and Supardjo were of Central Javanese ancestry, but they do not seem to have had a long-standing, intimate connection with the other officers. Soejono was in the air force and Supardjo was in the West Java division (Siliwangi) of the army. One of the battalions involved was from the East Java division (Brawijaya). Most putsches or coups have been staged by officers united by some strong, previously tested, fraternal bond: they had been students in the same graduating class of the military academy or officers in the same unit or participants in a particular military operation.[42] The movement consisted of a fairly disparate group of officers.

If Anderson and McVey are correct in arguing that military officers led the movement, why was its military strategy so poorly designed? The officers should have been capable of designing a sensible military action that would not have been so vulnerable to a counterattack. An action planned according to purely military considerations would presumably have turned out differently.

A major stumbling block for the Anderson and McVey thesis revolves around the afternoon radio announcements. Why would army officers who wanted to purge the army of corrupt, anti-Sukarno generals also decide to announce a new government of "Revolution Councils"? Why were they not content to eliminate the generals and then allow Sukarno full authority to take further action? Why did they bother to interfere with the president's prerogative in choosing his cabinet? Lacking definite answers to these questions, Anderson and McVey speculated that the statements were the result of "muddle and ineptness." They were a "panicked reaction" to Suharto's emerging counterattack and the president's refusal to issue a public statement fully supporting them. The "main aim" of the statements "seems to have been to try to compensate for the President's growing unwillingness to cooperate, by eliciting support from 'outside' groups within the society." By announcing the names of forty-five members of the Indonesian Revolution Council, an "extraordinary spectrum of unlikely characters," the movement hoped to broaden its base of support.[43] If that was the case, the question arises: Why did the movement try to broaden its base of support by impinging on the president's authority and claiming that all state power had fallen into its hands? Wouldn't that have unnecessarily antagonized all of Sukarno's many supporters? It would seem that the movement could have found a better way to drum up support short of proclaiming such a drastic change in the civilian government.

Anderson, in a more recent article, has altered his interpretation of the afternoon radio announcements. He now sees them as an indication that the movement was a setup. The announcements were meant to be ludicrous and counterproductive. He writes that the movement's long string of "stupidities" and "blunders" creates the suspicion "that this string was deliberately arranged to ensure the Movement's failure." The announcements "merely confused the public, paralyzed the masses, and provided easy pretexts for smashing the September 30th Movement itself." He explains the incoherence of the events as the intended handiwork of unknown army officers who wished to create a pretext for attacking the PKI. In proposing that the movement was designed to fail, Anderson has aligned himself with Wertheim's argumentation, which I will examine in more detail later in this chapter.[44] Anderson remains committed to the idea that the PKI was not the mastermind. In a 1996 interview he noted, "I cannot absolutely say that the PKI had no connection with the Movement. But I am still of the opinion that it was not the main designer of the Movement."[45]

The Movement as an Alliance of Army Officers and the PKI

Like Anderson and McVey, Harold Crouch found the army's insistence that the PKI was the mastermind to be unsupported by the evidence. He noted in his book *The Army and Politics in Indonesia* (1978) that there was "no strong evidence to show that the officers involved in the Thirtieth of September Movement were committed supporters of the PKI." There was "little to indicate that they were prepared to blindly follow instructions from the party."[46] In formulating an alternative to the regime's official version, Crouch did not believe that the opposite should be posited, that the army officers were the masterminds who had brought in the PKI members as dupes. According to Crouch, the evidence that had emerged in the Mahmillub trials held after Anderson and McVey wrote their report indicated that the PKI members involved in the movement could not be depicted as having been bamboozled. Courtroom testimony revealed that the involvement of the PKI, especially its members Sjam and Pono, was too deep to be written off as inadvertent and coincidental. Crouch could not endorse the Cornell paper's full exculpation of the PKI. Nevertheless, his overall conclusion was consonant with the basic premise of the Cornell paper. He argued that the "original initiative arose within the Army."[47] The PKI was heavily involved but remained a secondary player.

Crouch regarded the military officers involved in the movement as allies of the PKI, not its servants: "It is clear that they were willing to cooperate with representatives of the party in order to achieve their ends. It seems probable that all the main participants in the movement had been sounded out by the Special Bureau much earlier and were regarded favorably by Sjam and his colleagues. . . . While the Special Bureau representatives were important members of the plotting group, there is little evidence to show that their role was dominant."[48] Crouch portrayed the movement as the result of a solid collaboration between "progressive" army officers and the PKI's Special Bureau.

Crouch's version can be squared with the version put forth by Sudisman, a surviving member of the PKI Politburo's Working Committee (Dewan Harian), which was the nucleus of the party leadership. (Three other members—Aidit, Lukman, and Njoto—were secretly executed by the military sometime in late 1965. The fifth member, Oloan Hutapea, was executed in 1968 in East Java.) In his final speech before his 1967 military tribunal, Sudisman introduced a distinction between certain party leaders who became involved in the movement in a private capacity and the party as an institution, which "knew nothing about the September 30th Movement." The party as an institution, he argued, considered the movement as "an internal Army matter." He explained that the Central Committee had never discussed the movement and the party's rank-and-file had never been instructed to support it. Thus the party was not responsible as an institution. Sudisman admitted that some "prominent PKI leaders," including himself, had participated in ways that he did not specify.[49] According to Sudisman's statement, a group of progressive military officers acted on their own initiative, and certain members of the party, acting as individuals and without informing or coordinating with formal party organizations, provided assistance to those officers. Individual PKI leaders, at the very least Aidit and Sudisman, involved themselves in this clandestine military operation and brought with them selected groups of PKI supporters. For this handful of PKI leaders the movement was not an official party operation; it was an army putsch that would produce beneficial results for the party. The party leaders wanted to support the movement but did not want to involve the entire party in it. Sudisman affirmed that the initiative and leadership of the movement remained with the military officers.

Crouch's interpretation has been the most judicious and well-founded one available. Its problems lie in its limitations. While Crouch neatly resolved the matter of the mastermind, he left other matters unresolved. He could not explain why the movement was poorly designed and why it issued the afternoon radio announcements. Like Anderson and McVey's, his account does not sufficiently explain how the disparate group of military officers in the movement came together in the first place. If they originated the plan and had their own autonomy vis-à-vis the PKI, what was the basis of their commonality?

The Movement as a Frame-up of the PKI

The Suharto regime's version began to look particularly suspicious in the late 1960s when information emerged about Suharto's background. W. F. Wertheim, the prominent Dutch scholar on Indonesia, revealed in a short article in 1970 that Suharto had been a friend of two of the movement's leaders: Lieutenant Colonel Untung and Colonel Latief.[50] Suharto had traveled from Jakarta to a small town in Central Java (Kebumen) in late April 1964 to attend Untung's wedding. The connection between the two men must have been close since an army general would not have made such a long trip for frivolous reasons.[51] Suharto also knew Colonel Latief as a close friend. The two had known each other since the days of guerrilla warfare against the Dutch in the late 1940s. Suharto twice mentioned to foreign journalists that Latief had come to see him the night before the movement began. Suharto's explanation was that Latief wanted to either kill him or check on his position. He did not admit to speaking to Latief.[52] That Latief was kept imprisoned in an isolation cell for many years before being allowed to emerge in public suggests that Suharto was in a dilemma: he did not want to have Latief executed like the others but did not want him speaking in public.

Wertheim noted other suspicious aspects of the movement. Suharto was not among the generals abducted, although he was a key commander of troops in Jakarta and a potential threat to any mutiny or coup attempt. The movement's troops did not blockade Kostrad headquarters, although it was not far from their position in front of the palace. Suharto operated freely from his office in Kostrad while the rebel troops were milling about in Merdeka Square directly in front of him. Suharto, Wertheim thought, operated with "uncanny efficiency in extremely confusing circumstances."[53] Most military officers in Jakarta had little idea how to react. But Suharto seemed to know exactly what was needed to defeat the movement.

The mystery of the identity of Sjam provoked Wertheim's suspicions. The Suharto regime produced Sjam before the public in 1967 and claimed he was a confidante of Aidit's, entrusted with maintaining contacts within the military. Wertheim suggested the reverse may have been true: that Sjam was a military man entrusted to infiltrate the PKI. No one "who played a role within PKI or had close relations with it, had ever heard about this Sjam."[54] Sjam's testimony could not be trusted. He could have been a double agent who was acting on behalf of certain elements within the military. If so, he could have played a "provocateur's role" to get the PKI involved in an action that was programmed to fail.[55] In a follow-up article of 1979 Wertheim again accused Sjam of being a military plant within the PKI. There was "one specific person as the shrewd manipulator of the conspiracy: the mystery man Sjam acting as the agent of the Armed Forces."[56] Sjam acted on behalf of the anti-Communist elements of the army and was rewarded by special treatment in prison: "He has been treated with respect by interrogators and no one has ever seen him being maltreated or tortured during or after interrogations. He had been recompensed for his 'co-operative' attitude during the trials by highly privileged treatment both at Nirbaya prison near Jakarta and, later, in Rumah Tahanan Militer, the military detention house where he was transferred at his own request because he apparently felt safer there. All this happened in spite of the death sentence he had received."[57]

Wertheim seems correct on one point: Suharto was close to both Latief and Untung. At his trial in 1978 Latief confirmed what Suharto had already admitted: that the two had seen each other on the night of September 30, 1965. But he contradicted Suharto's claim that the two had not spoken with each other. Latief testified that he had informed Suharto that some army officers were about to act against the Council of Generals: "One day before the event I directly reported to Major General Suharto when he was at the Army Hospital waiting for his son who had been scalded by hot soup. Having reported to him, I obtained moral support because there wasn't any reaction from him."[58] Latief went further. He claimed that he also had discussed the issue of the Council of Generals with Suharto the day before (on September 29) at Suharto's residence in Jakarta:

> Two days before the October 1, 1965 event, I along with my family visited General Suharto's house on Jalan Haji Agus Salim. At that time he was the commander of Kostrad. Besides paying a family visit, I intended to ask him about information concerning the Council of Generals and at the same time report to him what I knew. It was he himself who informed me that a former subordinate of his from Yogyakarta named Subagiyo had informed him the day before I came to his house of the existence of the Council of Generals that would stage a coup d'état against the government of President Sukarno. His opinion was that inquiries

needed to be made. Because there were many guests in the room, our conversation was steered to other matters.[59]

Latief explained in court how he had become a family friend of Suharto's. He had served with Suharto since the late 1940s:

> As a subordinate, I was rarely outside the chain of command under General Suharto; wherever he was, I was always with him. From this arose a familiarity between us and our families beyond official duties. Indeed, I am a former subordinate who served directly under his leadership when, at the time of the guerrilla struggle [in the late 1940s] I was commander of Company 100 which was, organizationally and tactically, directly under Brigade X. . . . I have been familiar with him since we were together in Central Java. If he was ever in a different chain of command, I would still visit him often. Usually, subordinate officers of my rank (battalion commander) would rarely visit him—I was the exception. The others said they were reluctant because General Suharto was considered too intimidating. In my opinion, he wasn't. One proof is that when he had his son Sigit circumcised, even my family attended the ceremony. I wasn't able to go because my mother in Surabaya was very sick. Likewise, when I had my son circumcised he and Ibu Tien [Suharto's wife] came to my house. So my conclusion was that we were like family and didn't have any problem at all. Indeed, we had a very close relationship.[60]

Latief was so close to Suharto that he proposed during that September 29 visit to exchange houses with Suharto. As an officer in the Jakarta district command, Latief had been given a large house that had been the former residence of the British ambassador. Latief claimed that he had planned to give that house to Suharto and then move his family into Suharto's more modest house. Latief wanted his old friend and superior officer to have the better house.[61]

Untung, according to Latief, was also a former subordinate on close terms with Suharto: "Lieutenant Colonel Untung as well was once his [Suharto's] immediate subordinate in the Korem of Solo. Later Lieutenant Colonel Untung was chosen as one of the guerrilla leaders who parachuted into Halmana [in Irian Jaya] during the Trikora campaign. I once heard from Lieutenant Colonel Untung himself that General Suharto was angry when, after his tour of duty in Trikora was completed, he [Untung] was transferred to the palace guard. Suharto had wanted to appoint him to a Kostrad unit and bring him under his command."[62]

Suspicions about Suharto abound: he was on close terms with Untung and Latief, two of the battalions used by the movement had been brought to Jakarta on his orders, and he benefited most from the action. For Wertheim these facts indicated that Suharto was among the masterminds of the movement. The real puppet masters were "some high military men who used a double agent like Sjam for their own ends." Their intention was to create a pretext by which they could attack the PKI and undermine Sukarno's power: "The whole affair rather looks like a well-planned plot, specifically aimed at hopelessly compromising both the PKI and President Sukarno himself, and thus providing the occasion and excuse for eliminating their influence in Indonesian politics."[63] The movement appeared so incoherent and ineffectual because it was a fake operation that was meant to be easily defeated.[64]

Wertheim did not speculate on the precise roles that Suharto, Untung, and Latief played in the movement. Wertheim's story line implied that Suharto was somehow in league with his friends in organizing the movement; perhaps Suharto initiated the movement, placed his two old friends and Sjam in the leadership of it, and then betrayed them. Or perhaps Suharto revealed to his friends that the movement would indeed fail but promised them that they would be saved and given comfortable positions in the new government.[65]

While Wertheim's solution to the puzzle is elegant enough, explaining some of the oddities in a consistent narrative, it has to face some obvious objections. First, it seems improbable. In Wertheim's scenario Suharto becomes a figure of superhuman genius. Everything worked according to his plan. The movement did not just implicate the PKI and quickly collapse, it opened the way for Suharto to become army commander. Suharto's superior officer (Yani) and most of his peers and rivals were eliminated in one fell swoop. It is difficult to believe that Suharto could have been so clever in arranging a clandestine action that worked so perfectly for him. Suharto did not have a reputation for being a particularly intelligent schemer.

Second, if Suharto worked with other generals in what Wertheim calls a "generals' conspiracy" to organize the movement, it seems improbable that they would have designed a plan that called for killing seven other generals. If the goal was a pretext for crushing the PKI and bringing the army into state power, why would they be willing to seriously damage the army in the process? Why would they be willing to sacrifice their fellow anti-Communist officers? Wertheim realized the obvious point, that Yani's general staff could not have organized the movement because so many of them became its victims. What other generals would have conspired to organize the movement? The only reason to kill the generals would be to clear the path for Suharto's ascendance. The mastermind could only have been Suharto himself since it is unlikely he would have received help from any other general for a plan that put the lives of seven generals at risk. Wertheim acknowledged that Suharto was the only general with the motivation to organize the movement but resiled from the argument that Suharto did in fact organize it. Instead, Wertheim proposed the more modest claim that Suharto, "even if he was not personally involved in the conspiracy," had foreknowledge of the action. For Wertheim, Suharto's culpability lay, at the very least, in not informing his superior officers about the plot.[66] That is a far lesser claim than that some pro-Suharto military officers used Sjam as a double agent to create a fake coup.

Third, the goal of implicating the PKI in a coup attempt could have been achieved in a much more straightforward, unequivocal fashion. If certain army generals, or Suharto himself, had designed the movement with that goal in mind, they should have had Untung's group announce over the radio that they were working for the PKI and wished to overthrow Sukarno. The movement carefully hid its links to the PKI and never clearly stated that it wanted to stage a coup against Sukarno. Its first statement claimed that Untung wanted to protect Sukarno. None of its statements mentioned the PKI.

Fourth, the movement leaders did not think that they were acting on behalf of Suharto. If they had, they would have demanded that Sukarno appoint Suharto as Yani's replacement. Through Supardjo the movement leaders recommended the names of three generals as candidates for the position of the army's temporary caretaker: Pranoto, Basuki Rachmat, and U. Rukman.[67] They did not propose Suharto's name. While mulling over all the possibilities, Sukarno rejected Suharto because he was "too stubborn," and Supardjo does not appear to have pleaded on Suharto's behalf.[68] It is hard to believe that the movement would kill off army generals for Suharto's benefit and then not lobby Sukarno to appoint him interim commander.

Wertheim's proposed narrative—the movement as a "well-organized plot" to frame the PKI—remains at the level of speculation, as Wertheim himself acknowledged.[69] Suharto's actions could just as easily be explained by accepting Latief's story. Latief argued at his tribunal that he and Untung acted independently from Suharto and obtained from him only tacit support ("there wasn't any reaction from him"). Latief explained that he and Untung had come to view Suharto as a firm supporter of President Sukarno's and trusted that he would support them in their action against the Council of Generals: "Indeed, I believed that among all people he was the one most loyal to the leadership of President Sukarno. I had known him since Yogyakarta [in the late 1940s] and I knew the real General Suharto."[70] According to Latief, he had simply misjudged Suharto.

Latief's and Untung's friendship with Suharto and their trust in his loyalty to President Sukarno could explain why the movement did not target Suharto for abduction and execution. Since the movement counted on Suharto's support, Latief and Untung may have thought their plan was foolproof and that they needed only a small number of troops to successfully occupy Jakarta. That the two main battalions involved in the movement were under Kostrad command does not prove that Suharto was complicit. The conspirators could have struck up an agreement with the battalion commanders without Suharto's knowledge or the knowledge of any other officer at Kostrad headquarters. Latief's tip-off to Suharto would explain why he was able to act with "uncanny efficiency in extremely confusing circumstances." A residual familial affection, and perhaps some gratitude for the tip-off, would explain why Suharto did not have Latief executed. Although the evidence does not support the claim that Suharto was the mastermind, it suggests, at the very least, that he had foreknowledge of the movement, gave his tacit support, and then betrayed his naive former confidantes.

Each of these four narrative strategies fails to account for all the movement's anomalies. The plausibility of each depends upon highlighting a limited range of facts while ignoring, glossing over, or incorrectly explaining other facts. In the decades that have passed since the event, no one has been able to arrive at a wholly satisfactory narrative. The movement has become like an unsolvable Rubik's cube, one on which the six colors cannot be aligned with the six sides. No one has been able to square (or cube, shall we say?) the facts with a plausible narrative.

One obstacle to solving the puzzle has been the forceful imposition of a false solution immediately after the event. As Suharto's army asserted its own narrative—the PKI as the *dalang* (the puppet master)—it invented facts (like the Lubang Buaya torture story and the confessions of PKI leaders). With its volumes of propaganda the Suharto regime has booby-trapped the historians' path with false clues, dead-end diversions, and doctored bits of evidence. The falsity of Suharto's solution is apparent in its imprecise use of the term *PKI*. According to the official version, the *PKI* masterminded the movement. But it is obvious that the PKI, as an institution that consisted of millions of people, could not have organized a secretive military rebellion.

If the PKI in the aggregate was not responsible, what was the precise connection between the PKI leaders and the movement? For instance, what was Aidit doing at Halim Air Force Base? Anderson and McVey presented him as "a dupe" of the rebel officers. But they wrote their analysis before information emerged about the important role played by Sjam and the Special Bureau and before Sudisman admitted that particular party leaders had been involved "in a personal capacity." Crouch reconciled this new information with the Cornell paper's analysis by arguing that certain PKI leaders and members actively assisted, but did not direct, a putsch by junior army officers. Crouch's proposed narrative has been the best informed so far but, like the Cornell paper, it has not been able to explain why a pro-Sukarno military rebellion should aim to decommission Sukarno's cabinet.

Wertheim's narrative managed to resolve this anomaly by depicting it as a deliberate provocation: the decommissioning of the cabinet was meant to guarantee that the public would not support the movement. According to Wertheim, certain PKI leaders became involved in the movement because they were, as the Cornell paper had argued, duped. But they were duped not by the rebel officers but by a cabal of anti-PKI officers and their double agent, Sjam. The officers who wanted to destroy the PKI and overthrow Sukarno designed the movement so that it would it implicate the PKI in a crime and then collapse. Sjam lured Aidit and other elements of the PKI into a trap. While Wertheim's story line solves the anomaly of the cabinet's decommissioning, it generates other anomalies. If the movement was a setup, it had to have been designed by Suharto or officers working for him. Yet the officers in the movement did not propose that Sukarno appoint Suharto as Yani's replacement. Ultimately, Wertheim's solution fails to account for many pieces of the puzzle.

3

The Supardjo Document

The blaring overture that announced the contest dies away in a pusil-
lanimous snarl as soon as the struggle has to begin, the actors cease to
take themselves *au serieux,* and the action collapses completely, like a
pricked bubble. . . . The revolution itself paralyzes its own bearers and
endows only its adversaries with passionate forcefulness.

Karl Marx, *The Eighteenth Brumaire of Louis Bonaparte* (1852)

Torture-induced confessions, dissimulating testimonies, fabricated
media stories by army psychological warfare specialists—amid the
abundance of information about the movement, precious little can be
considered reliable evidence. Analysts have been unable propose anything more than educated guesses about the identity of the real leaders
and their motivations. Were Sjam and Aidit in charge, as Sjam himself
testified at his trial? Or were Untung and the other military officers in
charge, as they testified at their trials? Or were they working together as
a team with neither clearly in charge? Or was Suharto somehow behind
them as the *dalang,* the puppet master, of the entire miserable drama?
In the absence of any unimpeachable evidence, these questions cannot
be answered with any certainty.

Given that the evidence about the movement has been confused and
suspect, it should not be surprising to discover that a crucial piece of evidence has been overlooked. One of the conspirators of the movement
present at Halim air base on the day of October 1, Brigadier General Supardjo, wrote a postmortem analysis of their failure. He titled it "Some
Factors That Influenced the Defeat of 'the September 30th Movement'
as Viewed from a Military Perspective" (see appendix 1). Analysts have so

far not recognized this document for what it is: the most important primary source on the movement. It is the only document that has surfaced to date that was written by a participant in the movement before his arrest. As such, the information that it contains is of unique reliability and frankness. Supardjo was writing for the benefit of his colleagues, not for hostile interrogators and prosecutors. If we are to analyze the movement afresh, we should begin with this document, see what conclusions can be drawn from it, and then reexamine the remaining evidence in light of it.

It hardly needs to be said that the Supardjo document cannot answer all the questions about the movement. The author was an individual with his own particular angle of vision. Supardjo was not one of the core organizers. Only five individuals led the movement and, presumably, understood all or most of its intricacies and subterfuges: Sjam, Pono, Lieutenant Colonel Untung, Colonel Latief, and Major Soejono. On the day of the action Supardjo was with these five individuals at Halim Air Force Base in Jakarta, and he served as their representative to President Sukarno. But he had not attended any of their planning meetings in the weeks before. He had arrived in Jakarta only three days before the action. While Supardjo was able to fulfill the promise of the title—"factors that contributed to the failure" of the movement—he did not understand all the reasons for that failure. As he saw the action unfold, he was mystified as to the underlying logic of certain decisions. This is where his unfamiliarity with the discussions and planning sessions during the previous weeks proved to be a limitation to his analysis. Moreover, he knew little about the status of the movement in Central Java, the province where it was strongest. Supardjo attempted to be strictly rational in writing his analysis: in the first section of the text he reports the events that he witnessed and then in the second section he lists his interpretations of those events. Of course, he might have misperceived certain events or misinterpreted what he had perceived.

In this chapter I present background information about Supardjo and then describe the document's significant claims concerning the leadership of the movement, the movement's plan of action, the implementation of that plan, and the movement's strategies in regard to President Sukarno and Major General Suharto.

Supardjo's Background and His Analysis

When I first began researching the events of the mid-1960s, I was struck by the oddity of Supardjo's participation in the movement. He was named in the second radio announcement (Decree no. 1) of October 1, 1965, as the number two man in the hierarchy of the movement; he was the deputy commander whose name immediately followed that of the commander, Lieutenant Colonel Untung. Why would a higher-ranking officer be willing to put himself under a lower-ranking officer? The fourth announcement (Decision no. 2), read over the radio in the early afternoon, canceled all ranks above lieutenant colonel. Why would a decorated, career military officer who had painstakingly worked his way up the hierarchy for twenty years participate in an action that would result in his demotion? What meaning could such a cancellation of higher ranks have when, at about the time of the announcement, Supardjo was sitting before the president in his uniform with its brigadier general's insignia on full display?

The very presence of Supardjo in Jakarta at the time of the action was curious because he was normally stationed far away, in West Kalimantan, as the commander of the troops along the border with Malaysia. His official title was commander of the Fourth Combat Command of the Mandala Vigilance Command (Panglima Komando Tempur IV Komando Mandala Siaga).[1] The other officers involved in the action, such as Lieutenant Colonel Untung, Colonel Latief, and Major Soejono, commanded troops in Jakarta. But Supardjo seemingly could not provide any troops for the action. What was the purpose of his involvement if he was merely an individual player and did not have any troops to contribute? He could not have been significantly involved in planning the action of October 1 since he had spent nearly all his time during the previous months along the border with Malaysia. And if he was not involved in planning it, why would he be willing to participate in it? He was not a long-standing, close, and trusted friend of the other officers. He was from the army's West Java command (Siliwangi), whereas Latief and Untung were from the Central Java command (Diponegoro), and Soejono was an air force officer based in Jakarta. How did Supardjo get mixed up with this group in the first place?

Supardjo's unique position as an outsider and an insider make this document particularly valuable. He was able to view the events from the perspective of a detached spectator. He begins his essay by stating that he was involved with the movement for only three days—meaning September 30, October 1, and October 2—and that this was a very short time "compared with the length of time of all the preparations." On the other hand, Supardjo was an insider. He was with the core organizers in their Halim air base hideout, conversing with them minute by minute about how the action should proceed. They trusted him to talk to President Sukarno on their behalf. On the day of the action no other person was as close to the core organizers as Supardjo.

At the very least, this document can help clear up some misconceptions about Supardjo's role. Because he was the highest-ranking officer in the movement, many commentators have mistakenly assumed that he was a key leader, if not *the* key leader. The U.S. ambassador to Indonesia at the time describes Supardjo in his memoir as "the coup's real tactical commander."[2] Suharto's autobiography claims that Sukarno once said in private that the entire movement was under the command of Supardjo.[3] Others assert that he was the commander of the troops that occupied Merdeka Square.[4] Back in 1966 Untung's lawyer, in a desperate bid to protect his client, argued in court that Supardjo had been the mastermind of the entire plot and that Untung had merely followed orders from a superior officer.[5] Supardjo's own document reveals that he was not the leader of the movement and did not command any of its troops.[6]

Supardjo's own explanation of how he came to Jakarta might be accurate. He stated in court that he left Kalimantan because his youngest child was seriously sick and thought to be dying. His wife had sent a radiogram asking him to return to Jakarta.[7] Once in the capital, he took advantage of his visit to learn the latest news about the planning against the Council of Generals. He acknowledged that he met with his old friend Sjam, who told him about the upcoming action. Supardjo claimed that he would have returned to his base in Kalimantan before October 1 if his superior officer, Omar Dani, had not asked him to stay until October 3 for a meeting the president. Dani and Supardjo both wanted to talk to Sukarno about what could be done to prevent a coup by the Council of Generals. Supardjo was keeping track of two separate efforts to counter the right-wing generals: Dani's plan on one side and the movement on the other. The movement moved first and preempted Dani's plan.[8] Perhaps Supardjo was being disingenuous in his courtroom testimony; he might have come to Jakarta precisely so that he could collaborate with Sjam. He might have been committed to the movement from the start. However it may be, Supardjo's role in the movement was limited, even superfluous.

Supardjo functioned as an adviser or assistant rather than as a commander. On the morning of October 1 he was driven to the palace with two battalion commanders who could have easily served as the movement's liaisons with the president. In all likelihood the movement's original plan relied on only these two officers, Captain Sukirno and

Major Supeno, to meet the president. Supardjo's participation could not be counted upon since he was far off in Kalimantan and had no orders to return to Jakarta. The battalion commanders had been ordered to come to Jakarta with their troops for the October 5 Armed Forces Day parade. Arriving in Jakarta only three days before the action, Supardjo may have been a last-minute addition to the plan.

Supardjo's postmortem analysis suggests that he had not been responsible for organizing the movement. He wrote as an army officer perplexed by all the movement's deviations from standard military practice. If he had been in charge, one can assume that it would have been a more professional operation. Supardjo had become a brigadier general at forty-four precisely because he had been highly successful in combat. By 1965 he had served in the army for twenty years, from the time of the war of independence, when he had distinguished himself in the fighting in West Java against Dutch troops. Against a seemingly unassailable Dutch encampment, he had used a modern industrial variation on the Trojan horse tactic. He commandeered a train, secretly boarded three hundred soldiers into the cars, and then surprised a far larger force of Dutch troops as the train passed near their fort.[9] Later, as a district commander in West Java in the late 1950s and early 1960s, he had played a crucial role in the counterinsurgency warfare that defeated the Darul Islam movement. He had also studied the theory of warfare, having spent a year at the staff college of Pakistan's army in Quetta, where he wrote a manuscript on guerrilla warfare.[10] When it came to military matters, the slim general with the pencil mustache was an expert.

Supardjo wrote his analysis of the movement while he was on the run. His life was in near ruins: the movement had collapsed; he had been stripped of his rank and dismissed from the army; he was cut off from his wife and nine children (who were put under constant surveillance); his coconspirators, such as Untung, were being put on trial and sentenced to death. The army was hunting all over the country for Supardjo. Despite what must have been his great disappointment, he wrote about the movement without spite or rancor.

Since the document is not dated, we are left to speculate when it was composed. Supardjo wrote this analysis at least one month after the event; he mentioned that a letter he had written to Sukarno in early October 1965 was delivered a month late. We can assume that he wrote the analysis for the benefit of Sudisman, who, as the senior surviving member of the nucleus of the PKI's Politburo, took up the responsibility in 1966 to write a critique of the PKI's earlier policies. Supardjo noted in

5. Supardjo and Ibu Supardjo, ca. 1962. Photo
credit: Supardjo family collection

the first paragraph that his analysis was meant to help the "comrades of
the leadership" develop a "comprehensive analysis" of the movement.
The Politburo's critique was issued in September 1966, so Supardjo's
analysis was probably written before then.[11]

During the questioning at his Mahmillub trial, Supardjo admitted
to orally communicating his criticisms of the movement to another
party leader, Soejono Pradigdo, in September 1966 and to meeting Sudisman one month after that through Pradigdo's mediation. The head
judge asked Supardjo twice on the last day of his questioning whether he
had ever written "a self-criticism about the failure of the September 30th
Movement" and whether Sudisman had asked him to write "a sort of
self-criticism." Supardjo curtly replied no.[12] There is no reason to trust
either Supardjo's chronology here of meeting Sudisman or Supardjo's
denial that he had written such a document. Throughout the questioning at the trial Supardjo's answers were, naturally enough, always terse

and often evasive. His answers became especially evasive when the questions concerned his relationship to the PKI.

Supardjo's repudiation of the document is understandable because particular passages were highly incriminating. The open question is why the Mahmillub judges and prosecutors decided not to adduce the document as evidence and thereby make its existence public knowledge, especially since it showed that Supardjo was sympathetic to the PKI and that Sjam had played a leading role in the movement. The judges did not pursue the questioning of Supardjo about the document and did not reveal to the public that the court was in possession of it.[13] Perhaps they believed it would have complicated their story line and opened up a whole new set of questions. Perhaps they were wary of the effect such a document would have had on the PKI activists still struggling against Suharto's army. Supardjo wrote it to help them learn from their mistakes. Since the Mahmillub trials were for show and not for getting at the truth of the event, one should not be overly surprised that the prosecutors did not use the document to advance their case. The verdict was predetermined; they needed only to go through the motions. Moreover, the military court did not follow strict rules of evidence; the judges would have read the document in private and did not have to have it entered into the court record for it to become part of their deliberations—if any were held. The prosecutors and judges decided what evidence would appear in court based upon considerations of its utility for public opinion. The Suharto regime never wanted the Indonesian public to soberly and rationally examine the events of early October 1965. Suharto's army whipped up a hysterical witchhunt against the PKI and then instituted bizarre anti-Communist laws that went so far as to discriminate against the grandchildren of those stamped by the government with the label PKI. Until 1994 the regime did not present a white book on the movement to convince the Indonesian public through rational argumentation that the PKI had led the movement, and even then the book it published was an absurd mishmash of unsubstantiated, unreferenced statements.[14]

There is little doubt about the authenticity of the Supardjo document, despite his own disavowals. The text is too convoluted to have been forged. The army's attempts at forgery—the confessions of Aidit and Njono—were remarkably crude. Moreover, army intelligence agents would not have gone to such great lengths to draft such an intricate document and then never use it. Both Lieutenant Colonel Heru Atmodjo, who was imprisoned with Supardjo, and Supardjo's son, Sugiarto, have confirmed that Supardjo wrote the document.

The Leadership of the Movement

Although Supardjo observed the movement at close range, he admitted that even he was confused about who was actually leading it. The movement, which disregarded standard principles of military organization, did not have a single overall commander giving orders within a clear chain of command. The collaboration between the PKI group (Sjam and Pono) and the military group (Untung, Latief, and Soejono) was loosely structured, to the point that the two groups were constantly debating what to do, even at critical moments when decisions needed to be made quickly. Supardjo, ever the military man, was frustrated at not being able to determine who had the final authority. Describing the last day, October 2, when they were under siege and Suharto's troops were approaching, Supardjo wrote: "What happened at that time was a debate, or a discussion that was langiradis [*langdradig*, without end], to the point that we were confused on witnessing it: Who is really the commander: Comrade Sjam, Comrade Untung, Comrade Latief, or Pak Djojo [Major Soejono]?"

Supardjo thought the candidates for the position of commander should have been either Untung or Sjam: "The operation should have been under one person. Since this was a military movement, it was best if the combat command was given to Comrade Untung while Comrade Sjam acted as a political commissioner. Or vice versa, Comrade Sjam being the one holding the supreme command." Supardjo was greatly bothered by this problem of leadership. He came back to it in a later section: "First it should have been decided who would be the commander who would directly lead the action (campaign). Whether Comrade Sjam or Comrade Untung. Then his assistants or staff should have been appointed." Obviously, Sjam played a very important role within the core group if Supardjo considered him to be on par with Untung, the nominal leader of the movement. Although Untung's name was placed before the public as the commander (in the first statement read over the radio), it appears that Sjam, whose name was not publicized, was at least of equal importance in the decision-making process on the day of the action.

Instead of a chain of command, the movement created what Supardjo called *rows*. The word he used, *sjaf*, evokes rows like those of Muslims praying in a mosque. Supardjo perceived three rows: "a) the Head Group [Kelompok Ketua], b) the Sjam and friends group, c) the Untung and friends group." By "Sjam and friends" Supardjo apparently meant the Special Bureau: Sjam, Pono, and Bono. By "Untung and friends," he apparently meant the military officers Untung, Latief, and Soejono. The first group, "the Head Group," was not identified by a person's name, as the other two were. Though Supardjo implied that these three rows did not constitute a tight line of command (descending from a to b to c), the term *Head Group* certainly suggests that it was above the other two in some way. Who was above Sjam and Untung? By the end of the document the answer is clear. Supardjo later reveals that the Head Group was the PKI leadership: the movement was an "operation that was led directly by the party [*operasi yang langsung di-pimpin oleh partai*]." Supardjo put the Special Bureau personnel second on the list because they functioned as the linchpin between the PKI leadership and the military personnel. Although Sjam may have shared the command of the movement with Untung on the day of the action, he actually stood above Untung because he was part of "the party," which was the real leader of the movement.

One should not assume that Supardjo had direct, detailed knowledge of the party's involvement in the movement. Since his only contact with the PKI was Sjam, Supardjo's claim that "the party" led the movement must have been based on inference. Observing Sjam's playing a leading role in the movement and believing that Sjam was acting on orders of higher-ups in the PKI, Supardjo inferred that "the party" was the real leader. He knew, at least, that Aidit was at Halim and that Sjam was conferring with Aidit during the day of the action. (Supardjo met Omar Dani the night of October 1 to request an air force plane to transport Aidit to Central Java.) However, Supardjo could not have known who else in the party, if anyone, was involved. Nothing in the document suggests that he understood the respective roles played by Aidit, the Politburo, and the Central Committee. As a military man, he would not have had any knowledge of the party's internal decision-making processes. When Supardjo speaks about "the party," one should not interpret that to mean that he knew for certain that the party leadership as a whole designed the movement, much less supported it or knew about it. For him, "the party" was shorthand for Aidit and unknown other people above Sjam. Supardjo's allegation that "the party" led the movement does not prove that the PKI was responsible *as an institution*. He could have known for certain only that Sjam was leading the movement and was somehow working with Aidit.

As Supardjo saw it, Sjam was the liaison between the Head Group and the military officers who were willing to put themselves at the service of the party. Sjam thus had more authority within the movement than the officers. Given Supardjo's statement, Sjam's own testimony on this point might well be correct: "I held the political leadership and Untung held the military leadership, but the military leadership was under the political leadership. So it is I who am responsible for all of what occurred during the movement."[15]

At his trial Supardjo acknowledged that he had become involved in the action because of his connection to Sjam. He claimed that he had first met Sjam in 1956 and had occasionally used him thereafter as a source of military intelligence. For Supardjo, Sjam was someone who was well connected and in possession of a great deal of information about political and military affairs. He knew Sjam both as a representative *(wakil)* of the PKI and as an "informer of the army" who possessed an army identification card.[16] When Supardjo flew into Jakarta on September 28, 1965, from the Malaysian front, he headed for Sjam's house within only hours of landing. He visited Sjam again the following night and held discussions with him about the upcoming action. On the night of September 30, Supardjo again went to Sjam's house and traveled with him to Halim Air Force Base for the beginning of the action. Supardjo was not well acquainted, if acquainted at all, with the other officers in the movement such as Untung and Latief.

In his postmortem analysis Supardjo explains that he was willing to join the movement because he thought the party knew what it was doing. The PKI at that time had a reputation for being highly disciplined and tightly organized. After all, it was a vast organization with millions of members throughout the country, from ministers in Sukarno's cabinet down to illiterate peasants in remote, inaccessible villages, and it was sustaining an impressive variety of activities: it ran its own schools, published newspapers, and staged cultural performances. Many scholars have had difficulty believing that the PKI organized the movement precisely because it was such an incoherent and amateurish operation. Supardjo assumed that the party was more far-sighted than he and had devised a brilliant, foolproof plan. He acknowledges that it was a terrible mistake on his part to have "overestimated the ability of the comrades of the leadership of the operation." When he joined the action, he had full faith in "the leadership" despite his doubts about the prospects for success: "Even though the actual facts did not add up, we still believed that the leadership must have a superior set of calculations and that it would be made known to us at the appropriate moment. The mystery would be revealed later. After all, the slogan of the leadership was always: 'Enough, we just have to begin and everything else will just fall into place.'"

Supardjo's explanation of his own willingness to follow the plan may provide clues to the reason that other military officers, such as Untung, Latief, and Soejono, were willing to participate. Supardjo mentioned that the military officers were highly doubtful of the success of the plan that Sjam proposed and at least one had decided to withdraw.[17] Officers such as Supardjo stayed on, despite their doubts, only because they trusted the wisdom of a party leadership that had been so successful in organizing millions of people.

The core leaders' indecisiveness on the day of the action appears to have been the result of an ambiguity in their respective roles. Supardjo presents the movement as having been plagued with an inherent inconsistency. On the one hand, Sjam was the overall leader who had prodded the military officers into joining with assurances of success; the officers thus deferred to his leadership. On the other hand, Sjam, having initiated the operation, depended upon the military officers for its execution. He had to defer to them while the operation was underway since he was a civilian who could not command troops himself. Supardjo, although he was aware that Sjam was the leader, was confused about the core group's decision making and had to ask, "Who is really the commander?"

The list of deputy commanders announced over the radio bore no relation to the real chain of command. The four men on the list had no authority within the movement. Supardjo, at the top of the list, did not command any of the movement's troops. (He acknowledges in his analysis that he asked to be given command of the remaining troops on the last day but did not receive a clear response from Sjam and Untung.) In his courtroom testimony Supardjo denied that he had ever been consulted about the list of deputy commanders; his name "was written down there according to their own whims."[18] (Supardjo did not identify the "they" to whom he was referring. One may assume he meant Sjam and Pono.) When I interviewed another officer listed as a deputy commander, Lieutenant Colonel Atmodjo, he denied that he knew about the list of deputy commanders, much less signed it. He claimed that Sjam and Pono put his name on the list and that later, when he was in prison, Pono apologized to him for including his name without permission.[19] Sjam needed the names of four officers, one from each branch of the military, to give the appearance that the movement had wide support within the armed forces. The symbolism was more important than their concrete contributions to the movement. Sjam probably assumed that they would be happy to be known as the deputy commanders if the movement was successful. Supardjo notes that "the leadership" (again this must be Sjam), would say, "Yeah, brother, if you want a revolution, a lot of people want to stay back, but once you've already won, everybody wants to join."

One of the most interesting aspects of Supardjo's analysis is the distinction he makes between an original plan and a revised plan. The error of "the party," according to Supardjo, was usurping a preexisting plan of "democratic-revolutionary" military officers for dealing with the right-wing army leadership. He mentions the existence of an original two-stage plan whose first stage was "limited to the officer corps" and was "of an internal army nature." This first stage was intended to eliminate the pro-American army generals and was not to have involved the PKI in any way. Military officers supportive of Sukarno were to carry out this first stage by themselves. By a process Supardjo does not explain, that plan was abandoned. There was a "shift of the operational plan, which was originally of an internal army nature, to an operation that was led directly by the party, and that dragged the party into this and resulted in the destruction of the party."

Going by this explanation, it would appear that Sjam and his immediate superior, Aidit, were aware of "democratic-revolutionary" officers and were waiting for them to act. Supardjo does not explain how, within the terms of the original plan, these officers were to "seize the army leadership." Perhaps they intended to follow an administrative route: they would pressure Sukarno into replacing Yani and Nasution with officers who were sincerely committed to his policies, and these replacements would then reassign or dismiss pro-American officers. Or perhaps the "democratic-revolutionary" officers intended to follow the model of the classic putsch and use their troops to forcibly "seize the army leadership" with methods similar to those that the movement employed. Supardjo does not explain which officers were involved in this original plan.

That Supardjo objected to the PKI's takeover of what had been planned as an internal military operation was confirmed to me by a former PKI Politburo member, Rewang, who spoke with Supardjo sometime in 1967 while they were both confined in the Military Detention Center (Rumah Tahanan Militer) in Jakarta. Supardjo told him that it would have been better if the PKI had not intervened *(campur tangan)* and had allowed military officers to counter the Council of Generals on their own.[20]

According to Supardjo, in the first stage of the original plan, the broadest possible front of pro-Sukarno forces would depose the generals who had been conspiring with the United States and Britain. Once this first stage was accomplished and the army was in the hands of Sukarnoist and left-leaning officers, the PKI would be able to mobilize its masses without fear of army repression. The demonstrations and actions of the PKI "would be shadowed by progressive military troops." If the first stage of the revolution was to have been a purely nationalist movement of military officers, the second stage was to be "a purely PKI movement." Supardjo does not mention when and precisely how this original plan was abandoned.

In his courtroom testimony Supardjo stated that he and other military officers had been thinking about how to counter the anti-Sukarno generals. He contended that he and Omar Dani were scheduled to meet the president on October 3 to talk to him about the Council of Generals.[21] Sukarno himself was worried about an army coup in mid-1965. He was convinced that the CIA was plotting against him, especially after Marshall Green arrived as U.S. ambassador in July.[22] Green had been the ambassador to South Korea in 1961 when General Park Chung Hee staged a coup against the civilian government of Chang Myon and replaced it with a military junta.[23] One can assume that Sukarno's loyalists in the military held many discussions about the likelihood of a coup and floated many ideas about how to counter the right-wing army generals. For Supardjo the movement resulted from the initiative of the party (meaning, from Supardjo's perspective, Sjam). The party interfered with the plan of some pro-Sukarno officers to deal with the Council of Generals by themselves.

Supardjo's conclusion is credible: the movement failed precisely because it had been led by a civilian, Sjam, who knew little of proper military procedures. By putting himself in charge of a military action, Sjam created confusion within the core group itself about the chain of command. He did not define the precise nature of his role and the extent of his authority. The officers suspended their strictly military calculations and put their trust in Sjam because he claimed to work on behalf of a powerful, well-organized, and well-informed political party. With Sjam's intervention the movement's military character became compromised.

The Plan

Supardjo's picture of the unnamed leader of the movement is not flattering. He was stubborn, arrogant, dismissive of skeptics, and determined to carry out the plan. Supardjo writes: "When opinions were solicited, someone asked, are these forces really enough to balance the other forces, the answer was delivered in an intimidating tone: if you want to make a revolution, few will want to join in, but if the revolution is successful, just wait and see, many people will want to join in." At another point in the deliberations doubters were intimidated into silence. When someone (probably Supardjo) asked what the leader would do if the West Java military troops just outside Jakarta launched a counterattack, the response did not address the question; it only ordered the person not to lose commitment: "Enough, don't think about backing off!" It was as if the mere thought of contingency planning was considered an invitation to defeatism. Supardjo mentions that doubts about the loyalty of the troops to the action "were suppressed with the slogan 'Whatever happens, we can't turn back.'" The leader was so hell-bent on the action that he did not brook questioning, much less criticism. The bullying reached such an extent that the operatives in the regions reporting to "the leadership" in Jakarta felt compelled to report that they were prepared to take action. Supardjo notes, "When the information was received from the regions, it turned out that the regions were not ready. . . . Bandung was [not] fully ready but in order to avoid facing harsh questioning simply responded, 'It's all taken care of.'" Given that Supardjo argues that "the party" led the movement, this unnamed arrogant leader must be Sjam.[24]

Going by Supardjo's account, the Special Bureau deceived itself by taking its ambitions to be accomplishments. It believed that the promise of support from one officer automatically meant that all his subordinate officers and soldiers would join the action. Given the pressures to please a browbeating leadership, some Special Bureau members promised more than they could deliver. The leadership never carefully studied which troops would actually be able to join. Supardjo notes, "Usually, if there were only ten people in one platoon whom we were able to contact, it was reported that the entire platoon was with us. If there was one battalion commander whom we contacted, then it was thought that all those below him were already on our side." Supardjo's comment is believable since the movement was probably counting on the participation of Latief's brigade (consisting of three battalions) or least a portion of it and must have been disappointed when no more than a few platoons appeared.

As Special Bureau members from around the country sent in optimistic reports, Sjam seems to have become convinced that the movement could not fail. He was under the impression that troops throughout the country were ready for a revolt. Supardjo concluded that the movement was designed more as the fuse of a bomb rather than the bomb itself. The action in Jakarta was supposed to ignite a series of similar actions outside Jakarta. The movement did not think it had to carefully coordinate the various actions and create a detailed blueprint for how the movement was to spread. Supardjo writes: "The strategy that was followed in the entire movement was this type of strategy: 'Light the Fuse.' It was enough for the fuse to be lit in Jakarta and then hope that the firecrackers will go off by themselves in the regions."

The movement leaders did not verify beforehand that the firecrackers were ready to explode; it simply trusted "unconfirmed reports" that they were ready. The leaders did not set up clear-cut channels of communication between Jakarta and the regions so that they could ensure that the regions understood the plan. Sjam did not use phones or radios to convey instructions to the regions; he sent couriers carrying instructions. Not all the couriers arrived at their destinations in time: "There were still many couriers who had not arrived at their appointed destinations by the time the event occurred (the courier sent to Palembang had only just reached Tanjung Karang [the southern tip of Sumatra])." The decision to begin the action on October 1 appears to have been made only the day before. For couriers who had to rely on buses, trains, and interisland ferries to travel long distances, one day was not enough time.

Supardjo's discussion of his "fuse theory" is ambiguous. At times it appears as if he is speaking of the firecrackers as revolts by civilians. He uses the term *people's revolt* in one passage: "In my opinion, the strategy of the leadership team was a strategy to 'light the fuse of the firecracker' in the capital city, and then hope that the firecrackers would go off by themselves, that is, a people's revolt, and resistance in the regions would emerge after hearing the signal." Given that this quote appears in a paragraph about troop strength, it is likely that Supardjo was thinking of "revolt and resistance" by military troops, not civilians. A "people's revolt" would have meant a revolt by the progressive-minded troops who would rally the masses behind them. The next sentence explains the consequence of this strategy of lighting the fuse: The movement's leaders "did not go ahead with a concrete calculation of the troops they had." Thus it appears that Supardjo's references to firecrackers meant military troops, not civilians.

If one is to believe Sjam's courtroom testimony, he had calculated that the movement would have six battalions: one from Latief's brigade, one from Untung's palace guard, one from Soejono's air force troops, one from Central Java, one from East Java, and one consisting of civilians from PKI and PKI-affiliated organizations.[25] It is doubtful that six battalions would have been sufficient, especially when only five consisted of real troops and none included an armored unit. (Sjam did not address the absence of tanks in his testimony.) At the time of the action the movement was unable to mobilize all six battalions. The movement had only a portion of the companies under Untung and a small fraction of Latief's troops. Except for one company that was sent to Gambir, the battalion of civilian militiamen spent the day on standby. Soejono's troops stayed at Halim air base and provided little tangible assistance to the movement apart from supplying some arms and ammunition.

Although the movement organizers assumed they would have more troops than those that materialized at Lubang Buaya on the night of September 30, they were not overly concerned about troop strength. They did not think they needed an overwhelming force to take the capital city. Supardjo acknowledges in his document that he could have flown in three battalions from Kalimantan. These soldiers, numbering about twenty-five hundred, would have increased the movement's troop strength by about 100 percent. The movement proceeded without these troops. Perhaps the organizers thought that such a large-scale troop movement from Kalimantan to Jakarta would have attracted undue attention. Supardjo's argument, however, appears to be that such troops could have been flown in after the action began. If the movement had kept fighting and had not collapsed so quickly, it would have had the opportunity to substantially augment its troops.

Supardjo also mentions that the organizers did not have a contingency plan in case of defeat. They did not think the action through carefully enough to figure out its weak points and how it could fail. There was no plan B. Supardjo felt he had to instruct the surviving members of the party leadership in basic military lessons: "According to the requirements of military operations, we are always thinking about retreat when we are victorious and moving forward, and we are thinking about advancing and attacking when we're defeated and retreating. What I mean by this is that thinking about retreating in the course of attacking is not shameful, but it is standard procedure for every attack or campaign." Sjam, who seems to the target of Supardjo's criticisms, was so negligent that he did not create a "picture of the battle" that would prepare him to face any contingency. Supardjo implies that Sjam thought the mere thought of retreat to be a sign of shameful weakness. With this headlong rush into battle Sjam followed Napoleon's spirit of *"on s'engage et puis on voit"* (one commits oneself and then sees what happens) but lacked the general's legendary ingenuity and, of course, his legions of trained, well-organized soldiers.

Not only was there no plan B but plan A was not even fully worked out. Supardjo writes in a crucial passage: "It turned out that the plan for the operation wasn't clear. It was too superficial. The centerpiece of the whole plan was the simple kidnapping of the seven generals. What would happen after that, if it was successful, wasn't clear." He added: "Because there was no clear explanation of how the action would be carried out, there was a lack of agreement about the movement itself among the officer comrades in the army."

Much of Supardjo's critique of the movement is based on the paradigm of a proper military operation: there should have been a clear chain of command, a hierarchy of personnel for an effective division of labor, a detailed agenda for how the action would proceed from start to finish, and careful contingency planning that included alternative scenarios and a plan for retreat. Supardjo attributes the failure of the movement to draw up a viable plan to the hubris of the leadership, meaning, in particular, Sjam. Arrogant, determined to forge ahead, deaf to criticism, Sjam had convinced himself that the action was foolproof.

Implementing the Plan

The lack of careful planning and the indifference of the leadership to military procedures resulted in a terribly bungled operation. If one were to make a film based on Supardjo's analysis, it would not look like the film commissioned by the Suharto regime, *The Treason of the September 30th Movement/PKI* (Pengkhianatan G30S/PKI). That film depicts the organizers of the action as a ruthless collection of devious schemers who plotted every move down to the last detail. Supardjo's analysis reveals the plotters to have been thoroughly flummoxed, indecisive, and disorganized. Rather than being ingenious villains in the tradition of espionage films, they were more like clumsy amateurs committing, in tragic fashion, a comedy of errors. For Supardjo the movement largely defeated itself and should serve as a case study of how not to carry out a military operation.

The very limited military goals of the operation were not fully achieved. The "centerpiece of the whole strategy," as Supardjo describes it, was the kidnapping of seven generals. This failed because of the hastiness of the preparations. Supardjo, at Lubang Buaya in the early morning hours of October 1, was appalled by the chaos. Even at that late stage "various important matters had not yet been settled." The codes had not been determined, the ammunition had not arrived, and the air force troops had arrived late. The soldiers and civilian youths were haphazardly divided into the kidnapping teams: "The decision about which platoons would be assigned to which targets was not done carefully. For example, it so happened that the main target [presumably Nasution] was first assigned to a platoon of youths who had only just learned how to hold a gun, then it was reassigned to an army platoon, but then that platoon was not one that was mentally prepared beforehand for special assignments." The team sent to kidnap Nasution was led by a private when all six of the other teams were led by a corporal, sergeant, or lieutenant. The movement leaders knew that kidnapping Nasution and Yani would be the more difficult tasks since these two generals had armed guards posted in front of their residences. That is why the kidnapping teams for Nasution and Yani were substantially larger than the others; about one hundred men were sent in four trucks to capture Nasution, compared with just nineteen men for Suprapto. The most experienced and talented soldiers were not assigned to lead the high-priority teams. Nasution escaped, and Yani was shot at his house.

Supardjo does not explain what the movement's intention was, but one assumes that it was to capture the generals alive. The kidnapping teams used violence only when faced with resistance, and even then they do not appear to have intended to kill the generals. One soldier involved in the kidnapping, Sergeant Major Bungkus of the palace guard, told me that he assumed that the original plan was to bring the generals before Sukarno. That plan had to be abandoned because three generals were either badly wounded or dead. The movement could not drag three bloodied bodies before the president. Once the original plan was aborted, the three generals who had been taken alive were considered useless. Someone in the movement decided at that point that the best option was to kill all the generals, along with the mistakenly abducted lieutenant, and hide their corpses. The movement, however, may not have planned to bring the generals before Sukarno. Bungkus also noted that the soldiers were told during the briefing sessions that these generals were about to stage a coup and that they could not be allowed to escape capture.[26]

Another blunder, according to Supardjo, was that the movement did not take advantage of the bulk of its troops. The companies from the battalions of Central and East Java were not assigned to accomplish any strategic objective and wound up being useless decorative pieces. Most were ordered to guard the empty presidential palace. The troops stood idle in the field in front of the palace until the afternoon. The organizers probably knew that Sukarno was not inside the palace by about 9:30 A.M. at the latest, when Supardjo returned to Halim from the palace by helicopter. But the two battalions were not reassigned. Indeed, it appears that the leadership did not have any special purpose for them from the beginning. As Supardjo describes the plan, "It was estimated that one battalion from Central Java and one from East Java could be used as extras [*figuran*]." Their task, it seems, was simply to influence the public with the psychological impact of seeing troops occupying the nation's center of power.

As an experienced tactician, Supardjo does not fault the movement for having too few troops. He knew that troop strength was not necessarily the crucial factor in determining victory or defeat. Skillful deployment, quick movement, and the element of surprise can compensate for the lack of troops. He notes that "one battalion that panics can be overwhelmed by just one team of soldiers." The movement did not need vast numbers of troops, he believed, only troops that were wisely used.

Just as the movement did not take full advantage of the troops under its command, it did not take full advantage of the radio station. Supardjo recognized the value of radio communications in the exercise of power. Control of the nation's radio transmitters was "equal to dozens of divisions." Yet the movement used the radio only "to read out a few announcements." Supardjo thought that a properly organized action would have prepared a steady stream of propaganda and would have presented a careful, detailed explanation of its goals. The public could hardly understand, much less support, the movement based on its brief, puzzling announcements. Supardjo notes this failing yet had no explanation for it.

That the movement squandered what power it did have was one problem. Another was that its power was precarious to begin with. The movement was not in command of troops that understood and supported its objectives. Astonishingly enough, of all the troops involved, Supardjo thought only one company was ideologically committed to the movement: "If the movement is reexamined, it is found that, actually, the only unit that was fully with us was just one company from the palace guard." The other troops, such as those from the Jakarta garrison (under Latief) and the air force (under Soejono) were simply following the lead of their commanding officers and had little or no commitment of their own to the movement. The officers of Battalion 530, who spent the day idling in front of the palace, agreed to defect in the afternoon and bring the entire battalion inside Kostrad, the army reserve head-quarters, on the eastern side of Merdeka Square.

The desertion of Battalion 530 was not just the result of the lack of ideological commitment on the part of the officers and soldiers; it also derived from their lack of food. It has been well known that these troops turned themselves over to Kostrad headquarters when they were suffering from hunger. After being posted to guard the palace in the early morning, the troops were not given breakfast or lunch. Supardjo, whose military experience must have drilled into him the utmost importance of food supplies, stresses this error: "All the hindrances in the movement of our troops were caused by, among other things, *the lack of food* [underlined in original]. They didn't eat in the morning, the afternoon, or the night." Supardjo mentions that the core group of plotters at Halim learned that the troops had not been fed only after Supardjo proposed they attack Kostrad: "This fact was only discovered at night when there was some thought about mobilizing troops for an attack inside the city. At that time the Central Java battalion [454] was at Halim. The East Java battalion [530] had already been drawn into Kostrad in order to eat."

With its troops poorly deployed, ideologically unprepared, and demoralized from hunger, the movement proved to be a disaster in military terms. It could not sustain itself long enough for anyone in the public to rally behind it. The movement announced its existence over the national radio station at about 7:15 A.M., and about twelve hours later troops loyal to Suharto retook the station and proclaimed over the airwaves that the movement had been defeated.

Civilian Participation

The movement was not designed as a purely military action. The conspirators had recruited members of PKI-affiliated organizations to serve as auxiliary troops and to provide logistical support, especially food and water. Supardjo notes that the troops went hungry because the civilians who were supposed to supply them did not show up. According to Supardjo, Jakarta had been divided into three sectors (north, central, and south) and a commander had been assigned to each sector. The sector commanders "had been assigned to take care of administrative matters for the troops in their individual sectors." But on the day of the action these sector commanders were nowhere to be found: "When these sectors were contacted, not one was at its station." The commanders of the sectors had disappeared. It turned out that "all these sectors that had been drawn up beforehand existed only on paper." Supardjo criticizes the organizers of the action for not inspecting the sectors beforehand and ensuring that the sector leaders knew exactly what they were supposed to do.

Supardjo's analysis of the sectors appears to be inaccurate, again reflecting his unfamiliarity with the PKI and certain aspects of the movement. Njono, the head of the PKI's Jakarta chapter and a member of the Politburo, claimed at his Mahmillub trial that he had divided the city into sectors.[27] But he stated that there were six sectors, not three, as Supardjo states, and that the personnel grouped into the sectors were civilian militiamen who were not responsible for supplying the regular troops with food.[28] Njono had mobilized two thousand men, largely from the PKI's youth organization, Pemuda Rakjat, to serve as reserve manpower for the military operations. These youths had received military training at Lubang Buaya in the previous months. The militiamen who had occupied the telecommunications building were from one sector (the Gambir sector). Some confusion among the movement participants can be seen in their conflicting recollections about the sectors. While Supardjo thought the sectors were supposed to supply food to the troops, Njono thought the opposite, that the troops at Lubang Buaya were supposed to supply food to the sectors. Njono recalled that his militiamen spent the day idle while waiting to receive rice, uniforms, and weapons from the troops at Lubang Buaya. During the day of October 1 the instruction from those officers was for the sectors to stand by. Njono became aware that the movement had become "jammed up" when these supplies did not arrive by the afternoon. According to his testimony, the civilian recruits remained inactive: they "didn't do anything."[29] It is a known fact that the only militiamen who surfaced in support of the movement were those who occupied the buildings near Merdeka Square in the afternoon. Njono's story about the "Gambir sector" and the confusion about supplies is a credible explanation for the general passivity of the sectors.

One civilian involved in the Gambir sector was Juwono, a pseudonym for a twenty-year-old member of the PKI's youth wing, Pemuda Rakjat, in the Menteng district of Jakarta. He followed the organization's instructions to participate in the military trainings held at Lubang Buaya. In the weeks before the movement Pemuda Rakjat held frequent meetings to discuss the political situation, especially the danger of a coup by the Council of Generals. On September 29 a leader of the military training instructed Juwono to report to the neighborhood of Pejompongan, not far from the city's main stadium. Once there, he found a gathering of hundreds of youths from all over the city. He recalled that *Gambir* was the term for the group. On the afternoon of October 1 he and about thirty other youths were given weapons and told to guard the telecommunications building. They stood around the building, doing nothing, until troops suddenly arrived. Juwono and the others were unprepared for an actual gunfight. After surrendering their weapons, they were trucked to the military police headquarters, where they were jailed, interrogated, and tortured. Juwono spent the next thirteen years as a political prisoner.[30]

In addition to mobilizing youths to act as a militia, the movement appears to have asked Gerwani, the Indonesian Women's Movement, to open communal kitchens around the city. The kitchens were to feed both the troops and the militias. In a conservative-minded patriarchal gesture the movement left the cooking to women.[31] The Dutch scholar Saskia Wieringa interviewed former Gerwani members in the early 1980s who claimed to have been asked by the Jakarta branch of the PKI to be at Lubang Buaya for duties related to the anti-Malaysia campaign.[32] Perhaps the kitchens did not materialize because so few women showed up. Wieringa reports that only about seventy women were at Lubang Buaya on October 1. They included members of Gerwani; the PKI's youth organization, Pemuda Rakjat; the trade union organization SOBSI (Sentral Organisasi Buruh Seluruh Indonesia, the All-Indonesia Central Workers Organization); and the peasant's association BTI (Barisan Tani Indonesia—the Indonesian Peasants Front). Also among them were wives of the palace guard troops. These women were assigned tasks other than cooking. Some sewed tricolor striped badges onto the uniforms of the movement troops.[33]

It would be surprising if there was not frequent miscommunication between the movement and the civilians recruited to assist it. The movement could not reveal the plan in any detail to the civilian members of the party without increasing the risk of exposure. The tight military secrecy that allowed the kidnappings to achieve the element of surprise simultaneously doomed mass civilian participation. Since the party members were not told exactly what would happen, they were confused about their tasks. A former high-level PKI leader confirmed that many people in Jakarta assigned to the sectors were hopelessly confused and decided, by default, to do nothing.[34] By combining a mass movement with a military conspiracy, the movement leaders were attempting the impossible. The party members (including the highest levels of the leadership) could not be informed of the details of the conspiracy without endangering the secrecy on which its success depended. The bizarre character of the movement that has so confounded all observers partly derives from its not having been designed as an exclusively military operation. Many civilians were integrated into the action, in ways that were confusing to all the participants.

Sjam may have inserted the civilians into the design of the movement over the objections of the military officers. One member of the PKI Politburo, Peris Pardede, testified at the first Mahmillub trial that Sudisman (a member of the Politburo) had informed him in September that the officers in the movement did not have sufficient troops for their action. Sudisman had explained that the party would supply a contingent of civilian youths to supplement their strength "even though the officers don't actually like it and would prefer just to act by themselves."[35]

Given the paradigm that the movement established in Jakarta, it appears that the intended role for civilians within the movement, apart from assisting the troops, was to rally behind the officers who declared themselves supporters of the movement. In response to Untung's call, officers around the country would initiate the formation of revolution councils. Civilians would then meet these officers and decide how the councils would govern. In Jakarta the movement appointed forty-five people to serve as members of the national Indonesian Revolution Council. The officers in the regions, in forming local revolution councils, were supposed to accommodate nationalists, Muslims, and Communists under Sukarno's Nasakom formula.

If the movement had been able to sustain itself longer, mass demonstrations might have occurred in a number of cities in support of the movement and its revolution councils. Njono claimed that he drew up not only six sectors for the militiamen in Jakarta but also a network of what he called posts (presumably members' houses and party offices). The personnel at these posts were PKI members at the level of the Section Committee (Comite Seksi). They were instructed to stay at their posts on the day of the action and keep listening to their radios.[36] It seems that Njono would have mobilized the PKI masses for demonstrations if the movement had not collapsed prematurely.

Supardjo was under the impression that the movement was counting on mass demonstrations once the military operation had been completed. He notes at one point in his analysis that Sjam and the Special
Bureau thought that the PKI masses were ready for some sort of militant action: "The mistaken strategy of the September 30th Movement
also derived from the fact that many comrades in the regions reported
that the masses could no longer be restrained. If the leadership did not
take action, the people would proceed on their own (for the revolution)." By using the term *revolution,* Supardjo does not necessarily mean
a Communist revolution. *Revolution* was a commonly used term in the
Sukarnoist discourse of the time. From constant usage its meaning
had become polyvalent, jargonistic, and ambiguous. Even Suharto, in
suppressing the movement, claimed to be defending the "revolution"
against an attempted "counterrevolution."

Sjam does appear to have been expecting some sort of mass action in
support of the movement. In his courtroom testimony he described the
collapse of the movement: "And after weighing the options on how to
keep the movement going while its strength kept decreasing [during the
night of October 1 and early morning October 2], when meanwhile
there were no signs that the mass movement would support and join the
September 30th Movement, I finally decided to stage a retreat."[37]

The PKI, as is well known, did not call its members out into the
streets to support the movement. However, its public line—that the
movement was an internal army action—did not preclude the possibility of organizing demonstrations in support of it. Demonstrations did
occur in Yogyakarta. The movement in Jakarta appears to have counted
on a "mass movement" as a kind of secondary phase. Judging from the
party's passivity in Jakarta (and everywhere else except Yogyakarta), the
movement was probably designed to succeed on the basis of its military
operations alone. Demonstrations, to be organized later, would provide
public legitimation for the insurgents and help convince enemies that
any counterattack would not enjoy popular support. As the movement
was collapsing, Sjam held out the hope that the "mass movement" could
reinvigorate it, but most likely he had not planned from the start on civilian actions as the key to its victory.

The Movement and Sukarno

The movement has usually been described as a coup attempt. The
writers aligned with the Suharto regime insisted upon using this term;

Notosusanto and Saleh titled their book *The Coup Attempt of the "September 30th Movement" in Indonesia,* and the State Secretariat subtitled its 1994 report *The Attempted Coup by the Indonesian Communist Party.* Even those historians who have disagreed with the regime's analysis have used the term. Harold Crouch titled his chapter about the movement "The Coup Attempt." When thinking about the events of 1965, the unwary are likely to believe that the term *coup* can be unproblematically applied to the September 30th Movement. The CIA study of the movement argued that the term *coup* is "technically correct" if the meaning is understood as "a sudden, forceful stroke in politics" but that the term *coup d'état* is incorrect: "For it now seems clear that the Indonesian coup was not a move to overthrow Sukarno and/or the established government of Indonesia. Essentially it was a purge of the Army leadership, which was intended to bring about certain changes in the cabinet."[38] In reviewing the movement's actions, one does not find any effort to depose the president apart from the radio announcement decommissioning his cabinet (Decree no. 1). The movement took no direct action against the president. Supardjo met with Sukarno that morning on behalf of the organizers, presented him with a fait accompli, and then allowed him to take whatever further action he so desired. Supardjo did not dictate terms to Sukarno.

Supardjo's account of the interaction between the movement and Sukarno on October 1 is particularly valuable because he was the only person speaking to both. He was the channel of communication between the movement's core organizers and the president. The account in this document is similar to his testimony in court, but the document contains a number of new elements.

An important revelation concerns the reaction of the movement's organizers once Supardjo reported his conversation with Sukarno to them. According to Supardjo, they debated what to do but could not come to any clear decision. They were effectively paralyzed by their own indecisiveness. Since no overall commander had been designated before then, none of the plotters was in a position to make the final decision. Since Sukarno's refusal to support their action prompted such confusion, it is reasonable to assume that they had counted on receiving his blessing. They would capture all seven generals alive, present them before Sukarno, and demand that they be dismissed or imprisoned. After all, Sukarno and his advisers had been very worried about the Council of Generals for the last six months. Sjam's confidence that the plan was foolproof must have derived in part from the certainty that

Sukarno would welcome an action against the army high command. But Sukarno could not support their action once he learned of the bloodshed. Without his support the movement leaders did not know how to proceed.

It is surprising to discover in the Supardjo document that Sjam was of the opinion that the movement should continue even if it meant disobeying Sukarno and incurring his opposition: "Comrade Sjam insisted the revolution would have to proceed without Bung Karno [Sukarno]." The main point of Supardjo's passage is to register his disagreement with Sjam's proposed line. He argues that the movement should have made a definite decision to keep Sukarno as an ally. If the movement had followed Sjam's line, it would have confronted the hostility of nearly the entire army and would have been isolated easily. If, however, the movement was able to convince Sukarno that the movement needed to continue to finish off the Suharto and Nasution combine, the right-wing army officers would have been isolated: "If we brought Bung Karno on board, the main contradiction would have become one between the left and the Revolutionary Democratic groups on one side, and merely the right-wing group alone on the other side." The problem was that the core group never made a decision to either proceed without Sukarno or to gain Sukarno's assent for further action: "There wasn't a decision by us on which line to take." In the manner of Leibniz's theology of god as the great watchmaker (creating the universe, setting it in motion, and then abandoning it), the organizers of the movement did nothing during the afternoon and night of October 1 and allowed the initiative to pass into the hands of Suharto and Nasution.

According to the Suharto regime's white book on the September 30th Movement, the organizers "decided to disobey President Sukarno's order." The anonymous authors argued, in the vague phrasing that was their specialty, that Sjam insisted that the organizers disobey the order because he did not want to "create an atmosphere of hesitation among the leaders of the movement."[39] It is difficult to follow the logic of their argument. They were apparently contending that Sjam succeeded in uniting all the movement's leaders behind a single program (the councils) at a time when they were uncertain about how to proceed. The actual decision making was, according to Supardjo's analysis, the exact opposite: the organizers did not *decide* to disobey Sukarno's order. They did not decide anything. They were deadlocked.

Supardjo's comment on Sjam's position ("Comrade Sjam insisted the revolution would have to proceed without Bung Karno") may explain the radio announcements in the afternoon that decommissioned the president's cabinet and proclaimed that all power had fallen into the hands of the Indonesian Revolution Council. Supardjo does not specifically address those announcements, but one can presume, reading between the lines, that Supardjo thought Sjam was responsible. While Supardjo and the other military officers remained loyal to Sukarno, Sjam wished to bypass him and create an entirely new form of government. The plotters were deadlocked in their discussions because of this difference of opinion. At his Mahmillub trial Supardjo claimed that he had not agreed with the idea of the Indonesian Revolution Council and had refused to sign the document that Sjam had passed around, apparently sometime in the late morning or early afternoon on October 1: "The Revolution Council was just the wish of Sjam and it had never been discussed at a meeting." Supardjo recalled that he noticed a division between Sjam and the military officers in the movement since the other officers, like Supardjo, were unwilling to sign the document.[40] Untung and Latief were willing to follow Sukarno's demand to end the movement, but Sjam "was not happy with it."[41] The officers had motivated their troops with the idea that Sukarno needed to be protected from a coup by the right-wing generals. Supardjo opposed Sjam's line because the general recognized what was obvious: the most powerful loyalty among the military troops and officers was to Sukarno, not to the PKI.

The basic idea of the Revolution Council must have received the assent of the officers beforehand as the term was mentioned in the first radio announcement. However, if the officers agreed to the idea, they probably did not envision the council's displacing Sukarno's authority. In trying to continue with the movement, Sjam may have altered the original plan for the councils. Since Sukarno did not support the movement, Sjam quickly redesigned the original plan so that it would not rely upon the president. The radio announcements in the afternoon may reflect Sjam's own improvised departure from the plan that the military officers had initially agreed upon. Instead of institutions to support Sukarno, the councils were abruptly recast as the basis of a new form of government.

With Supardjo's analysis, one can venture the hypothesis that the radio announcement in the afternoon that decommissioned Sukarno's cabinet was Sjam's response to Sukarno's refusal to support the movement. If the movement had gone according to plan and Sukarno had supported it, the revolution councils would have been set up to complement the existing cabinet rather than replace it. The later radio announcements must have been intended to be read in the morning, not long after the first announcement. They were delayed because of the protracted debate and indecision among the movement's leaders after Sukarno had ordered the action to be called off. Eventually, Sjam ignored the wishes of the officers and tried to keep the movement going by having a revised announcement broadcast. The decommissioning of the cabinet was perhaps a last-minute, last-ditch attempt by Sjam to give a new direction to the movement while his coconspirators from the military dithered. For the positions of deputy commanders of the movement, Sjam chose officers who happened to be around him that day (Supardjo and Atmodjo) or who had reputations as progressives (Sunardi and Anwas).

The movement was paralyzed. On the one hand, Sjam was hoping that a "mass movement" of soldiers and civilians would magically appear and save the movement. On the other hand, his military coconspirators were exhausted, confused, and nervous. They were unwilling to support the continuation of the movement if that would lead to a confrontation with Sukarno. When their supreme commander ordered them to call off the movement, they obeyed. And so the discussions among the core leaders rambled on. The leaders did not issue a statement to call off the movement, organize concrete actions to continue it, or attempt to persuade Sukarno to support a wider war against Suharto and Nasution. They simply drifted ineluctably onward toward disaster.

Pranoto's Appointment

By default the movement relied on Sukarno to protect it from the onslaught of Suharto's troops. Yet the organizers knew by the afternoon of October 1 that Sukarno had lost the power to command the army. Suharto refused to permit Major General Pranoto, Sukarno's appointee as temporary commander of the army, to fulfill the president's summons. As the historian of Indonesia's military, Harold Crouch, put it, "Suharto blatantly disobeyed Sukarno's instructions. Pranoto's appointment was ignored, and Suharto issued a veiled command to the president that he should leave Halim. The relationship between the president and the commander of the army that had prevailed through most of the Guided Democracy period ended on 1 October 1965."[42]

When he was writing his postmortem analysis, Supardjo still believed that the movement could have been saved if Pranoto had asserted the power that Sukarno had invested in him. On the afternoon of October 1 the movement was hoping that Pranoto would oppose Suharto and take command of the army. While he was conferring with Sukarno, Supardjo had suggested Pranoto and two other generals as candidates for army caretaker. Pranoto was one of the few members of the army general staff who was not an anti-Communist. In Supardjo's opinion Pranoto should have taken more initiative. If Pranoto had exercised "some authority, the situation would not have become as bad as it did. With that letter of instruction [from Sukarno], he should have quickly delivered a speech over the radio and announced his appointment. The second step should have been to order the two sides not to engage in combat. Pranoto also should have arranged the force of the brigades near him and directly taken command of them. . . . Then he should have immediately, using temporary expedients, filled the vacant positions on the army's general staff." Unfortunately for the movement and for Pranoto himself, who was later imprisoned for twelve years, he allowed Suharto to retain control of the army.[43]

Given Pranoto's position in the army and the uncertain context of that day, it was unfair of Supardjo to have expected him to seize the army command from Suharto. Pranoto was Yani's assistant in charge of personnel. He was neither the direct successor to Yani's position nor the most senior officer. Pranoto recounted in a brief essay years later that he and a group of officers at army headquarters sent a note to Suharto on the morning of October 1, once Yani's disappearance was confirmed, asking Suharto to serve as the temporary army commander. After all, Suharto had served as the caretaker of the army on previous occasions when Yani was out of the country. Pranoto had already placed himself under Suharto's command by the time Sukarno appointed Pranoto as caretaker. Pranoto's response was to wait until he received a written order from Sukarno. Although Supardjo referred to a "letter of instruction," Pranoto did not receive a written order, only an oral message from a courier. It is understandable that Pranoto did not immediately challenge Suharto and side with Sukarno because Pranoto could not have understood the stakes involved—he could not have predicted that Suharto would eventually overthrow Sukarno and orchestrate the killing of hundreds of thousands of people. Pranoto was one of the movement's last hopes, but he can hardly be blamed for not fulfilling the role that Sukarno had assigned him.

The Movement and Suharto

One of the odd silences in Supardjo's analysis, a silence that will greatly disappoint readers today, concerns Suharto. Supardjo criticizes the movement for many things but not for failing to kidnap or in some way neutralize Suharto beforehand. Implicitly, Supardjo chalks up the movement's failure to deal with Suharto to the more general failure to do any detailed contingency planning. He mentions neither Untung and Latief's close relationship with Suharto nor the story that Latief disclosed much later at his trial in 1978, that he had told Suharto about the movement beforehand. Because Supardjo was not involved in the planning meetings in August and September and had no connection with Untung and Latief, Supardjo may have known little or nothing about those matters. In this document he does not reveal a knowledge of what the core organizers had decided before the action with regard to Suharto. Supardjo's discussion of Suharto focuses on one argument: that the movement should have attacked Suharto's Kostrad headquarters in the afternoon or evening of October 1. Supardjo frankly admitted in his courtroom testimony that he thought the movement should have bombed Kostrad.[44]

In his written analysis he explains why he urged an aerial attack on Suharto's headquarters. He was fairly confident that the movement could have defeated Suharto and Nasution if it had attacked them before their consolidation of power in the evening. Supardjo thought the army was in a state of panic for twelve hours after the operation began (or had been detected), which would have meant from about 5 A.M. to 5 P.M. Suharto began to move confidently only after Battalion 530 surrendered around 4 P.M. Nasution arrived at Kostrad in the evening and the radio station was retaken around 7 P.M. Supardjo demanded that the movement attack Suharto before he could reverse its progress. If the movement had attacked Suharto that afternoon, "it is very likely that the opponent would have raised his hands in surrender, because at that time Nato [Nasution-Suharto] did not have a *grip* on the Indonesian military in the city." The movement stood a good chance of eliminating its antagonists: "In the first hours, Nato [Nasution and Suharto] and company reorganized their command. Their position at that time was very weak. At that moment, the leadership of the operation should have ambushed the enemy without thinking at all about the risk to our troops." Supardjo may have been demanding a bombing run over Kostrad well into the night. Suharto caught wind of the discussions at

Halim and abandoned his headquarters around 11:30 P.M. (according to the journalist John Hughes) for fear of an aerial attack by the air force.[45]

It is debatable whether the movement could have emerged victorious from a showdown with Suharto since Supardjo demonstrated that the movement itself did not have a solid command structure, the troops were lacking both food and morale, and the propaganda material broadcast over the radio was too brief and ambiguous to be of any use. Launching an offensive might have resulted in a defeat as crushing as the one the movement ultimately experienced. Given its own weaknesses in ground troops, the movement would have had to rely on the air force's aerial bombardments of Suharto's headquarters to buy time to mobilize more infantry troops and regroup. It is possible that aerial attacks could have provided the movement with a margin of victory. Supardjo's point was that the organizers had to attempt an attack because they had no other means of defending themselves; they had to fight and make the best of a bad situation, regardless of "the risk to our troops." When one is heading for defeat, there is little point in rejecting a potentially effective tactic for fear that it will not guarantee victory.

According to Supardjo, the air force commander, Omar Dani, was involved in these discussions at Halim air base and was in favor of attacking Kostrad. The movement's organizers, however, were not: "After hearing the news that General Harto [Suharto] was preparing a counterattack and Vice Marshal Dani's offer of integration [of air force and September 30th Movement troops] for fending it off, the offer should have been accepted at that time." Dani was supposedly serious about his offer: "Dani had already made preparations to the point of ordering rockets to be installed on the planes."[46] Omar Dani was deeply loyal to Sukarno and may well have believed that the president needed protection from the right-wing army generals. Supardjo mentions that Dani's recommendation to the movement organizers was that they "continue the revolution together with Bung Karno." Dani's assent to a bombing run on Kostrad (if indeed he did assent to one) was probably motivated by a desire to protect the president, who was still at Halim. Ultimately, the air force decided against an attack on Kostrad. Heru Atmodjo recalls that the officers at Halim were worried about the possibility of civilian casualties. If a bomb missed its target, it could easily land in the nearby residential areas.[47]

Supardjo insisted even up to the last moments that the movement resist the troops that Suharto had sent to attack Halim. Supardjo mentions that he offered to take command of the remaining troops near the air base to fight off Suharto's troops. For Supardjo it was better to attempt resistance and lose than to flee helter-skelter. The movement's organizers, Sjam and Untung especially, neither accepted nor rejected Supardjo's proposal. As was the case during all previous rounds of decision making, they did not come to a decision. They did nothing. When the troops of the army's Special Forces began to enter the area around Halim, the movement's troops, many of whom were from the Central Java battalion, scattered in all directions in a desperate flight for their lives. As Supardjo notes, the soldiers unfamiliar with the city became the easy prey of Suharto's troops.

It is significant that Supardjo never mentions Suharto without pairing him with Nasution. He viewed them as a team, as a "joint command." He abbreviated the two names to make a clever neologism that referred to their pro-Western orientation: they were "Nato" (*Na*sution-Suhar*to*). The term *enemy* in the document always refers to Nato, not Suharto himself. Supardjo appears not to have considered Suharto a powerful commander in his own right. Supardjo was under the mistaken impression that Nasution, not Suharto, had forbidden Pranoto to go to Halim and meet Sukarno. The lack of any extended discussion of Suharto in the document suggests that Supardjo, even after the defeat of the movement, did not view Suharto as the key adversary. Heru Atmodjo told me that Supardjo had a low opinion of Suharto's capabilities as an officer and thought that his position as Kostrad commander was insignificant.[48]

Supardjo's assessment of Suharto is not altogether surprising. For the first two weeks of October the U.S. embassy was under the impression that its old ally Nasution was in charge and that Suharto was just carrying out his orders. On the basis of embassy reporting, Secretary of State Dean Rusk wrote on October 13 that Nasution appeared to be the one "calling the shots."[49] Ambassador Green reversed that judgment in early November: "Suharto, not Nasution, is one who gives orders, conceives his own strategy and faces Sukarno directly."[50] Compared with Nasution, who had been prominent on the stage of Indonesian politics since the early 1950s, Suharto was a minor figure. At first, many people could not believe that he was acting on his own initiative.

Supardjo might not have known that Latief had tipped off Suharto and, if he had known, either before or after the action, he might not have thought it a decisive factor. Perhaps the movement did not abduct Suharto or otherwise neutralize him because it underestimated his power. Kostrad did not possess any troops of its own; it borrowed troops from the regional commands. Most troops in Jakarta on October 1 under Kostrad command were precisely the ones that the movement was going to use (Battalions 454 and 530). Even if Sjam thought Suharto might turn against the movement, Sjam, like Supardjo, might have thought that Suharto had neither the fortitude nor intelligence to defeat the movement. Suharto was known as stubborn (Sukarno's description of him) and stern (Latief's description of him) but not as a right-wing officer allied with Nasution.[51] Indeed, it was widely thought that the two were enemies since Nasution had removed Suharto from his post as commander of the Central Java division in 1959 for corruption.[52]

Supardjo, writing his analysis in mid-1966, seems unaware that Nasution's role in the attack on the movement was negligible compared with the role of Suharto and his Kostrad officers (namely, Yoga Sugama and Ali Moertopo). The image of Nasution as the army's grand patriarch was so indelibly printed in the minds of the movement plotters that they could not imagine that Suharto, a relative nobody, could suddenly emerge as the leader of an ambitious plot to overthrow Sukarno and attack the PKI. They could have profited from thinking in terms of the chess game once proposed by Bertold Brecht: "A game in which the positions do not always remain the same; where the function of the pieces changes if they have stood for a while on the same square: then they become either more effective or weaker."[53]

Supardjo also seems unaware of Suharto's role in sabotaging the president's bellicose policy toward Malaysia before October 1965. The army high command was opposed to Sukarno's Confrontation with Malaysia as the hostilities were escalating in 1964–65. The generals were, however, not confident enough to challenge the president. Yani and Major General S. Parman, the head of army intelligence, covertly undermined Confrontation by deputing Suharto to send agents to contact Malaysian and British officials and assure them that the army did not want war. Suharto's Kostrad was the center of the army's effort to maintain clandestine contact with the other side. Moreover, Suharto, as the vice commander of the forces used for Confrontation, ensured that the troops along the border with Malaysia were understaffed and underequipped. Supardjo was the commander for Confrontation troops stationed in Kalimantan. He knew that his superiors were trying to put the brakes on Sukarno's policy, but he does not appear to have known that Suharto was the key player in that effort. I will return to this issue in chapter 6.

For Supardjo the movement largely collapsed under the weight of its own incompetence: it did not have a well-thought-out plan apart from kidnapping the seven generals, did not take advantage of the radio, could not make decisions, and did not feed its troops. He saw the failure of the movement as an abject lesson in what happens when civilians design a military action. Sjam placed himself at the head of the movement, browbeat his subordinates in the Special Bureau to submit reports in accordance with his own agenda, and dismissed criticisms from the military officers willing to work with him. In bewildering fashion he adulterated the paradigm of a secretive military action with that of an open mobilization of civilians. Supardjo, and presumably the other officers as well, initially followed Sjam's lead because they assumed his confidence was based on expert knowledge. They assumed the PKI leadership knew what it was doing. But when the movement did not go according to plan on October 1 and President Sukarno demanded it be called off, the military officers refused to follow Sjam any further. The discussions between the movement's leaders became deadlocked because neither Sjam nor the officers had the power to overrule the other. Sjam may have been responsible for the radio announcement decommissioning Sukarno's cabinet at very moment that Supardjo was negotiating with Sukarno.

What is clear from the Supardjo document is that Sjam was the one person most responsible for initiating and designing the movement. By presenting the role of Sjam as more important than that of the military personnel involved, the document suggests that Harold Crouch's contention that the army officers were the originators of movement is incorrect. While many pro-Sukarno and pro-PKI officers were sharing information in mid-1965, bouncing ideas off one another, and contemplating a variety of strategies for dealing with the right-wing army generals, the movement represented Sjam's particular invention. The officers who participated in the movement (Untung, Latief, Soejono, Supardjo) were those who were willing to follow Sjam's lead.

Supardjo concluded that the movement was led "directly by the party" because he knew Sjam was a representative of the PKI. But he did not specify how "the party" led the operation. Given the need for pro-PKI military officers such as Supardjo to keep their contact with the party secret, it is unlikely that he had contact with anyone other than Sjam. He probably knew little about Sjam's relationship to the party's leaders. In stating that the movement was led by the PKI, Supardjo was not affirming that the Politburo and the Central Committee had discussed the action and approved it (as the Suharto regime alleged). All that Supardjo could have known was that among the five core leaders, Sjam was the one most responsible for the movement. From that fact Supardjo inferred the leadership of the party. Nothing in the document suggests that he had firsthand knowledge of the role of Sjam's superiors in the movement.

In blaming a civilian for the failure of the movement, Supardjo was not trying to uphold the dignity of his own institution, the Indonesian military. He wrote the document as a committed Communist Party follower who wished to edify the "comrades in the leadership." Despite his regrets that he had placed too much trust in Sjam even after he realized that the plan for the movement "did not add up," Supardjo did not regret his loyalty to the party. In one passage he condemns his fellow officers for being unable to carry out "revolutionary duties" and overcome an ingrained deference to their superior officers. Supardjo took his profession seriously; he was well versed in military strategy. But he believed that the military should serve revolutionary politics rather than the elitist, pro-Western politics that Nasution advocated. Supardjo's postmortem analysis of the movement cannot be read as an officer's attempt to clear the military's name by blaming civilians. It was instead an internal critique: it represented the perspective of a party loyalist angered and disappointed by the actions of certain party leaders.

4

Sjam and the Special Bureau

His very existence was improbable, inexplicable, and altogether bewildering. He was an insoluble problem. It was inconceivable how he had existed, how he had succeeded in getting so far.

Joseph Conrad, *Heart of Darkness* (1902)

The Supardjo document enables us to solve one mystery: the relationship between the military officers (Untung, Latief, and Soejono) and civilians (Sjam and Pono) within the leadership of the movement. Of the five core leaders, Sjam was the most important one. Unfortunately, the document does not help us answer the questions that logically follow: Who was Sjam? Was Sjam a loyal servant of Aidit's and only following orders? Was Aidit, then, the real leader of the movement, pulling Sjam's strings from behind the screen? Or did Sjam have autonomy, such that he was able to design the movement by himself and keep Aidit in the dark about the details? Was Sjam working for the army rather than Aidit? Or was he working for a third party? What was his Special Bureau and how did it function inside the party?

Given the lack of evidence, it has been possible to imagine a wide variety of scenarios with differing levels of culpability for the actors involved. Aidit, for instance, can be represented as either the mastermind of the entire operation, personally involved in every aspect, or as the hapless fall guy in an elaborate setup engineered by Sjam. The inner workings of the party have been completely obscure, at least to those concerned with facts and not obliged to believe the fairy tales imposed on the Indonesian public by the Suharto regime.

In this chapter I present new information that can help reduce the number of plausible scenarios. Many holes remain but some elements of the story can be clarified. Much of the information comes from a former PKI member who had detailed and intimate knowledge of Sjam and the Special Bureau. I spoke to him on numerous occasions over a period of several years. After he was confident that I could be trusted with his story, and I was confident that his story could be trusted, we recorded an interview. He also gave me a sixty-one-page typed autobiographical essay. Because he has requested anonymity, I cannot describe his position in the party and explain how he came upon his knowledge. I can only affirm that I am certain that he was in a position to know the workings of the Special Bureau first hand. Since his story is the only primary source so far available about bureau members, apart from their testimonies at Mahmillub trials, it deserves careful examination. Based as it is on memory, it probably contains a number of inaccuracies. However, I believe that his story is largely credible. Parts of it can be corroborated by other sources. The pseudonym used for him here, Hasan, was chosen at random.

Background on Sjam and the Special Bureau

When did the Special Bureau begin? According to Hasan, Sjam was technically correct when he claimed, in the course of his courtroom testimony, that it began in 1964.[1] Hasan affirms that the name originated around 1964 but says that the organization itself had been functioning since at least the early 1950s, when the party was reorganized under Aidit's leadership. One branch of the party was assigned the task of cultivating supporters within the military. This clandestine branch functioned within the PKI's aboveground Organizational Department, which handled matters such as the recruitment, posting, and training of members. Until 1964 this branch had been known as the Military Section (Bagian Militer) of the Organizational Department. Most of the department's staff did not know that this branch existed. It was headed by a man named Karto. Sjam testified that he had been in the Organizational Department since 1960. What he did not say was that he had been working under Karto as a secret member of that department. He became head when Karto died around 1963 or 1964.

Hasan describes Karto as a senior PKI member who joined the Communist Party in the 1920s. Karto was originally from Solo and had been active in the armed revolt against the Dutch forces from 1945 to

1949. Hasan, a member of a *laskar* (people's militia) in Central Java, knew Karto during those years of armed struggle and occasionally met him in later years:

> At that time [in the 1940s] he was a member of the Central Committee of the PKI, from the peasants' sector. He had great influence in the rural areas. He was already old then, already experienced, so a lot of the cadres in the military were his followers. Karto was considered a father figure in Central Java, an old man, from the generation of 1926–27—he might have even been sent to Boven Digul.[2] He had known suffering, very thin he was. He lived in the BTI [Barisan Tani Indonesia—the Indonesian Peasants Front] office and never married. Later he came down with cancer and was taken to the Soviet Union for treatment. But the doctors there weren't able to do anything for him. He was there for six months and then came back to Indonesia and then after about another six months finally passed away. That was in 1963 or 1964.[3]

Two former PKI leaders told me that Karto's nickname was Hadi Bengkring because he was so thin. (*Bengkring* means emaciated in Javanese.) Hasan recalls that Karto died of lung cancer because of a lifetime of chain-smoking—a habit that he refused to break even while suffering from cancer.[4]

While in prison with former PKI leaders after 1965, Siauw Giok Tjhan, the head of a pro-Sukarno organization of Chinese Indonesians, learned that Karto had been the head of the Military Section. Siauw had known very little about the Communist Party before 1965 and certainly knew nothing of Karto. In prison Siauw became something of a social scientist who collected information about the movement to figure out how it occurred. He wrote in his unpublished analysis that Karto had been "an old man, a founder of the PKI who was respected by many figures in the PKI."[5]

A former member of parliament for the Communist Party, Oey Hay Djoen, recalled that Karto was a well-known figure within the party: "He was the kind of fellow who was everywhere and anywhere, all the time and any time. But he didn't act cocky. He was a quiet fellow; sometimes he'd smile. But he was always present around the party. And he was respected. People knew that he was an important person, even though he didn't have an official position. We didn't make a issue of that."[6]

Precisely because of his familiarity with many military figures of the Indonesian revolution, Karto became responsible for continuing the party's relationship with them after national independence had been won. In the 1950s and early 1960s, while remaining an aboveground party leader in Jakarta, he maintained a secret nationwide network of contacts among the military. In each province several party members contacted officers. Hasan explains: "In general, Karto would assign a person native to that region to head up the Military Section there. But his assistant would be someone sent from Java, someone personally trained by Karto. The head would certainly be a local person: in Padang, definitely a Padang person, in Medan, a Medan person. But Karto would send fellows from Yogyakarta, Solo, East Java out to the other islands to keep an eye on the activities of the local Military Section and make sure they didn't make any mistakes. He sent them to Riau, Banjarmasin, North Sulawesi, and so on."

In his aboveground work Karto was an exacting leader who paid careful attention to the character of the party's personnel. Hasan continues: "Karto, my goodness! He was a stickler for details. Little things, he'd ask the cadres about the little things. It was that spirit of 1926–27, very strict. Toward the members he could be harsh. He would go into depth about their work: 'In your village who are the cadre? What have they done? What have you done in the village that has benefited the peasants?' My goodness, most of them would have to say, 'Nothing yet.' A week later he'd remember the conversation and ask them again about the same details."

From Hasan's description Karto appears to have shared much in common with the perspective of Tan Ling Djie, the party leader ousted by Aidit and his colleagues in 1951. The original model of the party was of an organization of carefully selected, well-trained, committed militants who lived among the peasants and workers and built up their power from below. The older generation believed the party should be designed to survive bouts of repression, such as those under Dutch colonialism and the Japanese occupation, and to work toward an armed seizure of state power. Some viewed Aidit's strategy as the embourgeoisement of the party: members became government officials, lived in large houses in Jakarta, obtained funding from businessmen, and supported Sukarno's populist politics. Many of the older generation of Communist Party figures did not survive in the party leadership once Aidit's generation took over. Karto must have found some way of remaining an important party figure, perhaps by compromising while still holding to his dissenting opinions. Moreover, his vast network of contacts in the military must have made it difficult for the younger generation to dislodge him.

The Military Section, the proto-Special Bureau, naturally emerged out of the party's experience with the nation's sprawling, improvised armed struggle from 1945 to 1949. Many young men supportive of the left-wing movement joined militias and managed to enter the regular military. Once the armed struggle ended, the party did not want to lose these supporters, and vice versa. To develop the Military Section the PKI leaders did not consult the esoteric realms of Communist Party theory. It was simply a matter of sustaining contact with military personnel who had not yet been divorced from their affiliations with civilian politics. The former Politburo member Iskandar Subekti says in his confidential 1986 account of the movement that the "Special Bureau was a body that specialized in looking after the comrades within the military."[7]

Contrary to the propaganda of the Suharto regime, the Special Bureau was not some strangely fiendish scheme exclusive to the Communist Party. Other political parties had similar networks inside the military. The Socialist Party of Indonesia, for instance, had its own network of officers.[8] Precisely these connections facilitated the collaboration between the Socialist Party of Indonesia and the rebel colonels of the 1967-58 revolts in Sumatra and Sulawesi (see chapter 6 on these revolts). The Suharto regime, in constructing a sacred aura around the military, presented the Special Bureau as an aberrant external infiltration of the military by a determined and peculiarly evil foe. In fact, the postindependence military was full of different cliques based upon political predilections. As Daniel Lev has noted, officers were "in constant contact with civilian groups in the highly politicized atmosphere of postrevolutionary Indonesia." Military officers "maintained or developed connections with political parties, either on their own or through family and social connections."[9]

After Karto died, Aidit appointed Sjam as his replacement. Among the PKI political prisoners, it was rumored that Karto had told Aidit before his death not to select Sjam.[10] The story may be true. Hasan notes that Sjam's temperament—boastful, aggressive, and impatient—was the opposite of Karto's. According to Hasan, Sjam's appointment to the Special Bureau was attributable to Aidit's fondness for him. Sjam was known as Aidit's man. He had a long-standing friendship with Aidit, unlike Pono and Bono, who were considered Karto's men.

Sjam testified that he began working as head of the Special Bureau in November 1964. Hasan, however, is certain that it had to have been sometime before May 1964. For unknown reasons, by unknown hands, Karto's network was renamed the Special Bureau around the time of the transition in leadership. Whereas Karto was an experienced, well-known, and well-liked party member who combined aboveground work with secret military networking, Sjam was an anonymous figure in the party who stuck to the shadows.

Little is known for certain about Sjam's childhood and youth. In his courtroom testimony he provided a rough outline of his life. He was born in Tuban, a town on the north coast of East Java, around 1924. He attended junior high school and agronomy school in Surabaya. When Japan invaded Java in 1942 and the agronomy school was forced to close down, he had to abandon his studies before obtaining his degree. He shifted to Yogyakarta around that time and enrolled in a business school there. In the course of my oral history research with ex-political prisoners, I met Sukrisno, a man who turned out to be a close friend of Sjam's in Yogyakarta.[11] (Like Hasan, Sukrisno does not want to be identified by his real name.) He confirmed that Sjam was born in 1924 and that he attended business school *(sekolah dagang)* in Yogyakarta. The two became friends there. Sukrisno also confirmed what some historians have already learned, that Sjam was a member of the so-called Pathuk group.[12] Sukrisno recalls that around 1943 the youths of the city who wished to resist the Japanese occupation began gathering in the Pathuk neighborhood. The leaders of this group were Djohan Sjahrouza and Daino, both of whom were associated with the Socialist Party (Partai Sosialis). On occasion, senior national-level Socialist Party leaders such as Sjahrir would visit. According to Daino's widow, Ibu Oemiyah, Sjam was indeed part of the Pathuk group.[13] Both she and Sukrisno recall that Sjam participated in the attack on the Japanese government's main office in Yogyakarta in September 1945. A crowd of people surrounded the office while a group of young militants, among them members of the Pathuk group, lowered the Japanese flag and raised the Indonesian flag.

Sjam's activities after leaving Yogyakarta have been a mystery. Sjam claimed in his courtroom testimony to have joined the Communist Party in 1949. According to Benedict Anderson, there is documentary evidence showing that he was working as a civil servant of the Dutch puppet state in West Java in 1949 and was serving as the head of the Banten branch of the Socialist Party of Indonesia in 1950–51.[14] Such evidence suggests that he was neither a militant nationalist during the years of the armed struggle nor a Communist Party member in the early 1950s. The Socialists and Communists split after the Madiun affair in 1948. Although he had been close to the Socialists while he was in Yogyakarta, Sjam could not have been simultaneously aligned with both the Socialist Party of Indonesia and the Communist Party in the early 1950s.

Sukrisno cleared up the confusion around Sjam's activities. He and Sjam left Yogyakarta together in 1947 and moved to Jakarta. They lived in the same house, worked in the same office, studied Marxism-Leninism from the same teacher, and together established a trade union for dockworkers. He was perhaps Sjam's closest friend from 1943 to 1950. According to Sukrisno, Socialist Party leaders of the Pathuk group sent five youths to Jakarta in 1947. The Dutch had already occupied the city but allowed the Indonesian Republic, based in Yogyakarta, to maintain the offices of certain ministries there. The Socialist Party leaders wanted these five youths to help the Republican officials in Jakarta smuggle supplies and money back into Yogyakarta. The five were chosen because they were reliable, resourceful, and fairly well educated; they were not just young militants only good for fighting. The five, all in their early twenties, were Munir, Hartoyo, Widoyo, Sjam, and Sukrisno himself. After arriving in Jakarta, they contacted the Republican officials from various ministries. Sjam and Sukrisno began working in the Ministry of Information, whose branch office for West Java was headquartered in Jakarta. They received a salary and a fairly high civil service rank even though their work was a kind of combination of office boy and covert operative. Sukrisno recalls that Sjam was once instructed to take a huge sum of cash out of the office to buy automobile tires and then arrange for them to be put on a train heading for the interior of Java. The train workers at the Manggarai station in Jakarta helped carry supplies for the Republican forces.

The five lived on Jalan Guntur in a house vacated by the resident of Bogor, an Indonesian nationalist who shifted to the Republic's capital of Yogyakarta. They soon met several men who had returned from studies in the Netherlands, where they had become members of the Communist Party of the Netherlands (CPN) and had joined the underground antifascist struggle during the war years. One of these men, Hadiono Kusuma Utoyo, worked with Sjam and Sukrisno at the Jakarta office of the Ministry of Information. He became their mentor in Marxism and Leninism.[15] Once a week, on a regular schedule, the five walked to Utoyo's house on Jalan Kebon Sirih to study under his direction. Sukrisno recalls that one book they read was Lenin's *State and*

Revolution in Dutch translation. From Communists back in the Netherlands they used to receive suitcases full of books that sailors would help smuggle into the city. This political education was an eye-opening experience for them. The Socialist Party leaders of the Pathuk group had provided Sukrisno and his comrades with little more than a place to gather and a general spirit of populism. He said that his initial aspiration was to become an important leader in the postindependence state with a high rank and a high salary. In learning about communism from the recently returned CPN members, Sukrisno felt that he was gaining advanced, scientific knowledge. He changed his career plans. He and Sjam quit their jobs at the Ministry of Information, joined the Communist Party, and started organizing trade unions, first at the colonial government's motor vehicle repair shops and then at the port of Jakarta, Tanjung Priok. They founded the Shipworkers and Sailors Trade Union (Serikat Buruh Kapal dan Pelayaran) in late 1948 and were the leading officers of it until February 1950, when it merged with the parallel union that had operated in Republican territory, Port Workers and Sailors Trade Union (Serikat Buruh Pelabuhan dan Pelayaran, SBPP). Sukrisno and Sjam did not contest the elections for the new union (which maintained the name SBPP). Instead, they were appointed to positions in the Communist Party. With the dissolution of their union they went their separate ways. Sukrisno occasionally ran into Sjam in later years. Sjam once asked for his help in contacting some old friends of the Pathuk group who had become military officers. Sukrisno guessed that Sjam's role within the Communist Party was to handle the military officers, but he was unaware of Sjam's precise role and ignorant of the existence of the Special Bureau.

Sukrisno is certain that Sjam was not working for the Dutch puppet government of Pasundan in 1949. He was employed in Jakarta as a civil servant of the Republican government from 1947 to 1948 and was preoccupied with trade union organizing from 1948 to 1950. The confusion perhaps arose because Sjam was working within Dutch-held territory and was working for the West Java branch of the Ministry of Information. Sukrisno is also certain that Sjam was not a member of the Socialist Party of Indonesia in the early 1950s. Sjam was correct when he testified that he joined the Communist Party in 1949. Sukrisno joined at the same time. Although all five Pathuk group members sent to Jakarta joined the PKI in the late 1940s, they remained on friendly terms with the Socialists who had guided them in Yogyakarta.[16] The five continued to socialize with figures in the Socialist Party of Indonesia even while relations between their respective political parties were deeply antagonistic.

How Sjam came to know Aidit is a matter of some conjecture. Sukrisno confirms what the historian Jacques Leclerc has reported, that Sjam helped Aidit resurface in mid-1950 after two years of an underground existence. In the wake of the Madiun affair in 1948, when the army under Sukarno and Hatta attacked the Communist Party, Aidit fled Central Java and went into hiding in Jakarta—a city he knew well from his time there as a nationalist activist in the mid-1940s. Once the Dutch departed in 1949 and it was safe to reemerge, Aidit and another Communist Party leader, Lukman, chose to appear first at the port of Tanjung Priok, as if they had just disembarked from a ship. They claimed that they had been in Vietnam and China and had witnessed first hand the Communist revolutions there. Sukrisno claims that Sjam was assigned the task of escorting Aidit through the port: "I went with Sjam to Tanjung Priok that day, but I did not accompany him to the docks to meet Aidit. Since I had never seen Aidit, I did not know what he looked like. I stayed outside." Sjam apparently had met Aidit before because he was able to recognize him. According to Leclerc, Sjam facilitated Aidit and Lukman's passage through the immigration office where they faced some trouble, given that they lacked the proper papers.[17] At least from that moment in Tanjung Priok, Aidit must have felt indebted to Sjam for his help in pulling off this bit of theater.

Sjam appears to have joined the Military Section under Karto sometime in the 1950s. Although Sjam claimed to have joined the Communist Party's Organizational Department (under which the Military Section operated) in 1960, it is likely that he joined well before that. Supardjo stated at his trial that he had known Sjam as a covert agent of the PKI since 1956.[18] Sukrisno notes that Sjam would have had a ready-made pool of contacts in the military just from his friends and acquaintances in the Pathuk group who joined the military. It is doubtful that Sjam would have been appointed head of the Special Bureau in 1963 or 1964 if he had not had a long record of covert work on behalf of the party. Sjam must have proved himself to Aidit over the years, to the point that Aidit had full faith in Sjam's loyalty to the party and in his capabilities in contacting military officers.

The Functioning of the Special Bureau under Sjam

At the time of the movement Sjam was neither a high-ranking military officer nor a prominent civilian politician. No one had even contemplated the idea that this apparent nobody was the leader of an ambitious military operation to seize "all power" until Sjam himself testified to that effect in 1967. Most observers had assumed that he had been nothing more than a faceless, replaceable functionary of the party whom Aidit had happened to choose as a go-between. Since Sjam's appearance at Mahmillub trials, his role within the party has been the source of much speculation. The information from Hasan clears up some of the mystery around Sjam and the Special Bureau.

According to Hasan, the Special Bureau had a five-man team in Jakarta, called the Biro Chusus Pusat (Central Special Bureau). Pono was Sjam's assistant, Bono the secretary, Wandi the treasurer, and Hamim the trainer of the bureau's cadre.[19] Of the five men, only Sjam, Pono, and Bono contacted military personnel for the purposes of intelligence gathering. Wandi and Hamim worked as their support staff. In most provinces there was a three-man team called the Biro Chusus Daerah (Regional Special Bureau). Although the Central Special Bureau concentrated on the officers in Jakarta, a regional branch for Jakarta supplemented its work.

All five members of the Central Special Bureau were not generally known as members of the Communist Party. They made a conscious effort to ensure that they were not perceived in public as party members or supporters. Each appeared to be a businessman. Hasan explains: "Sjam had a factory for making roof tiles, Bono had a car repair shop, Pono had a restaurant, Hamim had a bus transport business—they were living amid the society with these camouflages. Even their neighbors thought they were just regular businessmen. Every morning they'd leave for work at six o'clock. They all had cars paid for by the profits from their own businesses." To complete the disguise Sjam wore a tie and jacket and drove a luxury sports car. It would have been a stretch to suspect that he was a member of a party that detested conspicuous consumption and kept strict tabs on its members' income. That the Special Bureau members owned businesses was confirmed by a former political prisoner, Martin Aleida, who shared a cell in 1967 with a man named Suherman who managed a large store in the Jakarta neighborhood of Pasar Baru, one of the city's main commercial centers. Suherman explained to Aleida that he managed the store on behalf of the Special Bureau. He also mentioned that next to his store was another business owned by the Special Bureau, a workshop where many retired air force mechanics worked.[20]

Those in the Special Bureau who had previously been aboveground party members were rumored to have been dismissed from the party. They were accused of either betraying the party or committing a disciplinary infraction (womanizing, for instance). If they happened to meet former comrades, they would say they no longer agreed with the party or even that they loathed it. Hasan recalls: "Pono was originally from the PKI in Pekalongan [a city on the north coast of Central Java], so when he came to Jakarta no one knew where he came from. No one knew that he had been in the PKI. Those back in his area didn't know where he went. It just seemed like he left the party. Then bad things were said about him." Like Pono, Hamim had been known as a Communist Party member. He had taught at the party's school for Marxism-Leninism in Jakarta (the Aliarcham Academy) in the early 1960s. But he left the school under mysterious circumstances in 1964. The former vice director of the school, Sucipto, told me that he was under the impression that Hamim had severed all connections with the party. If Hamim ran into PKI members, he would tell them that he no longer agreed with the party. Sucipto was surprised when Hamim's name came up after 1965 as a member of the Special Bureau.[21]

The three-member teams of the regional branches also consisted of people who were not known as PKI cadre. They worked, for instance, as hotel managers, businessmen, and teachers while keeping their connection to the PKI hidden. Even the provincial Communist Party leaders might not know who was in the provincial Special Bureau. Some members of the Provincial Committee (Comite Daerah Besar) knew their identity, some did not.[22]

The wives of these party members were not allowed to be affiliated with the PKI. Sjam forced his wife to quit her activist work in the BTI, the peasants' union. Apparently, this had disastrous consequences for her. According to Hasan, "Sjam married a schoolteacher in West Java. She was Sundanese. She had to give up all of her activism. People could not know that she was a Communist or supportive of the Communists. She wasn't happy at all: 'How can a revolutionary activist like me wind up like this? Confined to the house, I can't do this, I can't do that. I can't even write articles.' She protested. She died of sickness sometime before 1965, cancer or something like that."[23]

The five members of the Central Special Bureau met once a month. For security reasons they did not have an office of their own. They met in various places around the city. The meetings were not occasions for debate or freewheeling discussions. There was only an exchange of information among the five concerning their progress in fulfilling their assigned tasks. Sjam would relay information from Aidit and present the party's line on current political issues. He would then assign the others to carry out certain tasks during the course of the next month.

Hasan confirmed Sjam's contention that the Special Bureau operated solely under Aidit. Some members of the Politburo and the Central Committee were aware that the Special Bureau existed, but they did
not necessarily know who was in it. The Special Bureau reported only
to Aidit and took orders only from Aidit. As Sjam put it in his testimony, "The Special Bureau was an instrument of the head of the
party."[24] Iskandar Subekti also affirms that it was "a body assisting the
head of the Central Committee [Aidit] that was formed outside of the
regulations of the party's constitution, for there is not even one article of
the party's constitution that mentions this body. It was assigned the task
of looking after, cultivating, and recruiting party members within the
military in illegal fashion (since it was impossible to do so legally). Aidit
asked Sjam to handle the party's forces within the military."[25]

Those in the Central Special Bureau in Jakarta took a number of
precautions to guard the secrecy of their operations. Their main concern was that the anti-Communist officers in army intelligence would
discover that they were working for the Communist Party. So that the
five of them would not appear to be working together, they rarely met as
a group outside their monthly meetings. Their practice in meeting one
another or their contacts was to wait no more than ten minutes for the
other person to show up. They would interpret a delay as a possibility
that the person had been arrested and forced to reveal his secrets.

Hasan is uncertain how Sjam arranged to meet Aidit so that
Sjam's cover as a private businessman would not be compromised.
Hasan believes that Sjam would go to Aidit's house—they lived close to
each other in an upscale part of Jakarta—and the meeting would seem
to be a neighborly visit. Because many other people, from a wide variety
of backgrounds, came to the house to see Aidit, Sjam would not be noticed. As a powerful politician, Aidit was naturally in great demand. It
would have been difficult for an intelligence agent to keep track of each
person visiting him.

For all that anyone could see on the outside, Sjam, Pono, and Bono
were private businessmen who doubled as army intelligence agents but
had no significant relationship with the PKI. If a relationship with the
Communist Party was known, it may not have been clear whether the
men were spies for the army working inside the PKI or vice versa. Such
ambiguity was crucial since Sjam, Bono, and Pono did not maintain
perfect covers. Several former high-level party members recalled in
interviews with me that they were vaguely familiar with these three men
and knew them to be part of the PKI's Organizational Department

(although my informants were unaware of the existence of the Special Bureau). While the three men did not have a prominent and vocal presence at the PKI's headquarters, the very fact that they occasionally showed up there must have compromised their cover. That several party members I spoke to, including Sukrisno, knew they were affiliated with the Communist Party suggests that other members also knew.

The army intelligence agents monitoring the PKI headquarters and Aidit's house may have had a record of Sjam, Pono, and Bono. But it is not known whether any such agent also knew them to be frequenters of military offices or knew for certain that they were working for the PKI. It is obvious that the army intelligence network under Major General Parman did not know their identities. The army high command was worried about the Communist Party in 1965 and knew that it had connections with some military officers. If Parman, the intelligence czar, knew Sjam was the party's key man for handling military contacts, Parman would have been keeping close tabs on him. Anyone following Sjam in August and September 1965 would have noticed that something was afoot. Parman's death at the hands of the movement by itself suggests that he was ignorant of Sjam's identity.[26]

The proliferation of intelligence agents and informants in Jakarta worked in favor of maintaining the secrecy surrounding the Special Bureau. There were so many spies and double agents that it was difficult for any one agency to keep track of even a portion of them. Parman of the army had his agency. General Nasution, as the defense minister, had his own intelligence network. Suharto at Kostrad, the army reserve, had his own, the military police had its own. The first deputy prime minister and foreign minister, Soebandrio, had an intelligence agency under him, the BPI (Badan Pusat Intelijen). The navy, air force, and police all had their own networks. The Supreme Operations Command (Koti) had its own. Some agencies were rivals and were spying on each other. Rumors were constantly circulating. Each agency operated under a partial cloud of confusion. Even with his plants at PKI headquarters, Parman seems not to have detected the Special Bureau personnel.

It is likely that someone warned Yani on the night of September 30 about the impending action. According to Omar Dani, an officer in the military police told Yani that an action was imminent and offered an extra set of guards for his house. Reportedly, Yani dismissed the offer because he presumed that the information was just another rumor.[27] The generals at the army high command had been receiving such reports for weeks, and none had turned out to be true.[28] The movement appears to have been able to abduct six generals because its planning had been obscured by an excessive amount of "intelligence noise."[29]

Sjam, Pono, and Bono—the nucleus of the Special Bureau—were responsible for maintaining contacts with military officers. Each had official military cards identifying him as an intelligence agent. With those cards they could move unhindered in and out of military facilities. According to Hasan, "Those three had identification cards given to them by friends in the intelligence departments of the various services. Each was given identification cards showing that he was an intelligence agent for the army, or the navy, or the air force. They had cards, for instance, from the Jakarta garrison. They could walk into a military complex, show the card, and say, 'I'm an intelligence agent for so and so, for colonel so and so, or for general so and so.' They could visit the offices and homes of the officers."[30]

Each of the three men had his own group of contacts: "They had generals, colonels, captains—even down to the lower ranks. This was in Jakarta, but in the regions it was of course left up to the Regional Special Bureaus. Just like at the Central Bureau, the regional branches also had generals—this officer, that officer—who were under their influence. A regional branch had to follow orders from the Central Bureau. In the monthly meetings they talked about how far the PKI's influence had reached inside the military, was it growing or not? Those in the Special Bureau were ordered to go back and further expand the party's influence in the four services: the air force, police, army, and navy."

In his 1967 courtroom testimony Sjam described how the Special Bureau recruited officers. Hasan has confirmed that Sjam's description of the process, quoted in part here, is largely accurate:

> Every member and leader of the Special Bureau had an obligation to expand the organization within the ranks of the armed forces. You studied the various officers and found out about them, and then you tried to approach them and get to know them. If you succeeded in becoming acquainted with an officer, then you would begin talking about general social and political issues. Once you could see what kind of military officer he was, whether he was an anti-Communist or a democrat, then you would keep exchanging ideas with him about political issues facing the country and about progressive ideas. Once it was clear that the officer was, from the perspective of the PKI, progressive, then you would go on to talk to him about issues related to the party. If it appeared that the officer didn't reject such discussions,

that he didn't evidence a negative reaction, you would continue with deeper issues, that is, with questions of Marxist theory.[31]

Hasan contends that the goal was not to turn the officers into party members. It was to make them willing to provide information to the Special Bureau and carry out assignments. The officers were not educated in "questions of Marxist theory," as Sjam asserted. As of September 1965 the party had not yet implemented plans to conduct clandestine classes in Marxism-Leninism for military personnel. The bureau usually contented itself with Sukarnoist officers who supported the Communist Party because it was supporting Sukarno. Hasan observed: "What was important, generally speaking, was that the military personnel were pro-Sukarno, meaning not necessarily pro-PKI. At that time the PKI was cooperating with Sukarno, so what was being done by Sukarno was similar to the PKI's program. . . . Within the Special Bureau, no one said, 'This fellow is a member of the party.' No, nothing like that. What was important was whether or not he would obey Sjam."

The Special Bureau members used their military contacts not only to gain information about the internal machinations of the military but also to act on behalf of the Communist Party. Hasan cited an example from December 1964. Aidit needed help when Sukarno's third deputy prime minister, Chairul Saleh, accused the PKI of having a step-by-step plan to seize state power. Saleh, who was close to the anti-Communist Murba Party, claimed there was a document that revealed the PKI's secret plan. Because of this allegation the military police interrogated Aidit and was thinking about bringing a case against him. Aidit instructed Sjam to order the Special Bureau's contacts inside the military to thwart the case. The effort succeeded brilliantly: Aidit was cleared of the charges and came out of the case vindicated. Saleh had to apologize for disseminating a forged document.[32]

Aidit, according to Hasan, also used personnel in the Special Bureau as back-up bodyguards. As a minister in Sukarno's cabinet, Aidit was assigned, as a matter of protocol, a military detachment to protect him when he was traveling outside Jakarta. However, given the anticommunism of the army leadership, he did not trust the guards assigned to protect him. He would order Sjam to have the Special Bureau's military contacts in the region shadow the guards and guarantee that he was not harmed.

However much the Special Bureau took advantage of its supporters in the military, it also offered something in return. It had complex give-and-take relations with its military contacts. It provided information

that helped the officers understand the political situation and even advance their careers. As Hasan notes, "If they wanted to attract an officer
to join the Special Bureau's network, they would give them information
that was useful for them in fulfilling their military assignments." For instance, when battling the revolts of Darul Islam, PRRI, and Permesta,
some army officers cooperated with the mass organizations affiliated
with the Communist Party. The Darul Islam (House of Islam) movement (1948–62), active in West Java, demanded an Islamic state in Indonesia. (It went by the acronym DI, while its military wing, Tentara
Islam Indonesia, or the Islamic Army of Indonesia, was abbreviated as
TII. Today the movement is usually referred to as DI/TII.) Both the
guerrillas of the Darul Islam movement and the rebel military officers
behind the PRRI and Permesta revolts were strict anti-Communists.
The Communist Party had an urgent interest in helping the military
suppress these revolts.

During military operations some officers drew upon the networks of
local PKI cadre for intelligence information and for recruits for civilian
militias. The Special Bureau facilitated these contacts between the military personnel and the PKI. Hasan elaborated on this point:

> Attracting a military officer worked like this. Say, for example,
> his assignment was to attack DI/TII in a certain district in West
> Java. That was his assignment. Someone from the Special Bu-
> reau would approach him and explain how DI/TII operated,
> what its strategy was. Now the military fellow would listen care-
> fully. Someone like Sjam would tell him, look, that group doesn't
> have any mass base, so if you want to attack it, you should mo-
> bilize the masses first, get the masses involved. If the officer
> agreed, he would come back to talk with Sjam about how to mo-
> bilize civilian militia groups (Organisasi Perlawanan Rakyat),
> and Sjam would explain, well, you have to do this, this, and this.
> The information from the military itself about political issues
> was next to nothing, especially for an officer in a remote district
> in West Java. Sjam would inform him that DI/TII was being
> sponsored by the United States and the Netherlands. And this
> officer would become convinced that it was indeed the enemy
> and had to be destroyed. After all, that was what Sukarno or-
> dered, that it be destroyed. So if the officer, with the backing of
> the PKI masses, succeeded in attacking and destroying DI/TII,
> then he would get a promotion. He would feel indebted to Sjam

since he got the promotion because of Sjam's help. He felt that he had benefited, that he better understood the political situation, and could better perform his military duties. It was the members of the Special Bureau who gave them a political education.

It is likely that the relationship between Sjam and Supardjo proceeded along the lines that Hasan describes. As the commander of the West Java district Garut, where the DI/TII had an important base, Supardjo played a major role in ending the prolonged DI/TII insurgency in the early 1960s. The army in West Java began deploying large numbers of civilians in a "fence of legs" tactic in 1960. Supardjo, with the PKI's help, used this tactic in Garut. The civilians lined up with little distance between them and then swept through an area as teams of armed soldiers advanced ahead and followed behind. With this tactic the armed insurgents were flushed out of their bases and concentrated in increasingly smaller zones.[33] Supardjo organized some of these "fence of legs" operations by using Communist Party cadre who were militantly opposed to the DI/TII and were often the targets of its hit-and-run attacks.[34] On the basis of his success in finishing off the DII/TII, Supardjo was promoted to colonel and later handed the high-profile post of commanding the troops assembled along the Malaysian border during Confrontation. He was an army commander who took combat strategy and organizational discipline seriously. His experience with counterinsurgency warfare taught him first hand the importance of civilian support.

It was no secret at the time that some units of the army, in suppressing these right-wing revolts of the 1950s and early 1960s, solicited the help of the PKI.[35] What was not generally known was that the PKI had a special department that was serving as a clandestine liaison with the officers and asking them to do favors for the PKI in return. Colonel Abdul Latief, while assigned to Sumatra to suppress the PRRI rebellion in 1958, worked with the mass organizations of the PKI there. One former member of the PKI from North Sumatra recalled meeting Latief during that time and coordinating the actions of a PKI youth group with him.[36]

When an officer who had been collaborating with the PKI was transferred, the relationship did not necessarily end. His previously established contact in the Special Bureau would arrange for the Special Bureau in the new area to meet him. Given the cell structure of the Special Bureau, a three-man team in one regional branch did not know the identities of teams in other regions. The organization developed a method for staying in contact with officers who were being moved around the country. Hasan explains: "Let's say a Javanese officer is posted to fight in Menado. Well, there is a Special Bureau there. Before he leaves Java, he would be given a code. It was like this: here is a sheet of paper; the letter *A* is written on the upper half in red, and another *A* written on the lower half in black. The paper is then torn in half. One half is given to the officer, and the other is sent to the regional branch via the center. The Special Bureau person, once he receives the paper, is told the name of the officer. And he goes looking for him. He keeps looking for him until he finds him. Once he meets up with him, he brings out this piece of paper and they would match up their separate halves."

It is not surprising that some military personnel, even high-ranking officers, supported the Communist Party. The party fervently supported every major military campaign that Sukarno launched. In addition to backing the campaigns against the DI/TII, PRRI, and Permesta revolts, the party backed the military's seizure of West New Guinea (now known as West Papua) from the Dutch in 1962 and the Confrontation against Malaysia, which began in 1963. The party had garnered much respect among some officers as a patriotic and pro-Sukarno force that could build public support for the wars that the military was waging. It appeared to be a disciplined and responsible party.[37]

For those higher-ranking officers with an international perspective, the attractions of the PKI lay not just in terms of national politics. Some officers were deeply impressed by the victorious guerrilla war of the Chinese Communists and the implacable Vietnamese resistance to the U.S. military. Their experience during the national revolution had made them committed anti-imperialists. President Sukarno himself constantly implored Indonesians not to allow the country to be controlled by Western capitalists. Sukarno had organized the 1955 Asia-Africa Conference in Bandung as an explicit rejection of the old colonial powers. The anti-imperialist revolutions in China and Vietnam thus struck a responsive chord in those Indonesian officers who took their Sukarnoism seriously. The successes of Communists in other countries raised the prestige of the Communist Party, which was assumed to share the same spirit and wisdom.

Supardjo, who visited both China and Vietnam, was in awe of the military capabilities of the Communist parties there. According to Heru Atmodjo, who was imprisoned with Supardjo in Cimahi prison (near Bandung), Supardjo had great respect for Sjam because he thought

Sjam had been trained in China as a political commissar to military troops. Sjam probably misrepresented himself. According to Hasan, Sjam had never been to China for anything more than medical care.[38] However, it appears that he had been to Vietnam. Subekti writes that "Sjam himself had been delegated by the party once to observe Vietnam when it was still fighting a war against the United States."[39] Whatever his misconceptions about Sjam, Supardjo's exposure to the Chinese and Vietnamese militaries convinced him that Communist parties, in their remarkable ability to integrate civilians into military operations, represented a paradigm relevant for Indonesia.[40]

Supardjo may have been impressed by Sjam simply because the general assumed that Sjam was representing the PKI, an institution that impressed Supardjo. Some people who knew Sjam before 1965 were not impressed in the least. They remember him as bombastic, arrogant, and not particularly bright.[41] Benedict Anderson witnessed Sjam's testimony at the 1967 Mahmillub sessions and could not believe that Sjam was a high-ranking Communist Party leader since his rhetoric came straight from the nationalist activism of the late 1940s, unmediated by the party's current discourse: "Sjam spoke in a manner completely unlike the other witnesses—boastful, a tad megalomaniac, but above all in a 'frozen' version of the kind of talk that was used in 1945-49. . . . It felt like entering a kind of aural antique shop."[42]

There is an explanation for Sjam's antiquated language. Hasan told me that Sjam never read books and barely read the party literature. He was too busy meeting people and arranging subterfuges to be bothered with theory. Sjam's position in the party was such that he did not have to think about the party's program and defend it in public; he did not sit on a decision-making body, write party literature, hold a seat in parliament, or organize conferences. His job was to take orders from Aidit, keep secrets, and cozy up to left-wing officers. Sjam was ordering powerful generals and colonels to do favors for Aidit. He did not feel that he had anything to learn from literature and theoreticians. Hasan saw Sjam as someone who felt himself to be the paragon of the Communist activist doing practical work to build up the strength of world's third-largest Communist party.

Hasan believes that Sjam was not a mysterious figure at all; he operated by a simple principle: follow Aidit. Sjam was unwaveringly loyal to Aidit. He viewed Aidit as the Indonesian version of Stalin or Mao, a great figure of epic proportions with a glorious future ahead of him. Sjam felt proud to serve as Aidit's righthand man. Sjam was a classic apparatchik who understood the party as an organization that was fight-ing for state power. He would have grasped Machiavelli better than Marx.

Understanding Sjam as a party functionary motivated by a personal loyalty to Aidit, and largely devoid of the humanist idealism and collec-tive spirit that motivated other members, allows us to see the logic be-hind one of Sjam's answers during the questioning by the Mahmillub prosecutor. Sjam was asked what education the Special Bureau provided its supporters in the military:

SJAM: It was about theory and ideology.
PROSECUTOR: Theory and ideology. What was the theory?
SJAM: Marxism-Leninism.
PROSECUTOR: And the ideology?
SJAM: Love the party.

Love the party *(cinta kepada partai)*. That was Sjam's idea of the party's ideology. It was the thinking of someone so devoted to the organization that the democratic ideals for which it stood were mere rhetorical dross.

Sjam's behavior after his capture in 1967 suggests that he was an op-portunist. With the party that he supposedly loved in ruins, along with his chances of rising to power, he devoted himself to saving his own skin, even when that meant betraying former comrades. During his first Mahmillub testimony he named two military officers who had been part of the Special Bureau's network—officers who had not yet been identified as pro-PKI. One appears to have been arrested and impris-oned because of Sjam's disclosures.[43] In later appearances as a witness at Mahmillub trials, Sjam named more names. Subekti notes that he never approached Sjam, his fellow inmate at Cipinang prison, to find out more about the events of 1965 because he viewed Sjam as entirely unreliable.[44]

Hasan explained that Sjam's strategy was to keep providing his cap-tors with useful information: "He once told me, 'Actually, I want to live a long life.' Because of that, he revealed certain issues both while he was in prison and in court. It was so he could prolong the stay of execution. He was actually afraid, afraid to be shot by the firing squad." Sjam thought that if he could postpone the execution long enough, he might be able to outlast the Suharto regime, which he did not believe capable of lasting very long.

In his testimonies at various trials (about ten by 1972), Sjam added a new detail each time so that military intelligence agents would think that he had more information to reveal.[45] His fellow political prisoners noticed this tactic. Siauw Giok Tjhan, in his analysis, mentioned that when another prisoner criticized Sjam for revealing the names of so many military officers, he justified his actions by saying, "Each person has a right to defend his right to life. As a person who has been given a death sentence, I want to postpone it and, if possible, get it canceled. If I sense that the sentence is about to be carried out, that I'm about to be executed, I raise another big issue so that, for the sake of another interrogation, the sentence against me won't be implemented."[46] Sjam followed the classic strategy of Scheherazade, the woman in the legend of the *Arabian Nights* who was married off to a deranged king who executed his wives after sleeping with them. She was able to forestall her execution by telling stories to the king every night. Instead of having her beheaded, the king kept her alive so that he could hear the rest of her stories. After 1,001 nights he vowed not to execute her. This strategy worked almost as well for Sjam. Although he was executed in 1986, after being sentenced in 1968, he had bought himself a reprieve much longer than 1,001 nights.

Some observers (such as Wertheim) have assumed that Sjam's self-serving behavior was evidence that he was not a real member of the PKI. But they have not appreciated the extent to which characters such as Sjam were by no means unique within the party. Other former high-level Communist Party leaders betrayed the party after their arrests: Sujono Pradigdo (head of the Verification Committee), Peris Pardede (head of the Control Committee), Sampir Suwarto (head of security at party headquarters), Kusnan (private secretary to Sudisman and member of the Verification Committee), and Burhan Komalasakti (member of the Central Committee), among others.[47] Such betrayals can be considered understandable responses to torture or physical threats to loved ones. However, other party leaders, even rank-and-file members, did not succumb to torture. For die-hard party loyalists like Hasan, who was also tortured, the betrayals of the leaders were indications that the party had become too bourgeois by 1965. The leaders should have attained their high positions precisely by proving their courage and commitment to the party. That the party was led by people who could not face the military repression with nerves of steel suggests to Hasan, a follower of the Maoist line on armed struggle, that the party contained fundamental flaws.

Hasan's account of Sjam's personality and work for the Communist Party allows us to read Sjam's first testimony before the Mahmillub in a new light. Hasan confirms many of the claims in that testimony: the Special Bureau maintained contacts with military officers, it worked exclusively under the direction of Aidit, it was not accountable to the other institutions of the party, it was headed by Sjam, and Sjam was loyal to Aidit. By itself Sjam's testimony, like all the testimonies at the Mahmillub trials, cannot be treated as valid evidence. Scholars have been justified in not relying upon Sjam's version of events. Hasan's corroboration of his version, however, suggests that Sjam was not just telling tall tales. Subekti's account of the movement also confirms many claims in Sjam's testimony. Of course, not all Sjam's claims should be considered truthful—Hasan contradicts several. I have translated the bulk of Sjam's testimony and included it as appendix 2 so that readers can familiarize themselves with his precise claims (rather than those filtered through Suharto regime propaganda).

5

Aidit, the PKI, and the Movement

For the PKI, work can only be performed properly and with excellence if it is accompanied by loyalty or solidarity. . . . It is this basis of Communist morality that conditions the practice of democratic centralism — centralism based on democracy, and democracy with a center—in which collective and individual responsibility are made one.

Sudisman, *Analysis of Responsibility* (1967)

The evidence so far suggests that Aidit at least approved of Sjam's collaboration with military officers for staging a preemptive strike against the army high command. Sjam was the primary organizer of the movement, according to the Supardjo document. He was Aidit's loyal subordinate, according to Hasan. If these two claims are true, one has to suspect that Aidit was more than a gullible dupe of the movement. At this point the unanswered question is whether Aidit initiated the movement and ordered Sjam to carry it out (as the Suharto regime's version claimed) or allowed Sjam to work with the military officers on the assumption that the officers were leading the movement. What did Aidit know about the relationship between the Special Bureau members and the military officers? What did Sjam tell him? What information did he hear from other sources about the disposition of military officers who joined the movement? Was Aidit the mastermind, commanding and supervising Sjam's every move, or was he a supporter of the movement and under the impression that the military officers were masterminding the action?

It is difficult to assess Aidit's role because there is no direct, conclusive evidence about it. Given the clandestine nature of the organizing, only two men were in a position to fully understand Aidit's role: Sjam and Aidit himself. The army executed Aidit in November 1965 before he had a chance to give an account of his actions. Sjam, appearing at a Mahmillub trial in 1967, asserted that he had acted on orders from Aidit. His assertion is impossible to verify. The only approach to the question of Aidit's role is indirect, a matter of piecing together bits of evidence and considering the plausibility of different possibilities. In this chapter I consider statements by former PKI leaders, Aidit's political strategy in the months before the movement, and his views on military coups. I also consider the party's statement about the movement in the October 2, 1965, edition of its daily newspaper, *Harian Rakjat.*

Sudisman's Analysis

The most significant statement by a PKI leader about the movement was by Sudisman, the party's secretary general who managed to survive the great massacres. He was captured in December 1966 and brought before the Mahmillub in July 1967. He was one of a group of five young men who had taken over the leadership of the party in 1951. These five—Aidit, Lukman, Njoto, Sakirman, and Sudisman himself—enjoyed great success in rebuilding the party. In his defense plea Sudisman referred to the unity among these five men as similar to that of the five Pandawa brothers of the great Indian epic the *Mahabharata:* "The four of them are I, and I am the four of them. . . . With the four of them, I have been five-in-one. . . . We five have always been together."[1] The Communist Party's success from 1951 to 1965 was in part due to this unity of the leadership. No splits fragmented the party into rival organizations (such as occurred in the Communist movement in India), even in the midst of the Sino-Soviet conflict.

Sudisman's defense plea, though presented in the Mahmillub—"in the grip of the enemy," as the ex-PKI activists would say—is a candid, well-written document that exhibits remarkable intelligence and composure. He did not shrink before the court in fear, shift blame onto others, feign ignorance, or plead for his life. As the highest party leader left alive, he felt a responsibility to the party's supporters to explain what went wrong. Aware that he was going to be sentenced to death, he composed his defense plea as a political statement to the broader public outside the courtroom. Indeed, because he refused to recognize the legitimacy of the Mahmillub, he denied that it should be called a defense plea *(pledoi)*. He called it an "analysis of responsibility" *(uraian tanggundjawab)*.[2]

Sudisman acknowledged that, in some unspecified way, he was "involved" *(terlibat)* in the movement and that other unnamed Communist Party leaders were also "directly involved" in it.[3] By using the word *involved* he did not mean that the PKI leaders had directed the movement. He upheld the party's statement of October 6, 1965, that the movement was "an internal army matter" and that the PKI as a party "knew nothing" about it.[4] He contended that the initiators and main organizers of the movement, its "moving spirits," were "progressive officers" who wanted to foil the coup plot by the Council of Generals.[5] This group behind the movement largely consisted of "non-Communist officers" (meaning Sukarno loyalists) but also included "a few who were Communists."[6] Sudisman's implication was that certain Communist Party leaders as individuals decided to support these progressive officers. He did not explain exactly how he and the other party leaders struck up an alliance with the officers and provided this support. His focus was on justifying the Politburo's strategy of supporting the movement rather than describing the manner in which it was implemented.

He claimed that he had become convinced that the action by the "progressive officers" was the best method of countering right-wing army generals who had proved themselves to be the single largest obstacle to the party's programs. They blocked Sukarno's anti-imperialist foreign policy, the government's economic policies designed to benefit peasants and workers (such as land reform), and the PKI's continued expansion. The strategy of supporting the "progressive officers," Sudisman argued, seemed correct at the time. In retrospect, however, he considered it misguided. The failure of the movement and the vulnerability of the party to military repression revealed something wrong in the very nature of the party's organization and ideology. Sudisman suggested that the problem was not that the party leaders just happened to bet on the wrong horse; the problem was that they were betting in the first place. Caught up in their long streak of success, they had lost the ability "calculate scientifically the concrete balance of forces on each side."[7] Their emphasis on national unity had led them to become too accommodating of the middle class and neglectful of building up the autonomous organized strength of the peasants and workers.[8] By supporting a secretive putsch divorced from "the masses," the leaders had opted for a kind of risky short-cut to the revolution—a risk they never would have taken had the party not been preoccupied with the machinations of elite politicians in Jakarta. In the ruins of the movement stood revealed the "accumulated mistakes of the PKI over a long period of time."[9]

Sudisman believed that the masterminds of the movement were the military officers such as Untung and Supardjo. In evaluating the accuracy of his belief, one has to ask what Sudisman knew about the movement. On what information was his belief based? According to his *Analysis of Responsibility*, his knowledge of the movement was derived solely from Aidit. Sudisman noted that in Politburo meetings Aidit had "explained that there were progressive officers who wanted to take preventive action to forestall a coup d'état by the Council of Generals."[10] In Sudisman's experience Aidit "was always extremely careful and precise in estimating the balance of power"; he was "extremely meticulous in such matters."[11] By virtue of his position as a coordinating minister in Sukarno's cabinet, Aidit "had many channels for checking his information."[12] Sudisman trusted Aidit's opinion that the movement deserved to receive support: "Comrade Aidit explained to us [presumably, members of the Politburo] quite convincingly that the existence of the Council of Generals had called into being the progressive officers and the September 30th Movement, which would carry out a military operation and form a Revolution Council."[13] Aidit was consistent in informing the Politburo that the movement was internal to the military: "Aidit always said that the progressive officers wished to carry out a military operation, never once that the PKI wished to carry out such an operation. Nor did Comrade Aidit ever state that the PKI wished to start a revolution at that time."[14] Sudisman positioned Aidit as the one person in the party who was in touch with the officers and who determined what actions PKI personnel would take to support the movement. He mentioned that Aidit instructed "a number of cadres to be sent to the provinces a few days before the outbreak of the September 30th Movement, with the line 'listen to the announcements over the Radio of the Republic of Indonesia and support the Revolution Council.'"[15] For Sudisman the movement was similar to the coup by Colonel Qasim in Iraq in 1958 that overthrew the monarchy and canceled Iraq's participation in the military alliance for containing the Soviet Union (the Baghdad Pact of 1955, which included Turkey and Great Britain, among others).[16] Some coups have a progressive political agenda—they are against feudalism, imperialism, and capitalism—while some coups have a reactionary agenda. The movement, though not a coup, was a military action that the party considered to be progressive.

Sudisman did not claim to have direct contact with the officers involved in the movement. Perhaps he was not even in contact with Sjam and the personnel of the Special Bureau. He did not mention them. Although Sudisman must have known more about the party's connection to the movement than he revealed in his *Analysis of Responsibility*, without additional evidence one cannot presume that Sudisman's judgment on the movement's "moving spirits" was based on information other than what Aidit provided him. During the Mahmillub sessions Sudisman, in response to Sjam's testimony, claimed to have no direct knowledge of the movement, to have been following orders from Aidit, and to have believed that Sjam was also following orders from Aidit: "Even though I myself did not know [about the movement], what was done by the witness, Comrade Sjam, was on the instructions of Aidit, and even I carried out instructions from Comrade Aidit, from the perspective of responsibility, I will take over the responsibility for all of it."[17]

I will comment later on Sudisman's enigmatic assumption of responsibility for a movement about which he admitted to knowing so little. For now the important point to note is that Sudisman was not necessarily in a position to know how the movement was organized. There is no reason to consider as authoritative and well informed his opinion that the military officers were acting on their own. Sudisman's evaluation of the movement as having been led by the military does not constitute a convincing refutation of Supardjo's evaluation of it as having been led by Sjam. Since Supardjo was much closer to the movement's organizers and witnessed their decision-making process first hand, his evaluation should be given more weight.[18]

The question about Aidit's knowledge remains unresolved in Sudisman's analysis. Perhaps Aidit too believed that the military officers were acting on their own. He depended on information from Sjam. Perhaps Sjam did not explain to him that he was actually playing a dominant role in organizing the officers. Alternatively, Aidit might have known that the officers behind the movement were those connected to the Special Bureau but might have wished to hide that fact from others in the Politburo in order to maintain the secrecy around the Special Bureau's operations.

Sjam and Hasan's Analyses

Toward the end of his Mahmillub trial Sudisman read aloud his "analysis of responsibility" before the judges and spectators. His analysis can be understood in part as a refutation of the testimony that Sjam had provided at the same trial. Brought into the courtroom as a witness, Sjam had testified that Aidit did much more than support the movement. According to Sjam's version of events, Aidit had initiated the movement. He had supposedly ordered Sjam to mobilize military personnel affiliated with the Special Bureau to stage a military action against the right-wing army generals. Sjam stated: "After August [1965], we [in the Special Bureau] received information from Comrade Aidit that the situation was coming to a head. And all the signs pointed to the Council of Generals as having already begun its final preparations for a final seizure of state power. With such issues in mind we had a question: In facing such a situation, should we wait to get hit or should we hit first? Since our conclusion was that we have to hit first, we made preparations by holding meetings between myself, Pono, Untung, Latief, Soejono, Sigit, and Wahyudi, as preparatory meetings to carry out a movement that would ultimately be named the September 30th Movement. I was the one who led those meetings."[19] Sjam claimed to have chosen the officers who participated in those meetings and to have designed, with Aidit's help, the idea of the Revolution Council.

Sjam's testimony, by itself, should be treated with skepticism. His claim to have been the boss of the military officers can be dismissed as the delusion of a megalomaniac, someone who wished to be seen as an important political player. His claim that he was following orders from Aidit can be dismissed as an effort to legitimate actions that may have actually fallen outside Aidit's purview. Perhaps Sjam implicated Aidit in order to please the military prosecutors who wanted confirmation of their accusation that Aidit was the mastermind of the movement. Sjam's claims, however, cannot be so easily dismissed in light of Supardjo's postmortem analysis (which I reviewed in chapter 3) and Hasan's corroboration of certain parts of Sjam's testimony pertaining to the functioning of the Special Bureau (reviewed in chapter 4). Perhaps Sjam was not a sham. In the autobiographical essay that he wrote in the mid-1990s, Hasan has corroborated a number of Sjam's claims about his role in the movement. Hasan believes that Sjam was following Aidit's orders and that the officers were, in turn, following Sjam's lead:

At a certain time, about the month of July 1965, in a meeting of the Central Special Bureau, Sjam explained that President Sukarno's sickness was worsening and could well kill him. This event would be used by the anti-Sukarno military who worked hand in hand with the neocolonial forces—the United States, Britain, Japan, the Netherlands—to overthrow Sukarno's state and replace it with a pro-Western, fascistic, military government. The democratic people's movement guided by the principle of Nasakom, in which the PKI had become the vanguard, would be violently repressed to the point of utter destruction.

To face this critical and urgent situation, the PKI as the vanguard of the people's movement had to take a position. The PKI's position was that it had to resist the coup movement of the army against the Sukarno government in a military way. Aidit assigned the task to the Central Special Bureau, which had been cultivating military personnel. In the course of subsequent events, as the situation became more critical, the order changed: the Special Bureau would not just wait for the coup by the military but would act preemptively against the pro-neocolonial generals.[20]

Sukarno was ill from August 3 to August 9, so the first meeting to which Hasan refers must have occurred in early August. The possibility of Sukarno's death in early August might have provoked Aidit's initial determination to prepare for a military action, as Hasan suggests, but it could not have sustained that determination through late September. The rumors that Sukarno was dying evaporated as soon as he regained his health. Some advisers thought all along that he was suffering from nothing more than a bad case of the flu. After August 9 Sukarno showed no sign of a serious relapse and resumed a grueling schedule filled with passionately delivered public speeches, including one the night of September 30 itself.

For Aidit to have continued the plan for a military action, if that is what he did, he must have been convinced that the anti-Communist army generals would strike regardless of Sukarno's health. Aidit, according to Hasan, changed the original plan; the Special Bureau went from anticipating the generals' coup d'état to preempting it. This echoes Sjam's contention that the party faced the question of whether to wait for the coup and then act or to preempt it. It also echoes Supardjo's contention that "the party" at some point shifted its strategy from remaining informed about the plans of the "progressive officers" to imposing its own plan.

The accounts of Sjam and Hasan, taken together, cannot be considered definitive proof that Aidit initiated the movement, that Sjam followed Aidit's order, and that the military officers affiliated with the

Special Bureau followed Sjam. Perhaps the officers acted on the basis of unjustified inferences. When speaking before the officers and other members of the Special Bureau (the people whom Hasan knew), Sjam might have boasted of orders from Aidit in order to get the others to follow him. Recall that Supardjo was under the impression that the party had a larger plan that went beyond what Sjam had explained to him. Sjam might well have pretended that the party leadership was more involved in the movement than it was. Hasan's corroboration of the basics of Sjam's account, however, suggests at the very least that the idea of Aidit's being one of the movement's leaders is not far-fetched. To get a better idea of Aidit's role one has to consider the accounts by those in the Politburo itself.

Iskandar Subekti's Analysis

Two members of the Politburo are known to have played a direct role in the movement: Njono, who organized about two thousand youths to serve as a civilian militia, and Iskandar Subekti, who accompanied Aidit at Halim Air Force Base. Both men provided accounts of the party's decision-making process in their courtroom testimony. Njono, the first Communist Party leader to be tried by the Mahmillub, tried to clear other party leaders of any blame. He presented himself as a rogue element who had acted in defiance of a Politburo decision to remain uninvolved in the Sukarnoist officers' action against the Council of Generals.[21] His implausible "loose cannon" scenario is best put aside. It was understandable, even admirable, of him to accept full responsibility, but it is impossible to believe he acted in complete isolation from Aidit and other party leaders, especially because Sudisman later admitted that the Politburo had decided to support the movement.

Subekti's account merits more attention. Subekti was the note taker *(panitera)* and archivist for the Politburo. He was suited for this role not merely because he knew shorthand; he was well educated, fluent in several European languages, and deeply knowledgeable about the party's history and programs. When he was put on trial in 1972, this keeper of the party's secrets could afford to be more frank than Njono had been. Sudisman's "analysis of responsibility" had already been issued, and the party had already been destroyed.

In his courtroom defense plea Subekti stated that at a meeting sometime in August 1965 the Politburo had decided that the party would provide "political support" to an action being plotted by progressive officers.

Figure 3. Organizational Structure of the Leadership of the Communist Party of Indonesia, September 1965

Chairman of the Central Committee
D. N. Aidit

Working Committee of the Politburo (Dewan Harian Politbiro)
Five members: D. N. Aidit, Lukman, Njoto, Sudisman, Oloan Hutapea

Politburo (Politbiro)
Twelve full members: D. N. Aidit, Lukman, Njoto, Sudisman, Oloan Hutapea, Sakirman, Njono, Mohamad Munir, Ruslan Wijayasastra, Jusuf Ajitorop, Asmu, Rewang
Four candidate members: Peris Pardede, Sanusi, A. Sucipto Munandar, F. Runturambi
Note taker: Iskandar Subekti

Central Committee *(Comite Central)*
85 members

Source: Subekti, "G-30-S Bukan Buatan PKI," 2–3.

While he did not explain the precise meaning of "political support," Subekti distinguished it from "physical support," which the Politburo declined to provide. The implication was that officers would act by themselves, while the party would champion their cause in the press and in government meetings: "The party's position was to provide political support, not physical support or some other type of support, to the young officers who wanted to foil the Council of Generals' plot against President Sukarno. The PKI would provide support to an action by revolutionary and democratic forces to oppose counterrevolutionary forces. Such a position was proper and normal, given the developing situation at that time and the PKI's political line to support the government of Sukarno."[22]

Subekti claimed that Aidit explained the Politburo's decision to a group of Central Committee members on either August 27 or 28.[23] Subekti emphasized that this meeting was a briefing by Aidit and not a formal meeting of either an expanded Politburo or a miniature Central Committee (see figure 3 for the PKI's leadership structure). The briefing was meant to apprise certain leaders of the party's position. Aidit explained to those assembled that a clique of progressive officers was organizing an action against the Council of Generals and that the party would provide "political support." According to Subekti, no discussion was held and no decisions were made in that forum.

Subekti stated that the Politburo did not meet during September. Njono also stated that the Politburo, though it met three times in August, met not once in September. This suggests that Aidit was acting alone during the weeks before the movement, outside the Politburo's supervision. According to Subekti, "The subsequent implementation of the Politburo decision [in August] about which Aidit held the briefing [on August 28] was entrusted to the Politburo Working Committee. As usual, the Politburo Working Committee carried out the day-to-day implementation of Politburo decisions. There wasn't another Politburo meeting [after the August 28 briefing] to hear reports about the implementation by the Politburo Working Committee. Nor did the Head of the Central Committee [Aidit] give the Politburo an opportunity to evaluate the policy of the Politburo Working Committee and the head of the Central Committee in implementing the Politburo decision."[24] In other words, Aidit acted alone throughout September when it came to the planning for the movement.

If Subekti is correct in claiming that the Politburo did not meet during September, the members could not have been informed as a group about Sjam's role in the movement. Sjam started to hold meetings with the officers only in September (according to his own testimony, at least). The Politburo as a body could not have known of, much less approved, Aidit and Sjam's precise actions.

If the Politburo, during its meetings in August, gave its approval to the idea of "political support" for a military action by progressive officers, the details of the party's collaboration were left to Aidit to determine. Subekti noted in a revealing passage that Aidit was the only party leader entitled to handle the PKI's relations with the military:

Handing over military problems to D. N. Aidit was, in my experience, an ordinary matter, an everyday thing. Since military problems—meaning problems that were tied to certain positions that had to be adopted by the party toward the military, or to the cooperation between them—were matters that had to be handled delicately, they were entrusted to the head of the Central Committee, D. N. Aidit. In everyday practice this could be seen in speeches, writings, or explanations of the party's position toward the military that were expressed in the editorials of *Harian Rakjat*. The only one allowed to write about military issues was the head of the Central Committee, D. N. Aidit, no one else, not even the editors of *Harian Rakjat* themselves.[25]

Subekti's main point was the same as Sudisman's: the movement was not the work of the Communist Party *as an institution,* even though certain party leaders were involved in it. Neither the Politburo nor the Central Committee devised a plan of action for initiating, organizing, and leading the movement.

Subekti's 1972 courtroom speech appears to accurately reflect his honest opinions about the movement. He reiterated many of the same opinions when he wrote a confidential document in 1986 for a small group of surviving party loyalists, including former Politburo member Jusuf Ajitorop.[26] The front page of the handwritten text states that it was not to be circulated to the public and that it was meant exclusively for the "party's documentation." Subekti had decided to write this analysis of the movement soon after all three leaders of the Special Bureau (Sjam, Pono, and Bono) were executed in September 1986.[27] Aware that these three (his fellow inmates at Cipinang prison) had taken their secrets to the grave and that few other PKI leaders had survived, Subekti felt compelled to put his own recollections and opinions on record. For a limited audience of party loyalists Subekti affirmed the point that he had made years before in public:

> The movement was not a product or a creation of the PKI. . . . If it had been a movement by the PKI, or a movement "masterminded" by the PKI, then it should have been discussed and decided upon by the highest body in the party's leadership, the Central Committee. . . . But this matter was never discussed in the Central Committee, much less decided upon by that eighty-five-member body. . . . There were even full members and candidate members of the Politburo who knew nothing about it. Despite the fact that some Central Committee and Politburo members were caught up in the movement, the majority of them were just implementers of orders, not thinkers who participated in determining, discussing, or planning the movement.[28]

Subekti's point on the institutional culpability of the Communist Party is valid enough. The question it begs is how Aidit and certain other leaders became "caught up" *(tersangkut)* in the movement. While both Subekti and Sudisman implicitly suggested in public that Aidit made his own policy when it came to the movement, neither was explicit about the precise nature of Aidit's involvement. On this issue Subekti was more forthcoming in his 1986 confidential document. He implicated Aidit and other party leaders much more deeply in the design of the movement. Subekti's version of events is worth considering in detail because he was in a position to know more about Aidit's actions in August and September than anyone else. As the note taker for the Politburo, he also served as a kind of personal secretary for Aidit.

Subekti claimed in his confidential analysis that Aidit met Sjam in August 1965 to discuss the feasibility of a military action against the Council of Generals. Aidit was still exploring his options at that point. Sjam assured Aidit that he could mobilize the party's supporters in the military for such an action. Aidit then approached the Politburo. Under the impression that the military action would be carried out by the military officers themselves, independently of the party, the Politburo agreed at a meeting in August to provide "political support." Aidit then formed a special handpicked team from the Politburo members to discuss the means by which the party would support the officers. Subekti knew about this team because he was on it. He joined the team's discussions "not as a contributor of ideas and opinions but rather as a note taker of the decisions taken by this collective."[29] The members of the team, as Subekti recalled, were Aidit, Sudisman, Oloan Hutapea, Lukman, and Rewang. This team met frequently from late August to late September with the three core members of the Special Bureau, Sjam, Pono, and Bono. Aidit thus excluded both the Politburo and its full Working Committee from the decision-making process. Some members of these bodies were left in the dark. Njoto in particular was cut out of the loop. Subekti noted: "Aidit consciously excluded Comrade Njoto from all these discussions because of ideological considerations. Njoto was not trusted because, on the basis of experience, he was considered more of a Sukarnoist than a Communist."[30] Oey Hay Djoen (who was close to Njoto) told me that Aidit relied only upon his trusted confidantes in the weeks before the action.[31]

It is reasonable to assume that Subekti is correct about this claim of a special team chosen by Aidit to discuss the movement. As a covert operation that required secrecy, the movement could not have been known by many people. It should be obvious that the PKI's Central Committee, consisting of about eighty-five members, could not have been told the details of the movement and permitted to deliberate on them—that would have been the equivalent of a public announcement, given that the army had moles inside the party. The presence of Sakirman in the Politburo would have made it impossible for Aidit to discuss the plans for the movement in any detail in that forum. One key target of the movement was Sakirman's younger brother, General Parman, the head of army intelligence. Parman himself once told a U.S. military officer in mid-1965 that he had thoroughly infiltrated the Communist Party and knew within hours of the decisions made at key meetings. Parman also mentioned that the PKI knew that it had been infiltrated and had formed a small core group for deliberating sensitive issues.[32]

Subekti noted that one topic of discussion within the special team was Aidit's proposal for a revolution council: "D. N. Aidit had conceptualized *(mengkonsepkan)* a list of people who were to be the members of the Revolution Council. This concept was accepted by the aforementioned collective body."[33] The idea behind this list of names was that the movement should appear to be a purely military action: "From the very start, when still in the first stages of the discussions between D. N. Aidit and Kamaruzaman [Sjam], it was already decided that the movement had to be a military movement and could not be seen as a movement originating from the PKI."[34] The people chosen to be members of the Indonesian Revolution Council were thus political figures who represented a broad cross-section of ideological tendencies. The movement was not meant to be an action that would immediately put the PKI in the palace. It was meant only to eliminate the anti-Communist army generals and thereby create a political environment in which the PKI could expand. Subekti emphasized that the special team of Politburo Working Committee members never discussed the idea of decommissioning Sukarno's cabinet. He blamed Aidit for inserting that idea in the October 1 radio announcement at the last moment, but Subekti did not explain why or how Aidit did that. The Revolution Council, as it was formulated by the special team, was intended to pressure the Sukarno government to move further left, not to replace the existing cabinet of ministers.

The special team, in Subekti's judgment, did not function as a constraint on Aidit's freedom to maneuver. He portrayed Aidit as a leader who was initiating the idea of a military action to preempt the Council of Generals. The special team appears to have been more like a sounding board for Aidit than a cohesive body that was making decisions as a collective. Since the Special Bureau was entirely under his direction, Aidit was in a position to exercise exclusive control over the movement. Subekti wrote that Sjam "was appointed by Aidit as the chief leader *(pemimpin utama)* in the command of the movement."[35] Note that Subekti did not claim that the special team appointed Sjam the leader. Subekti claimed that Aidit himself did that. Even if the members of the special team were involved in planning the action in the weeks before October 1, they do not seem to have assigned themselves any role in executing it. At least two other members of the team were inactive on October 1: Lukman was touring Central Java, and Sudisman was holed up in a house in Jakarta, listening to the radio (according to Hasan, who was with Sudisman that day). In his courtroom defense plea Subekti contended that he was following orders when he accompanied Aidit to Halim Air Force Base: "I was needed to help Aidit and I did the typing on the personal orders of Aidit, not on the basis of a decision by the Politburo or as a duty that had been assigned by the Central Committee Secretariat." Aidit regarded Subekti as a loyal follower who did not ask a lot of questions: "Aidit actually had enough assistants, with Bono and Kusno. Aidit requested me as well and no one else because, I suppose, he had a special 'affection' [English in original] or liking for me, since he had known me as a comrade since our time at Menteng 31 [a house in Jakarta that was the center for nationalist youth] before the proclamation [of national independence] on August 17, 1945, and who knew me as someone who liked to work hard without being troublesome."[36] For Subekti the special team of Politburo members was not the mastermind of the movement. It was more like a consultative body for Aidit and Sjam as they plotted the movement with certain military officers.

Subekti's confidential analysis is strong evidence for the claim that Aidit and Sjam's role in the movement was greater than that of the military officers'. Subekti, unlike Supardjo, was in a position to know the internal dynamics of the PKI's leadership. Supardjo simply noted that "the party" was more dominant. Subekti was more precise in identifying who in the party was responsible. Writing for an internal party audience in 1986, he was under no pressure to be dishonest. He wished to be frank for the sake of the party's own process of self-rectification. His perspective, nonetheless, was limited. Subekti would not have been present at any meetings between Sjam and the military officers, so he would not have known the nature of that interaction. Nevertheless, from the discussions of the special team alone he could have sensed that Aidit and Sjam had initiated the action and were gaining the cooperation of military officers supportive of the PKI. Subekti, like the other four PKI leaders on the special team, must have realized that the military officers within the movement were not entirely independent of the party; they were Sjam's contacts.

Subekti could have exaggerated Aidit and Sjam's role since he bore a powerful grudge against both. The bilious tone of certain passages of the 1986 analysis (his denunciations of nearly all other former PKI leaders as cowardly, petty bourgeois, and unprincipled) seems to be the result of his great frustration and disappointment in witnessing the collapse of the party.[37] One could say that Aidit and Sjam were his scapegoats. Still, his reasons for blaming Aidit and Sjam may have been well founded. Other former party leaders, such as Sudisman, also held those two men responsible.

Consider Sudisman's statement, as quoted earlier: "Even though I myself did not know [about the movement], what was done by the witness, Comrade Sjam, was on the instructions of Aidit, and even I carried out instructions from Comrade Aidit, from the perspective of responsibility, I will take over the responsibility for all of it." Sudisman's claim of ignorance should be taken to mean that he did not know some details of the movement. He admitted that he had been involved. But the manner in which Sudisman assumed a moral responsibility for the movement suggests that he believed that Aidit acted alone. Sudisman elaborated on this matter in the Politburo's "self-criticism" document (issued in September 1966) and in his defense plea at the Mahmillub trial. He felt responsible as a party leader who had allowed Aidit far too much leeway to act on his own. In Sudisman's opinion the party's principle of "democratic centralism" had leaned more toward centralism than democracy. The PKI leaders had surrendered too much power to Aidit. The implicit message of Sudisman's argument was that Aidit had determined the party's policy toward the movement and the Politburo had permitted him to proceed. Since Sudisman believed that "democratic centralism" was the ideal organizational form in which "collective and individual responsibility are made one," he felt that his responsibility for party policy was equal to that of Aidit's. If Aidit had made a mistake, it was because the other leaders had allowed him to make a mistake. Aidit's adventurism, to use Sudisman's term, reflected profound problems with the party since Aidit could not be singled out as an individual and assigned full blame. Sudisman felt that he and the other PKI leaders had allowed the principle of "democratic centralism" to degenerate.

At the time of Sudisman's trial in 1967, the surviving PKI leaders in prison were heatedly debating this issue of responsibility. The military had collected about seventy-five political prisoners, both PKI leaders and military officers, in one location, the Military Detention Center (Rumah Tahanan Militer) in downtown Jakarta, so that they could be presented as witnesses at Sudisman's trial. Once gathered in a single building, they had frequent opportunities to discuss among themselves the party's decision-making process and to figure out who should be blamed for their defeat. One of the prisoners there was Tan Swie Ling, who had been arrested with Sudisman in December 1966. He had been sheltering Sudisman in his house. Tan recalled that the general opinion among the PKI leaders held at the detention center was that Aidit as an individual should be blamed: "They all felt disappointed, angry, and because of that what they uttered was just curses. Of course, the curses were all directed toward D. N. Aidit. He was condemned for his errors and such—ultimately, it was all his fault. I never heard an explanation that really made sense. . . . I met one leader who I respected, and who was respected by many people, Joko Soejono, who dealt with the workers and who had been a member of the Central Committee. I once asked him: Actually, why did the movement happen? Yeah, he just replied, 'because Democratic Centralism was tilted to one side; what functioned was only centralism; there wasn't any democracy.'"

Sudisman, as Tan recollects, acknowledged that Aidit had enjoyed too much power within the party, but Sudisman blamed the other party leaders for not being competent enough to challenge Aidit: "As for Sudisman, he provided an explanation. He said, 'If the comrades feel that the centralism was too strong and that the democracy didn't function well, the source of the problem was not because Aidit was a dictator.' This was according to Sudisman. 'Instead, it was because Aidit's mastery of theory was so much greater than the others'. They weren't equal. The gap was too big. Every time there was a discussion, every time there was a debate, Aidit always won.'"[38]

Although Sudisman believed that Aidit dominated the PKI because he was so intelligent, it is possible to locate other reasons. The simple fact was that the party was growing under Aidit's leadership. Many Politburo and Central Committee members were willing to defer to Aidit because he seemed to possess the formula for success. Whatever the precise reasons for Aidit's dominance, the surviving PKI leaders identified it as the cause of the party's downfall. By late September the party leadership had come to resemble a military hierarchy, with Aidit as the commander-in-chief, giving orders even to senior Politburo members. (As Sudisman noted, even he took "orders" from Aidit.) Aidit, as the linchpin between the Special Bureau and the aboveground party leadership, was in a uniquely powerful position. The rest of the party leaders had to defer to his judgment when it came to a military action. Once that action failed, these leaders believed that it had failed because Aidit had worked on his own, outside the control of the rest of the party's institutions, and had organized the movement with the help of the Special Bureau, a wing of the party that was entirely under his direction.

The Advantages of Preemption

If Aidit was indeed the main organizer of the movement, what was his motive? Both Subekti and Sudisman argued that the movement was intended as a preemptive military strike against a Council of Generals that was plotting a coup d'état. Many politicians in Jakarta in 1965, including Sukarno himself, worried that certain army generals were plotting with Western powers to overthrow him. It is highly likely that Aidit was convinced that such a Council of Generals existed and that it represented an immediate threat to both Sukarno and the Communist Party. Both Sudisman and Subekti affirmed that they were convinced by August and September 1965 that the army high command was plotting a coup. The puzzling question is why Aidit believed that a preemptive military strike was the best option for responding to this threat. Did he not trust President Sukarno to handle the generals on his own? Did Aidit not trust the ability of the PKI to face an assault from the military? The party had been under near-constant attack since the late 1940s: the post-Madiun affair repression in 1948, the mass arrests in Jakarta in August 1951, the banning of the party in three provinces in 1960. Somehow the party managed to survive and grow amid these setbacks. Why did Aidit not wait until the generals made their move and then lead the PKI masses in resistance? If the pro-Sukarno, left-wing military officers were plotting against the right-wing generals, why did Aidit not just leave them to their plotting? Why did he feel that he and certain other party members should play a role? Aidit, as Sudisman affirmed, had a reputation as a careful strategist and must have calculated the costs and benefits of his chosen option.[39]

One option was to allow Sukarno to deal with the right-wing generals by himself. Sukarno could have dismissed Yani as army commander and replaced him with a more left-leaning general such as Pranoto or Rukman and then could have insisted that the new commander reshuffle his staff. Sukarno may have intended to meet Yani at the palace on October 1, quiz him again (as in May 1965) about the rumors of a Council of Generals, and inform him that he would be replaced.[40] The political analyst Rex Mortimer, writing in the mid-1970s, thought that this administrative approach would have been Aidit's preference since the Communist Party had come to depend so heavily on Sukarno's protection. Relying on Sukarno to deal with the generals would have been safer and easier than organizing a secret attack: "It would have been a comparatively simple matter for Sukarno to immobilize the army by placing its leaders under close arrest, retailing to the nation in his inimitable style the basis for his action and stringing out the resolution of the affair while he reorganized the service more to his liking."[41] Mortimer assumed that Sukarno held absolute power over the army, that an order from Sukarno to the military police to arrest the generals suspected of plotting a coup, or an order dismissing Yani, would have put an end to the matter. That was not necessarily the case. Sukarno's hold over the military was precarious. His die-hard supporters in the army were not sufficiently numerous or strategically placed to guarantee that an order of his would be followed. What if Yani had decided to countermand an order from Sukarno (in the way that Suharto did on October 1)? Would Sukarno have been able to force Yani to back down without risking a bloody battle between different military units (what Sukarno wanted to avoid at all costs on October 1)? Aidit may have had good reasons for rejecting a strategy that relied on Sukarno. Perhaps he feared that a move to arrest or reappoint the army commanders would only provoke the generals into launching a coup or that Sukarno would not have the fortitude to face a showdown with the army high command.

Another option was to rely on the strength of the party's supporters, those twenty-seven million people Aidit invoked in his speeches. If brought into the streets en masse, they would have posed a formidable challenge to the army generals. The former journalist Joesoef Isak recalls that he was informed by members of the party's Central Committee in August and September that some sort of mass action against the "capitalist bureaucrats" and the "counterrevolutionaries" was imminent. Isak was then head of the Asia-Africa Journalists Association (PWAA, Persatuan Wartawan Asia-Afrika), an organization that grew out of the famous Asia-Africa Conference held in Bandung in 1955. The office of the organization in downtown Jakarta hosted five journalists from Asian countries and five from African countries.[42] Isak regularly briefed these ten individuals, known as the association's "foreign secretaries," about political developments in Indonesia. Some information that he passed on derived from confidential reports that he received from the PKI's Central Committee. Isak was not a full-fledged member of the Communist Party, but he was trusted as a solid supporter. He was a conduit for information from the party to the foreign secretaries, many of whom were members of Communist parties in their home countries. A Central Committee member, Nursuhud, kept Isak informed of the party's latest positions.[43] He was thus privy to sensitive information.

Isak recalled that the political atmosphere in mid-1965 was "indeed revolutionary." The PKI felt confident that it was winning the competition with the army, that events were moving in its favor.

The party leaders felt they had reached a stage where they could deliver a final blow to the army high command. Sudisman too, in his analysis, noted that the party leaders "regarded the political situation at that time as a revolutionary situation" in which actions by "broad masses of people" were coming increasingly to determine government policy.[44] During the two months before the movement, Isak heard that some sort of major action was in the offing:

> I was told that in just a little while the whole situation would change. I understood that there would be a massive movement *(gerakan hebat)*. It would be the final blow. I kept bugging the party [meaning his briefer, Nursuhud], asking when? You said in just a little while, well, it's been a week, a month, and still nothing has happened. I kept going after the party, asking when. The foreign secretaries [of PWAA] kept asking me when it was going to happen.
>
> The party told me, "We will raise the revolutionary actions all the way up to their peak. We will lynch the capitalist bureaucrats and the counterrevolutionaries." I asked, how are you going to do that? "Descend into the streets," that was the story told to me, "descend into the streets. We are going to go directly into the offices of the ministers, the directors general of government departments, and grab them. We are going to take [Sukarno's third deputy prime minister] Chairul Saleh out and dunk him in the Ciliwung River."[45]

Like every other politically aware person in Jakarta, Isak knew that the PKI's main enemy was the army leadership. Whatever form the "final blow" took, it would be aimed at the army high command. The information from Isak's briefer was that the party's action would involve mass demonstrations. Isak did not expect a clandestine military operation.

If Aidit was indeed mulling this option of mobilizing massive demonstrations, he ultimately decided against it. He must have realized that the Communist Party, however large and influential it had grown, remained an unarmed organization that could not hope to prevail against machine guns and tanks. If the right-wing generals launched a massive assault on the PKI, they could inflict heavy losses from which the party might require another generation to recover. Organizing the party masses for a direct challenge to the army high command might well have been regarded as leading sheep to slaughter. The political scientist Daniel Lev noted in early 1966 that the Communist Party could not compete with the army on the terrain of raw force: "In bedrock political terms, the PKI did not possess the physical power to deal with the army, whose weapons made up in any final showdown for its lack of political finesse."[46]

By itself the prospect of another round of anti-Communist repression in 1965 was probably not frightening for Aidit. What was cause for concern was the possibility that Sukarno would be overthrown. However precarious his hold over the army had become, he had provided some measure of protection for the party since the late 1950s. If Sukarno was no longer in control of the state, the Communist Party would have to face the army by itself. In the absence of any restraining power from above, the repression could prove much worse than on previous occasions. The right-wing generals would be able to dismiss all the top-level pro-Sukarno and pro-PKI officials in the government and military so that the full force of the state could be turned against the party. A coup by the Council of Generals in 1965 portended to be a full-scale counter-revolution, meaning a complete overturning of both the Sukarnoist and Communist influence within the state.

It appears that the option that Aidit preferred was one that used progressive military officers to attack the right-wing generals. The advantage was that this plan would not risk the lives of unarmed party masses. The PKI already had contacts in the military who were opposed to the Council of Generals. Why not use them? Once the army command was in the hands of officers sympathetic to the PKI, the masses could be called out for demonstrations without fear of bloody reprisals. Sukarno could peacefully proceed with reshuffling the army commanders. If the Council of Generals moved first and seized control of the army command, those progressive officers would be lost to the party. Some would be removed from important command positions. Others, in the interests of preserving their career, would sever connections with the Special Bureau and follow the new chain of command. It would become nearly impossible for the party to use them again for a major action. For the party to have such substantial assets in the military and not use them productively must have seemed absurd to Aidit. Although Aidit's decision in favor of preemption was retrospectively criticized as adventurist by other party leaders, it made good sense, at least in principle. The enemy camp, the army officer corps, was divided. It was reasonable to exploit that division, especially when a direct attack (by civilians against the army) would only force the allies inside the enemy camp to close ranks against the party.

Aidit had to assess whether this option, which looked attractive in theory, was feasible in practice. He had to determine whether the progressive officers were strong enough to carry out an action against the right-wing generals. For this Aidit had to rely on Sjam. Aidit must have received assurances from Sjam that well-placed officers had enough troops at their command to carry out an action. Aidit would have heard from a variety of sources that the junior officers and the rank-and-file were furious about the economic gap between themselves and the generals. He would have heard about a lot of discontent in the army regarding the generals' opposition to Sukarno's policies. The troops seemed ready for a revolt. As a prominent civilian leader, Aidit would have had neither the time nor ability to contact many officers himself and cross-check Sjam's evaluation. In his courtroom testimony Sjam mentioned that he "carried out an inspection of the organization, meaning, a judging of our strength within the armed forces, especially the army."[47] He judged the strength of his contacts to be sufficient. While Aidit was not particularly adventurist, he put himself in the position of relying on someone who was.

For Aidit another attraction of the preemption strategy was the chance to steal a march on the party's allies in Sukarno's camp. The PKI would come out of the action as the savior of Sukarno and the entire Sukarnoist program. As Hasan noted in a passage that I quoted earlier, the PKI leadership viewed itself as the vanguard *(pelopor)* of the Sukarnoist forces (the "democratic people's movement" guided by Nasakom). With the preemptive action against the right-wing generals, Aidit would prove that the PKI was indeed the leading component of the Nasakom grouping. Sudisman mentioned in his analysis that the Communist Party leaders, in supporting the movement, were thinking about "how to safeguard or 'safe-stellen' President Sukarno's left-wing policies."[48]

Sukarno believed that the PKI was somehow involved in the movement, but he did not consider the party's action tantamount to treason. He did not denounce the party for betraying the nation. In his final statement before the parliament as president in 1967, he described the PKI leaders as *keblinger*.[49] It was an interesting choice of words by someone who chose his words carefully. *Keblinger* is a Javanese adjective used in Indonesian that means dizzy, being in a state where one has lost proper perspective, or, in colloquial English, over the top. Sukarno's implication was not that Aidit was unpatriotic (the charge leveled by the Suharto regime) but that he had lost his sense of proportion. Aidit's response to the rumors about the Council of Generals was far in excess of what was necessary.

It is possible to excuse Aidit's strategy of preemption as the result of a provocation by the right-wing generals. We now know, on the basis of declassified U.S. documents (reviewed in chapter 6), that Yani's clique did not have plans to launch an old-fashioned coup d'état against Sukarno. Yani's generals certainly wanted to overthrow Sukarno, given his encouragement to the PKI, but they were waiting for a suitable pretext. Their preferred pretext was an unsuccessful PKI coup attempt. The right-wing generals may have been stoking the rumor mill in 1965 to provoke the Communist Party into attempting some sort of military action. They may have planted stories to encourage Jakarta's political circles to think that Sukarno's days as president were numbered. If the PKI leaders believed that Sukarno could not provide protection for them against the army, perhaps they would be tempted into some sort of direct action against the army.

Still, the possibility that Aidit was provoked into preemptive action does not absolve him of Sukarno's charge of being *keblinger*. In responding to the rumors about the Council of Generals, Aidit could have opted for a safer strategy. He was responsible for choosing a strategy that, however defensible in principle, contained fatal flaws. It relied on the wisdom of Sjam, a self-deluded braggart and unthinking apparatchik, and brought the party into the shadowy world of double agents, where it was nothing more than a low-level, easily outwitted amateur. It moved the party away from the terrain where it was strongest—in aboveground, open politics involving the public—and into the intrigues of Jakarta's political and military elite.

Aidit probably assumed that few risks were involved with this military option. He and the other party leaders felt that the right-wing army commanders were vulnerable because so many officers were pro-Sukarno. Oey Hay Djoen described the general opinion of the party leaders in 1965: "The army couldn't defeat us. Why? Because the army was opposed not only by the navy but also by the air force. And not just that. Within the army itself, there were splits. So they couldn't, they couldn't unite to attack the PKI."[50] A preemptive action by army troops against the right-wing generals would ensure that the military was irreparably sundered and incapable of attacking the party. Such an action would unite the Sukarnoist officers in all the services and isolate Yani's high command. With the army neutralized the party could proceed further with its mass campaign against the "counterrevolutionaries" and "capitalist bureaucrats."

The Algerian Coup as a Precedent

One insight into Aidit's strategic thinking came to light in a 1994 book written by Manai Sophiaan, a Sukarnoist politician and former ambassador to the Soviet Union.[51] Sophiaan argued that Aidit, in supporting a military action against the right-wing generals, was inspired by the military coup in Algeria in June 1965. Sophiaan based this argument on his interview with the former head of the Indonesian Journalists Association (Persatuan Wartawan Indonesia), Karim D. P., who spoke with Aidit shortly after the Algerian coup. Karim D. P. did not release this information himself because he was a political prisoner during the Suharto years. Even after his release he was banned from speaking and writing in public. He started publishing his writings only after Suharto fell from power. In a public address delivered in 1999 Karim D. P. claimed that Aidit reacted favorably to the news of the military coup in Algeria. The significance of this bit of information requires some explanation of the events in Algeria and Indonesia's relationship to them.

The Algerian coup occurred on June 19, 1965, less than a week before the Second Asia-Africa Conference was scheduled to begin in the capital city of Algiers.[52] The usurper, Colonel Boumedienne, promised that he would hold the conference as his ousted predecessor, Ahmed Ben Bella, had originally planned. Sukarno was to be a special guest because he had been the host of the famous first conference, the Bandung summit in 1955. Back in Jakarta, the coup became a burning topic of conversation among government officials because Sukarno had to decide whether to attend the conference, and thereby implicitly legitimize Colonel Boumedienne, or to boycott it as a gesture of protest. Was Boumedienne a CIA stooge, as so many coup makers in Africa were, or was he an independent nationalist who could be accepted according to the Asia-Africa Conference's principle of nonalignment? Sukarno's officials were not quite sure who Boumedienne was, but they were willing to give him the benefit of the doubt, especially since he was willing to continue to host the conference. Sukarno decided to attend.

Both Aidit (as a representative of the Communist Party) and Karim D. P. (as a journalist) were part of President Sukarno's delegation to the conference that left Jakarta on June 23. The delegation had to cancel its visit to Algeria en route because the venue for the conference in Algiers had been mysteriously bombed. With the conference postponed, most Indonesian delegates flew to Paris, where they could

spend a few enjoyable days before heading back to Jakarta. Sukarno
took advantage of the Parisian stay to convene a meeting of all the Indonesian ambassadors in Europe. It was in Paris that Karim D. P. spoke
with Aidit about his interpretation of the Algerian coup.

Aidit had just returned to his hotel from a meeting at the headquarters of the French Communist Party. He told Karim D. P. that he had
just met six comrades from Algeria, presumably members of the Algerian Communist Party:

> First of all, he said that he had asked the six comrades to imme-
> diately return to their country and support Boumedienne. Aidit
> said that according to the information and materials presented
> by the Algerian comrades, the character of the Boumedienne
> coup d'état could be classified as a progressive coup d'état. Be-
> cause of that, it should be supported by the people. If 30 percent
> of the people supported it, then the coup d'état could be trans-
> formed and its character turned into a people's revolution that
> would benefit the struggle of the Algerian people. That's what
> Aidit said. He promised that he would explain his theory later,
> back in Indonesia. At the time he was in a hurry since he had to
> get to the airport quickly and travel onward to Moscow. Aidit
> told me that it was known in Indonesia that the Council of Gen-
> erals planned to launch a coup d'état to overthrow President Su-
> karno. That coup d'état desired by the Council of Generals was a
> reactionary coup d'état, different from the one that occurred in
> Algeria.[53]

Going by Karim D. P.'s story, one can presume that Aidit was favorably disposed to the idea of a "progressive coup d'état." He believed
that, in certain circumstances, a military coup could create a political
environment more conducive to the growth of the Communist Party. If
the military officers behind the coup were ideologically progressive and
open to an alliance with a mass movement, they could be considered
preferable to an ineffectual civilian government.

To understand Aidit's position better, we should turn to Joesoef
Isak, who also met Aidit in Paris at that time. Isak, as I noted earlier,
was the head of the Asia-Africa Journalists Association, which was
headquartered in Jakarta. He was carefully following the events in Algeria since his organization had been involved in the preparations for this
high-profile, long-delayed international conference. He had traveled to

many African countries in recent years and had become familiar with
the continent's political events and personages. After leaving Jakarta to
attend the conference, he learned en route, like the other Indonesian
delegates, that it had been postponed indefinitely. He wound up idling
away his time in Paris with them. Isak arranged a meeting between
Aidit and Jacques Vergès, a French lawyer and journalist whom Isak had
known from his previous travels in Africa. Vergès had become famous
in 1957 for going to Algiers to defend Algerian nationalists accused of
a bombing. He turned public attention away from Algerian acts of resistance to the criminal acts of the French colonial state, such as the
torture that had been inflicted on the defendants.[54] Vergès became supportive of the Algerian nationalist struggle, left the French Communist
Party (which was not supporting the struggle), and aligned himself with
the Beijing line, which, unlike Moscow's détente, extolled national liberation movements that were fighting Western imperialist powers. He
lived in Algiers after independence in 1962, worked for the foreign ministry, and edited a journal published by the organization that had led the
anticolonial struggle, the FLN (Front de Libération Nationale). By 1965
Vergès was back in Paris and working as the editor of *Révolution,* a journal that he founded, apparently with financial assistance from China.[55]

During the meeting with Aidit, whom Vergès viewed as a great
Communist statesman, a kind of younger brother to Mao Zedong,
Vergès discussed the significance of the Algerian coup. Isak recalls that
their interpretation of the coup was shaped by their perspective on the
Sino-Soviet split. Both Aidit and Vergès were opposed to the Soviet
principle of peaceful coexistence. While Aidit retained a public posture
of neutrality in the Sino-Soviet conflict, he was widely known to be
much closer to the Maoist line.[56] Vergès was in Paris because he had fallen out of favor with the FLN in Algeria over the Sino-Soviet issue.[57]
The ousted Algerian president, Ben Bella, was close to the country's
Soviet-aligned Communist Party. For Maoists, Ben Bella's overthrow
was not necessarily a setback for the country. While the Eastern bloc
countries had denounced the Boumedienne coup, Aidit had praised it
in a public statement on June 22, only three days after the event, while
he was still in Jakarta. He denounced Ben Bella for his "rightwing policy opposed to the aspirations of the Algerian people" and praised the
usurper: "We must thank Colonel Boumedienne."[58] China also welcomed the coup and hoped that it would be treated more favorably by
Boumedienne than it had been by Ben Bella.[59]

However much the China-aligned Communists favored Boumedienne, he remained an unknown figure. For Aidit the colonel's experience as the commander of the anticolonial guerrilla forces suggested
that Boumedienne would not be a supporter of peaceful coexistence.
Aidit thought that the coup opened up an opportunity for the Beijing-
oriented Communists to increase their power over the Algerian state.
Isak's account of Aidit's statements to Vergès is worth quoting at length:

> I brought Vergès to Aidit's hotel room. He entered. Actually, I
> was aware of my status—after I brought him there I was going to
> leave. But Aidit said, "No, stay, come and sit down." So that's
> why I was present. You can surely imagine it, Aidit's charisma
> was extraordinary. He was the head of the largest Communist
> Party outside of Eastern Europe and China. I mean, his perspec-
> tive on things was from a very high level. So, Jacques Vergès said,
> "Comrade Chairman, you've just come from Algeria.[60] What is
> your advice for the Algerian comrades?" He was the one who
> asked. He lowered himself, asking Aidit like that, the PKI chair-
> man, whom he considered more senior than himself.
>
> Aidit portrayed the situation like this, "Look"—his eyes were
> really red, as if his eyeballs were going to pop out, they were
> bulging, he never slept, they were very red—"Look. This isn't a
> revolution. This, if you want to use the term *revolution*, is a revo-
> lution from above. This is a coup d'état, not a revolution. That is
> the first point. Second: between Boumedienne and Ben Bella,
> both are from the same class: the bourgeoisie. But between these
> two, Boumedienne is better. When the armed struggle was going
> on, Ben Bella was in a Paris prison cell. The one who led the
> armed struggle in Algeria was Boumedienne. . . . The one who
> held high the banner of Marxism was this nationalist, this bour-
> geois person. He's better than Ben Bella.
>
> "But don't think that this coup alone is going to move Algeria
> to the left since it is Boumedienne who is implementing Marx-
> ism. What happened in Algeria is just the starting point of a new
> momentum that has the potential to move Algeria more to the
> left. If"—Aidit had a condition—"If the comrades take advan-
> tage of this momentum . . . Comrade Jacques, you must immedi-
> ately return to Algeria. Make sure there isn't a wall that's free of
> graffiti. Make sure there isn't a main road that isn't full of banners
> [with the slogan] 'Support the coup d'état of Boumedienne.'"

The way Aidit expressed it was that the people should feel that this coup d'état was their own. It should be turned into a people's coup d'état. He said the comrades there had to descend into the streets. That was his basic message as I grasped it. The coup had to become owned by the people.[61]

Going by Isak's account, it is possible to see Aidit's support for the Boumedienne coup as consonant with Aidit's commitment to Leninist theory. By itself the coup was not a positive development for the Algerian left or for the Chinese line in the international Communist movement. But it had the potential to become positive since Boumedienne was more progressive than Ben Bella. The coup presented an opportunity for those Algerian Communists who did not support the Soviet Union's peaceful co-existence line to mobilize more people and gain greater access to state power.

Aidit's view of the coup was the opposite of the Soviet Union's. The scholar Ruth First, a member of the pro-Soviet South African Communist Party, interpreted the coup as a method to prevent Algeria from moving further to the left. She argued that President Ben Bella had been planning to use the forum of the Asia-African Conference to announce his plan for transforming the political party that he led (the FLN) into "a party with a firm organic commitment to the left, including the Algerian Communist Party; with stronger disciplinary controls; and Marxist training of functionaries and the rank and file."[62] In searching for a firm mass base for his presidency, Ben Bella wanted to turn the FLN into the functional equivalent of a Communist Party. He was also planning to dismiss Boumedienne from his position as commander of the army. According to Ruth First, the coup was a "putsch to pre-empt the Ben Bella move."[63]

Aidit's interpretation of the coup, whether it was correct or well informed or not, was based on a hard-headed political analysis: he evaluated the coup according to whether it would lead to greater power for his side (the China-aligned international anti-imperialist movement). The coup did not present Aidit with a new paradigm for political action. He was probably already familiar with at least the 1958 Qasim coup in Iraq. The argument proposed by Sophiaan, that the Boumedienne coup inspired Aidit to initiate the September 30th Movement, seems inaccurate. Aidit already understood that a military coup, under certain circumstances, could be a positive development. He did not need the Algerian example to realize that. The one way in which it may have been an inspiration was in terms of nomenclature. Boumedienne, upon overthrowing Ben Bella, created a twenty-three-man "Council of the Revolution." That term was probably the source for the movement's "Revolution Council" (Dewan Revolusi).

The important insight that emerges from this inquiry into Aidit's view of the Algerian coup was expressed by Isak: "Aidit didn't have any objection to a movement from above, but it had to be quickly turned into a people's movement." It is reasonable to assume that Aidit understood in 1965 that a military action of some sort in Indonesia could create a better environment for the Communist Party's growth. The ultimate goal was not a military-led state, of course, but a PKI-led state. A military action could be a temporary expedient for reaching a wider goal.

The Antinomies of Revolutionary Populism

Aidit's ideas about how a military coup could be transformed into a people's movement can help explain the meaning of the movement's decree about the Revolution Council. The movement was intended to be a military operation guided by a revolutionary political program — a program over which Aidit must have had control. That was his area of expertise. Most likely, the original intention of the movement was not to decommission Sukarno's cabinet. Both Subekti and Munir affirmed that Aidit discussed the idea of the Revolution Council with certain Politburo members in August and September 1965. Munir, the former Politburo member and head of the PKI-affiliated trade union federation (SOBSI — Sentral Organisasi Buruh Seluruh Indonesia, All-Indonesia Central Workers Organization), stated in his courtroom defense plea in 1973 that Aidit had once justified the role of the Revolution Council to him: "It should first be explained what was suggested to me by D. N. Aidit: 'The Revolution Council forms a rival organization to the Council of Generals and simultaneously functions as a catalyst for accelerating the process of forming a Nasakom cabinet.'"[64] Note that the council was not supposed to replace the existing cabinet but act as a catalyst for changing its composition. Subekti and Munir contended that the council was conceived only as a kind of pressure group on the central government. Sudisman noted that the Revolution Council did not consist of the leading pro-Sukarno figures; it consisted of "lightweight Nasakom notables."[65] One can assume that if Aidit had planned that such a council would replace the existing cabinet and acquire all powers of the state, he would have chosen more important people for it. It appears that the idea of decommissioning the cabinet emerged only on the morning of October 1 itself, once Sukarno refused to support the continuation of the movement. The text of Decree no. 1, drafted beforehand, could have been altered at the last minute.

The Revolution Council had a precedent. The military councils set up by rebel colonels in 1957–58 in Sumatra and Sulawesi initially demanded changes in the composition of the central government (namely, the restoration of Hatta's authority) and in relations between Jakarta and the provinces. Those councils did not at first demand independence for the provinces in which they were based. Their call for independence came later (as I will explain further in chapter 6).

In formulating the Revolution Council, Aidit was not planning to immediately establish the Communist Party as the ruling party. He wanted to continue the same Nasakom paradigm that Sukarno already had in place. Once the military power behind the anti-Communist elements in the government was eliminated, the Nasakom paradigm would function more smoothly for the "kom" element, which would no longer stand in constant fear of being suppressed. The movement's listing of the forty-five members of the national-level Revolution Council has always seemed strange because it included such a great diversity of figures, everyone from the right to the left. But it was intended to represent a broad cross-section of the political spectrum. The goal of the movement was a coalition government in which the Communist Party would have greater freedom to maneuver, not a pure PKI-dominated state.

The Communist Party's strategy since Aidit took control in 1951 had been a "united national front." The party, in the words of the key Fifth Congress in 1954, wished to build an alliance of "the working class, the peasantry, the petty bourgeoisie and the national bourgeoisie." This alliance would combat imperialists, the section of the bourgeoisie that collaborated with the imperialists, and feudal landlords. Whatever the Marxist-Leninist rhetoric, the party's program was, strictly speaking, populist: it took as its revolutionary subject "the Indonesian people" as a whole. It did not promote the sectarian interests of peasants and workers. The ultimate objective was what it called a "people's democracy" in which there was ample room for "national capitalism."[66]

The PKI was not very different from other postcolonial Communist parties that prioritized nationalism over socialism. Like those other parties, it faced a tension between its revolutionary rhetoric and its populist program. Such a tension was not highly pronounced before 1965 because the party's united front program was succeeding so well: the membership was rising rapidly, the party leadership was staying united (even after the Sino-Soviet split), and President Sukarno was promoting a similar brand of populism. The emphasis on national unity in the face of imperialism was paying dividends when imperialism was a continuing presence on the country's borders (witness the West Irian campaign and the Confrontation against Malaysia) and a palpable threat (witness the CIA's backing of the PRRI/Permesta rebellions; see chapter 6). The Communist Party's strategy seemed neatly matched to Indonesia's political conditions.

The tension, nevertheless, could not be transcended. By 1965 the party's rhetoric was at times stridently sectarian, to the point that the petty bourgeoisie in the villages was being considered the enemy. The PKI promoted campaigns against "seven village devils": bad landlords, usurers, advance buyers of the harvest, capitalist bureaucrats, bad rich peasants, village bandits, and bad officials.[67] Although still within the logic of populism (there were good landlords and bad landlords, good officials and bad officials), the sloganeering tended to make many people worried that they would be tagged with the label *devil*. The current of sectarianism unnecessarily antagonized potential allies within the united front strategy.

Aidit attempted in the early 1960s to bring the party's Marxist-Leninist theory fully in line with its populist practice. Aidit and several party ideologues developed a theory that they called the "dual aspect of the state": one aspect was "pro-people" and the other was "anti-people." The PKI's task was to support the pro-people elements within the state against the anti-people elements.[68] The party thinkers contended that their theory, though it dispensed with a class analysis of the state, was a legitimate innovation within the Marxist-Leninist tradition. Sugiono, a teacher at the party's own school of theory (the Aliarcham Academy), wrote a thesis on the "dual aspect of the state" and hoped to have an official institute of a Communist country legitimize it. He submitted it for a degree at a North Korean university but was disappointed when the Communist Party ideologues of Pyongyang rejected it as un-Marxist.[69] Although the theoretical discussions about the "dual aspect of the state" do not appear to have reached much beyond the Central Committee, Aidit often invoked it in his speeches and writings. In 1963, for instance, a Politburo statement asserted that "the pro-people's aspect [of state power] is already becoming steadily greater and holds the initiative and offensive, while the anti-people's aspect, although moderately strong, is being relentlessly pressed into a tight corner."[70]

6. This cartoon appeared in the independence day issue of the PKI newspaper commemorating the twentieth anniversary of the nation. The left-wing movement punches, kicks, and slashes its way through the years as it defeats imperialists and their local collaborators. The final image is of the people united behind Sukarno's principles (Five Charms of the Revolution), punching the U.S. and British governments and dislodging Indonesian "capitalist bureaucrats" and "village devils." The slogan is "Intensify the Revolutionary Offensive in All Fields." Source: *Harian Rakjat,* August 17, 1965.

The "dual aspect of the state" theory can help explain why Aidit was willing to promote an action by military troops. According to that theory, some soldiers and officers inside the existing Indonesian military were pro-people and some were anti-people. The task of a revolution, as Aidit saw it, was to support those pro-people military personnel and use them as a catalyst for turning the whole state pro-people. Aidit was not working under the logic of a soldiers' mutiny or a coup d'état — the standard paradigms by which observers have tried to comprehend the event. The movement was something of a hybrid: it was a partial coup meant to result, at some later stage, in a partial revolution. Aidit supported the pro-people troops so that they could both remove their anti-people commanding officers and force the creation of a new coalition cabinet. These two developments would open up a new political space for the party to expand and gain greater powers.

Interpreting the *Harian Rakjat* editorial

The edition of the PKI's newspaper published on Saturday, October 2, 1965, carried a headline that stretched across the width of the paper: "Lt. Col. Untung, the Commander of the Palace Guard, Saves the President and the Republic of Indonesia from the Council of Generals' Coup." A smaller headline directly underneath read: "The September 30th Movement Is a Movement Completely Internal to the Army." From the headlines alone it was apparent that the PKI leaders were supporting the movement while distancing themselves from it. A brief twenty-line editorial tucked away near the lower left corner of the first page, just below an inconsequential report about a press conference held by the Chinese foreign minister in Beijing, reiterated the message of the headlines, that the movement was a laudable effort to save the president and was an internal army matter: "We the people fully understand what was asserted by Lt. Col. Untung in carrying out his patriotic movement. But, whatever the case may be, this matter is an internal army matter. But we the people who are aware of the politics and tasks of the revolution are certain of the correctness of the action taken by the September 30th Movement to safeguard the revolution and the people."

The awkward language of the editorial — two "buts" in a row and an extraneous "whatever the case may be" — suggest the writer was striving to emphasize that the Communist Party's support for the movement did not mean that the party was involved in it. Along the bottom of the front page ran the customary Saturday feature, seven cartoon panels depicting

7. This cartoon appeared on the bottom of the front page of the *Harian Rakjat* newspaper on Saturday, October 2, 1965. The movement, upholding the national interest (RI is the Republic of Indonesia), punches the Council of Generals, which is propped up by the U.S. government. Indonesian currency notes are in the general's pocket and a dollar sign is on his epaulette. His affiliation with the CIA is revealed as his hat flies off. The caption reads: "Lieutenant Colonel Untung and a battalion of the palace guard safeguard the president and the Republic of Indonesia from a coup by the Council of Generals."

the day-by-day progress of the left during the past week. The combined panel for Thursday and Friday (September 30 and October 1) showed the fist of the September 30th Movement smashing into the face of the Council of Generals. The cartoon in the next panel for Saturday was a gorier scene: the generals, with U.S. dollars and CIA receipts falling out of their pockets, were being hurled by a burly soldier onto a sea of spikes.

The oddity of this *Harian Rakjat* front page was its publication after the movement in Jakarta had already been defeated. Major General Umar Wirahadikusumah had issued an order at 6 P.M. on October 1 that banned all papers, except the two army-owned papers, from publishing. Suharto's troops had retaken the radio station at about 7 P.M. and broadcast a denunciation of the movement around 8:45 P.M. Why did the editors of *Harian Rakjat* defy the army's ban, only to publish a statement in support of a failed action? The office was located in the neighborhood

8. The caption along the bottom reads: "This week's film," which alludes to the popular Indonesian custom of watching films on Saturday. This film is a grisly one: a soldier smiles triumphantly while watching two CIA-funded generals fall onto spikes. Within the panel the title of the film, "De Over Val," which is Dutch for "surprise attack" *(overval)*, has been changed to "De Generals Val," which is a double entendre that means both "the generals' trap" and "the generals' fall." The parenthetic phrase translates the latter meaning into Indonesian: "the generals' fall."

of Pintu Besar Selatan, about half a mile from Merdeka Square. The reporters on the paper must have been following the events of the day and must have known that the movement in Jakarta had collapsed.

Benedict Anderson and Ruth McVey thought that the army must have seized the *Harian Rakjat* office on Friday night. The army had already suspected by then that the Communist Party had some sort of role in the movement (given that the militiamen arrested at the tele-communications building were from Pemuda Rakjat). For the Saturday edition to appear, either it must have been printed and distributed be-fore the army arrived or it was printed and distributed while the army officers were occupying the office. Anderson and McVey leaned toward the former possibility since the Saturday edition of *Harian Rakjat* was probably printed on Friday afternoon. In most offices at that time em-ployees worked only a half-day on Fridays. The Cornell scholars specu-lated that the October 2 edition came out before the editors were certain that the movement had failed.[71]

What happened that night of October 1 at the *Harian Rakjat* office? A former journalist on the paper, Martin Aleida, recalls a conversation that he had with an editor who was at the office that night.[72] Aleida himself was out of town. He had been sent to study at a PKI school in Semarang about two months earlier. He managed to survive the 1965–66 massacres and several years in prison. Once out of prison, he ran into one of his former colleagues, Wahyudi, who had been a senior editor on the paper in 1965. According to Wahyudi's account, a group of army personnel arrived at the office at about 11 P.M. and demanded that the paper shut down. Wahyudi and another editor refused, insisting that they would close the paper only if they were presented with a written order. The army personnel did not occupy the premises, forcibly evict the staff, or interfere with the publication of the paper. The office con-tinued working as normal.

Wahyudi stated, according to Aleida, that the editorial supporting the movement had been delivered to the paper's office at about 9 P.M. by the usual courier. Wahyudi did not know who wrote the editorial, but he suspected that it was Dahono, the paper's reporter who usually spent his days at the Central Committee Secretariat (on Jalan Kramat), ob-taining the party's official positions on various issues. Dahono was not a very good writer. He had been appointed to the *Harian Rakjat* staff by the Central Committee for his enthusiastic loyalty to the party and bonhomie, not for his journalistic skills. Thus the language of the edito-rial may have been so awkward because Dahono wrote it.

Aleida was not told whether the paper was printed before or after the army arrived. He remembers that the usual deadline for submission of articles was around 11 P.M. and that the paper usually came off the press around 1 to 2 A.M. If the paper followed the usual pattern on that Friday night, the army would have arrived just as the Saturday edition was being edited and typeset.

The question concerning the party's decision to publish a statement of support for a failed military action remains open. Perhaps it was not clear on Friday night that the movement had actually failed. The troops and militiamen in Merdeka Square had been cleared out, but the leaders of the action were still together at Halim. Untung had not been captured. The actions in Central Java were still underway. In laying out the front page, the editors did not emphasize the party's support for the movement. The editorial was very brief, cautiously worded, and placed toward the bottom of the page. The lead stories reported on Untung's action in a matter-of-fact manner and emphasized that it was an internal army matter. It is difficult to believe that the editors or their superiors at the Central Committee thought they were putting themselves at risk by going ahead with the edition. They could not have predicted that the movement would collapse so quickly, the army would attack the PKI so suddenly and ruthlessly, and that the *Harian Rakjat* would never be given a chance to revise its position in light of subsequent events. They could not have understood that the entire Sukarno-centered political system to which they had become accustomed was being fundamentally transformed on that night of October 1.

At least three former PKI Politburo members, Sudisman, Subekti, and Munir, stated in their courtroom defense pleas that the party as a whole was not involved in the movement but that certain unnamed leaders were involved as individuals. Their assessment seems correct. The movement appears to have been Aidit's own project. He believed that a military action by progressive officers was the best strategy to eliminate the threat of the Council of Generals. As a covert military operation, no one in the party was allowed to know the details except for a handful of his trusted confidantes largely from the Politburo Working Committee. Aidit recruited individual party leaders, such as Njono and Sukatno, who mobilized youths into a militia force, without informing them of the overall operation. Information was conveyed on a need-to-know basis. None of the official leadership bodies of the Communist Party—the Politburo, its Working Committee, and the Central Committee—was involved in the planning and organizing of the movement.

In principle, the movement was justifiable in terms of the PKI's self-interest. The party's contacts in the military could be put to good use in eliminating the anti-Communist army high command. The movement turned into a fiasco for reasons that Aidit did not foresee. First, he was blind to the faults of Sjam. He authorized Sjam to proceed with the military action without having sufficient means of verifying Sjam's word. Aidit, I suspect, did not realize that Sjam had dragooned the military officers into joining and had deluded them into thinking that the PKI would ensure the success of the action. When linking Aidit and the officers, Sjam distorted their perceptions of each other.

Second, Aidit did not perhaps sufficiently appreciate beforehand that the army was riddled from end to end with double agents and that the personal networks inside the army criss-crossed the officers' political allegiances. Any action by "progressive officers" was highly vulnerable to betrayal. Untung and Latief, the two key officers willing to stick with Sjam even as others dropped out, thought that Suharto was their ally.

Third, given the inherent risks of a military action, Aidit's involvement needed to have a much greater degree of plausible deniability; he did not take enough precautions to protect himself and the party in case of a failure. If he had stayed away from Halim and had decided not to go underground in Central Java, he could have been more convincing when asserting that the party was not involved.

Fourth, Aidit had developed a populist theory in which a military coup could be a positive development if it had a revolutionary program and the backing of the masses. He and Sjam inserted a political content into the movement—the Revolution Council, a term borrowed from the Algerian precedent. This political agenda placed too great a burden on what was, after all, a very limited military operation to kidnap the army high command. Aidit was too caught up in the fuzziness of populism to recognize the strategic errors in exploiting the military for political purposes. The movement was not organized as a coup and commanded by a single military officer (such as the successful coups with which Aidit was familiar, Qasim's in Iraq in 1958 and Boumedienne's in Algeria in 1965). The political agenda adulterated the purely military aspects of the movement. Its plan for success was predicated on gaining Sukarno's assent to it; the president would ensure that rival officers would not counterattack. The movement was not designed to succeed on the basis of its own raw military power.

My explanation of the Communist Party's role in the movement does not confirm the Suharto regime's version that accuses *the PKI* of being the mastermind. The party as an institution was not responsible. Only two individuals in the party, Aidit and Sjam, were responsible for organizing it. As Sudisman argued, the party's formal decision-making bodies were responsible only in the sense that they had allowed Aidit far too much leeway to work on his own.

6

Suharto, the Indonesian Army, and the United States

> From our viewpoint, of course, an unsuccessful coup attempt by the PKI might be the most effective development to start a reversal of political trends in Indonesia.
>
> Howard P. Jones, U.S. ambassador to Indonesia, March 10, 1965

For Aidit the covert use of progressive officers to dislodge the right-wing army high command must have seemed a clever strategy. Both the party and President Sukarno could be saved from the Council of Generals with one swift, backhanded stroke. In its first stages the movement was on its way to success: it mobilized troops without being detected and achieved the element of surprise—the corpses of six generals are sufficient proof of that. The surprise, however, was short lived. Aidit was apparently unaware that others in the army leadership and the U.S. embassy had been patiently waiting for an event like the movement and had already prepared a plan for responding to it. While the generals and the embassy staff did not anticipate that the movement would erupt on October 1 and would kill half of Yani's staff, they did anticipate some sort of dramatic action involving the PKI. They were waiting for a pretext for attacking the party and undermining Sukarno's rule. Aidit unwittingly played into their hands.

As declassified U.S. government documents reveal, in 1965 the generals realized that they could not stage an old-fashioned coup d'état against Sukarno—he was far too popular. They needed a pretext. The best pretext they hit upon was an unsuccessful coup attempt that could be blamed on the PKI. The army, in its contingency planning, had already drawn up a game plan: blame the PKI for an attempted coup, begin a full-scale war on the party, keep Sukarno as a figurehead president, and incrementally leverage the army into the government. The army kept the U.S. embassy abreast of its plan and knew that it could count on U.S. diplomatic, military, and economic support when the time came to implement it. The movement broke upon an army that knew exactly how to react. Even if the PKI had no involvement with the movement, it almost certainly would have been blamed for it.

When reading these documents about high-level army planning that was done before the outbreak of the movement, one is struck by how closely the events of 1965–67 followed the army's game plan. I do not believe this tight correspondence between the events and the plan can be explained by arguing that certain army generals designed the movement themselves. Of course, it is tempting to interpret the movement as a fake coup attempt that was designed to fail. But such a "hidden hand" argument is not only difficult to believe (given the complicated logistics required), it is impossible to square with the facts. As I argued in chapter 2, the movement would have been designed very differently if it had been meant to be a setup. When dealing with the covert operations of intelligence agencies, one should be careful not to push conspiracy theories too far. The U.S. embassy and the army generals were not controlling all the events through double agents. The movement originated with Aidit, his Special Bureau, and a group of progressive officers and was designed to succeed. It failed not because it was preprogrammed to fail but because it was poorly organized and because the army had prepared for a counterattack. Even if Suharto had not known about the movement's plans beforehand, he and his fellow generals would have reacted in a similar manner. The army might not have been able to defeat the movement so quickly and effortlessly, but it would have organized an anti-PKI and anti-Sukarno campaign all the same.

In rejecting extreme conspiracy theorizing, one should not jump to the other extreme and argue that U.S. officials and army generals were surprised on October 1 and had to improvise all their responses. A point that has been obscured in much of the literature on the movement, especially in accounts by U.S. officials, is that the U.S. government had been preparing the Indonesian army for a showdown with the PKI and a takeover of state power.[1] From 1958 to 1965 the United States trained, funded, advised, and supplied the army precisely so that it could turn itself into a state within a state. Under Nasution and Yani the army gradually expanded its powers, consolidated its officer corps, and made itself the government-in-waiting. In the months before October, the United States and the army wanted an incident like the movement to occur. They were busy creating the conditions for it and preparing themselves for dealing with it. The United States did not leave the contest between the army and the PKI to pure chance.

Within this one event of October 1, 1965, is embodied the lengthy, complex, global history of the competition between Communists and anti-Communists, extending from village-level rivalries to the high politics of U.S. foreign policy. This chapter is a brief analysis of the postcolonial contest in Indonesia between army officers and the PKI and is largely based on U.S. government declassified documents. The analysis begins by examining how the United States developed a solid alliance with the army in the late 1950s and ends by examining how the army responded to the outbreak of the movement in 1965. Ultimately, this chapter is meant to explain how the army came to fetishize a relatively small-scale putsch into the greatest evil of Indonesian history, something requiring a response of mass arrests and massacres.

Origins of the U.S. Alliance with the Army

Until the late 1950s it did not seem that the U.S. government and the Indonesian army had a bright future together. Key officials in the Eisenhower administration (1952–60) were thinking about how to break up Indonesia into smaller states. For them, President Sukarno was an anathema. His nonaligned foreign policy (on assertive display at the 1955 Asia-Africa Conference), repeated denunciations of Western imperialism, and willingness to include the Communist Party as an integral component of Indonesian politics were construed in Washington as proof of his allegiance to Moscow and Beijing. Eisenhower and the Dulles brothers—Allen at the head of the CIA and John Foster at the head of the State Department—viewed all nationalist Third World leaders who wished to remain neutral in the cold war as Communist stooges. In full confidence of their right to handpick the leaders of foreign countries, Eisenhower and the Dulleses repeatedly used CIA covert operations to overthrow such leaders: Mossadegh in Iran in 1953, Arbenz in Guatemala in 1954, and Souvanna Phouma in Laos in 1960. The Dulles brothers viewed Sukarno as yet another irritating character who needed to be removed from the world stage.[2]

After the PKI's gains in the mid-1957 provincial elections, the Dulles brothers thought it was time to move against Sukarno. His softness on communism and support for democratic elections appeared to be giving the Communist Party a direct path the presidential palace. The brothers rejected the sober advice of the U.S. ambassador in Jakarta, John Allison, who counseled that the Communist threat was not severe enough to warrant overthrowing Sukarno. In the wildly overheated imaginations of the cold warriors in Washington, the PKI had won an "absolute majority" of the Javanese votes in the 1957 regional elections.[3] (It had won only 27 percent.) The Dulles brothers became convinced that Java had fallen to the Communists and that it was best to separate it from the rest of Indonesia. When facing Communists in Asia, the guiding principle of the Eisenhower administration was the division of a country into Communist and non-Communist zones. The lesson from the loss of China in 1949 was that it was better to cut one's losses and allow some territory to fall to the Communists than to sustain a protracted fight for the whole country. The United States was thus willing to divide Korea and Vietnam into northern and southern halves. By late 1957 the Eisenhower administration thought that the rise of the PKI, especially in Java, meant that it was time to break the Indonesian archipelago up into smaller units.

Rebellions by regionally based army colonels in Sumatra and Sulawesi appeared to the Eisenhower administration as the perfect vehicles for isolating Java. Lieutenant Colonel Ahmad Husein, the commander of West Sumatra, seized power from the civilian governor on December 20, 1956. Colonel Simbolon, the commander of the entire northern half of Sumatra (headquartered in Medan), proclaimed himself the governor of his region two days later. Lieutenant Colonel Barlian, the commander of the southern half of Sumatra (headquartered in Palembang), followed suit by ousting the governor there in March 1957. All three colonels demanded greater autonomy for the provinces vis-à-vis the central government, the dissolution of the existing cabinet, and the return to power of Muhammad Hatta, a Sumatran politician who had resigned from the vice presidency on December 1, 1956.

For similar reasons the military commander for the entire eastern half of the country (including Sulawesi, Maluku, and the Lesser Sundas) usurped the civilian government and declared martial law in March 1957. Lieutenant Colonel Sumual, based in the city of Makassar, announced what he called a "universal struggle" (Perjuangan Semesta

Alam, known by its acronym, Permesta), which reiterated the demands of the three Sumatran colonels. All these rebel officers were essentially looking for a reformed central government in Indonesia, not for rump, breakaway independent states.

Back in Washington, the significance of these rebellions was greatly exaggerated. Allen Dulles stated at a National Security Council meeting in March 1957 that "the process of disintegration has continued in Indonesia to a point where only the island of Java remains under the control of the Central Government. The armed forces of all the outlying islands have declared their independence of the Central Government in Jakarta."[4] Such an inaccurate assessment convinced the policy makers that the United States should turn against Indonesian nationalism.

Sukarno was initially receptive to the rebels' demands. The formation of a new cabinet in April, the holding of a reconciliation conference soon afterward, the dispatch of more funds to the regions, and the continued prospect for the colonels' own career advancement within the national army were all factors mitigating the intransigence of the rebels. But the Eisenhower administration, through its covert contacts with the dissident colonels, insisted that they resist Sukarno's blandishments. An ad hoc committee on Indonesia within the National Security Council concluded in September 1957 that the United States should "strengthen the determination, will and cohesion of the anti-Communist forces in the outer islands" so that they could serve as a "rallying point if the Communists should take over Java."[5] U.S. material support gave the rebels the confidence to reject any negotiated resolution. The CIA gave Colonel Simbolon in North Sumatra a down payment of $50,000 in early October 1957 and began transferring weapons the following month.

Although these rebellions did not begin with the intention of overthrowing the Jakarta government, they acquired that intention by early 1958, largely because of the influence of the U.S. government. The colonels, flush with dollars and guns from the CIA, became more ambitious. On February 15, 1958, Colonel Husein announced a new national government, the Revolutionary Government of the Republic of Indonesia (shortened to its initials, PRRI). He demanded that foreign countries freeze Jakarta's assets abroad and relocate their embassies from Jakarta to West Sumatra. Faced with a virtual declaration of war, Sukarno's government decided that its only option was to respond with military force. The Indonesian military's offensive began one week after Husein's announcement.

The air force bombed key PRRI targets and airlifted Javanese battalions into Sumatra. Lacking planes, antiaircraft weapons, and subma-
rines, the rebel colonels in Sumatra were vulnerable to aerial and naval
bombardments. An added liability was morale: many troops under the
colonels were unwilling to fight against the Indonesian military. The
main cities of Sumatra fell one by one in March and April until the capital of PRRI, the hill station of Bukittinggi, was retaken on May 4. Although scattered remnants of rebel troops moved into the forests and
waged a sporadic guerrilla war for another three years, the PRRI in Sumatra was effectively finished at that point.

Jakarta's victory in eastern Indonesian took longer because the CIA
provided airpower to the rebels. Operating from airports in Menado,
the city on the northern tip of Sulawesi close to U.S. air bases in the
Philippines, the CIA ran a fleet of about eight or nine planes piloted by
Americans, Taiwanese, and Filipinos. This small fleet severely ham-
pered the military by bombing ships and airports throughout eastern
Indonesia. The CIA abruptly removed its air support in late May 1958
when an American pilot, Allen Pope, was shot down and captured alive
after his bombing raid on the city of Ambon—a gratuitous raid that
killed about seven hundred civilians. Once the CIA's planes were out of
commission, Jakarta was able to quickly defeat the rebels in Menado.

The Eisenhower administration started reassessing its strategy
as the rebel colonels were going down to defeat. The adventure-filled
dream world of covert U.S. action began to crumble. Seeing that the Indonesian officers who were suppressing the rebel colonels were anti-
Communists (such as Nasution and Yani), Washington realized that
sabotaging the national army was counterproductive. The U.S. backing
of the rebellions pitted anti-Communist officers against one another.
The PKI emerged with greater popularity because its line about U.S.
imperialism became confirmed by experience. With U.S. arms found in
Sumatra and a U.S. pilot shot down over Ambon, Indonesians could see
that the United States was indeed trying to break up the country.

The result of the reassessment was a policy reversal in Washington. Instead of trying to dismember Indonesia, the United States would
support the anti-Communist army officers in Jakarta and rely on them
to keep the PKI in check. This new policy received systematic formulation in a National Security Council (NSC) document, the "Special
Report on Indonesia," written in January 1959.[6] The NSC saw the army
as the "principle obstacle to the continued growth of Communist
strength." The civilian non-Communists in the political parties "could,

with the backing of the Army, turn the tide against the Communist party in the political field." The NSC document urged Eisenhower to strengthen U.S. ties to the military so that it could "combat Communist activity." To ensure that the army leadership was willing and able to fulfill its role as the vanguard of the anti-Communist forces, the White House donated massive amounts of equipment.[7]

The new U.S. strategy for combating the PKI was sophisticated, especially in light of the crudeness of the former U.S. strategy. The NSC realized that the Communist Party had already acquired unimpeachable nationalist credentials. The party was well organized, highly disciplined, and extremely popular. In the NSC's assessment the PKI "would probably have emerged as the largest party in Indonesia" if Sukarno had not canceled the election scheduled for 1959.[8] The army could not simply attack the Communists in pit-bull fashion: "Open measures of repression against the PKI would be difficult to justify on internal political grounds, and would expose any government undertaking them to charges of truckling to Western pressure."[9] The army would have to approach the PKI with the subtlety of a fox. Any attack on the party would have to be justified in the very terms of Indonesian nationalism that the party itself championed.

The trick was to keep provoking the Communist Party into taking some sort of rash action that would make it appear antinational. The NSC document of 1959 emphasized that the United States, in providing aid to the Indonesian army, should prioritize "requests for assistance in programs and projects which offer opportunities to isolate the PKI, drive it into positions of open opposition to the Indonesian Government, thereby creating grounds for repressive measures politically justifiable in terms of Indonesian self-interest."[10] The consistent U.S. strategy from 1959 to 1965 was to help the army officers prepare themselves for a violent attack upon the PKI. Howard Jones, the ambassador in Jakarta for seven years (1958–65) and one of the main architects of the policy, supplied an important element of continuity for three administrations (Eisenhower, Kennedy, and Johnson).

Setting the Stage for a Showdown

In accordance with the policy of building up the army as the bulwark against the PKI, the U.S. government trained army officers in the United States, donated and sold weapons, and provided financial aid. General Nasution, the commander of the army, was America's "golden boy"; his firm anticommunism had convinced policy makers in Washington that the army was indeed the best hope for containing the Communist Party. Nasution repeatedly assured U.S. officials that the army would never allow the PKI to take power. The U.S. Joint Chiefs of Staff justified aid to the Indonesian army in 1958 as encouragement to Nasution to "carry out his 'plan' for the control of Communism."[11] After Sukarno shunted Nasution aside in June 1962, promoting him to an administrative position as chief of the armed forces and thereby removing him from troop command, his successor, Lieutenant General Yani, continued the same anti-Communist posture.

In August 1958 the United States began a military assistance program that supplied equipment to the military, especially the army, and trained officers in the United States. From 1958 to 1965 the United States annually spent between $10 million and $20 million on military assistance to Indonesia.[12] The program for training Indonesian army officers in schools such as those at Fort Bragg and Fort Leavenworth was extensive. From 1950 to 1965 about twenty-eight hundred Indonesian army officers were brought to the United States for training—most of them after 1958. That number represented about one-fifth to one-quarter of all army officers.[13] Through this training the United States was able to develop extensive contacts within the Indonesian army. Of course, not all the officers trained in the United States became loyal partisans of the anti-Communist crusade. But such a large-scale program must have influenced the political orientation of some officers. In the early 1960s U.S. officials certainly thought they were enjoying some success with the program. Dean Rusk wrote a memo to President Johnson in 1964 explaining that U.S. aid to the Indonesian military was of little significance in military terms but was *"permitting us to maintain some contact with key elements in Indonesia which are interested in and capable of resisting Communist takeover"* (emphasis in original).[14]

In addition to training officers, the U.S. government promoted "civic action." Although the United States had originally formulated civic action for militaries fighting guerrilla warfare, it wished to apply it in Indonesia as a prophylactic against the Communist Party's political influence. The U.S. government defined *civic action* as the use of a military "on projects useful to local population at all levels in such fields as education, training, public works, agriculture, transportation, communications, health, sanitation and others contributing to economic and social development, which would also serve to improve the standing of the military forces with the population."[15] It was a program, as the cliché went, to win hearts and minds. Under civic action the Indonesian army was to involve itself in activities normally reserved for civilians. Soldiers were to become officials within the civilian government, such as village heads, and build infrastructure projects, such as bridges and roads. In 1962 the National Security Council endorsed the idea of strengthening the Indonesian army's role in "economic and social development activities."[16]

Guided by Nasution's conception of "territorial warfare," the Indonesian army had in fact been inserting itself in civilian life since the early 1950s. What the Kennedy administration was proposing in the early 1960s was U.S. support for the Indonesian army's existing programs.[17] The Indonesian army's newly christened civic action program was largely under the control of Colonel George Benson, whose official title from August 1962 to July 1965 was special assistant to the U.S. ambassador for civic action. Benson enjoyed the full confidence of the army commander, Yani, whom Benson knew from his days as U.S. military attaché at the Jakarta embassy (1956–59), and so was allowed a free hand to work within the Indonesian army.[18]

One virtue of civic action was the cover it provided for covert operations against the Communist Party. The NSC committee on counter-insurgency agreed in December 1961 to spend money in Indonesia "to support civic action and anti-Communist activities" that would involve the "covert training of selected personnel and civilians, who will be placed in key positions in the [here the censor notes the deletion of 'less than 1 line of source text'] civic action program."[19] The many excised passages in this declassified document suggest that the civic action program involved sensitive covert operations in Indonesia.

The Indonesian army was following its own version of a Gramscian strategy: contesting strategic sites in civil society before launching a bid for state power. The army had its own "functional group" (Golkar), which was similar to a political party; trade union (Sentral Organisasi Karyawan Sosialis Indonesia, the Central Organization of Socialist Employees of Indonesia); newspapers *(Angkatan Bersenjata* and *Berita Yudha);* and a group of cultural figures who worked closely with anti-Communist officers (such as the writer Wiratmo Sukito, the initiator of the Cultural Manifesto that set off a storm of controversy in 1963). By sprouting a great variety of wings and fronts, the army was transforming itself into a mirror image of the PKI. The martial law declared in March 1957 in response to the PRRI/Permesta rebellions allowed the army extraordinary powers to intervene in civilian politics. As Daniel Lev noted, "Martial law was to become the army's political charter."[20] Regional army commanders restricted the press, arrested politicians, and imposed their own unwritten laws. The nationalization of Dutch businesses in December 1957 provided an opportunity for the army to enter the economy. Many army commanders became businessmen, turning handsome profits from plantations, factories, import and export ventures, and illegal smuggling.[21] They accumulated sizable funds to bankroll their efforts to invade strategic sites of civil society. In the late 1950s and early 1960s the army under Nasution pushed for a corporatist, military state in which political parties would be abolished and the public sphere evacuated of political contestation.[22] The veteran politician Sjahrir warned in 1958 that Nasution's officers harbored "a militaristic and fascist ideal" for the Indonesian government.[23]

Many in the Kennedy administration believed that political order and economic development in certain Third World countries could be best achieved through military governments. These U.S. officials assumed that the military was often the best-organized institution and thus the most deserving of running the government. The political scientist Lucien Pye of the Massachusetts Institute of Technology suggested that armies in preindustrial countries could be "modernizing agents" since they tend "to emphasize a rational outlook and to champion responsible change and national development." Army officers appreciated "technological advancement," could promote "a sense of citizenship," and were capable of "strengthening essentially administrative functions."[24] Walt Rostow headed a team at the State Department that wrote a report in January 1963, "The Role of the Military in the Underdeveloped Areas," that endorsed the idea of encouraging the militaries of some countries to take over the functions of the state and disregard the principle of civilian supremacy.[25] The Kennedy administration looked to the Indonesian army as a state within a state.

The high command of the Indonesian army viewed itself in the same way. In the early 1960s it was preparing itself for taking state power. Guy Pauker, a key U.S. specialist on the Indonesian army who was affiliated with both the Rand Corporation and University of California–Berkeley, noticed that Nasution was following a clever long-term strategy "in making the Indonesian Army into the organization which could eventually stabilize and develop the country."[26] Nasution did not want to take state power until the army was tightly knit as a centralized institution and "capable of governing Indonesia." The general had realized that the army could not stage a coup d'état against

President Sukarno because he was too popular: "Any direct political attack on him is doomed to fail."[27] It could not depose Sukarno without provoking an uncontrollable civil war. Pauker was not optimistic about the success of Nasution's long-term strategy—both Sukarno and the PKI stood a chance of foiling it—but Pauker noted that the army was the only real hope for defeating the Communists. The army was "the rallying point of anti-Communist elements" in the civil society.[28]

Pauker struck up an alliance with the vice director of the army's staff college, Colonel Suwarto, who was grooming his fellow officers for their future role as rulers.[29] Suwarto, a 1959 graduate of a training program at Fort Leavenworth, was known as a personal enemy of President Sukarno's. Only with Yani's protection was Suwarto able to continue to hold influential positions within the army and continue to scheme against Sukarno.[30] The army, of course, could not openly discuss plans for taking state power. Suwarto and his like-minded colleagues at the college, which was known as Seskoad (for Sekolah Staf Komando Angkatan Darat), worked in subtle fashion. For instance, they arranged for U.S.-trained economists at the University of Indonesia in Jakarta to come to Bandung and teach seminars for the officers. These economists had been educated largely at Berkeley, courtesy of the Ford Foundation. A Berkeley professor who chaired the project, Bruce Glassburner, spent three years in Indonesia (1958–61) and later recalled that the army officers at Seskoad wanted to learn about economics so they could rule wisely once they took state power: "Given the parlous state of the Indonesian economy in the early and mid-1960s, the military readily recognized that in the event of a political shift which would bring them to power, prompt solution of the worst of the economic problems would be of highest priority."[31] The economists who taught at Seskoad, such as Muhammad Sadli, later became the so-called technocrats and Berkeley mafia of the Suharto regime.[32]

Among the officers participating in Seskoad seminars was Suharto. He had recently been dismissed from his position as army commander in Central Java on charges of corruption, but his superiors had decided that his smuggling operations at the port of Semarang were not serious enough to warrant prosecution. They did not publicly announce the reason for his dismissal. The charges were hushed up, and he was sent off to Seskoad in late 1959. There he came under the influence of Suwarto. A historian of the Indonesian military, Ulf Sundhaussen, noted that at Seskoad Suharto was "involved in the formation of the Doctrine of Territorial Warfare and the Army's policy on Civic Mission (that is, penetration of army officers into all fields of government activities and responsibilities)."[33] Suwarto taught the officers to think of the army as an institution that had the right and ability to involve itself in governing the country. Although Suharto did not go to the United States for training, he would have known about U.S. hopes for the army as both an anti-Communist bastion and a shadow government.

Yani and his staff later recruited Suharto to play a crucial, covert role in their efforts to undermine Confrontation, Sukarno's anti-Malaysia campaign. The army generals did not at first object to the campaign, launched in September 1963, since it resulted in increased funding. But as the hostilities intensified in mid- to late 1964, they wished to prevent it from leading to a full-scale war with the British military, which was protecting Malaysia. To avoid a clash with Sukarno, who was known to meddle with army appointments if displeased, the generals retained a public face of support for Confrontation. Meanwhile, they devised several hidden methods for sabotaging it. They lobbied Sukarno to reorganize the military command for Confrontation. Sukarno saw the need for change after the humiliating failure of covert raids into Malaysia in mid-1964 and agreed to the army's proposal, renaming the multiservice command Kolaga (Komando Mandala Siaga) in September 1964. He also authorized the insertion of Suharto as vice commander of Kolaga on January 1, 1965.[34]

From his position as second in command, Suharto proceeded to assert greater authority than the commander of Kolaga, Air Force Vice Marshal Omar Dani.[35] Suharto determined the deployment of the army personnel and weaponry brought into the anti-Malaysian campaign. At the time Suharto's base of operations was Kostrad, the army's reserve troops, of which he had been commander since May 1963. Suharto slowed down the deployments and kept the forces stationed near the Malaysian borders constantly understaffed and underequipped. Dani, as commander of the air force, could not force the army to comply with the targets he set. The troops stationed in Sumatra under the command of Colonel Kemal Idris, an old enemy of Sukarno's whose appointment was another tactic to sabotage Confrontation, were denied transport ships, which prevented them from invading Malaysia.[36]

Suharto and his intelligence agents at Kostrad also sabotaged Confrontation by secretly contacting representatives of Malaysia and Britain and assuring them that the army was opposed to the hostilities and would try to limit them. Perhaps Yani and his intelligence chief, Parman, entrusted Suharto with this sensitive task so that they could enjoy plausible deniability if the plot became exposed. In July or August 1964 Suharto ordered his intelligence officer at Kostrad, Major Ali Moertopo, to inform the enemy of the army's real intentions.[37] To facilitate communication with Malaysian officials, Moertopo used Indonesian civilians who had been involved in the PRRI/Permesta revolts of 1957–58 and had opted for exile in Singapore and Malaysia.[38] In January 1965 Suharto summoned his old friend Colonel Yoga Sugama from Belgrade, where he was military attaché, to return to Indonesia precisely so that he could help "put the brakes" on Confrontation.[39] Yoga took over Moertopo's work. Additionally, Major Benny Moerdani, a Kostrad officer since January 1965, was sent to Bangkok to make contact there with pro-Western officials. For cover he worked as a sales manager in the Indonesian airlines office.[40]

One reason that Suharto and his Kostrad officers were opposed to Confrontation was that it was diverting the army's resources from the campaign against the Communist Party. The intelligence section at Suharto's Kostrad wrote a secret report in mid-1964 arguing that Confrontation was jeopardizing the army's efforts to keep the PKI under control.[41] Too many troops were concentrated along the border with Malaysia instead of being stationed within Indonesian, especially Javanese, civil society. A later confidential U.S. government report noted that the military preferred to end Confrontation so that the troops could be returned to their home bases "to be prepared for a future confrontation with the PKI and other extremists."[42]

The Year of the Showdown

Trained, armed, funded, and encouraged by the United States to attack the Communist Party, the army high command decided in January 1965 to begin contingency planning for doing so. A series of events prompted Yani and his inner circle to believe that President Sukarno's rule was becoming less stable and that, as a consequence, the threat of the PKI was increasing. Sukarno's health was failing, as evidenced by a kidney ailment that required an operation in December 1964. He was also becoming more isolated on the international stage. In response to the UN Security Council's approval of a council seat for Malaysia, Sukarno announced on January 7 that Indonesia was withdrawing from the United Nations. His policy of Confrontation against Malaysia was emboldening the Communist Party to demand that thousands, if not millions, of civilians be armed and organized into a new fifth service of the military. With the possibility of the PKI's becoming armed, the army generals realized that Confrontation was spinning out of their control.

According to the CIA's published analysis of the movement, Yani and four other generals began meeting in January 1965 "to discuss the deteriorating political situation and what the Army should do about it. The group, known as the 'brain-trust,' included four other generals: Gen. Suprapto, Gen. Harjono, Gen. Parman, and Gen. Sukendro." These generals met "regularly, in secret."[43] The first three generals were on Yani's general staff. The last, Sukendro, had led the crackdown on the PKI in July–September 1960 and had, with other hard-line anti-Communists within the army, demanded that Nasution stage a coup d'état against Sukarno at that time. Sukarno negotiated a compromise with the army that led to ending the repression against the Communist Party and to sending Sukendro into exile for three years.[44] Those were the years that Sukendro spent at the University of Pittsburgh, where he developed close contacts with U.S. officials and the CIA. Yani brought Sukendro back into the army in 1963 and later entrusted him with the top-level plotting to resume what he had attempted so crudely back in 1960: crush the PKI and overthrow Sukarno.

Information leaked out about Yani's select group of generals. Sukarno heard the rumors about the Council of Generals and summoned Yani to the palace on May 22 for an explanation. As the CIA acknowledged, Yani's brain trust was "almost certainly the group the PKI was warning Sukarno about."[45] Yani conjectured that some people had misconstrued the army's committee for senior promotions (Wanjakti) as the Council of Generals.

The U.S. ambassador, Howard Jones, learned of the discussions of Yani's brain trust in January. Jones wired his superiors in Washington that an embassy informant, who had just come from a meeting with General Parman, had reported that the army was "developing specific plans for takeover of government moment Sukarno steps off stage." Although this contingency planning was being done "with an eye to post-Sukarno era," some officers in the "top military command" were pushing for a coup before Sukarno's death if the Communist Party succeeded in forming an armed civilian militia. The informant explained that if the military did takeover before Sukarno died, the "coup would be handled in such a way as to preserve Sukarno's leadership intact." It would be a coup that would not appear to be a coup. Jones's informant stated that even the president's detractors in the army "were convinced that there was no possibility of any coup succeeding against Sukarno. He was still beloved of the masses." Jones considered the information credible because the informant was an "excellent source."[46]

The experienced diplomat Ellsworth Bunker, sent to Jakarta in April 1965 for an overall evaluation of U.S.-Indonesia relations, confirmed this assessment of Sukarno's unassailability. "There is little question of his hold on the loyalty of the Indonesian people," he wrote in his report to President Johnson. Indonesians "in large measure look to him for leadership, trust his leadership, and are willing to follow him. No force in the country can attack him nor is there evidence that any significant group would want to do so."[47]

For a coup d'état to succeed in Indonesia, it would have to be disguised as its opposite: an effort to save President Sukarno. The military would have to appear as Sukarno's savior instead of his grave digger. The problem for the army was that such a disguised coup needed a pretext. As I noted earlier, by 1959 the U.S. National Security Council had recognized that the repression of the PKI had to be "politically justifiable in terms of Indonesian self-interest"; the Communist Party had to be driven "into positions of open opposition to the Indonesian Government." The logical pretext for a coup would be a coup attempt by the PKI. Ambassador Jones told a closed-door meeting of State Department officials in the Philippines in March 1965, "From our viewpoint, of course, an unsuccessful coup attempt by the PKI might be the most effective development to start a reversal of political trends in Indonesia." Jones hoped the PKI would give the army a "clear-cut kind of challenge which could galvanize effective reaction."[48]

Jones was not alone in thinking about an "unsuccessful coup attempt by the PKI" as the ideal pretext. The idea circulated widely among the diplomatic corps of countries allied with the United States. Edward Peck, the assistant secretary of state in the Foreign Office in Britain, suggested "there might therefore be much to be said for encouraging a premature PKI coup during Sukarno's lifetime."[49] Responding to Peck in December 1964, the New Zealand high commissioner in London averred that a premature PKI coup "might be the most helpful solution for the West—provided the coup failed."[50] The idea even reached as far as the Pakistani foreign service. A Dutch intelligence officer with the North Atlantic Treaty Organization informed a Pakistani ambassador in Western Europe about it in December 1964. The ambassador dutifully reported to his superiors in Islamabad that a "premature communist coup" that would be "foredoomed to fail" would provide "a legitimate and welcome opportunity to army to crush the communists and make Sukarno a prisoner of the army's good will."[51] Apparently, the idea was considered so clever that it became the banter of the cocktail circuit. This may explain why Jones used the phrase "of course" while broaching the subject with his State Department colleagues, as if they were already familiar with it.

Both the United States government and the Indonesian army's high command spent 1965 waiting for some sort of dramatic action from the PKI that would provide a justification for repressing it. Some even helpfully suggested that the United States serve as a catalyst for this longed-for clash. A State Department analyst in Washington wondered in March, "Is there anything that would make [such a] clash inevitable?"[52] Ellsworth Bunker, in his report of April, suggested that the "U.S. should be directed toward creating conditions which will give the elements of potential strength the most favorable conditions for confrontation."[53]

The United States was "creating conditions" through covert operations. An NSC committee approved a proposal in March 1965 for covert actions such as "support to existing anti-Communist groups," "black letter operations," and "media operations." The plan was to "portray the PKI as an increasingly ambitious, dangerous opponent of Sukarno and legitimate nationalism" and thereby unite all the non-Communist elements against the PKI. The proposal mentioned that "leading nationalist personalities" in Indonesia had already been given "some funds" through "secure channels" so that they could "take obstructive action against the PKI."[54]

The U.S. government became eager for a showdown between the army and the Communist Party in 1965 since U.S. relations with the Sukarno government were rapidly deteriorating. Militant demonstrators attacked many consulates and libraries of the U.S. government. Sukarno's blasé reaction to these attacks in February and March suggested that he was encouraging them. The United States adopted what it called a "low-posture policy." This entailed the withdrawal of most embassy personnel (who numbered four hundred in April and thirty-five in August), suspension of aid to Sukarno's government, and continuation of contacts with the army leaders in the hope that they would act against the PKI and Sukarno. The CIA station was kept at its full contingent of twelve members (eight operatives plus four administrative staff) so that it could continue its covert operations.[55]

Hunkering down, U.S. embassy officials believed the final showdown against the Communist Party was imminent. Bunker wrote in

April: "U.S. visibility should be reduced so that those opposed to the communists and extremists may be free to handle a confrontation, which they believe will come, without the incubus of being attacked as defenders of the neo-colonialists and imperialists."[56] Marshall Green, who replaced Jones as U.S. ambassador in July 1965, was deputed to take a harder line with Sukarno. Green's assessment after about one month in Jakarta was that the U.S. priority had to be to "maintain whatever contact possible with the military and other elements in the power structure, looking toward the post-Sukarno period."[57] During Green's tenure the U.S. embassy laid low while hoping that its friends in the army would act against the PKI and Sukarno. As one NSC staffer explained to President Johnson, the "main objective remains to ride out the long storm with battened hatches (reduced diplomatic staffing) in an effort to play for the long-term post-Sukarno stakes."[58] The United States decided against a complete severance of relations with Indonesia so that it could maintain contact with its anti-Communist allies in the army.

One of the Americans with the closest contacts in the Indonesian army was George Benson, the civic action adviser to the Indonesian army. He was on close personal terms with Yani and many officers on the general staff. Before returning to the United States in July 1965, Benson had lunch with Yani and Parman. Benson recalled that Yani assured him that the army was solidly anti-Communist. Yani explained that he and his general staff had appointed all 120 battalion commanders in the country and considered them trustworthy. Yani also said, according to Benson, "We *have the guns*, and we have kept the guns out of their [the Communists'] hands. So if there's a clash, we'll wipe them out."[59]

The U.S. government, of course, did not know exactly when and how the clash would occur between the army and the Communist Party. The United States was certain, however, that such a confrontation would occur and was fairly confident that the Indonesian army would somehow prevail. Already in January 1965, a CIA assessment about the "beginnings of a scramble for succession to Sukarno" predicted that the "initial struggle to replace him would be won by Army and non-Communist elements."[60] The simple fact, bluntly expressed by Yani to Benson, was that the army had a monopoly of arms. Frederick Bunnell has accurately described U.S. policy in 1965: "There was always the cautious confidence that the army could and would prevail in a post-Sukarno showdown, but the form and timing of such a showdown could not be predicted."[61]

Given that the embassy wanted to provoke a showdown, it is reasonable to assume that the CIA station's covert operations involved measures that would prompt the PKI to think that it and Sukarno were in serious danger. Some of the CIA's "black letter operations" and "media operations" must have been designed to convince PKI leaders that the army generals and the United States were mad dogs spoiling for a coup.

U.S. officials repeatedly informed the army generals that the United States would support them if they moved against the PKI. Howard Jones had assured Nasution back in March 1964 during a private ninety-minute meeting that there would be "U.S. support in time of crisis." In turn, Nasution assured Jones that the army was "still anti-communist in outlook" and was indoctrinating the officers "to ensure military will be ready to meet challenge when it came."[62] At another meeting Nasution assured Jones that the army's attack on the Communist Party in 1948, an attack largely conducted by Nasution's own West Java troops, "would be mild compared with an army crackdown today."[63]

The open question was whether the PKI would give the army a pretext for an attack. While Jones saw that an "unsuccessful coup attempt by the PKI" would be the ideal event, he was pessimistic about the chances of its happening. He noted in his March 1965 State Department speech that the PKI was not likely to attempt any action against Sukarno: "The PKI is doing too well through its present tactics of cooperation with Sukarno. Unless the PKI leadership is rasher than I think they are they will not give the army the clear-cut kind of challenge which could galvanize effective reaction."[64] Contrary to Jones's expectations, the PKI, more specifically, Aidit and Sjam, did walk into the trap.

Exploiting the September 30th Movement

Before the outbreak of the movement, U.S. officials and their allied Indonesian officers had already written a script that contained the following plot elements: blame the PKI for a coup attempt, launch a general repression of the PKI throughout the country, retain Sukarno as a figurehead president while eroding his authority, and establish a new army-dominated, corporatist government. This was their ideal scenario. Events unfolded in such a way that they were able to turn this scenario into reality. Although the movement had come as a surprise, they knew immediately how to take advantage of it. The movement was not a straightforward coup attempt by the PKI, but it was similar enough to serve their purposes. The movement allowed U.S. officials

and their Indonesian generals to set in motion their long-standing plan
for displacing Sukarno and attacking the Communist Party.

In the early days of October the U.S. embassy and policy makers
back in Washington were concerned that the Indonesian army would
not take full advantage of the opportunity to attack the PKI. Even before the United States had solid evidence that the PKI was responsible,
it was blaming the PKI and encouraging the army to destroy the party.
An embassy report of October 4 observed that the army had not
"reached a decision on whether to maintain its drive for complete victory over the PKI."[65] While U.S. officials were confident that their old
ally Nasution would push for a full-scale attack, they fretted that other
elements in the army would stymie him. The CIA station in Jakarta
noted the next day that "the Army must act quickly if it is to exploit its
opportunity to move against the PKI."[66] The CIA station (presumably
its head, B. Hugh Tovar) again worried on October 7 that there was a
danger the army would not unleash an assault on the PKI but would
settle for only limited action "against those directly involved in the murder of the Generals."[67] The very next day all the CIA's worries disappeared when it discovered that the army generals had already met on
October 5 and agreed to "implement plans to crush the PKI."[68] The
movement would be put to its proper purpose as the justification for the
planned repression of the PKI—repression that turned out just as Nasution promised: it made the 1948 repression of the PKI look mild.

Although the army generals did not need further assurances that the
United States would support them during their anti-PKI drive, the
embassy gave them such assurances nonetheless. Ambassador Green
cabled Washington on October 5 to propose that he "indicate clearly to
key people in army such as Nasution and Suharto our desire to be of assistance where we can." In response the State Department agreed with
the proposal but noted that the army generals must have already felt
certain that they could rely on the United States: "Over past years inter-
service relationships developed through training program, civic action
program and MILTAG [Military Assistance Group], as well as regular
assurances to Nasution, should have established clearly in minds Army
leaders that U.S. stands behind them if they should need help."[69] One
assurance that the embassy conveyed to an aide of Nasution's in mid-
October was that the British troops massed in Malaysia would not exploit the chaos in Jakarta and attack Indonesian troops involved in
Confrontation. The army could proceed with its drive against the PKI
without fretting about an offensive from Malaysia. According to the

embassy, Nasution's aide offered his thanks: "He [the aide] commented to the effect that this was just what was needed by way of assurances that we (the army) weren't going to be hit from all angles as we moved to straighten things out here."[70]

As the death squads fanned out across the country to hunt down PKI members, the embassy was delighted. Ambassador Green observed in early November that even the "smaller fry" in the PKI were "being systematically arrested and jailed or executed." In Central Java the army was mobilizing and arming militias of Muslim youths to "keep them out in front against PKI." Green noted in the same memo that the embassy had "made clear" to a contact in the army "that Embassy and USG [U.S. Government] generally sympathetic with and admiring of what army doing."[71] Green's only lingering worry was that the army would compromise with Sukarno and allow the PKI to retain some vestiges of its former power. Green assured Washington that the army was nevertheless "working hard at destroying PKI and I, for one, have increasing respect for its determination and organization in carrying out this crucial assignment."[72]

The United States backed up its words of encouragement with material aid. The army needed communications equipment to link its various headquarters around the country so that it could better coordinate the drive against the PKI.[73] Sometime in late 1965 the United States flew in state-of-the-art mobile radios from Clark Air Base in the Philippines and delivered them to Kostrad. An antenna was brought in and erected in front of Kostrad headquarters. The investigative journalist Kathy Kadane discovered from her interviews with former officials in the late 1980s that the United States had monitored the army's communications over those radios: "The CIA made sure the frequencies the Army would use were known in advance to the National Security Agency. NSA intercepted the broadcasts at a site in Southeast Asia, where its analysts subsequently translated them. The intercepts were then sent on to Washington." The United States thus had a blow-by-blow account of the army's assault on the PKI, overhearing, for instance, "commands from Suharto's intelligence unit to kill particular persons at given locations."[74] A member of the embassy's political affairs section, Robert Martens, helped the army by providing lists of the names of PKI members.[75] Martens admitted in a letter to the *Washington Post* that he handed over the names of "a few thousand" members, whom he disingenuously termed "leaders and senior cadre"—as if a list of that many names could include only the hard-core leadership.[76]

The embassy also transferred a large sum of money to the army-created civilian front called Action Front for Crushing the September 30th Movement (Kap-Gestapu). The actions of this organization were, as Ambassador Green noted, "fully consonant with and coordinated by the army." To help this front hold demonstrations and carry out its "current repressive efforts targeted against PKI," Green authorized in early December the granting of 50 million rupiah to the front's representative, Adam Malik.[77]

Although Suharto was not part of Yani's brain trust, Suharto was familiar with its game plan. As scripted, Suharto kept Sukarno as a figurehead president. Sukarno was not officially removed from office until March 1967. Ambassador Green recognized in early November 1965 that Suharto's strategy was to "assert carefully applied army pressure and control government but will not, if he can avoid it, take over in name so long as Sukarno is alive."[78] The continued presence of Sukarno as president lent credibility to Suharto's actions, as if they came with the president's approval. The army was able to concentrate its repression on the PKI while the other pro-Sukarno organizations either remained neutral or joined in the violence. For their part, the PKI leaders themselves still counted on Sukarno's using his presidential powers to save the party from the army's repression.

Green was also cognizant by early November that Suharto was not displacing Sukarno in order to restore democracy and reestablish a civilian government. In accordance with Nasution and Suwarto's teachings, Suharto was laying the foundations for a thoroughly army-dominated polity. Green informed Washington: "Army is not thinking purely in military terms or intending turn political future of Indonesia over to civilian elements. Army is moving its people into all aspects of government and organizational framework with view [to] keeping control on political trends and events."[79] Before he was unexpectedly thrown into command of the army in October 1965, Suharto was aware of the army's blueprints for creating its own dictatorship. Nasution and other generals would have filled him in on whatever details he did not know. Taking advantage of the outbreak of the movement, Suharto gradually implemented the preexisting plan for turning the army, already the shadow government, into the real government.

From the start of his takeover of state power in October 1965, Suharto wished to ally Indonesia with the United States and end Sukarno's nonaligned foreign policy. Suharto aimed to achieve economic growth, the prerequisite for a durable dictatorship, through a tight integration

with the Western economies. He signaled his strong support for
Western private investment quite early. Aware of the U.S. hostility
to Sukarno's moves to nationalize the oil industry, Suharto personally
intervened in a meeting of cabinet ministers in December 1965 that
planned to discuss the issue. Sukarno's third deputy prime minister,
Chairul Saleh, chaired a meeting on December 16 to decide upon the
nationalization of the oil companies Caltex and Stanvac. Soon after
Saleh opened the meeting, Suharto suddenly arrived by helicopter, entered the chamber, and peremptorily announced, as the gleeful U.S. embassy account has it, that the military "would not stand for precipitous
moves against oil companies." Faced with such a direct threat, Saleh indefinitely postponed the discussion of nationalizing the oil industry.[80]

For its power grab to be successful, the army needed to show that it
could improve economic conditions. The army could gain legitimacy
only if the public felt that it was bringing tangible, material benefits.[81]
This is where the U.S. government and the U.S.-trained Indonesian
economists played important roles. Representatives of the army began
approaching the embassy in November 1965, asking for covert deliveries
of rice.[82] Since the United States did not think any large-scale delivery
of supplies could be kept secret and kept solely within the army's hands,
the embassy turned down the requests. The United States wanted to
wait until the army was more fully in control of the government.[83] Once
Suharto decommissioned Sukarno's cabinet in mid-March 1966, im-
prisoning fifteen ministers and appointing his own replacements — all
the while keeping Sukarno as the president — the United States opened
the taps of economic aid: concessionary sales of 50,000 tons of rice in
April, and 75,000 tons of cotton and $60 million in emergency foreign
exchange credits from Germany, Japan, Britain, and United States in
June.[84] Suharto appointed the U.S.-trained economists to the ministries
related to economic affairs. They laid out the welcome mat for foreign
investment and oriented the country's economy around export production for Western markets.[85]

The Army's Coup

At a different time, in a different context, the movement might have
become just another temporary disturbance in Indonesian politics. It
could have been an uprising that suddenly erupted and then quietly
disappeared without causing any major changes in the structure of
power. By 1965 postindependence Indonesia had witnessed a number of

assassination attempts on the president, military mutinies, and guerrilla insurgencies, including, for example, the October 17, 1952, affair during which Nasution's army pointed tanks at the palace and demanded that Sukarno dismiss the parliament; Lieutenant Colonel Zulfiki Lubis's mutiny in November 1956; the Darul Islam insurgency from 1949 to 1962; the PRRI rebellion in Sumatra from 1956 to 1958; and the Permesta rebellion in Sulawesi from 1957 to 1961. The killing of six generals and a mutiny of troops in Central Java in 1965 could have become just another temporary crisis for Sukarno to overcome. But the army would not let the movement remain just another "ripple in the wide ocean." The event resulted in the end of Sukarno's presidency because it occurred at a time when the army was ready and willing to seize power.

Sukarno did his best to downplay the significance of the movement. His speeches from late 1965 onward contained vigorous condemnations of the anti-PKI violence that he believed, on the basis of his own commission of inquiry, had led to the deaths of more than a half-million people.[86] The violence was out of all proportion to the slayings of six generals and the mutiny in Central Java. Sukarno kept calling for calm: "In a state of calm it is possible to place all problems in their proper perspective." He wished to investigate the incident, determine who was responsible, and punish them. But he knew that the army, using its control of the media, was refusing to allow an atmosphere of calm to prevail. The media was inventing all sorts of absurd lies to whip up the anti-Communist campaign. The CIA noted in early November that the army had "instituted psychological warfare mechanisms, control of media prerequisite to influencing public opinion and have harassed or halted Communist output."[87]

Sukarno complained about particular stories in the newspapers, such as the one that said one hundred women of Gerwani (the Indonesian Women's Movement) were using razors to slice up the genitals of the generals: "Does the journalist think we're stupid? What's his point? To stir up hatred! Does it make sense, I mean, does it make sense that a penis was sliced one hundred times by razors? . . . Is our nation of such low quality that the newspapers write about imaginary things?"[88] He was infuriated by the steady stream of anti-Communist propaganda: the death of his former prime minister, Djuanda, was due to poisoning by agents of the Chinese Communist government; an electric chair for executing people was found in a PKI house.[89] In November Sukarno held a special meeting at the Bogor Palace for both military officers and journalists in order to discuss the incessant absurdities in the press:

9. This cartoon appeared in an army-approved newspaper supportive of the anti-PKI campaign. Its violent imagery is similar to the cartoons that had appeared in the Communist Party newspapers. The labels are now reversed: the PKI is the evil character betraying Sukarno's ideals and collaborating with imperialist powers. The September 30th Movement is depicted as a snake imprinted with the labels "stab from behind," "counterrevolutionary," and "slander." It is in league with the monster of Western imperialism and neocolonialism *(nekolim)* to the right. The warrior labeled "the people and the military" wields the sword of Sukarno's "Five Charms of the Revolution." The slogan at the bottom is "Never Forget Nekolim." Justifying the anti-PKI violence in terms of the PKI's own ideals (revolution, Sukarnoism, and anti-imperialism) shows how reluctant the army generals were to appear to contradict those principles, even as they were receiving assistance from the United States and undermining Sukarno. Source: *Kompas,* October 20, 1965.

"Now, then, look at this! Over and over it's the same thing. Yes, you know what I'm referring to. It's always Gestapu, Gestapu, Gestapu, Gestapu, Gestapu, razors, razors, razors, razors, razors, a grave for a thousand people, a grave for a thousand people, a grave for a thousand people, electric chair, electric chair, electric chair—over and over again, the same thing!"[90] Sukarno demanded that the journalists write only about true events and keep in mind their role in building the nation. But his pleas fell on deaf ears. In effect, the great orator was rendered voiceless: his speeches rarely entered the media. The army not only had the guns, it had the newspapers and radio.

Suharto's creeping coup d'état against Sukarno worked so well because the army high command had already drawn up a plan. Six generals in the high command became victims of the movement (an outcome certainly not envisioned in the plan), but the survivors, such as Suharto, Nasution, and Sukendro, were able to pick up the plan and put it into effect. While they no doubt faced some unexpected events and had to improvise at certain times, they had a definite strategy and set of goals.[91]

Suharto and his fellow generals understood the principle that the method of taking power greatly determines the sustainability of the new regime. They were not witless officers who could only follow the usual pattern for military coups: rolling the tanks into the streets of the capital, surrounding the palace, and capturing, perhaps killing, the president. They realized that the army did not have enough legitimacy and public support for a direct action against Sukarno. The army's strategy after the defeat of the regional rebellions in 1957–58 had been to construct itself as a state within a state. Army officers had become factory and plantation owners, bureaucrats in the civil administration, labor union leaders, newspaper owners, and students of neoclassical economics. The army had bided its time as it built up its capacity for governance. It did not want to take state power only to lose it because of internal disunity or widespread resistance.

The starting point for the army's game plan was an action that could be construed as a coup and blamed on the Communist Party. Taking the movement as their pretext, Suharto and his fellow officers created a hysterical, crisis-filled atmosphere wherein all non-Communists were led to believe that they were in mortal danger. Once begun, the psychological warfare campaign took on a life of its own, as army personnel convinced themselves that the Communists, even poor farmers in inaccessible villages, were hoarding Chinese-made weapons, digging mass graves, typing up lists of people to be killed, and practicing eye-gouging techniques. By mobilizing civilians to participate in the violence, the army ensured that the campaign would appear to have popular support. The army could appear as the savior of the nation, and the extermination of Communists could appear to be a patriotic duty.

With the legitimacy acquired from the anti-PKI campaign, the army was then in a position to move against Sukarno. As a White House analysis in mid-February 1966 observed, Nasution and Suharto, after "eliminating the PKI," were "using the political leverage they have gained against Sukarno."[92] Student demonstrations (partly paid for by the U.S. embassy) provided the appearance of mass public discontent with his presidency. Reduced to a figurehead—nothing more than a signature on documents, a photo on the wall, a uniformed mannequin at ceremonies—Sukarno was then discredited as a supporter of the PKI and the September 30th Movement.

The army, which was planning for the long-term stability of its rule, sought to ground its takeover of power in constitutional procedures. All of Suharto's moves were legitimated with signed presidential instructions: his promotion to commander of the army (October 2), his ratification as head of a new emergency military command called Kopkamtib (November 1), and his formation of the Extraordinary Military Court, Mahmillub (December 4). Suharto even used a presidential instruction as a justification for arresting fifteen members of Sukarno's cabinet and appointing his own ministers. Sukarno, of course, protested that his order of March 11, 1966, was not a transfer of authority, but words alone could not stop Suharto's forward march.[93] Suharto was scrupulous in stage-managing constitutional procedures, such as the session of Parliament that elected him acting president in March 1967 (a parliament stocked with handpicked delegates), so that the army's takeover of state power would not appear to be what it was: a coup d'état.

This clever combination of elements—mass terror against a demonized enemy, civilian complicity in the anti-PKI violence, anti-Sukarno student demonstrations, psychological warfare methods through the mass media, charades of legalistic procedures—reflected a mature understanding of how to take state power. In comparison with other coups in the world, the Indonesian army's was remarkably sophisticated. Suharto was able to stay in power for thirty-two years partly because he had carefully engineered the manner in which he seized power. The movement, elevated to the status of the nation's greatest betrayal, a manifestation of absolute evil, was a convenient pretext for him to begin the army's long-considered strategy for destroying the Communist Party, displacing President Sukarno, and founding an army dictatorship.

7

Assembling a New Narrative

> Now when the lord Chamberlen & these other lordes and knightes
> were thus behedded & ridde out of the way: then thought the protec-
> tour, yet while men mused what the mater ment, while the lordes of
> the realme wer about him out of their owne strenghtis, while no man
> wist what to thinke nor whome to trust, ere euer they should haue
> space to dispute & digest the mater & make parties: it wer best hastly
> to pursue his purpose, & put himself in possession of the crowne. . . .
> But now was al the study, by what meane thys matter being of it self so
> heinouse, might be first broken to the people, in such wise that it
> might be wel taken.
>
> Thomas More, The History of Richard III (1513)

The literary theorist Tzvetan Todorov has noted that works of detective
fiction combine two different narrative forms: the "story of the investigation" (how the detective comes to know what happened) and the
"story of the crime" (what actually happened).[1] The usual pattern of a
detective novel, as Slavoj Žižek notes, is to follow the detective in the
course of his investigation and then conclude with his reconstruction of
the crime. And so this book ends "not when we get the answer to
'Whodunit?' but when the detective is finally able to tell 'the real story'
in the form of a linear narration."[2] Each of my first four chapters focused on a particular piece of evidence or type of evidence. The chapters
progressed according to the logic of a detective's investigation rather
than the chronology of a storyteller's narration; each proposed a solution to one part of the puzzle after reviewing a limited range of evidence.
However, what follows in this chapter should not be considered "the
real story." My only claim here is that events *probably* happened in this

way. The limitations of the existing evidence make it impossible for the historian-detective to account for every anomaly, fill in every blank space, and identify the precise role of every person involved.

My investigation began with the Supardjo document, not because Supardjo was the most important figure in the movement but because his document is the richest and most reliable primary source available. Chapter 3 drew a number of narrow conclusions from his text. The most significant concerns the long-standing, unresolved question about the identity of the movement's leadership: Were the military officers (Untung, Latief, and company) or the PKI figures (Sjam, Pono, and the rest) leading the movement? The Supardjo document indicates that, of the five core leaders gathered at Halim air base, the main leader was Sjam. This invalidates the interpretations of Anderson and Crouch (described in chapter 2), which suggest that the military officers played the dominant role. With that conclusion in hand, chapter 4 turned to the question of Sjam's identity. That chapter, based largely on an oral interview with a former PKI leader who knew Sjam, drew another narrow conclusion: Sjam was a loyal subordinate of Aidit's. This invalidates Wertheim's hypothesis (also described in chapter 2) that Sjam was an army intelligence operative who was working to frame the PKI. Chapter 5 then focused on Aidit and presented evidence derived from statements by former PKI leaders, either in their courtroom defense statements or in oral interviews with me, that indicate that Aidit collaborated with Sjam to organize the movement as a preemptive strike against the right-wing army high command. This conclusion is not a confirmation of the interpretation of Suharto's regime as it points to the culpability of only Aidit and Sjam, not the entire party leadership.

The identity of the people participating in the movement and their reasons for joining were the focus of the investigation in chapters 3 to 5. The sixth chapter turned to a question pertaining to the army's response to the movement: Why did the army under Suharto's leadership exaggerate its significance and turn it into an epochal event? How did the movement become fetishized to the point that it could displace the mass killings of 1965–66 from Indonesia's social memory? Chapter 6, which draws largely upon declassified U.S. government documents, argued that the upper echelons of the army officer corps were waiting for an opportune moment to attack the PKI and displace President Sukarno. They were prepared to take state power. They turned the movement into their long-awaited pretext. Suharto probably knew beforehand that Latief and Untung were plotting some sort of action, but it is difficult to believe that he had a hand in designing the movement, much less masterminding it. The collapse of the movement can be explained without resorting to the hypothesis that Suharto himself, or other army officers, organized it so that it would fail. Suharto's quick and efficient response to the movement was a result of the army generals' preparation for such a contingency and his own foreknowledge of the movement.

The failing of most earlier investigations of the movement was their starting point: the assumption that there must have been a mastermind behind it. I am suggesting that there was no central "mind," whether one person or a tight cluster of people organized according to a clear division of labor and a hierarchy of powers. The movement was mysterious precisely because it lacked a single decision-making center. The one person closest to the core organizers at the time of the action, Supardjo, was mystified as to who the real leader of the movement was. As Supardjo noted, the central figure in the movement, to the extent it had one, was Sjam. Yet Sjam served as the connection between Aidit and the progressive officers. He was the center by virtue of being in the middle, not by virtue of being in control of all the forces of the movement. Aidit was in charge of the PKI personnel involved in the movement, whereas Untung, Latief, and Soejono were in charge of the military personnel. The two groups committed themselves to an action that, by default, turned their go-between into the leader. Sjam was a vanishing mediator: he brought the two groups together to stage the action but was in no position to command them once the action commenced. He was not like a military general who could lead a coup plot from start to finish in the way that Colonel Qasim did in Iraq in 1958 or Colonel Boumedienne did in Algeria in 1965. Once the action deviated from the plan and the participants had to improvise, they pulled in separate directions. The movement's disarray and indecision wound up paralyzing it in the face of Suharto's unexpected counterattack. The absence of a center confused the participants at the time and has continued to confuse historians trying to make sense of the movement.

It is now time to put together these separate findings and reconstruct the events of 1965. In this final chapter I present a brief chronological narrative that provides resolutions to many of the anomalies that I pointed out in the first two chapters. While doubling back to the starting point and closing the circle of this text, I will mark the gray areas of uncertainty that prevent this solution to the puzzle from being considered final.

The Triangular Configuration of Power

Imagine the following scene in Jakarta on May 23, 1965. The main stadium, which is not far from the presidential palace and the legislature, is overflowing with people. Tens of thousands are in the stands that circle the field, while thousands more stand in the field below. Outside in the parking lot and nearby streets more than 100,000 are milling about. It is a sea of humans. The occasion is the forty-fifth anniversary of the founding of the PKI. Judging by the size of the crowd, the party has never been healthier. To allow more people to gather around the stadium and prevent traffic jams, the party has discouraged people from driving there. Carrying small bundles of homemade food to eat for lunch, people have walked into the city from outlying villages. Red flags and big billboards with portraits of the party's heroes, such as Karl Marx and V. I. Lenin, line the city streets. A massive wood-framed, canvas-covered monument of the number *45* (painted red of course) stands on one of the main thoroughfares, dwarfing everything around it. Those marching to the stadium acquire the name "red ants" in popular discourse: countless in number, orderly, disciplined, and self-sacrificing but militant, and capable of stinging if disturbed. This army of red ants is, for President Sukarno, a glorious sight to behold. He graces the occasion and delivers a rousing speech from the podium, full of praise for the party's patriotism and spirit of resistance to the world's colonial and neocolonial powers. This May 23 celebration is almost a replay of the May Day celebration held in the same stadium only three weeks earlier. With two large-scale rallies in May the PKI has demonstrated in irrefutable fashion what many in Indonesia already suspect, that it is the largest and best-organized political party in the country. No other political party can hope to organize rallies of such scale. The *New York Times* reporter on the scene notes that the anniversary celebrations are "the most lavish ever staged by a political party here."[3] The party enjoys a rare combination of money, mass membership, and presidential favor.

This spectacular strength of the PKI was a central fact influencing the entire configuration of power in the country. A good portion of the army's officer corps looked upon the red ants with alarm. The party posed a threat to the army's own power in domestic politics and its profits from state-owned businesses, where army managers often faced workers organized by PKI-affiliated unions. Many officers were from privileged families. In their hometowns and villages their relatives

belonged to anti-Communist political parties. The highest commanders, Nasution and Yani, deeply antagonistic to the PKI, had been maneuvering to check its growth for years. They indoctrinated the officer
corps in anticommunism and ensured that the army functioned as a
protective patron of the civilian politicians who opposed the party. The
American scholar Daniel Lev noted that the non-Communist civilians
in the early 1960s "remained deeply afraid and resentful of the radical
threat which the PKI posed to their social, economic, and political
interests. They looked to the army, which frightened them less than the
PKI, for ultimate protection."[4] It was widely understood that the army
high command would never allow the Communist Party to take state
power, either by the ballot or the bullet. The two institutions were stale-
mated by 1965: The PKI dominated civilian politics, while the army
controlled more than 300,000 armed soldiers.

Between these two opposing forces stood President Sukarno. Ever
since Sukarno had dismissed the elected parliament in 1959 and concentrated power in the presidency, he had served as a buffer between the
two. Many anti-Communist military officers and politicians supported
his acquisition of dictatorial powers in the hope that he would block the
PKI. Sukarno himself had been no great fan of the party; he had supported the repression of it in 1948 (in the Madiun affair). The anti-
Communists were content with Sukarno's strong presidential system,
what he called Guided Democracy, because it was not based on elections. All observers believed at the time that the Communist Party
would win the plurality of votes if elections were held again. The party
had come out of the 1957 elections for provincial legislatures as the first-
ranked party in Central Java and the second-ranked in East and West
Java. For the anti-PKI elements Sukarno's handpicked national legislature was better than a democratically elected one controlled by the
PKI.[5] Anti-Communist elements sponsored the motion in the legislature in 1963 naming Sukarno "President for Life" to guarantee that a
Communist would never occupy the office.

The oddity of Indonesian politics under Guided Democracy from
1959 to 1965 was that Sukarno simultaneously served as a shield for the
anti-Communists and the Communists.[6] The PKI had been able to
grow during that period because it enjoyed Sukarno's protection. When
the army banned the party's provincial branches in 1960 and harassed
the leadership in Jakarta, Sukarno intervened. The army officers responsible for the repression, such as Colonel Sukendro, were punished.[7] The
president needed the Communist Party as a mass base for popularizing

his agenda, especially his battle against what he called the "old established forces" and the *nekolim* (neocolonial, colonial, and imperialist powers). The foreign policy of the president and the PKI were in harmony. Sukarno also needed the PKI as a bargaining chip in his dealings with the army. The party was his guarantee that the army would not be able to easily overthrow him.

By the time of the large rallies of red ants in Jakarta, the triangular balance of power—the PKI, the army, and Sukarno—was breaking apart. As the PKI grew ever larger, Sukarno was leaning more to the left than the right. The anti-Communists' attempt to woo him with a "Body for the Promotion of Sukarnoism" in December 1964 had failed. The putative beneficiary banned the body soon after it formed. He then banned the political party behind it (Murba) and reduced the powers of one of his deputy prime ministers, Chairul Saleh, who was affiliated with that party. The anti-Communist groups became more apprehensive in 1965, closed ranks behind the army, and believed that Sukarno had outlived his usefulness as a check on the Communist Party. The right side of the triangle began contemplating a political system beyond Sukarno, one without his mediating, all-pervasive presence.

Meanwhile, the PKI began chafing under the constraints imposed by this triangular configuration. It was boxed in. By 1965 it had grown to become the largest political party, yet it could not come to power by the ballot—there was no national election to contest. The parliamentary road to power had been blocked since 1959 and appeared as if it might never open again. Neither could the PKI come to power by the bullet. The party had no armed wing and had no intention of fighting a war against the government. All its members were civilians. The party had mass support but little to show for it. Despite their hard work in campaigning for Sukarno's policies, especially the Confrontation against Malaysia begun in 1963, Communist Party leaders had trouble acquiring positions in his cabinet. Only a few were appointed as ministers and none was given a position with real authority: Aidit and Njoto were ministers with only a coordinating or advisory role. To appease the anti-Communists, Sukarno handed all the key ministries that controlled large budgets or large numbers of state personnel (such as defense, home affairs, finance, industry, and plantations) to non-PKI figures. The PKI's influence at the uppermost level of the government was hardly commensurate with its influence in the society.

Lacking direct control of the levers of the state, the party used its mass following to push the state toward the left in 1965. Anti-American demonstrations led by the party and its affiliated organizations forced the closure of U.S. consulates outside Jakarta and the withdrawal of the Peace Corps. Actions by workers and party activists in Sumatra against U.S.-owned oil companies and plantations prompted the government to move toward nationalizing their assets. The PKI was mobilizing volunteers for the campaign against Malaysia and arranging to have them receive military training. Sukarno was toying with the PKI's idea of creating a "fifth force"—an armed militia outside the four existing military services (army, navy, air force, police)—and introducing "political commissars" into the army. Some party activists, feeling emboldened by their frequent demonstrations, which faced little resistance from the armed forces, imagined ever larger, more militant actions against "capitalist bureaucrats"—a term that included army officers because they owned so many businesses and occupied positions in the bureaucracy.

The momentum of events favored the PKI. Some non-Communist politicians, thinking the party's ascendance inevitable, softened their "Communist phobia" (Sukarno's term of opprobrium) and hoped that the party would remain willing to cooperate with other parties and downplay class struggle. The official line of the party was support for a "united front" of all anti-imperialist and patriotic forces. But some feared that the party remained a fundamentally sectarian organization bent on the seizure of state power.

Sukarno's buffering role was wearing thin. He remained, nevertheless, an unshakeable symbol of patriotism and national unity. He could not be easily removed by either side since both had spent the previous six years competing to be recognized as more Sukarnoist than the other. The PKI and anti-PKI forces had built up his popularity; neither could quickly reverse course. Sukarno retained an image of purity amid the economic crisis and administrative chaos. Those problems were not usually blamed on him but rather on elements of the government below him. Sukarno's direct and open manner of communication with the public and his long record as a leader in the anticolonial struggle made it difficult for anyone to doubt his sincerity. His cosmopolitan flair and courage to defy advanced, wealthy nations such as the United States made many citizens of this newly decolonized nation feel proud to be Indonesian. During the years of Guided Democracy, a cult was built around Sukarno to the point that he was capable of commanding widespread, unconditional loyalty.

The army high command, though frustrated by Sukarno's tilt toward the PKI in 1965, realized that he was too popular to be overthrown by a direct coup d'état. Such a coup would not guarantee a stable political order when many people, including junior officers of the army, were still passionate Sukarnoists. Experienced officers, such as Nasution, insisted that the army bide its time. By itself, overthrowing Sukarno was a simple task; establishing army rule for the long term was the more difficult proposition. The army high command did not want to win an easy battle only to lose the war. Under Yani's command the army spent 1965 resisting the PKI's demands for a civilian militia (the "fifth force") and the introduction of political commissars. Yani did not allow the army to be provoked into a rash action against Sukarno.

Regardless of Yani's strategy of patience, much of the Indonesian public believed by mid-1965 that the army would eventually stage a coup and put a violent halt to the ascendance of the PKI. The rumors were persistent, especially after Soebandrio, the number two man in the government (simultaneously first deputy prime minister and foreign minister), released in late May a copy of a confidential telegram that the British ambassador had sent to the Foreign Office in London. The telegram referred to "our local army friends" who were working on some unspecified, covert "enterprise."[8] The document may have been forged. Nonetheless, it was believed to be authentic at the time because it confirmed suspicions in Sukarnoist circles that the United States and the Britain were plotting a coup with the army's high command.

Aidit's Planning

The PKI leadership paid close attention to the rumors of a coup d'état. That the rumors came from every direction seemed to confirm their validity, even if people were only repeating vague ideas that they had heard second hand. The chairman of the party, D. N. Aidit, searched for more concrete, precise information in mid-1965. He ordered Sjam to have the Special Bureau canvass its contacts in the military and intelligence agencies to find out if the rumors were true. The Special Bureau, beginning under Karto's leadership from the early 1950s until about 1963–64, had developed a wide network of officers who were willing to provide intelligence information to the party. Sjam concluded from the information that he had gathered that the right-wing generals under Yani were indeed planning a coup.

Aidit had every reason to trust Sjam's information. It was easy to imagine that the army generals were plotting a coup. The question was how to respond. Aidit was weighing his options in mid-1965. He had two basic choices: wait for the coup to happen and then respond or take some sort of preemptive action to stop the coup from happening in the first place. Both had advantages and disadvantages. The disadvantage to the wait-and-see option was obvious. If Yani and his army commanders overthrew Sukarno, they would immediately turn their guns on the PKI. The repression could turn out to be extraordinarily bloody since the party had no arms with which to defend itself. Aidit was confident that the other services—the police, air force, and navy—would not support the army's coup and the anti-Communist repression. He was also confident that left-wing officers within the army itself would resist. Nonetheless, the prospect of such a postcoup battle for power must have worried him. Even if he thought the Communists and Sukarnoists stood a good chance of prevailing in the end, he must have realized that victory was not guaranteed and it might well be a Pyrrhic one. Before Yani's clique could be defeated, the battle for power could claim many victims. The only advantage of the wait-and-see approach was that it allowed the army to make the first move. The ambiguity of the rumors would end once the anti-Communist generals revealed their identities. By staging a coup these generals would prove to the entire country that they were enemies of the mainstream Sukarnoist and left-wing forces. The resistance to the coup would possess a certainty about the treasonous character of its antagonist.

On the other hand, the advantage of preemption was that it would save the nation from having to undergo such a civil war. For Aidit the progressive forces in the country—the Communist Party in alliance with Sukarno's supporters—represented the majority of the nation's citizens. They confronted an obstructionist minority faction in the army whose only strength lay in guns. If that faction could be halted before it fired a shot, the PKI's revolutionary subject, "the people," could avoid much suffering and chaos.

The disadvantage to preemption laid in its daunting logistical requirements: How could the party move against the top army commanders? The party could not simply call its masses out into the streets—a tactic at which it had become proficient by mid-1965—and expect to dislodge officers protected by guns and tanks. An administrative reshuffle did not hold out much promise, either. President Sukarno could not be relied upon to dismiss the commanders and appoint new ones because he would have no means to enforce his order if they refused to obey it. Besides, Sukarno did not deal with the army by delivering dictates. He had sidelined Nasution in 1962 only after delicate negotiations with the army generals and, even then, had allowed Nasution to choose his successor. The generals initially supported Sukarno's idea of Confrontation with Malaysia because they derived extra funding from the preparations for war. As soon as it threatened to turn into a real war with Malaysia and Britain in mid-1964, they sabotaged it. They complied with Sukarno's orders when they wished.

As Aidit was pondering the advantages and disadvantages of both options, he was speaking with Sjam about the possibilities of progressive officers' moving against the Council of Generals. Aidit asked Sjam around late August to sound out the pro-Sukarno and pro-PKI officers about whether they could foil the Council of Generals from within the army itself. When Sjam started discussions with the Special Bureau's contacts, he was a partner, sharing intelligence information and encouraging the officers to take some action against the right-wing generals. As no definite plan was emerging, Sjam decided to take the lead. He was impatient and convinced that something had to be done soon. He lobbied various officers to join an action against the Council of Generals.

Once Sjam was playing the role of coordinator, the only officers willing to commit themselves were those unquestioningly loyal to Sjam and the Communist Party. They assumed that they were being entrusted by the party with a great, historic task and were acting as part of an elaborate foolproof plan that the PKI leadership, in its wisdom, had developed. The give-and-take collaboration between the Special Bureau and the military officers in the years before 1965 helps to explain why certain officers were willing to involve themselves in the movement. They had grown to trust the Special Bureau. They could not have thought that following requests from Sjam was a serious breach of military discipline when they believed their top army commanders were conspiring against their supreme commander, President Sukarno. Sjam persuaded them to join by arguing that their action could not fail, given the vast reservoir of public support for Sukarno and the PKI. They simply needed a small action that would set off a chain reaction. The movement did not have to control Jakarta militarily. It only had to light a fuse, as Supardjo later put it. Subsequent actions would be carried out by others: Sukarno would support the action because he was worried about a coup, Major General Wirahadikusumah in Jakarta and Major General Adjie in Bandung would follow Sukarno's lead, Suharto would remain passive, the PKI masses would demonstrate in support of the action, and military officers around the country would clamor to join as they saw it growing. The movement would succeed once it had triggered many subsequent actions.

Throughout September 1965 Aidit, Sjam, and a group of military officers, particularly Untung, Latief, and Soejono, hammered out the precise plan for a preemptive move against the Council of Generals. It is not clear who among them was responsible for formulating which aspects of the plan. Since Aidit and the officers did not meet each other, one can assume that Sjam, as the go-between, was in a position to play the dominant role in the plan's formulation. The basic idea was to use the troops of the progressive officers to launch a surgical strike against those generals presumed to be plotting a coup. The core idea of the plan—what Supardjo called its centerpiece—was the night-time abductions of Nasution, Yani, and five other generals from their homes. A large gray area is on how the plotters determined that those seven generals were the members of the Council of Generals. It seems the plotters were largely relying on rumors and had no concrete evidence.

A point sometimes overlooked in histories of the September 30th Movement is that abduction was an honored tradition in Indonesian politics. Sukarno himself, with Hatta, had been abducted on August 16, 1945, by youths who insisted that they immediately declare national independence and lead a revolt against the Japanese troops. The two national leaders were driven to a small town on the outskirts of the city and held there against their will. They refused to submit to their abductors' demands. The youth had tried to organize a revolt in Jakarta. When that failed to materialize (not unlike the revolution councils of the September 30th Movement twenty years later), the youths brought the two national leaders back to the city unharmed.[9] Still, those youths were later considered heroes for their militant patriotism. One of them, Chairul Saleh, became Sukarno's third deputy prime minister. As Cribb and Brown note, "During the war of independence [1945–49], the kidnapping of conservative political figures in order to jolt them into a more radical stand had often occurred and the kidnapped figures were normally released unharmed, their self-confidence shaken, their prestige undermined and their ability to act decisively therefore reduced."[10] The movement was planning a time-honored tactic for forcing policy and personnel changes among the top leaders.

The other feature of the plan—the establishment of revolution councils throughout the country under the leadership of progressive officers—was meant to ensure the successful implementation of

whatever changes the movement demanded. These councils would prevent the right-wing officers from making a comeback and would pressure Sukarno into further purges of the army leadership. The councils
would give the appearance of mass support for the action. Initially, the
plotters did not intend for these councils to usurp Sukarno's cabinet or
any other government institution. The sole point was to provide popular support for the action against the right-wing generals and to pressure the existing government bodies to follow Sukarno's policies. Each
revolution council was to be led by a junior officer who would rally a
united front of patriotic forces in his district. This was in accordance
with Aidit's advice to the Algerian Communists in June 1965: the coup of
Colonel Boumedienne in their country should be made into a "people's
movement." Aidit's principle was that a military action should be accompanied by a wider demonstration of public support.

The idea for the revolution councils was more attributable to Aidit
and Sjam than the military officers. Untung and his fellow officers left
political matters up to the party while they focused on the narrow goal
of plotting the abductions. Aidit and Sjam hoped to use the councils
for pushing for broader changes in the composition of Sukarno's cabinet once the army commanders were purged. The Communist Party
wanted an improved Nasakom cabinet, which was another way of saying it wanted more ministries in the hands of the party and more anti-
Communist ministers dismissed.

Having decided by late August to support a preemptive strategy involving military officers, Aidit became more secretive. He did not convene a Politburo meeting in September, though he had usually con-
vened them three to four times a month. He did not inform all the party
leaders about the plan. If he thought certain leaders were needed for the
action, he briefed them and ordered them to carry out a specific task.
Njono, as the head of the Jakarta branch, and Sukatno, as head of the
party's youth wing (Pemuda Rakjat), were assigned the task of mobilizing a civilian militia that could boost the numbers of the movement's
troops. Even these leaders who became directly involved in the action
did not have a good sense about the entire plan. Party leaders believed
that a group of progressive officers would carry out a preemptive action,
while the party provided political support and some supplemental militiamen. That was what Aidit told a group of Politburo and Central
Committee members in late August, and that was the information circulating around party headquarters. Party members were told to wait
for an upcoming action originating from the military.

The movement's plotters wanted the action to be seen as a purely military action so that it could gain wide public acceptance. Even anti-Communist organizations would have difficulty opposing a patriotic officer like Untung, a hero in the campaign to take West Papua and a commander in the palace guard. The action would appear to be above party politics, motivated purely by patriotism. In the wake of the action, the party would leverage itself into a larger number of cabinet posts and would gradually displace its enemies from both the military and the civil administration.

While Aidit, Sjam, Untung, and the others were plotting what would be named the September 30th Movement, the army high command was biding its time. Nasution, Yani, and their colleagues were not actually planning to stage a coup d'état against Sukarno. They were waiting for the Communist Party to move first and provide them with some sort of pretext for cracking down on the party. The PKI may have interpreted their inactivity in early and mid-1965 as a sign of weakness, as PKI-led demonstrations forced a crisis in relations with the generals' main backer, the U.S. government. It is also possible that the army generals, in covert fashion, helped spread rumors about the Council of Generals. The army generals wanted to provoke the PKI into a rash action. To take advantage of their strength—raw military power—the generals needed a pretext. A direct attack on Sukarno and the PKI without a legitimate excuse would not result in a secure army-dominated polity.

It is still unclear whether any intelligence agents under the right-wing generals knew that Aidit and Sjam were plotting an action. Major General Parman, the army's chief of intelligence, had spies inside the party. But he must not have known about Sjam and the Special Bureau's organizing of the action. If he had known, he would have carefully monitored Sjam and been able to prevent his own kidnapping and slaying on October 1, 1965. The right-wing generals might have received some clues, but those clues were drowned out by a higher level of intelligence noise. Suharto's intelligence agents over at Kostrad—Yoga Sugama and Ali Moertopo, both from the Central Java Diponegoro division—might have had more definite information about the personnel of the Special Bureau and their plotting. Since Suharto knew both Untung and Latief, one can assume that Sugama and Moertopo knew them or knew about them. Suharto's group at Kostrad, the army reserves, may have also known about Sjam and the Special Bureau. The activities of Suharto, Yoga, and Moertopo in 1965 represent the largest gray zone remaining in our understanding of the movement.

The Plan Goes Awry

One reason that Parman remained in the dark about the plot may have been because many plotters themselves remained in the dark. In the effort to keep the plot secret, Aidit, Sjam, and the military officers did not reveal enough information to their coconspirators to allow them to participate effectively. Many blunders were committed because of the participants' lack of knowledge about their assignments. Since the organizers' plans were closely guarded secrets, their decisions on many logistical issues, even the starting date of the action, were revealed to their followers only at the last minute.

The plan went through a number of revisions. Some officers pulled out because they did not trust Sjam's leadership. As Supardjo noticed when he spoke with Sjam only days before the action, the plan "didn't add up." By the end of September the planners had not mobilized enough troops to face a possible counterattack. Significantly, they had no tanks. Without sufficient force behind it, the plan depended on Sukarno's endorsement of the abductions. His approval was expected to freeze the officers who could mobilize troops for a counterattack. The key officers commanding troops in or near the capital—Major General Wirahadikusumah of the Jakarta Kodam (the Jakarta garrison) and Major General Adjie of the West Java Kodam—were known as staunch Sukarnoists who would follow the president's lead. The plotters went ahead with the action in the expectation that no military force would be left to attack them.

Supardjo had joined the movement because he trusted Sjam and had become convinced that the right-wing generals would stage a coup. He had no previous connection with the other officers in the movement. Relying on the wisdom of the party that Sjam represented, Supardjo assumed that the plan was well designed, even if what he learned of it seemed strange. Although he was the highest-ranking officer in the movement, he was not the commander because he had not been a part of the planning over the previous weeks. Untung was chosen as the titular commander because his position as commander in the palace guard would give the action a greater measure of credibility. The action would appear to be a logical outgrowth of Untung's duty to protect Sukarno. Also, Sjam may have preferred Untung as the head because he was more pliable. Supardjo was a skilled military tactician with a mind of his own, whereas Untung was a soldier who had advanced through the ranks because of his bravery, not his intelligence.

As his fellow plotters pointed out the weaknesses in the plan, Sjam became ever more insistent. By holding meetings and inviting various officers to join (some of whom later withdrew), the conspirators had already put themselves at risk. Army intelligence agents would eventually uncover their plot. If they called off the action, they had no guarantee that they would not be arrested later. Sjam insisted they had to proceed. In late September, as the weaknesses of the final plan became more apparent, Sjam angrily dismissed all doubters as cowards. He was confident because he saw the PKI and the Sukarnoist forces as being too powerful to lose. Even if the action faltered, the Communist Party, with all its masses and political influence, would be able to step in and prevent total defeat.

Sjam had been serving Aidit for nearly fifteen years. He had been devoted to Aidit, taking orders from him, arranging for his personal security, digging for secret information that would be useful to him. Aidit had been Sjam's pole star. Sjam did not have much connection with anyone else in the PKI. He did not keep up with the party's literature and theoretical debates. Having promised Aidit that the plan for preempting the Council of Generals would succeed, he wanted to continue with the plan regardless of its weaknesses. He was not about to disappoint his boss. He had convinced himself and Aidit that the progressive officers could stop the right-wing generals who had been plotting a coup. He would lose Aidit's trust if he suddenly reported that the action could not be carried out. Aidit had been basing his political strategy throughout September on the expectation that this action would take place. If he had known beforehand that the action was too risky or not feasible, Aidit could have prepared a different strategy for dealing with the right-wing generals. If the action was called off at the last moment, the party would be unprepared to confront the anticipated coup d'état by the Council of Generals. Aidit might have had some inkling that the preparations for the action were deficient, but Sjam reassured him, just like he did the military officers involved, saying that everything would work out just fine. Aidit went ahead with the plan because the military officers were going ahead with the plan. The military officers went ahead because they thought Aidit wanted it to proceed.

The preparations were chaotic. Ultimately, the action had to be postponed a day—a delay that accounts for an October 1 event's being called the September 30th Movement. Untung, the titular commander, had not prepared himself. He had not slept well for days because he had continued with his normal duties in the palace guard. He began the action exhausted. The one-day postponement introduced even greater confusion into an already confused plan.

When the plan was implemented, all its flaws were revealed. Few aspects of the movement went according to plan. When the troops from various units assembled at Lubang Buaya at night, there was no clear chain of command to organize the kidnapping teams. The two most important teams—those for Nasution and Yani—wound up being led by inexperienced low-ranking soldiers. None of the teams had rehearsed the abduction. They were given their assignment at the last moment and then had to quickly improvise their strategy for approaching and entering the houses of the generals. The result was disastrous. Of the seven teams, only three succeeded in apprehending the generals and bringing them back alive. Nasution escaped. Yani and two other generals were shot when they resisted. The teams had not been trained beforehand to ensure that they would be able to capture the generals alive. They were simply ordered, as one sergeant of the palace guard recalled, "Grab them. And make sure not one of them gets away" *(Tangkap. Jangan sampai ada yang lolos).*[11]

When the movement's leaders discovered that one general had gotten away and that three of the six captured generals were dead or dying, they decided to abort the plan for presenting the generals to Sukarno. They could not take three bloodied corpses to the presidential palace. That was not in accordance with the time-honored custom of abducting one's seniors and then releasing them later unharmed. Thus they had to abandon one crucial part of the plan. The movement's leaders decided to have all their captives executed and the corpses concealed.

The plan to meet the president at the palace also failed. The original plan was to obtain a statement of support from Sukarno and immediately broadcast it over the radio station in the morning. Before army officers in and around the capital could even think about countering the movement, they would be presented with a fait accompli. The movement expected Sukarno to issue at least a neutral statement urging calm while he handled the matter. But the movement was unable to get a statement from Sukarno. In their confusion and exhaustion Untung and his soldiers from the palace guard did not notice that Sukarno had spent the night at the house of one of his wives. So the movement continued with the plan to station troops outside the palace and to send a delegation to the palace to meet him in the morning. Sukarno avoided returning to the palace precisely because of the unknown troops outside it. While his bodyguards shuttled him around to various hideouts, the movement's delegation wasted precious time sitting around the empty palace waiting for him.

That one member of the delegation, Supardjo, was finally able to meet with the president at around 10 A.M. was largely fortuitous. Supardjo was not part of the original plan. Neither was Heru Atmodjo, the air force officer who been tasked by Omar Dani to keep track of Supardjo. Yet it was these three officers (Supardjo, Atmodjo, and Dani) who managed to put the movement in contact with Sukarno. While Supardjo sat just inside the palace gates, idling away three precious hours that morning, Atmodjo contacted his superior officer, Dani, who had happened to learn of Sukarno's whereabouts. By chance, Sukarno decided to shift to Halim air base for safety. Dani and Atmodjo arranged a helicopter to fetch Supardjo from the palace and bring him to Halim so that he could meet the president. None of these moves was in the original plan. It was by chance that Supardjo was able to meet with Sukarno as early as he did. If not for Dani and Atmodjo, Supardjo might never have contacted Sukarno that day.

Because the centerpiece of the movement, the abductions, had failed, all the subsequent steps failed in quick succession. Sukarno could not support a group of junior officers who had killed off his army commanders. He ordered Supardjo to call off the movement and ensure that no more bloodshed occurred. Supardjo was willing to comply with Sukarno's order, as were the military officers in the movement's leadership, Latief, Untung, and Soejono. They were ready to cancel their badly botched operation.

Sjam and Aidit, however, wanted to continue with the movement. They wanted to issue a call over the radio for officers around the country to form revolution councils. Aidit had instructed party leaders to listen to the radio. Sjam had instructed personnel in the Special Bureau to spread the word among contacts in the military to wait for instructions over the radio. Both Aidit and Sjam thought that the next phase of the movement—the revolution councils—could succeed even if the first phase had failed. They imagined that revolutionary masses (both military and civilian) were sitting by their radios, ready to form these councils once they heard the signal. The action could continue without Sukarno's endorsement.

The delay in meeting Sukarno and the disagreement between Sjam and the military officers caused the movement's long silence over the radio waves. The radio station had been taken early in the morning and a statement read out a little after 7 A.M. The original plan must have been to quickly read out a succession of other announcements, including a statement from the president. But no further announcements were read out that morning. The movement was silent during the crucial early moments of the action. Untung and the other military officers were ready to quit: the generals had been killed and Sukarno had told them to call it off. Sjam tried but failed to convince these officers to continue with the movement.

I presume that Sjam, faced with the officers' reluctance to persist, drove to Aidit's hideout in Halim and redrafted the announcement about the revolution councils. The two of them came up with a new plan. Sukarno could not be counted upon to support a continuation of the movement so he would have to be bypassed. Instead of being pressure groups on Sukarno, the councils would become the nucleus of a new government. The announcement about the councils broadcast in the early afternoon, Decree no. 1, was devoid of details because it had been drafted so hurriedly. Aidit and Sjam improvised. They had Iskandar Subekti, the Politburo's secretary, type up the new announcement in Aidit's hideout. They included as "deputy commanders" the names of four military officers who they expected would be willing to support the movement. This listing of the commander (Untung) and his deputy commanders (Supardjo and company) bore no relation to the actual hierarchy within the movement; it had purely symbolic importance.

Since Sukarno had refused to endorse the movement, Aidit and Sjam would have to bypass him. The revolution councils meant to buttress Sukarno's rule were recast as instruments to replace his rule. Aidit and Sjam inserted new phrases into the text of the announcement about the councils (Decree no. 1): they "decommissioned" Sukarno's existing cabinet and gave "all authority" to the national Indonesian Revolution Council. Even though such a pronouncement contradicted the very raison d'être of the movement (the safeguarding of Sukarno and the ideals of his rule), Aidit and Sjam needed it as a last ditch effort to give new meaning to a faltering action.

The exhausted Untung reluctantly went along with Aidit and Sjam's revisions and signed at least two of the three documents they drafted (Decisions nos. 1 and 2). The former named the members of the Indonesian Revolution Council and the latter abolished ranks above lieutenant colonel. Untung was the only one to sign those two documents. Once typed up and signed, the documents were carried by courier to the radio station to be read over the air in the early afternoon.

Aidit and Sjam, seeing the action in Jakarta stumbling, hoped that progressive officers and civilians outside the capital city would initiate councils in their districts and frustrate any attempted counterattack by the army generals. It may have been a realistic hope, given that the movement did spread to Central Java. Aidit and Sjam gambled that the provinces would erupt. They relied on the power of the radio. But the radio announcements were not enough to get the party's followers demonstrating in the streets and forming Revolution Councils with military officers. Even for those party faithful who were listening to the radio and ready for action, the announcements did not clearly explain what they should do and why. Many cadre kept waiting for further instructions before acting. Aidit and Sjam could not issue further instructions about the councils that afternoon because they were preoccupied with the breakdown of the movement and the threat from Suharto.

That morning Sukarno had viewed the movement as a misguided but well-intentioned attempt by loyal troops to strengthen his hand vis-à-vis the obstreperous army high command. Although he did not issue a statement supporting the movement, he did not issue one denouncing it. Sukarno treated the movement as a new political force that had to be accommodated in his state but not one to which he would subordinate himself. He must have thought it represented many army officers because he asked the movement to recommend the names of generals who could replace Yani. If he had viewed the movement's leaders as hostile to his rule or bent on a coup, he certainly would not have requested their assistance in helping him choose a new army commander. When the radio announcement about the decommissioning of his cabinet aired in the early afternoon, he was angry but he must have seen that the movement's words were not in accordance with its actions; Supardjo remained deferential and did not attempt to force Sukarno to obey his wishes.

By late afternoon it was apparent to the movement's leaders that poor planning had resulted in the nonparticipation of the party's own personnel. The PKI youths readied by Njono and Sukatno in Jakarta to serve as militiamen did not come out into the streets. Of the six sectors readied, only one was deployed. The others remained on standby. The women instructed to open up communal kitchens did not show up. The lack of food for the troops stationed in Merdeka Square contributed to their willingness to surrender at Kostrad headquarters. Suharto launched his counterattack in the evening when the movement, by its own ineptitude, was already collapsing.

Suharto's Counterattack

Suharto was able to act on October 1 with "uncanny efficiency" (as Wertheim put it) because he already had some idea that the movement would occur and that he would not be targeted. He knew from the start that this was an action that could be blamed on the Communist Party. The question Suharto had to face in the morning was whether he could defeat it and launch the army's plan for attacking the PKI and overthrowing Sukarno. Suharto was not immediately certain how many troops and officers were involved. During the morning the Kostrad officers surveyed the movement's military strength and checked the loyalty of the key officers in the capital, especially that of Major General Wirahadikusumah. If the movement had been stronger and had received at least a qualified endorsement from the president in the morning, Suharto might have remained passive. He had only one battalion in Jakarta directly under his command (Battalion 328 from West Java) that he could use for an immediate counterattack. Noticing the movement's vulnerabilities, he realized he had sufficient time to mobilize other troops (such as the Special Forces, RPKAD, from their base south of the city) and gain sufficient backing from his fellow officers for an attack.

Once Suharto committed himself that morning to defeating the movement, he resolved to disregard Sukarno's orders, whatever they might be. The long-anticipated showdown with the PKI had come. Suharto was not going to allow the president to protect the participants in the movement or the party's members. Suharto's refusal to allow Pranoto and Wirahadikusumah to go to Halim and his insistence on Sukarno's departure from Halim indicate that Suharto was determined to ignore the president's will. A general without a preconceived plan would have deferred to Sukarno. Suharto responded to the movement on his own, without so much as consulting his commander-in-chief. From the morning of October 1 Suharto knew that the movement had the potential to serve as the longed-for pretext for bringing the army to power. The rapidity by which the army blamed the PKI, organized anti-Communist civilian groups, and orchestrated a propaganda campaign suggests preparation. The generals had done some contingency planning. The postmovement behavior of the army cannot be explained as a series of purely improvised responses.

The military officers in the movement who were meeting at Halim (Untung, Latief, Soejono) were ready to call off the operation before they knew about Suharto's counterattack. Sukarno had instructed them to quit late that morning. Unlike Aidit and Sjam, they were willing to abide by the president's instructions. Sometime in the late morning Untung signed the documents calling for the establishment of the Indonesian Revolution Council, but he considered his own participation in the movement finished. Even when he, Latief, and Soejono discovered that

Suharto was planning a counterattack, they did not organize their forces for self-defense. Supardjo insisted that they would have to fight Suharto and Nasution. He tried to regroup the movement troops that had been in Merdeka Square and form an alliance with Omar Dani's air force. But Supardjo found the core leaders unresponsive, confused, and tired. The officers were already angry with Sjam for betraying their original intentions with his radio announcement decommissioning Sukarno's cabinet. They had not bargained for a coup. In the midst of the emergency Latief talked at length about irrelevant matters. Untung and Latief had expected their old friend Suharto to either remain neutral or come out in support of them. When informed of his actions in the afternoon, they thought that Suharto might have some trick up his sleeve, that he might not actually attack the movement.

Once Suharto's troops retook the central square and the radio station around 6 P.M. and read out an announcement about an hour later denouncing the movement as counterrevolutionary, the five core leaders of the movement realized that they had been defeated in Jakarta. Dispirited and bewildered by all the deviations from the original plan, they were unable to decide upon a strategy for dealing with Suharto. They did not push the air force officers at Halim to bomb Kostrad on the night of October 1. They did not use Battalion 454, which was standing around a road just south of Halim, to defend themselves against the approaching Special Forces troops on the morning of October 2. The battalion commander, acting on his own initiative, nearly engaged the Special Forces troops in battle but retreated in response to the pleas of air force officers who did not want combat around the air base. Once Battalion 454 dispersed that morning, the movement had no sizable body of troops left.

Its only hope lay in the provinces. Central Java was where the PKI was the strongest and where the Special Bureau had the widest network of contacts in the military. It was, for this reason, the one province where the movement manifested itself. Aidit and Sjam, having already committed themselves to a continuation of the movement, decided that Aidit should fly out to Central Java and lead the resistance from there. At night they asked Supardjo, who was on good terms with Omar Dani, to ask him for assistance in flying Aidit out. Dani arranged for a plane for Aidit and, for good measure, one for himself. Although Dani had not been responsible for the movement, his statement of support for it, drafted before the announcements dismissing Sukarno's cabinet, had been aired on the radio. He fled to protect himself.

Once Aidit arrived in Yogyakarta, he did not know where to go or whom to meet. This move was not in the original plan. He wound up being unable to organize a movement of resistance. The military side of the movement quickly collapsed in Central Java too, and, as a result, the civilian side hesitated to come out in favor of it. The province was largely quiet from October 3 to the arrival of Special Forces troops in the provincial capital of Semarang on October 18. Aidit remained underground, waiting for Sukarno to bring the army into line and stop the repression of the PKI. Aidit did not organize or order resistance to the army. An all-out war between the PKI and the army would not only have led to the deaths of many party supporters, it would have made it difficult for Sukarno to reassert his authority over Suharto. The collapse of the movement forced Aidit into this about-face. On the afternoon of October 1 he thought the movement would spread and become power-ful enough to reshape the entire state. He assented to the radio an-nouncement decommissioning Sukarno's cabinet. But once the move-ment collapsed, he reverted to the party's traditional reliance on Sukarno to protect the party.

The disappearance of Aidit from Jakarta, the sudden about-face in strategy, and the aggressiveness of Suharto's army thoroughly confused the party leaders in Jakarta. The strength of the party had been based on its rigid hierarchy, with orders and information coming down from the top. Even the core members of the Politburo (such as Lukman, Njoto, and Sudisman) were perplexed by an action that, contrary to their ex-pectations, announced the decommissioning of Sukarno's cabinet and then quickly collapsed. With the PKI off guard and passive, Suharto's army had little trouble attacking it. If the PKI had decided to resist, it could have seriously hindered Suharto's troops. Railway workers could have sabotaged the trains carrying the troops to Central Java; unionized mechanics in the military's motor pools could have sabotaged the jeeps, trucks, and tanks; peasants could have dug up the roads to block troop movement; sympathetic officers and soldiers in the military could have attacked Suharto loyalists; youths of Pemuda Rakjat could have fought the anti-Communist youths mobilized by the army. Yet the party did not resist the army's offensive. Many people affiliated with the Com-munist Party or left-wing organizations willingly reported to army in-stallations and police stations when summoned in October–November 1965, believing that they would be released after a brief period of ques-tioning. Having done nothing to support the movement, they did not expect to be detained indefinitely without charge and accused of playing a role in some grand scheme to commit mass murder.[12] The commotion was thought to be a storm that would pass soon and leave Sukarno's authority intact.

The Aftermath

One could regard the army-orchestrated politicide of the PKI as the result of an amoral contest for state power: if the movement had succeeded and the PKI had won, the army and the non-Communist civilians siding with the army would have suffered similarly. Both sides could be viewed as boxers. The language used at the time suggests the analogy: "either hit or be hit" and "final blow." The PKI's newspaper depicted the movement as a fist punching the face of the Council of Generals. Because one does not feel sorry for a knocked-out boxer, one should not, so it would seem, feel sorry for the members of the PKI who were arrested and slaughtered by the army. This perspective has been common within Indonesia among the beneficiaries of the Suharto regime. The victims were not really victims at all; they were losers who would have committed similar or even worse violence against their opponents if they had had the chance.

Such a perspective misinterprets the anti-Communist politicide. The movement was organized as a putsch against the army high command. If Suharto's army had replied to the movement in kind, it would have captured the twelve members of the PKI's Politburo, as well as those soldiers and civilians who participated in the movement. That the army went after every member of the Communist Party and every member of every organization that had an affiliation with the PKI indicates that the army's response was not determined by the requirements of suppressing the movement. Thus we are dealing with a boxer who not only knocks out his opponent in the ring but goes on to attack all of that boxer's fans in the stadium, then hunts down and attacks his opponent's fans throughout the country, even those living far away who had not even heard about the match.

For Suharto the identity of the movement's real organizers was immaterial. He and his clique of army officers began the assault on the PKI within four days, even before they had evidence that the PKI had led the movement. That they never found evidence that anyone but Aidit and a handful of his trusted comrades were in some way complicit (as Sudisman and Sjam testified in 1967) was not a problem for Suharto and his officers. The army began fabricating evidence against the PKI in early October 1965. The movement was a convenient pretext for implementing a preexisting plan for the army to seize state power. The army generals had already determined that their power grab should target the PKI as the enemy while maintaining the pretense that they were protecting President Sukarno.

The tragedy of modern Indonesian history lies not just in the army-organized mass killings of 1965–66 but also in the rise to power of the killers, of people who viewed massacres and psychological warfare operations as legitimate and normal modes of governance. A regime that legitimated itself by pointing to a mass grave at Lubang Buaya and vowing "never again" left countless mass graves from one end of the country to the other, from Aceh on the western edge to Papua on the eastern edge. The occupation of East Timor from 1975 to 1999 left tens, if not hundreds, of thousands dead, many buried in unmarked graves. Each mass grave in the archipelago marks an arbitrary, unavowed, secretive exercise of state power and mocks the Suharto-era social imaginary in which only civilians commit atrocities and only the military holds the country together. The fetishization of a relatively minor event (the movement) and the erasure of a world-historical event (the mass killings of 1965–66) have blocked empathy for the victims, such as the relatives of those men and women who disappeared. While a monument stands next to the well in which the movement's troops dumped the bodies of seven army officers on October 1, 1965, no monument marks any of the mass graves that hold the hundreds of thousands of people killed in the name of suppressing the movement. As for the number of dead, their names, the location of the mass graves, the manner in which they were massacred, and the identity of the perpetrators, little is known in any detail or with any certainty. Beyond Lubang Buaya lie many larger, more complex mysteries.

Appendix 1

Some Factors That Influenced the Defeat of "the September 30th Movement" as Viewed from a Military Perspective (1966)

BRIGADIER GENERAL SUPARDJO

A Note on the Translation

The nonstandard grammar of Supardjo's prose and its mixing of terms from different languages makes this a difficult document to translate. The translation that follows aims to adhere as closely as possible to the original phrasing.

This translation is based on the document included in the records of the military court that tried Supardjo in 1967. Military officers obtained a copy of the original document either when they captured Supardjo in January 1967 or when they intercepted documents being smuggled into prisons by the friends and families of political prisoners. A staff member of the military court typed a copy of the original document. It is that copy that is contained in the court's records. I have not been able to find the original document. One person who read the original document (while in prison), Heru Atmodjo, confirms that the military court's copy, which I showed him, is identical to the original. Suparjdo's son, Sugiarto, on reading the military court's copy, recognized his father's style of writing and the arguments that his father communicated orally to his family while in prison.

The military court's typist might have introduced some typographical errors. The typist probably added the parenthetical Indonesian translations of Dutch terms. The parenthetical remarks that are more substantive and are longer than one or two words appear to have been Supardjo's. All comments in brackets are mine.

Words from five different languages appear in the text. To differentiate them, I use the following abbreviations:

[E]   English
[D]   Dutch
[J]   Javanese
[I]   Indonesian
[S]   Sundanese

Defeat contains the elements of victory.

> Motto: "When one falls, two rise."

Comrades of the leadership, I was with the "September 30th Movement" for one day before the event, "when the event was occurring," and "one day after the event occurred."[1] Compared to the length of time of all the preparations, the time of my involvement was very brief. Although what I know is only my experience during those three days, it was an experience of very decisive moments—moments when the guns began speaking and military matters determined the defeat or victory of subsequent actions. With this I am conveying some opinions, viewed from a military perspective, about the errors that were made, in order to complete materials for a comprehensive analysis by the leadership in the framework of surveying the incident of the September 30th Movement.[2]

The method of analysis: I will first present the facts of the event as I saw and experienced them, and then I will convey my opinion on those facts.

Facts about the First Night before the Action Began

1. When I met the comrades of the military leadership group on the night before the action began, they were worn out from lack of sleep. For example, Comrade Untung had attended the meetings of Bung Karno at Senayan for three straight days as part of his security duties.[3]
2. When the reports arrived about the individual troops in the regions, Bandung, for instance, it turned out they were forced to report they were ready, when in fact they were not.
3. Because there was no clear explanation of how the action would be carried out, there was a lack of agreement about the movement itself among the officer comrades in the army. It

reached the point where one officer comrade who had been kept on the leadership team clearly stated, at that decisive moment, that he was resigning.[4]

4. If the movement is reexamined, it is found that, actually, the only unit that was fully with us was just one company from the palace guard. Doubts had already emerged at that time, but they were suppressed with the slogan "Whatever happens, we can't turn back."

5. With the resignation of one comrade officer, one could sense a prejudice from the leadership team toward the other comrades of that group. Suggestions and questions were responded to by pointing out the irresolution of the questioner. For instance, if someone asked about the strength of the opponent, he was answered in a dismissive tone: "Yeah, brother, if you want a revolution, a lot of people want to stay back, but once you've already won, everybody wants to join." And another expression: "We're revolutionary while we're young, what's the point if we're already old?"[5]

6. The meeting at L.B. [Lubang Buaya] for the preparations appeared to have an extremely packed agenda. It was already late into the night, and the codes related to the execution of the action had not yet been determined. The decision about which platoons would be assigned to which targets was not done carefully. For example, it so happened that the main target was first assigned to a platoon of youths who had only just learned how to hold a gun, then it was reassigned to an army platoon, but then that platoon was not one that was mentally prepared beforehand for special assignments.[6]

Facts about the Day of Implementation

7. The first news that arrived was that General Nasution had been caught but had then escaped. The leadership team appeared rather confused and did not give any further orders.

8. The next news was that General Nasution had joined General Suharto and General Umar [Wirahadikusumah] at Kostrad. Even after receiving this news, the operations leadership did not reach any conclusion at all.

9. The news also came in that the troops of the Central Java battalion and the East Java battalion didn't receive any food,

then the news that followed was that the East Java battalion asked for food from Kostrad. The troops guarding the radio station RRI abandoned it without having received any instruction to do so.

10. According to the plan, Jakarta was divided into three sectors: South, Central, and North. But when these sectors were contacted, none of them was at its station.

11. The atmosphere of the city was quiet and the opponent was in a state of panic for twelve hours.

12. 7:00 P.M. on the second night [October 1], General Nasution-Harto and Umar formed a command. They showed signs of launching an offensive the next day.

13. On hearing this news, Vice Marshal Omar Dani suggested to Comrade Untung that the forces of AURI [air force] and "the September 30th Movement" be merged to confront the offensive from Nato (Nasution-Harto) and company.[7] But this did not receive a clear, concrete response. It turned out that the leadership team of the September 30th Movement no longer had a fighting spirit.[8]

14. Then there emerged a third problem. Yes, this was with the appearance of Bung Karno at the Halim Airfield. Bung Karno then took the following actions:

    a. Stopped the movements of both sides (with the explanation that if a civil war broke out, the neocolonial powers would benefit).

    b. Summoned the cabinet and armed services' ministers.[9] Nasution-Harto and Umar refused to comply with this call. General Pranoto was forbidden by Nasution to fulfill Bung Karno's summons.[10]

    c. Decided upon a caretaker for the leadership of the army.

The Second Day [October 2]

15. The comrades of the "September 30th Movement" leadership gathered at L.B. [Lubang Buaya]. RPKAD [Special Forces] began to attack and enter. The situation became *"wanordelik"* [D, *wanordelijk*] (*katjau* [I]) [chaotic]. The youth troops were not yet accustomed to facing real combat. At that crucial moment I proposed that I take control of the command of the

troops, and later, if the situation could be overcome, I would return it. There was no concrete response.

16. Then there was a meeting at which it was decided to stop the resistance and disperse the various units; they were to return to their homes and await further developments. The battalions from Central Java and East Java were to be urged to return to their home bases.

17. That day as well, an order was issued by Bung Karno for all the various troops to stay put and await negotiations. But the Nato side [Nasution-Harto] ignored this order and used the opportunity to continue attacking our troops and even the PKI.

Such are the facts that I myself witnessed and from these facts each person can draw his own lessons and come to different conclusions. Be that as it may, the conclusions that I have come to are as follows:

1. The exhaustion of the comrades of the leadership team that led the military side of the action had a great influence on the enthusiasm for the operation; this exhaustion influenced the command activities at the crucial moments when quick and clear decisions were needed from them.

2. When the information was received from the regions, it turned out that the regions were not ready. This was proven later when there were still many couriers who had not arrived at their appointed destinations by the time the event occurred (the courier sent to Palembang had only just reached Tanjung Karang). Bandung was [not] fully ready but in order to avoid facing harsh questioning simply responded, "It's all taken care of."

3. It turned out that the plan for the operation wasn't clear. It was too superficial. The centerpiece of the whole plan was the simple kidnapping of the seven generals. What would happen after that, if successful, wasn't clear. And what would be the plan if there was a counteroffensive, for instance, from Bandung? This question was dismissed by saying, "Enough, don't think about backing off!" According to the requirements of military operations, we are always thinking about retreat when we are victorious and moving forward, and we are thinking about advancing and attacking when we're defeated

and retreating. What I mean by this is that thinking about retreating in the course of attacking is not shameful but is standard procedure for every attack or campaign. Retreat does not mean defeat—it is a certain maneuver in an attack that can be reversed so that one can reattack and gain victory. This state of affairs caused some military comrades to withdraw from the action, but these doubters could have been persuaded if there was a clear and convincing plan for their path to victory.

4. If we review the units we could rely upon, we find it was only one company from Cakrabirawa. It was estimated that one battalion from Central Java and one from East Java could be used as extras. Add on to this five thousand armed youths. When opinions were solicited, someone asked, are these forces really enough to balance the other forces, the answer was delivered in an intimidating tone: If you want to make a revolution, few will want to join in, but if the revolution is successful, just wait and see, many people will want to join in. There was another explanation that was not of a technical character, for instance, "We're still young, what's the point of a revolution if we're already old?" To return again to the matter of our troop strength, it would have been enough to have army troops that were fairly trustworthy. From a technical, military point of view, the basic idea of an attack, where the highest commander is himself commanding the operation, the troop strength has to be focused upon a decisive target. In my opinion the strategy of the leadership team was a strategy to "light the fuse of the firecracker" in the capital city and then hope that the firecrackers would go off by themselves, that is, a people's revolt, and resistance in the regions would emerge after hearing the signal. Here were particular mistakes: first, they did not focus the main troop strength on the key target; second, they did not go ahead with a concrete calculation of the troops they had.

5. The comrades of the staff and I made the following errors: overestimated the ability of the comrades of the leadership of the operation. Even though the actual facts did not add up, we still believed that the leadership must have a superior set of calculations and that it would be made known to us at the appropriate moment. The mystery would be revealed later. After all, the slogan of the leadership was always: "Enough, we just have to begin and everything else will just fall into place."

We ourselves believed that because it was proven in the operations led by a fellow Communist Party, such as Comrade Mao Zedong, who began with just one regiment and then destroyed the power of Chiang Kai-sek whose troops numbered in the hundreds of thousands. After this bitter event, however, we all have to be more critical and work with concrete calculations. What I saw at Lubang Buaya was that the phase of self-preparation wasn't yet complete. On the last night various important matters had not yet been settled, most notably, the troops (from AURI) that were supposed to have arrived had not yet arrived. The assignments and the instructions were still being prepared. The boxes of bullets had not yet been opened and distributed. In this condition it was apparent that there wasn't any division of labor, everything was dependent on Pak Djojo [Major Soejono].[11] If Pak Djojo had not yet arrived, the work didn't proceed. And once Pak Djojo arrived, the time was already too short.

When we received the news that Nasution had escaped and fled, the leadership group lost its good judgment and didn't do anything. For twelve hours, for the entire day, the enemy was in a state of panic. The troops in the city were under a big question mark and not a few of them were confused (when I was at the palace, I saw for myself the state of the city).

Here we must note a fundamental mistake that can occur in a certain operation (campaign): that is, "Not to take full advantage of one's success." (Standard procedure in implementing the principles of combat and one that has to be followed by every combat commander.) This principle actually is based on the teachings of Marx, who said, "After a revolt occurs, the offensive cannot be allowed to halt even for a moment. This means that the masses who join in the revolt and decisively defeat the enemy cannot give any opportunity whatsoever to the ruling class to reassert its political power. They have to use that moment to the fullest to finish off the power of the regime in the country."[12]

I am of the opinion that one reason behind all these mistakes is the fact that the leadership was divided into three rows [*sjaf*]: a) the Head Group [Kelompok Ketua], b) the Sjam and friends group [Kelompok Sjam cs], c) the Untung and friends group [Kelompok Untung cs]. The operation should

have been under one person. Since this was a military
movement, it was best if the combat command was given to
Comrade Untung while Comrade Sjam acted as a political
commissioner. Or vice versa, Comrade Sjam being the one
holding the supreme command. With a command system
divided into rows, it turned out there were many discussions
that ate up a lot of time at the very moments when quick
decisions needed to be taken, and since the situation kept
changing by the minute, one thing after another, the problems
at every stage had to be handled one by one as quickly as
possible.

[There is no sixth point.]

7. For every battle engagement one has to have a "Picture of the
Battle" [E] well in advance. What happens after the event
breaks out, what is the condition of one's own troops, what
is the situation in Jakarta, what is the situation in Bandung
(remember, the center of Siliwangi[13]), what is the situation in
Central and East Java, what is the situation in the other areas
throughout the homeland (as could be followed by radio)?
With such a picture we can see the tactical position of Jakarta
and its relationship with the wider strategy. And vice versa—
seeing the interconnected strategy, seeing what is advantageous
or disadvantageous, we can quickly change tactics in the middle
of the battlefield.

 We should not have given any time to the enemy when
it was in a state of panic. We had to advance and complete
our victory. The enemy was in such a state—in an altogether
wrong position while we were in an altogether correct position.
One battalion that panics can be overwhelmed by just one
team of soldiers. But the advantage we held was not exploited.
Indeed, we did the exact opposite: 1) the Sector commanders
(South/Central/North), while we were in a winning position,
disappeared, remarkably enough. They had been assigned
to take care of administrative matters for the troops in their
individual sectors. But all these sectors that had been drawn
up beforehand existed only on paper. From this we can learn
the lesson, there was no communication between the different
troop units (*faktor verbinding-komunikasi* [cross-communication

factor]), and each became trapped in an unfamiliar location and became as good as blind to the situation and scared. 2) We did not take advantage of the RRI [Radio Republik Indonesia] station that we held. It was used over the course of the day only to read out a few announcements. A radio station is a means of communication. It should have been used to its maximum potential by the Agitation-Propaganda Front. If that had been done, its effectiveness would have been equal to dozens of divisions. (In this regard, the opponent has succeeded in the war over the radio and press.) 3) In the first hours Nato and company reorganized their command. Their position at that time was very weak. At that moment the leadership of the operation should have ambushed the enemy without thinking at all about the risk to our troops.

8. All the hindrances in the movement of our troops were caused by, among other things, *the lack of food.* They didn't eat in the morning, the afternoon, or the night. This fact was only discovered at night when there was some thought about mobilizing troops for an attack inside the city. At that time the Central Java battalion was at Halim. The East Java battalion had already been drawn into Kostrad in order to eat. Actually, there were two paths that could have been opened up: the battalion commander could have been given authority to obtain food in the places where he was. Contacting the residents or taking the initiative to open up food warehouses—half could have been consumed and the rest given to the people who helped cook it. With such a method there would have been sympathy and a sense of responsibility on both sides. The second path: the sector commanders should have managed this matter.

9. After hearing the news that General Harto [Suharto] was preparing a counterattack and Vice Marshal Dani's offer of integration [of air force and September 30th Movement troops] for fending it off, the offer should have been accepted at that time. By accepting it, all the troops of AURI throughout the country would have joined in. But since there was no faith that victory had to be achieved by blood, this offer of such great importance did not receive a positive response. Omar Dani had already made preparations to the point of ordering rockets to be installed on the planes.

10. Other factors that caused the operation to get stuck derived
from the fact that there was no division of labor. If we simply
followed the normal staff procedure that is mandatory for every
military unit, all the zigzagging could have been avoided. The
work should have been carried out according to the following
method: first, it should have been decided who the commander
would be who would directly lead the action (campaign),
whether Comrade Sjam or Comrade Untung. Then his
assistants or staff should have been appointed. One person
should have been appointed to be responsible for intelligence
work (research/information). Second, one person should have
been assigned and given responsibility for monitoring the
status of the enemy troops and our own troops. What are the
movements of the enemy troops, where are they located, and
then what would be the advice to the commander concerning
our own troops? A third comrade should have been appointed
to be responsible for all those things connected with personnel:
those wounded or killed, those troops absent, or whose morale
has fallen. Also the personnel of the opponent—the main issue
is: the matter of holding them prisoner, taking care of their
needs, guarding them, etc. Then, as for the fourth comrade,
he should have been assigned to think of all those things related
to logistics, the disbursement of weapons and ammunition,
clothes, food, vehicles, etc. Since victory and defeat in this day
and age also depends on the role of People's supplies, there
should have been a fifth person given the assignment to take
care of this matter. In short, the commander should have been
assisted by staff-1, staff-2, staff-3, staff-4, staff-5. Then, if he
found himself too busy, he could have appointed a deputy.
Furthermore, in the manner of the staff's work, the principles
of party work—the principle of democratic centralism—also
holds here. The staff offers its viewpoints and the commander
listens, evaluates them in his mind, and then comes to a
decision. Based on this decision, the staff gives directives for
its implementation to the lower-level staff. With this method
a commander avoids subjectivism. But he also avoids an
environment of liberalism. What happened at that time was a
debate or discussion that was *langiradis* [D, sic: *langdradig*] (*tak
berudjungpangkal* [I]) [without end], to the point that we were
confused on witnessing it: who is really the commander:

Comrade Sjam, Comrade Untung, Comrade Latief, or Pak Djojo [Major Soejono]? About this matter there has to be a detailed examination because the defeat in the capital largely resulted from the fact there was no normal division of command and labor.

11. There is one issue that is trivial but which still deserves attention. For instance, the style of discussion, especially that of Comrade Latief, did not prioritize fundamental problems and then attempt to solve those first. Some matters could have been postponed for later discussion. When the mouth of the cannon was pointed at us, what was urgent for us to discuss was how we could silence the cannon, not issues that could be discussed later.

12. With the appearance of Bung Karno at Halim, a different problem emerged. At that time we had to be quick in political judo, quick in deciding upon the basic point of our strategy. Do we proceed alone or do we proceed with Bung Karno? If we felt that we were capable, we could have quickly decided upon a line of going it alone. If, according to our judgment, we could not win a revolution on our own, then we had to quickly bring Bung Karno on board so that we could destroy the enemy forces together. In my opinion, at that time, the situation changed, as will be explained below:

1) Bung Karno:
  a) summoned the cabinet — the service ministers
  b) issued an order for both sides not to engage in combat
  c) temporarily took control of the army leadership and appointed a caretaker for the army's internal work.

2) Omar Dani: Did not wish us to confront Bung Karno, and his recommendation was that we continue the revolution together with Bung Karno.

3) Ibrahim Adjie: Issued a statement that Siliwangi would move on Jakarta if anything happened to Bung Karno.

4) M. Sabur:	Ordered RPKAD to be ready at any time if Bung Karno was in danger.
5) Nato and company:	Refused the summons of Bung Karno to appear at Halim.
6) September 30th Movement:	Comrade Sjam insisted the revolution would have to proceed without Bung Karno.
	The East Java battalion was in an exhausted state and had not yet resolved the problem of food.
	The leadership was in a nervous state.
7) The "Regions":	Nusatenggara had given a response. Bandung was quiet. East Java was also quiet. Central Java was quiet. The public in Jakarta was quiet At that time, in the regions over the whole Indonesian archipelago, the sound of return fire could not be heard.

Evaluation

If we had continued the revolution on our own, we would have confronted Nato and company, and the army.

If we brought Bung Karno on board, the main contradiction would have become one between the left and the Revolutionary Democratic groups on one side, and merely the right-wing group alone on the other side. But there wasn't a decision by us on which line to take. And even then the time was getting short and developments were crystallizing. Nato was arranging its forces—Bung Karno had gathered the cabinet members he needed.

At that time it was still not too late. There were openings into which we could have entered; the key issue was the appointment of a person to replace the chief of the army. Bung Karno asked us to name a candidate. Bung Karno's nominations were 1) Ibrahim Adjie and 2) Mursid. We nominated 1) Rukman, [2] Pranoto, and [3] Basuki Rachmat. Finally, Pranoto was agreed upon. Actually, we should have just left it up to

Bung Karno. That way, we wouldn't have asked for too much. And Bung Karno would have had the power to resolve this internal army problem and obstruct the escalating actions of Nato and company.[14] Even though the situation was like this, if Pranoto had been clever and tried to exercise some authority, the situation would not have become as bad as it did. With that letter of instruction [from Sukarno], he should have quickly delivered a speech over the radio and announced his appointment. The second step should have been to order the two sides not to engage in combat. Pranoto also should have arranged the force of the brigades near him and directly taken command of them.[15] With such actions his subsequent steps would have carried weight. Then he should have immediately, using temporary expedients, filled the vacant positions on the army's general staff. It was very unfortunate that this last opportunity was lost. Pranoto finally, after a long delay, made a speech over the radio. Even that was only because I pressured him through Comrade Endang.[16] But the contents of his speech were a complete mess—he even denounced the September 30th Movement as adventurist. These words automatically paralyzed the revolutionary energies in the regions, especially in Central Java. The idea sketched out above, the idea of embracing Bung Karno, was not at all a strategy of compromise in a negative sense, but of *"om te redden wat er te redden valt"* [D], to save what can be saved. In this case, if we lost, then there would have been a process of accountability, but only the perpetrators of the September 30th Movement would have to have been held accountable, and the solidity of the party would not have been affected. This tactic is none other than that expressed by the proverb, If we know we're only going to get the shell of an egg, it's better to try to get some of the contents, even if it's just half (*beter een halve ei dan een lege dop* [D, better half an egg than an empty shell]).

13. Eventually, Nato and company seized the initiative, ignored all else, and began their offensive. They hunted down the military troops of the September 30th Movement and did not waste the opportunity they had long awaited: the destruction of the PKI.
14. Meanwhile all the troops of the September 30th Movement gathered at L.B. [Lubang Buaya]. Every now and again one could hear the firing of the RPKAD troops as they searched for an engagement with our guns. Comrades Sjam and Untung and company began to meet to decide on a course of action. Present at this meeting was the commander of the Central Java

battalion and all the members of his battalion. The commander of the East Java battalion was also present but without his troops. There were, more or less, fifteen hundred volunteers who had been trained at Lubang Buaya. On seeing this situation, there were no other alternatives than to: a) fight an all-out war to the death, or b) quickly disappear and try to save our skins. The discussion continued for a long time without any resolution. Finally, I proposed that the command over all the troops be given to me and later, if the crisis could be overcome, I would return this authority to Comrade Untung. Comrade Untung did not agree since his opinion was that if the combat kept on going, there would no longer be any political basis to it. What he meant by these words, I don't quite know. On the other side, Comrade Sjam did not give any response to my proposal. Then I pressured them again to quickly make a decision: if we are too late, we are going to be trapped in a corner from which we will have no options other than to die fighting or die fleeing. Our position at that time was already precarious. The meeting then decided to call off the resistance, and every comrade was ordered to return to his individual place of residence. In this altogether belated state we then took the initiative to save the Leadership comrade (Sjam) and enter the city of Jakarta (Senon [Senin]). Comrade Untung committed a mistake even in disbanding his troops — he should have, as commander, directly given technical instructions on how to disperse and slip back outside. Since a lot of the comrade volunteers were from outside Jakarta — some were even from East Java — they naturally felt foreign in Jakarta and didn't know the streets. Because the order was just *"Pur manuk"* [S], or run away however you can, many became prisoners and easy prey for the tortures of the troops of Nato and company.

15. On the third and fourth days I suggested to the leadership that I come forward and accompany Bung Karno to try to help what needed to be helped. At that time the situation was not completely ruined. In the cabinet were still revolutionaries, but my proposal kept getting postponed until, in the end, Bung Karno didn't receive my letter to him until a month later. Bung Karno was in an already pinched position by then and was perhaps also worried about my approaching him.

16. Such was the process of the September 30th Movement's

action, from being successful to being suppressed, and
suppressed to such an extent that it was finally helpless and
submissive and the entire initiative was held by the opponent.

17. As general conclusions, I am of the opinion that:

   a. We carried out a *politik* [I] *strategisch verassing* [D][17]
   (*serangan tiba-tiba* [I: sudden attack]) that could be used by
   the opponent's propaganda and that led to putting the PKI
   into a cornered position.

   b. The original plan that was to be carried out: the Revolution
   would progress in stages and then suddenly change into
   a purely PKI movement. If the movement progressed in
   stages, then the first stage was limited to the army corps
   with the following technique: after successfully seizing the
   army leadership, the provincial army commanders and
   commanders who possessed a potential function would be
   replaced with elements, that is, democratic-revolutionary
   officers.[18] Then, in the second stage, the revolution would
   be led by the Party. Beginning with mass movements that
   would be shadowed by progressive military troops, precisely
   as is being done now against the government by the enemy.
   If the plan for revolution in stages was followed through
   to the end, the benefits would be: If we were attacked, the
   Party, remaining intact and legal, could protect the military
   comrades. If the action of the first stage succeeded, that
   would be a good stepping stone for jumping to the next
   stage of the revolution. In my judgment the defeat of our
   revolution this time was caused by, among other things,
   the shift of the operational plan, which was originally of an
   internal army nature, to an operation that was led directly by
   the party, and that dragged the party into this and resulted
   in the destruction of the party.

   c. The Topic of Preparation. The September 30th Movement
   was undertaken without having gone through a careful
   process of preparation. There was too much trust in the
   reports from lower-level cadres. In any situation whatsoever
   the leadership has to examine with their own eyes the
   progress of the preparations. The commander should have
   visited and seen for himself the headquarters of the three
   sectors, even if only for a few minutes so that he could verify
   that the posts were filled. The same goes for the other

preparations. It is customary in militaries throughout the
world to carry out inspections of the troops before they
begin their assignments. For example, if a team is about
to go on patrol, the commander of the platoon reviews the
team, inspects all its equipment, its supply of bullets, asks if
the orders have been understood, and only then is the team
allowed to go out on patrol. Such preparation was even more
incumbent on the September 30th Movement, a movement
that would decide the fate of millions of people—a
movement of not just national importance but also the
hope of the entire international proletariat. We should
not have acted hastily.

d. In the critical moments the leadership of an operation must
descend into the middle of the troops, inspire the rank-and-
file to rise and resist, even when the risk is the annihilation
of all of them. And if indeed they are destroyed, it is not that
important—the comrades who are still alive will continue
to strive for the revolution. And if we had acted in this way,
it is highly likely that the opponent would have raised his
hands in surrender, because at that time Nato did not have
a *grip* on the Indonesian military in the city. The whole
atmosphere was not yet anti-September 30th Movement.
In every revolutionary war a leader must be able to awaken
in his followers:
1. A spirit of heroism
2. A resolute thinking and firm determination
3. A spirit of self-sacrifice.

e. There is one issue that needs to be studied in detail. For
comrades who have all along lived in the organization of a
bourgeois army, it is very difficult and virtually impossible
to go against their friends of the same service: this happened
to the battalion from Central Java,[19] and also there was the
incident about which we heard later, when they faced the
Kodam [regional] commander Surjosumpeno.[20] Perhaps
this can be attributed to the weakness of their ideological
perspective, a weakness of their class perspective. The
teaching of Marxism-Leninism is: "If we don't eliminate
them, then they will eliminate us."[21] This point had not
yet penetrated the minds of most of the comrades in ABRI
[Armed Forces of the Republic of Indonesia] and had not

become a firm conviction. Given this experience, ideological education and class consciousness should become a priority for the Party.

f. The strategy that was followed in the entire movement was this type of strategy: "Light the fuse." It was enough for the fuse to be lit in Jakarta and then hope that the firecrackers would go off by themselves in the regions. Ultimately, this method did not succeed. There are two reasons for this: it could be that the fuse was not lit long enough to catch fire or the gunpowder in the firecrackers itself was still wet. I connect this with the work before the action: the manner of evaluating the masses and the comrades in ABRI was subjective. Given this experience, we have to make it a practice to verify the actual situation. Usually, if there were only ten people in one platoon whom we were able to contact, it was reported that the entire platoon was with us (an ally). If there was one battalion commander whom we contacted, it was thought that all those below him were already on our side. The mistaken strategy of the September 30th Movement also derived from the fact that many comrades in the regions reported that the masses could no longer be restrained. If the leadership did not take action, the people would proceed on their own (for the revolution). Following these unconfirmed reports, we were actually affected by mass "agitation," and likewise we did not faithfully follow the "mass line."

g. Considering the capability and immense size of the Party in recent times, I don't think the PKI would have been defeated as long as we were tactical in maneuvering it. I'll give an example: Let's say a cook has all the spices, the vegetables, and a complete set of ingredients. But if he's not smart in judging the temperature from the heat of the oil and the size of the flame, or how the spices have to be tossed in and which has to be cooked first, the food will not taste very good. This is an example: I commanded eighteen battalions,[22] three of which could have been mobilized for revolutionary duties, and their preparations were complete with an airplane—a Hercules carrier, thanks to the solidarity of the officer comrades in the army who possessed command positions. But all this was not taken advantage of, so

244 ❖ *Appendix 1*

ultimately it was not we who destroyed the enemy "one by one" but the reverse—we were destroyed "one by one."

For now, we close with the slogans,

> Once defeated, twice stronger.
> Forward on the path of the revolutionaries.

Appendix 2

The Testimony of Sjam (1967)

A Note on the Translation

Sjam made his first public statements about the movement on July 7, 1967. The military, which had captured him four months earlier, brought him before the military court that was trying the PKI Politburo member Sudisman. The text that follows is a translation of the testimony Sjam gave as a witness before the court. His later statements at his own trial in 1968 and as a witness in other trials did not substantially alter or amend this original testimony.

The questioning of Sjam lasted for nearly a full day. I have translated excerpts that are particularly informative about the movement. Most of the questioning was conducted by the military court's equivalent of a prosecutor *(oditur)*, although some judges asked questions. I have not thought it necessary to identify each questioner.

The Testimony

Q: What was your position in the party?
A: Leader of the PKI's Special Bureau.
Q: Leader or head?
A: Yes.
Q: Head of the Special Bureau?
A: Yes.
Q: About the PKI. PKI is the acronym for what?
A: Communist Party of Indonesia.
Q: Yes. You have been in the party since when?
A: 1949.
Q: 1949. Where was that?
A: In Jakarta.
Q: What was your position in the party when you first joined?
A: I didn't have a position then.

245

Q: You didn't have one? So you were what, then?

A: A regular member.

Q: A regular member. When did you become the head of the Special Bureau?

A: At the end of 1964.

Q: At the end of 1964. Around what month?

A: November.

Q: Before that what was your position?

A: A member of the Organizational Department.

Q: When did you become a member of the Organizational Department?

A: 1960.

Q: What was your elementary education?

A: People's School [Sekolah Rakjat].

Q: After that?

A: H.I.S.

Q: After that?

A: Agricultural school.

Q: Agricultural school. What was its name?

A: Landbouw School.

Q: Where was it?

A: In Surabaya.

Q: Did you graduate?

A: Almost.

Q: Almost. Also from the Landbouw School you almost graduated?

A: Almost.

Q: What class did you reach?

A: Class 3.

Q: Why didn't you graduate?

A: Japan invaded.

Q: After that, did you take any courses?

A: During the Japanese time I attended business school in Yogyakarta.

Q: Until completion?

A: I didn't complete that either, only up to class five.

Q: Why was that?

A: The revolution.

Q: What class?

A: Class two of the upper level.

Q: Where did the Special Bureau fit into the structure of the party?

A: Nowhere.

Q: How so?

A: The Special Bureau was an instrument of the head of the party.

Q: As the head of the Special Bureau, to whom were you responsible?

A: To the head of the party.

Q: Directly?

A: Directly.

Q: There wasn't anyone else?

A: No.

Q: Another agency?

A: No.

Q: So you received orders directly from the head of the party?

A: Yes.

Q: In that case, who was that?

A: Comrade D. N. Aidit.

Q: What was the task of the Special Bureau?

A: To work within the armed forces.

Q: To work within the armed forces. Could you explain further?

A: To search for members among armed forces personnel.

Q: And if you got them, then what?

A: Then organize them.

Q: And once they became organized, then?

A: Educate them.

Q: What education was provided?

A: It was about theory and ideology.

Q: Theory and ideology. What was the theory?

A: Marxism-Leninism.

Q: And the ideology?

A: Love the party.

Q: Meaning what party?

A: The PKI.

Q: Who helped you?

A: Comrade Pono and Comrade Walujo [Bono].

Q: Comrade Pono and Comrade Walujo—anyone else?

A: They were the only ones close to me.

Q: What was Pono's position?

A: Comrade Pono was my assistant.

Q: And Walujo?

A: Second assistant.

Q: Did others in the party know about the existence of the Special Bureau?

A: I don't know.

Q: You know Sudisman here?

A: Yes.

Q: How did you come to be acquainted with him, meaning, how did it happen that you could know him, the way in which you were introduced the first time and such, how did that happen?

A: At first I only knew his name. I once met him in the Organizational Department. It was only there that I became acquainted with him.

Q: You got to know him in the Organizational Department, that was all?

A: Yes.

Q: On other occasions?

A: There was none.

Q: Did Sudisman know you as the head of the Special Bureau?

A: I don't know.

Q: Oh, you don't know. Look here, won't you, at all of your interrogation reports? Just a little while ago you were saying that the task of the Special Bureau was to search for—what was it?

A: Search for members among the armed forces.

Q: Go ahead and describe, describe freely for the court, the work of the Special Bureau.

A: Well, the work of the Special Bureau was a certain type of work of the PKI, and it was within the armed forces. Every member and leader of the Special Bureau had an obligation to expand the organization within the ranks of the armed forces. You studied the various officers and found out about them, and then you tried to approach them and get to know them. If you succeeded in becoming acquainted with an officer, then you would begin talking about general social and political issues. Once you could see what kind of military officer he was, whether he was an anti-Communist or a democrat, then you would keep exchanging ideas with him about political issues facing the country and about progressive ideas. Once it was clear that the officer was, from the perspective of the PKI, progressive, then you would go on to talk to him about issues related to the party. If it appeared that the officer didn't reject such discussions, that he didn't evidence a negative reaction, you would continue with deeper issues, that is, with questions of Marxist theory. Also, once you knew that the officer had a good foundation for understanding Marxism, then you would raise his consciousness toward loving the party. That was the process for how someone in the Special Bureau would recruit members from the armed forces. Once you had a person, then you would raise his understanding of theory. Then you would give him some tasks to help the party—what was most important was help with ideas or material things, especially with paying membership dues. If some people could be attracted to the party, then you would form them into a group. This group would hold discussions about practical political issues and theoretical issues. Meaning, the practical politics was about the political situation at a certain time and the line or the political line of the Communist Party of Indonesia in facing that concrete situation at that time. So those were, roughly speaking, the methods of the Special Bureau in searching for members in the armed forces.

Q: Yes. But still, your answer was at a general level. What about implementation? What I mean is the practical implementation, how was that? What was done in the month or, I mean, in the beginning of 1965, along the lines of what you just explained?

A: I don't quite understand what you mean.

Q: In May 1965, do you recall, was there an order from the head of the party? What was that order?

A: There was information that there was a Council of Generals.

Q: How did that happen? Who gave the order?

A: Comrade D. N. Aidit.

Q: Please tell us about it.

A: In analyzing various activities—most important were those of the armed forces, with regard to national politics and agrarian issues, Nasakom issues, the issue of seconding military officers to the civil service, national front issues, the issue of arming workers and peasants, and issues of local government, it turned out that these activities didn't stand on their own, that is, they didn't appear to be purely localized activities, but all the activities could be seen as being activities directed by a centralized leadership. And also, the spreading of anti-Communist thinking, also the spreading of the idea that the PKI's activity was always about displaying its power. Thus the conclusion could be drawn that these activities were directed by a centralized leadership, and that central leadership was formed from the generals commanding the army. And the generals commanding the army, in directing these activities, were named or named themselves the Council of Generals. So with these centrally organized activities and the Council of Generals, we should be vigilant and prepared. That was what was explained to me.

Q: So you were ordered to be vigilant and—what was it?

A: Prepared.

Q: And the follow-up was what? Vigilant and prepared. What did you do, what steps did you take as the head of the Special Bureau after receiving such an order from the head of the party?

A: After there was this information from the head of the party, I then carried out an inspection of the organization, meaning, a judging of our strength within the armed forces, especially the army. After that we kept holding observations of our personnel in the army who at a later time could carry out a follow-up assignment from Comrade D. N. Aidit. And to determine what time that would be, I and Pono and Walujo held a discussion to choose which of our personnel were suitable and could fulfill conditions for being given an assignment or for receiving an order from Comrade D. N. Aidit. So from that discussion it was concluded to select personnel such as Latief, Untung, Soejono, Sigit, and Wahjudi, in addition to me and Comrade Pono. After reaching that decision about the personnel, we held preparatory meetings. After August we received information from Comrade Aidit that the situation was coming to a head. And all the signs pointed to the Council of Generals as having already begun its final preparations for a final seizure of state power. With these issues in mind we had a question: In facing such a situation, should we wait to get hit or should we hit first? Since our conclusion was that we have to hit first, we made preparations by holding meetings between myself, Pono, Untung, Latief, Soejono, Sigit, and Wahyudi, as preparatory meetings to carry out a movement that would ultimately be named the September 30th Movement. I was the one who led those meetings, and in the first meeting I explained that the situation had reached a climax and that we could not be inactive because for us in such a situation it is a matter of hit or be hit. And at such moments we have to be ready and alert. And the preparations that we need to take involve assembling our forces to confront the Council of Generals. And after the first meeting the conclusion was reached that all of us, that is, all the people present at the meeting, could accept this depiction of the situation and the line that we needed to follow. And in the meetings that followed, an inspection of our forces was begun. An inspection, meaning, an inspection of our strength and an inspection of our members who were in the armed forces, especially those in Jakarta. After we

could see that we did have forces, the following meetings became
more detailed about these forces, and whether we could expect
reinforcements to come from outside—outside, meaning outside
Jakarta. Eventually, it was concluded that there were an additional
two battalions, that is, 530 [from East Java] and 454 from Central
Java. So with the addition of these two battalions, there was a
total of about six battalions that could be assembled at that time.
With a strength of six combat battalions, it was considered
possible to carry out a movement. Having thought about our
armed strength, a conclusion could be drawn and a decision
taken. Only at that point, around mid-September to September
20, did I meet Comrade D. N. Aidit. I was asked to come up
with a concept because the Council of Generals already had a
concrete concept to face this situation. What about us? At that
time, after thinking about it at my home, I drew up a concept for
a movement and its political organization. The vehicle for this
movement I was thinking of naming the September Movement
and, concerning the political organization, I was thinking about
two names: Military Council or Revolution Council. At that time
I was leaning toward the name Military Council, as you'll see in
the notes in my notebook, which is in the hands of the military
police.[1]

But after I proposed that to Comrade D. N. Aidit, he didn't
agree with the name Military Council because Military Council
carried too narrow a meaning and suggested militarism, and was
too sectoral. So the name Revolution Council was chosen because
Revolution Council had a wider meaning and could encompass
all the various elements of the political organizations existing
within the society. Eventually, the decision was taken that the
name of the political body would be the Revolution Council.
I also proposed a concept about the names of people, and
ultimately that was also arranged. I would repeatedly propose
to Comrade D. N. Aidit changes here and there, and finally the
composition of the Revolution Council emerged, with the names
as they were announced over the radio. About the movement—
after that, it was decided on about the twenty-ninth that the
movement would be launched on September 30, so the movement
was named the September 30th Movement.

In the movement I held the political leadership, and Untung
held the military leadership, but the military leadership was under

the political leadership. So I was responsible for all of what occurred during the movement.

Once the movement was underway, the movement, according to the plan, carried out a safeguarding of the generals who were members of the Council of Generals. If at that time killing occurred, there was actually no prior plan for that because the aim of the movement was to take the generals into custody [*pengamanan*] and to search for facts and clear evidence about the Council of Generals. So the killing was a certain excess of the movement, certainly it was one result. However that may be, I as the leader am responsible for all that happened.

When the movement was going on, it didn't proceed as it should have. The reason why that was, even I can't understand to this day. To find the reason requires deep and careful study. But when the movement was going on and when the battalions that had been moved forward, that is, Battalions 454 and 530, already joined up with Kostrad, when it was clear that our strength was weakening, I decided to move the headquarters of the movement from Penas [the aerial survey division] to inside Halim air base.[2] And after weighing the options on how to keep the movement going if its strength kept on decreasing, when, meanwhile, there were no signs that the mass movement would support and join the September 30th Movement, I finally decided to stage a retreat. Also, after hearing from Supardjo what Sukarno had said to him about not continuing with the bloodshed, the decision was taken, I took the decision, to stage a retreat. Even though it was already clear far in advance that there would emerge complicated problems for the movement after the retreat, I took the decision precisely in the interests of saving this entire *nation*, meaning the entire *bangsa*, from chaos.

However, as it turned out, my effort, because of third parties who entered into this abnormal situation of our country, ended in that situation of chaos. Even if it didn't last long, it created conditions that were not wanted by anyone who loves his homeland. Along with the incident, I am also responsible for those types of conditions too. The aim, if the movement had been successful, was actually for the Revolution Council to become a council that would propose a concept to Bung Karno as president of the Republic of Indonesia to implement the politics of Nasakom and form a national coalition government centered on Nasakom.

There wasn't any intention of establishing a Communist state, nothing like that, but to establish a national coalition government centered on Nasakom. If that had been agreed to by Bung Karno as the president—but there were still other things that could be done in case Bung Karno did not agree. So fundamentally the Revolution Council was a temporary arrangement that was capable of being changed.

Such is what I recall. Perhaps there are still matters for which you'd like further comment. . . .

Q: Did the Special Bureau have branches in the provinces?

A: Yes.

Q: What form did they take?

A: They were called Provincial Special Bureaus.

Q: Were the Provincial Special Bureaus within the Provincial Committees of the party?

A: No.

Q: How so?

A: They were directly connected to the center.

Q: Directly connected to the center?

A: Yes.

Q: So the head of the party's Provincial Committee [Comite Daerah Besar] didn't know about it?

A: Some did, some didn't.

Q: Very well. Before, you said that the Special Bureau was not placed within the organizational structure of the party. Is that the case?

A: Yes.

Q: Could it be said that the Special Bureau was of an illegal nature?

A: Illegal in the negative sense, no, because its existence was based on the principle of the PKI's known as democratic centralism, where the head had the right to carry out actions or to engage in actions of an organizational nature. So there was a justification for it. But if considered more generally, according to law, it could be considered illegal but not in the negative sense.

Q: Please explain again what you mean by that special justification.

A: The justification was based on the organizational principle of the PKI, that is, *centralisme demokrasi*, or in other words, democratic centralism. In the case of centralism the head has the authority to take actions that are not provided for in the constitution of the PKI. That was guaranteed in the last clause of the party's constitution, that in an extraordinary situation, the party could be organized along extraordinary lines. Meanwhile, in 1964 it's possible that the party leadership, especially the head, thought that with symptoms such as the Council of Generals there existed an extraordinary situation and so the head used the authority in his possession under democratic centralism to determine organizational policy.

Q: Fine. Before, you said that the approaching of military officers began in 1957. Is that true?

A: Yes. It's true.

Q: Did that also happen in the provinces?

A: Not in all of them. Mainly, it was just in Java.

Q: In East Java who was approached?

A: Well, I don't know about the provinces.

Q: You don't know. In Central Java?

A: Again, I don't know.

Q: In Jakarta?

A: In Jakarta the officers that I myself approached directly were Pardjo, Major Suganda, Colonel Sidik, who had just been recently approached at that time. In the 1960s Colonel Mustafa, Brigadier General Djuhartono, Colonel Machmud Pasha were also officers whom I directly approached.

Q: By Pardjo you mean Brigadier General Supardjo?

A: Yes.

[Sjam explained that on the morning of August 26, he, Pono, and Walujo met to discuss the arrangements for the movement.]

Q: In the evening [of August 26] where did you go?

A: In the evening I went to meet the party head.

Q: The head being?

A: D. N. Aidit.

Q: Where?

A: At his house.

Q: At about what time?

A: Between 9 and 10.

Q: What street is the house on?

A: Pegangsaan Barat.

Q: Who came with you?

A: I was alone.

Q: What did you speak about? What did you report?

A: I reported about the meeting held in the morning.

Q: And what did Aidit say?

A: Yes, good, continue with the preparations.

Q: And? Was Aidit satisfied with the three personnel? [Untung, Latief, and Soejono]

A: Oh, no, he wasn't.

Q: And so?

A: Add more.

Q: Who gave that order? Who suggested to add more?

A: Head D. N. Aidit.

Q: To whom?

A: To me.

About the Involvement of the Party Leadership

Q: In this connection did you hear from Aidit that this movement had been decided upon by the party?

A: No.

Q: Now here in your interrogation report, Sjam, you say that when you received the instruction from D. N. Aidit in arranging the Revolution Council—

A: Yes.

Q: You asked Aidit something, correct?

A: Yes.

Q: What did you ask him?

A: Is this a decision of the party?

Q: And what was his answer?

A: He answered that it was the decision of the party.

Q: When did you hear of the party's decision—was it on the twenty-ninth [of August] or another time?

A: Before.

Q: Before, so when?

A: Before.

Q: Precisely?

A: About the twenty-seventh.

Q: The twenty-seventh. Are you sure or—?

A: About then.

Q: If I said it was the twenty-eighth or twenty-ninth?

A: I wouldn't object.

Q: You wouldn't object. So it is correct that you heard from Aidit that—the instruction from Aidit to you in the context of initiating the Revolution Council and its instrument, the September 30th Movement—Aidit answered that it was a decision of the party, correct?

A: Yes.

Q: You're not mistaken again?

A: No.

About the Troops Used for the Movement

Q: Before, you said that, to carry out the movement that later was named the September 30th Movement, six combat battalions were readied. Is that correct?

A: Yes.

Q: What were those six battalions?

A: From Cakrabirawa and Infantry Brigade 1.

Q: From Cakrabirawa how many battalions?

A: One company. From Infantry Brigade 1, one battalion, and one from P3.

Q: What is P3?

A: Pasukan Pembela Pangkalan [Airbase Defense Troops] of the air force. One battalion. Then there were two combat companies. And then there was 530 and 454. And one battalion of volunteers.

Q: Before you said that Battalion 530 was from where?

A: East Java.

Q: And 454 from where?

A: Central Java.

Q: You were in Jakarta. How did you assemble those battalions?

A: I didn't intentionally assemble them—I happened to be able to assemble them. Those two battalions happened to be assigned to Jakarta for Armed Forces Day [October 5]. And because we saw that this was a force we could use, we took advantage of the opportunity.

Q: You said it wasn't intentional. I don't quite understand. Why was it just an accident that you happened to assemble two battalions? How was that, please explain, how?

A: Actually, one month before Armed Forces Day there was the news that those two battalions, that is, the Raiders from East and Central Java, would be used for Armed Forces Day in Jakarta. Then we did some research into those two units. After that we thought that we could use them, and so we exploited the opportunity for using the troops, for reinforcing the troops, we had in Jakarta for the movement. So it wasn't intentional—it was an accident because they happened to be assigned to Jakarta, and we, taking advantage of that, determined that we could invite them to join the movement.

Q: You said that it was one month before. When was that?

A: Around September tenth to fifteenth, we received the news that 530 and 454 would be assigned to Jakarta.

Q: About September tenth to fifteenth, 1965, you heard the news that those two battalions would be assigned to Jakarta. Who did you hear that from?

A: From East Java and Central Java.

Q: More exactly from the Special Bureau?

A: From the Special Bureau in East Java and the one in Central Java.

Q: How exactly did the news go?

A: It was that Battalion 530 from East Java was assigned to join the ceremonies of October 5 and that it would leave for Jakarta.

Q: That's it?

A: Yes.

Q: There was no analysis or evaluation of the battalion?

A: I kept asking about the status of the battalion and was answered that it was a force that could be used for the movement.

Q: Who answered you?

A: The Special Bureau in East Java.

Q: For East Java, who was that?

A: Hasim.

Q: And for Central Java, who was that?

A: Salim.

Q: Did you ever receive a report that these battalions had been approached by the Special Bureau branches in the provinces?

A: Yes.

The Origins of the Special Bureau

Q: You said before that the Special Bureau was created in 1964. Correct?

A: Yes.

Q: You said that you worked with the armed forces in another capacity beginning in around 1957.

A: Yes.

Q: What was the organization or the organ of the party in which you were working before there was a Special Bureau? You worked at that time through what organ, if not with the Special Bureau?

A: I was at that time the assistant to the head.

Q: Oh, the assistant to the head. You weren't in the Organizational Department as you stated before?

A: Not yet.

About Aidit's Presence at Halim Air Force Base

Q: Is it true that Aidit was brought to Halim that night?

A: Yes, that's true.

Q: Who brought him?

A: Soejono.

Q: On whose orders?

A: Mine.

Q: What was the purpose of his presence at Halim?

A: To be near the leaders of the movement.

Q: To be near them. In your interrogation report it says to facilitate the connection between the central command [*cenko*] and Aidit and for controlling the plan of the movement.

A: Yes. . . .

Q: Sjam, did you know where Aidit was on October 1, 1965?

A: Yes.

Q: Where was he?

A: At Halim.

Q: When he left you knew?

A: Yes.

Q: Where did he leave to?

A: To Yogyakarta.

Q: How did he go there?

A: By plane.

Q: His leaving, according to what you know, was for what reason?

A: To avoid Jakarta.

Q: To?

A: To avoid Jakarta. To save himself.

Q: Why do that?

A: Because the movement had failed.

Q: Did he leave by his own accord or was he forced to leave? What did you see?

A: There wasn't anyone who forced him.

Q: No one forced him. So he left for Yogyakarta to save himself. Who else accompanied him on the flight?

A: He was with Walujo.

Q: Walujo. Anyone else?

A: With Kusno.

Q: Who was Kusno?

A: His adjutant.

Q: Adjutant. Anyone else?

A: No, that was all.

Sjam's Military Experience

Q: I'd like to ask the witness, have you any experience with military movements?

A: Yes, a little.

Q: Where?

A: At the time of the 1945 revolution.

Q: After that, you didn't have any more experience?

A: No, there was nothing more.

The Revolution Council List

Q: Why did you not make yourself known [on the list of members of the Indonesian Revolution Council] instead of hiding the Special Bureau?

A: Because, if I put my name down, a lot of questions would be raised because I was not someone who was well known. . . .

Q: I want to ask you, who among the members of the Revolution Council was, in your opinion, popular? Which ones were popular, Untung and Pardjo? According to your experience, during the time you associated with them, which was more, shall one say, intelligent, or better in certain respects like that?

A: Untung was more popular.

[Sudisman was asked to comment on Sjam's testimony. He corrected Sjam's listing of the members of the Working Committee of the Politburo. Sjam had stated that there were five members—Aidit, Sudisman, Lukman, Njoto, and Anwar Sanusi. Sudisman said Sanusi was not a member. His only other comment was on the question of responsibility.]

SUDISMAN: Even though I myself knew nothing [about the movement], what was done by Comrade Sjam was done on the instructions of Aidit, and even I carried out instructions from Comrade Aidit. On the matter of responsibility, I will assume responsibility for it all.

Notes

All translations from Indonesian-language sources are mine.

Introduction

1. Naming practices in Indonesia do not always follow the given name/family name pattern. The reader will find examples in this book of individuals with only one name (such as Sukarno, Untung, and Suharto), individuals known primarily by their first name (such as Pranoto Reksosamodra and Yoga Sugama), and individuals with abbreviated last names (such as Karim D. P.).

2. In his postmovement speeches Sukarno repeatedly referred to the event as a "rimpel in de geweldige oceaan" (a ripple in the wide ocean). He likened the revolutionary process in Indonesia to a churning ocean, continually producing peaks and valleys on the surface of the water. See his speech delivered at the time of Suharto's official inauguration as commander of the army on October 16, 1965, in Setiyono and Triyana, *Revolusi Belum Selesai*, 1:22–23, 38.

3. On the number of political prisoners, see Robert Cribb's introductory essay in his edited volume, *Indonesian Killings*, 42, and Fealy, *Release of Indonesia's Political Prisoners*, appendix.

4. All estimates of the number of people killed are guesses. No careful, comprehensive investigations have been conducted. The fact-finding commission appointed by President Sukarno reported in January 1966 that 78,500 individuals had been killed. This was an intentional underestimate by a commission dominated by military officers and reliant upon information from military officers. One of the two civilians on the commission, Oei Tjoe Tat, has claimed that he told Sukarno in private that the real number was closer to 500,000 or 600,000 (Toer and Prasetyo, *Memoar Oei Tjoe Tat*, 192). For a discussion of the estimates, see Cribb, "How Many Deaths?"

5. The core leaders, as I will explain in chapter 1, were two civilians, Sjam and Pono, and three military officers: Lieutenant Colonel Untung, Major Soejono, and Colonel Abdul Latief.

6. Colonel Latief's defense plea was privately published in Europe at the time of his trial. It was republished in Indonesia after the fall of Suharto (Latief, *Pledoi Kol. A. Latief*). Many people, including me, asked Latief to explain the movement in more detail. His standard response was to refer inquirers to his published defense. His refusal to write about the movement was not due to

261

a loss of memory. In the late 1980s, while still in prison, he wrote a detailed 118-page manuscript, complete with eight diagrams, about a single battle that occurred sixteen years before the movement ("Serangan Umum 1 Maret 1949") He was seventy-eight when he died of natural causes on April 6, 2005, in Jakarta.

7. On these stories see Wieringa, *Sexual Politics in Indonesia,* 291–327.

8. Ricklefs, *History of Modern Indonesia,* 268.

9. Cribb and Brown, *Modern Indonesia,* 97.

10. The government has published a history of the monument, Departemen Pendidikan dan Kebudayaan, *Hakekat Pembangunan Monumen Pancasila Sakti.*

11. The five principles—belief in one god, humanity, national unity, democracy, and social justice—were vague enough to be interpreted by Suharto in whatever way he saw fit.

12. McGregor, "Commemoration of 1 October, 'Hari Kesaktian Pancasila,'" 43.

13. A pamphlet sold at the museum (Pusat Sejarah dan Tradisi ABRI, *Buku Panduan Monumen Pancasila Sakti, Lubang Buaya*) conveniently lists the dioramas. Of the forty-two dioramas, fifteen depict incidents from 1945 to 1948 when the PKI was participating in Indonesia's armed struggle against the Dutch.

14. The National Monument History Museum, located in the base of the National Monument in the center of Merdeka Square, also excludes mention of PKI's anticolonial actions. The first plan for the museum, written by a Sukarno-supervised committee in 1964, called for a diorama depicting the PKI's 1926 revolt in Banten. After taking state power, Suharto shelved that plan and appointed a new committee in 1969 under the direction of the historian Nugroho Notosusanto. See McGregor, "Representing the Indonesian Past," 105–6.

15. Badiou, *Ethics,* 41.

16. The four novels Pramoedya Ananta Toer wrote while a political prisoner of the Suharto regime, the Buru quartet *(This Earth of Mankind, Child of All Nations, Footsteps, Glass House)*, can be read as a recovery of the origins of the nationalist movement. The very titles of the first two novels reflect the universalism behind that movement for a new particularity; the Indonesian nation, in Pramoedya's work, emerges not as an assertion of ethnic or cultural chauvinism but rather as an association of people opposed to such chauvinism. The first novel in the quartet is dedicated to Han, the nickname for the Dutch scholar Gertrudes Johan Resink.

17. Badiou, *Ethics,* 73–74. For an extended commentary on Badiou's ideas on events and truth, see Hallward, *Badiou,* 107–80.

18. The military's historical preservation department, Pusat Sejarah dan Tradisi ABRI, published a four-volume history of the PKI: *Bahaya Laten*

Komunisme di Indonesia. Also see Dinuth, *Kewaspadaan Nasional dan Bahaya Laten Komunis,* and Suyitno, *Pemasyarakatan Bahaya Laten Komunis.*

19. Suharto established Kopkamtib (Komando Operasi Pemulihan Keamanan dan Ketertiban, Operational Command for the Restoration of Security and Order) on October 10, 1965, and gained President Sukarno's approval for it on November 1. It maintained a ghostly existence. It was not an agency of the government with its own bureaucracy. Suharto designed it more as a special function of the military. Nearly all its personnel were officers who simultaneously held posts in the regular military structure. Southwood and Flanagan, in their fourth chapter of *Indonesia,* point out that its existence signified a permanent state of emergency, but they mistake it for a distinct agency. The regulations pertaining to it are compiled in Kopkamtib, *Himpunan Surat-Surat Keputusan/Perintah yang Berhubungan dengan Kopkamtib 1965–1969.* President Wahid disbanded the successor to Kopkamtib, Bakorstanas, in 2000.

20. Schmitt, *Political Theology,* 5.

21. Stewart Sutley's analysis of the 1965–66 emergency in terms of Schmitt's theory is astute: "Indonesian 'New Order' as New Sovereign Space." I would note only that he misses Suharto's normalization of the state of emergency.

22. Giorgio Agamben (*State of Exception,* 52–88) provides a penetrating analysis of both paradoxes: a law that states the law is suspended, and the exception that turns into the rule (thereby eliminating any distinction between the exception and the rule). Since Schmitt wished to contain the state of exception as a temporary expedient that would be productive for the rule of law, he could not admit the insight of one of Walter Benjamin's well-known theses on history, that the "tradition of the oppressed teaches us that the 'state of exception' in which we live is the rule." On Schmitt's domestication of the state of exception, see J. McCormick, "Dilemmas of Dictatorship."

23. Heryanto, "Where Communism Never Dies."

24. National Security Archives, interviews for the CNN television series *The Cold War,* Marshall Green interview, January 15, 1997, available at www.gwu.edu/~nsarchiv/coldwar/interviews/episode-15/green6.html.

25. This document was jointly prepared by the CIA, National Security Agency, Defense Intelligence Agency, and the State Department's intelligence section. Its title reflects its contents: "Prospects for and Strategic Implications of a Communist Takeover in Indonesia" (*Foreign Relations of the United States, 1964–1968* [hereafter, *FRUS*], 26:290, www.gwu.edu/~nsarchiv/NSAEBB/NSAEBB52/#FRUS).

26. Kolko, *Confronting the Third World,* 174. Also see T. McCormick, *America's Half-Century,* 100, 111, 114–18.

27. Quoted in Shoup and Minter, *Imperial Brain Trust,* 234–36.

28. Ibid., 236. The 1952 policy statement was NSC memorandum 124/1. The 1954 statement was NSC memorandum 5405.

29. Quoted in Scott, "Exporting Military-Economic Development," 241.

30. Nixon, "Asia after Vietnam," 111.

31. William Bundy, foreword to Marshall Green, *Indonesia*, xi. Bundy was assistant secretary of state for East Asian and Pacific affairs from 1964 to 1969.

32. McNamara, *In Retrospect*, 214.

33. Ibid., 270.

34. Ibid., 215. McGeorge Bundy, national security adviser to Kennedy and Johnson, has also affirmed that Vietnam was no longer of vital interest "at least from the time of the anti-Communist revolution in Indonesia" (quoted in John Mueller, "Reassessment of American Policy," 52). The Johnson administration's decisions of early to mid-1965 to dramatically escalate the war (by bombing North Vietnam and introducing U.S. ground troops into South Vietnam) were not guided by the domino theory. As George Kahin has shown, the administration was primarily concerned in 1965 with the symbolic consequences of the potential loss of South Vietnam to the Communists. U.S. officials wished to avoid a humiliation and to send a message to other nations that resistance to the U.S. military would carry a high price, even if that resistance was ultimately victorious (G. Kahin, *Intervention*, 283, 312–14, 356–58, 363, 375, 390–93). On the domino theory also see Porter, *Perils of Dominance*, 243–58.

35. *New York Times*, October 11, 1965, p. 1.

36. *New York Times*, June 19, 1966, p. 12E.

37. *Time* (Canada edition), July 15, 1966, p. 44.

38. Quoted in Chomsky, *Year 501*, 126.

39. Chomsky and Herman, *Political Economy of Human Rights*, 1:205–17.

40. I have coedited an Indonesian-language book of essays about the experiences of the victims: Roosa, Ratih, and Farid, *Tahun yang Tak Pernah Berakhir*.

41. Peter Dale Scott, who has studied both the movement and the Kennedy assassination, has proposed the term *deep politics* to refer to the covert aspects of states, "all those political practices and arrangements, deliberate or not, which are usually repressed rather than acknowledged." He means, for instance, a state's use of organized crime syndicates (*Deep Politics and the Death of JFK*, 7, 10). Scott's poetry book *Coming to Jakarta* is a profound meditation on the complicity of genteel, well-educated North Americans in the atrocities in countries such as Indonesia, Vietnam, and Chile.

42. Nasution, *Memenuhi Panggilan Tugas*, 6: 265–67. The Supardjo document is mentioned in passing in two recently published books, Katoppo, *Menyingkap Kabut Halim 1965*, 132–33, 255, and Sulistyo, *Palu Arit di Ladang Tebu*, 8. Sulistyo cites the document only to prove the minor point that the movement failed to supply food for its troops.

43. The records of Supardjo's 1967 trial before the Mahmillub (Mahkamah Militer Luar Biasa, the Extraordinary Military Courts) have been available at both the military archives in Jakarta (TNI Museum Satria Mandala,

Documentation Department) and Cornell University's Kroch Library. Crouch consulted certain sections of the Supardjo trial records. See his *Army and Politics in Indonesia,* 115, 127, 128, 132. There is a precedent for discovering important primary sources tucked away in Mahmillub records. While reading through the trial records of Lieutenant Colonel Heru Atmodjo in the early 1980s, Benedict Anderson found an autopsy report on the corpses of the seven officers killed in Jakarta by the movement. Suharto had suppressed the report, but the military entered it into some Mahmillub trial records as evidence, perhaps overlooking the implications of later public exposure (Anderson, "How Did the Generals Die?").

44. Fic, *Anatomy of the Jakarta Coup.* Victor Fic (1922–2005) was a political scientist who began writing about Indonesia in the 1960s. Except for the Supardjo document, his book contains nothing new, either by way of source material or analysis. It is based on the army's interrogation reports and Mahmillub records and reiterates the arguments of the Suharto regime's publications. Fic's claims, that both the Chinese government and President Sukarno were involved in the movement, are based on sheer speculation.

45. Supardjo's son, Sugiarto, has also confirmed in discussions with me that his father wrote the document.

46. Hasan has requested that I release his name and publish his memoir only after his death. Once his identity and life story are known, it will be obvious that he was in a position to have firsthand knowledge of the events that he describes.

47. Siauw, "Berbagai Catatan dari Berbagai Macam Cerita." Another of Siauw's unpublished essays, "The Smiling General Harus Dituntut ke Mahkamah," includes some of the same information.

48. Baperki stood for Badan Permusyawaratan Kewarganegaraan Indonesia, meaning Body for the Deliberation of Indonesian Citizenship. On its activities see Coppel, *Indonesian Chinese in Crisis.* The army banned it in late 1965 and arrested most of its members. On Siauw see the informative biography written by his son, Siauw Tiong Djin, *Siauw Giok Tjhan.*

49. Soebandrio, *Kesaksianku Tentang G-30-S.* The largest publisher in Indonesia, Gramedia, originally intended to publish this book. For reasons that its editors have not explained, it canceled the contract and destroyed the ten thousand copies it had already printed. See *Gamma,* November 8–14, 2000, 16–17, and *Tempo,* February 4, 2001, 68–69 (both newsmagazines are published in Jakarta). The manuscript has now become public property. Many individuals and groups in Indonesia have published their own editions.

50. Surodjo and Soeparno, *Tuhan Pergunakanlah Hati, Pikiran dan Tanganku.* The main weekly newsmagazine, *Tempo,* ran a special report on Dani on February 4, 2001, pp. 60–65.

51. Katoppo, *Menyingkap Kabut Halim 1965.*

52. The volume is *Indonesia, Malaysia-Singapore, Philippines, vol. 26 of* Department of State, *FRUS 1964–68*. See note 24 for how to access this material on the Internet.

53. Darnton, "It Happened One Night," 60. I thank Courtney Booker for calling my attention to this review essay.

54. Ritchie, *Rashomon*, 87.

55. Darnton, "It Happened One Night," 60.

56. At a February 12, 2002, press briefing, U.S. Secretary of Defense Rumsfeld stated: "There are known knowns. There are things we know we know. We also know there are known unknowns. That is to say, we know there are some things we do not know. But there are also unknown unknowns, the ones we don't know." As an excuse for doctored intelligence reports about weapons of mass destruction in Iraq, which is what he was addressing, this statement is an obfuscation. By itself, however, it is not the nonsense many of his critics have alleged it to be. The problem is its limitation. He did not mention the all-important fourth category central to psychoanalysis: the unknown knowns, or the things we know but do not admit to knowing (Žižek, "What Rumsfeld Doesn't Know That He Knows about Abu Ghraib").

57. The older genre of the detective story was preoccupied with individual criminals rather than collective agents. The usual difficulty in determining the perpetrator of mass killings is the impersonality of bureaucratic violence: the higher ranks disclaim knowledge of the lower, while the lower claim to be acting on orders from the higher. Perhaps the very ambiguity and impersonality inherent in bureaucratic violence has inhibited the formation of a literary genre that would star modern-day human rights investigators.

58. Sukarno used this analogy in a speech of October 27, 1965 (Setiyono and Triyana, *Revolusi Belum Selesai*, 1:61–62).

59. The victims were six army generals, a lieutenant, General Nasution's five-year-old daughter, a security guard at Leimena's house (next door to Nasution's house), a twenty-four-year-old nephew of Brigadier General Panjaitan's, and two army officers in Central Java. Another nephew of Panjaitan's was seriously wounded by gunfire. This list is based on the army's. During the ceremony at Lubang Buaya on October 1, 1966, the army distributed a short Indonesian-language report on the movement. This report was translated by the Canadian embassy (Canadian Embassy, Jakarta, to Under-Secretary of State for External Affairs, Ottawa, "Anniversary of Last Year's Abortive Coup," October 11, 1966). I thank David Webster for sending me a copy of this document.

60. Anderson and McVey, *Preliminary Analysis*, 63.

61. While lecturing before a group of government officials in Jakarta in 1980, Suharto's righthand man, Lieutenant Colonel Ali Moertopo, argued that the PKI's influence before 1965 was pervasive: "Indonesians had been influenced by communism as a system of thought for so long that it came to be

identified as the Indonesian way of thinking" (Bourchier and Hadiz, *Indonesian Politics and Society,* 110). This was actually an exaggeration. Sukarno had been much more influential than the PKI. Officials of the Suharto regime like Moertopo never made a point of condemning Sukarno, but their anticommunism necessitated a hostility toward one of his cherished principles, Nasakom, the unity of nationalists, religious-minded individuals, and communists. As early as 1926 Sukarno had called for people in all three groups to recognize the commonality of their concerns and unite for the sake of the nationalist struggle. He legitimated the role of the PKI in national politics (Soekarno, *Nationalism, Islam and Marxism*).

62. For thoughtful reflections on the psychology of denial, see Cohen, *States of Denial.*

63. The prime example of this studied silence is Notosusanto and Saleh, *Coup Attempt of the "September 30 Movement."*

64. Soeharto, *My Thoughts, Words, and Deeds,* 114.

65. "Surat Perintah 11 Maret untuk mengatasi situasi konflik ketika itu" [The Decree of March 11 Meant to Overcome the Situation of Conflict at That Time], *Kompas,* March 11, 1971, pp. 1, 12.

66. Cribb, *Indonesian Killings,* 16.

67. Karnow, "First Report on Horror in Indonesia," *Washington Post,* April 17, 1966, 1, 20; Seth King, "The Great Purge in Indonesia," *New York Times Magazine,* May 8, 1966, 25; Seymour Topping, "Slaughter of Reds Gives Indonesia a Grim Legacy," *New York Times,* August 24, 1966, 1, 16.

68. Karnow, "First Report on Horror," 20.

69. Topping, "Slaughter of Reds," 16.

70. Ibid.

71. Quoted in Newfield, *Robert Kennedy,* 71.

72. *Time* (Canada edition), July 15, 1966, 30–31.

73. C. L. Sulzberger, "Foreign Affairs: When a Nation Runs Amok," *New York Times,* April 13, 1966, 40.

74. Don Moser, "Where the Rivers Ran Crimson from Butchery," *Life,* July 1, 1966, 26–28.

75. Shaplen, *Time Out of Hand,* 128. This book is based on Shaplen's *New Yorker* articles on Southeast Asia.

76. Ibid., 26.

77. Shaplen, *Time out of Hand,* 128.

78. Geertz, *After the Fact,* 10.

79. Geertz, *Interpretation of Cultures,* 452n43.

80. Friend, *Indonesian Destinies,* 99, 113, 115.

81. An account that was published by the army notes that the Army Paracommando Regiment (RPKAD) began rounding up thousands of suspected members of the PKI in Central Java on October 18, 1965: "In carrying out its cleaning up movements, the RPKAD [Special Forces] did not meet

with any resistance from the remnants of the rebels." In other words, the "rebels" were not in the process of rebelling at the time of their capture (Dinas Sejarah Militer TNI–Angkatan Darat, *Cuplikan Sejarah Perjuangan TNI–Angkatan Darat,* 506.

82. Gestapu is an obviously artificial acronym. Indonesians usually form acronyms by combining syllables, sometimes letters, from a set of words in the order that the syllables appear. In Gestapu the *s* is out of order.

83. The most detailed account of the military's propaganda in the months after the movement is Wieringa, *Sexual Politics in Indonesia,* 291–317.

84. An article based on recent oral history research provides a detailed confirmation of Anderson and McVey's point. See Hasworo, "Penangkapan dan Pembunuhan di Jawa Tengah Setelah G-30-S."

85. Djayadi and Rusyana interviews. Both are pseudonyms for former PKI members.

86. Hughes, "Frenzy on Bali," chap. 15 of *End of Sukarno.* Also see Elson, *Suharto,* 125.

87. The most precise analysis of the killing in Bali is by Robinson, *Dark Side of Paradise,* 273–303.

88. This is based on my oral interviews with the widows of two former PKI leaders in Denpasar, Bali, Ibu Tiara (pseudonym) and Ibu Puger.

89. The date I owe to Wayan, the pseudonym for a man who was in a detention camp with one of the men killed in Kapal, I Gde Puger. Wayan kept a record of the date when Puger was taken out at night by the military for execution (Wayan interview).

90. Dana, Pugeg, Suwira, Reti, and Poniti interviews.

91. Robinson, *Dark Side of Paradise,* 295.

92. Cribb, "Genocide in Indonesia," 235.

93. The most notorious case occurred during the referendum on independence in occupied East Timor in 1999. The military mobilized militias to intimidate voters to support continued integration with Indonesia. Once the vote in favor of independence was announced, both the military and militia personnel laid waste to East Timor as an act of revenge, killing hundreds, forcibly deporting about 250,000 people into West Timor, and burning down about 70 percent of the buildings (Martinkus, *Dirty Little War;* Bartu, "Militia, the Military, and the People of Bobonaro").

94. Trouillot, *Silencing the Past,* 2.

95. Ibid., 26.

96. Suharto, in a statement addressed to the people of Central Java in November 1965, called for the destruction of the September 30th Movement "down to its roots" (*sampai pada ke akar-akarnya*) (Dinuth, *Dokumen Terpilih Sekitar G-30-S/PKI,* 137).

97. Prunier, *Rwandan Crisis,* 241. In arguing that the Hutu chauvinists behind the killings expected international passivity, Prunier asks the rhetorical

question, "Who remembers the half-million Chinese killed on the orders of President Suharto of Indonesia in 1965?" (229). Prunier's question about remembering is intriguing in that it reveals just how poorly the mass killings of Indonesia have been remembered. A common misconception is that only Chinese Indonesians were killed. While some ethnic Chinese were killed, they were not targeted as a group. Some Chinese Indonesians willingly collaborated with the army. The vast majority of the victims were Javanese and Balinese. Those Chinese Indonesians who were killed tended to be associated with left-wing organizations, such as Baperki. If the Hutu Power militants had succeeded in maintaining themselves in power as Suharto did, then perhaps the killings in Rwanda would be similarly misremembered today as a mysterious, spontaneous eruption of popular vengeance. One should also note in regard to Prunier's comment that Suharto was not president in 1965.

98. The introductory essay to my coedited book offers a more extended, albeit still preliminary, analysis of the killings: Roosa, Ratih, and Farid, *Tahun yang Tak Pernah Berakhir*, 8–18. Much more detailed oral history research needs to be done on the killings in a wide variety of localities before a clearer picture can emerge.

99. The perverse character of the social memory in Indonesia about the killings can be seen in a book by Taufiq Ismail, one of the country's most well-known poets. Amid a disorganized scrapbook of images, documents, and short essays (some pertaining to the irrelevant issue of narcotics), Ismail claims that Marxism-Leninism is an inherently evil ideology that necessarily produces genocide. The anti-Communist mass killings of 1965–66 were therefore prophylactic: they were done to prevent even greater mass killings by the Communists (Ismail, *Katastrofi Mendunia*). The historian Iwan Gardono Sujatmiko has also called the Indonesian mass killings prophylactic in "Kehancuran PKI Tahun 1965–1966" (11). No doubt, all the mass killings that have ever occurred can be justified in the same way. Perpetrators always claim to be acting in self-defense. Ismail's and Sujatmiko's explicit justification of the politicide is uncommon in Indonesian public discourse—the event is usually just ignored—but it accurately reflects what those who participated in the killings state when pressed to explain their actions.

100. R. Evans, *Coming of the Third Reich*, 328–33.

101. Quoted in R. Evans, *Coming of the Third Reich*, 332.

102. Setiawan, *Kamus Gestok*, 99–100.

103. See the speeches collected in Setiyono and Triyana, *Revolusi Belum Selesai*.

104. Sukarno's strategy in dealing with Suharto from late 1965 to March 1968 requires more attention than it has so far received. In the most detailed analysis so far, Crouch contends that Sukarno believed he could outmaneuver Suharto (Crouch, *Army and Politics in Indonesia*, 158–220; also see Legge, *Sukarno*, 430–58). Still, one has to wonder why Sukarno resiled from dismissing

Suharto or calling for resistance to the army-organized massacres. Sukarno's main method of resistance was delivering speeches—which he knew was futile since the army, in control of the media, suppressed or distorted his statements. Whatever Sukarno's reasons for his strategy of compromise, it is difficult to avoid the conclusion that he acted cowardly in the face of the massacres.

105. In 2000 the government discontinued the name Sacred Pancasila Day (Hari Kesaktian Pancasila) to avoid the connotation that Pancasila was sacred and thus on the same level as religion. The new name—Commemoration of the National Tragedy Due to the Betrayal of Pancasila (Peringatan Menge-nang Tragedi Nasional Akibat Pengkhianatan Terhadap Pancasila)—reaffirms the Suharto regime's propaganda; the September 30th Movement, not the mass killing that followed, was *the* national tragedy ("Betrayal of Pancasila Tragedy Commemorated," *Jakarta Post*, October 2, 2000). While Sukarno's daughter, Megawati, was president, she led the ceremony at Lubang Buaya in 2001 and 2003 but dispatched her coordinating minister for politics and security to lead it in 2002 and 2004 ("Megawati dan Hamzah Tak Hadir di Lubang Buaya," *Kompas*, October 1, 2004). Also see Adam, "Dilema Megawati di Lu-bang Buaya," *Kompas*, October 8, 2003; McGregor, "Commemoration of 1 October," 61–64.

106. Budiawan, "When Memory Challenges History"; van Klinken, "Battle for History after Suharto." Also see the flurry of newspaper articles in April 2000 when President Wahid suggested revoking the law banning Marxism-Leninism: "New Wave of Protests Target Plan on Communism," *Jakarta Post*, April 8, 2000, 1; Sulastomo, "Tap XXV/MPRS/1966," *Kompas*, April 12, 2000, p. 4; Franz Magnis-Suseno, "Mencabut Tap No XXV/MPRS/1966?" *Kompas*, April 14, 2000; "Dari Secangkir Kopi ke Hawa Nafsu," *Kompas*, April 14, 2000, p. 7; "Clamour about Marxism," *Jakarta Post*, April 18, 2000, p. 4.

107. In 1965–66, as a university student in Jakarta, Soe Hok Gie was an enthusiastic supporter of the army's moves against the PKI and President Su-karno. See the collection of his writings from that time, *Catatan Seorang De-monstran*. But unlike so many of his fellow anti-Communist youths, the so-called Generation of 1966, he was outraged once he learned of the mass killings and realized that Sukarno's rule was being replaced by an army dictatorship. Soe Hok Gie's writings of 1967–69, later collected and published under the title *Zaman Peralihan*, struck a strongly dissenting note. Many of that "Generation of 1966" denounced the tyranny of Sukarno, then comfortably adjusted themselves to well-paid positions in the Suharto tyranny.

1. The Incoherence of the Facts

1. For translations of the statements issued by the movement, see "Selected Documents," 134–39.

2. The square at that time was called Medan Merdeka, which could be translated as Independence Field. Following convention, I will refer to it as Merdeka Square. Today it is commonly known as Medan Monas (*Mo*numen *Nasi*onal) for the tall monument at the center of the field.

3. A detailed account of the kidnapping raids can be found in Anderson and McVey, *Preliminary Analysis*, 12–18.

4. Anderson and McVey assumed that Supardjo's role was to "control the Palace and Radio Station" (*Preliminary Analysis*, 11). That is inaccurate. By the time Supardjo arrived, Battalions 454 and 530 already controlled the area outside the palace and the radio station. It does not appear that Supardjo's intended role was anything more than to speak with Sukarno inside the palace. He did not command the troops that occupied the radio station.

5. Mahmillub transcript, Supardjo trial, defense plea *(pleidooi dari tertuduh)*, 13, 28. In this instance and nearly all other instances, I draw upon the transcripts from the Mahmillub (Mahkamah Militer Luar Biasa, the Extraordinary Military Courts) only to suggest possibilities, not to establish facts. As I note in the introduction, the testimonies of the defendants and witnesses at the Mahmillub trials are unreliable, and throughout this book I will be noting the many errors in their testimonies. However, some parts of the testimonies can be considered accurate when supported by other forms of evidence. In each trial transcript the most important section is the defense plea written by the defendant himself to present his general interpretation of the movement and reveal something of his personality.

6. By 1965 Sukarno had four wives: Fatmawati, Hartini, Dewi, and Harjati. None lived in the presidential palace in Jakarta.

7. Saelan, *Dari Revolusi '45 Sampai Kudeta '66*, 309–10. Colonel Saelan was the vice commander of the palace guard but was the acting commander that night because the commander, Brigadier General Sabur, was out of town. Within the palace guard, called Cakrabirawa, was a smaller unit of the president's personal bodyguards known as Detasemen Kawal Pribadi Presiden (DKP). This smaller unit formed the immediate circle around the body of the president. The commander of the DKP, Lieutenant Colonel Mangil Martowidjojo, has written a detailed account in his memoirs of Sukarno's movements on the morning of October 1, 1965 (see Martowidjojo, *Kesaksian Tentang Bung Karno*, 378–98).

8. Colonel Saelan has claimed that one of Untung's subordinates, Captain Suwarno, approached him at about 5:45 A.M. to ask where the president was (Saelan, *Dari Revolusi '45 Sampai Kudeta '66*, 309). This may suggest that Untung's group was looking for the president at the last minute. It was Suwarno who met Supardjo at the palace and explained that the president was absent.

9. Atmodjo interview, December 14, 2002.

10. See the interview with Dani in Katoppo, *Menyingkap Kabut Halim 1965*, 240.

11. See Sukarno's statement of October 3, 1965, in Setiyono and Triyana, *Revolusi Belum Selesai*, 1:18.

12. The times here are approximate. Lieutenant Colonel Martowidjojo recalls that Sukarno arrived at Halim air base around 9 A.M. (Martowidjojo, *Kesaksian Tentang Bung Karno*, 389). Supardjo appears to have arrived sometime before Sukarno. When Supardjo arrived, he briefly met Omar Dani at the main office and then went to meet with the movement's core leaders. Supardjo had already left the main office by the time Sukarno and his entourage arrived there.

13. The precise time of the killings is unknown. The Central Intelligence Agency, in its published report about the movement, claimed the generals were killed at about 7 A.M. (CIA, *Indonesia—1965*, 21). One soldier in the palace guard who was present at Lubang Buaya, Sergeant Major Bungkus, recalls that it occurred around 9:30 A.M. (Bungkus interview). For Bungkus's published comments on the killings, see Anderson, "World of Sergeant-Major Bungkus," 27–28.

14. The dates of the meetings, the topics of discussion, the names of all who attended, and the various opinions expressed cannot be known with any certainty. The Suharto regime's accounts were based on Sjam's testimony. But we have no reason to trust Sjam's word on these matters. Notosusanto and Saleh claimed that the plotters met ten times from August 17 to September 29 (see *Tragedi Nasional*, 11–13). The CIA report claims that they met eight times from September 6 to September 29 (*Indonesia—1965*, 110–57).

15. Atmodjo interview, December 14, 2002.

16. On Kusno's presence see Siauw Giok Tjhan, "Berbagai Catatan," 5–7. Subekti, at his trial, admitted to being at Halim with Aidit (Subekti, "Jalan Pembebasan Rakyat Indonesia," 45–46). This is a Mahmillub statement that is reliable. Subekti had no reason to admit that he was at Halim with Aidit. Much of Subekti's defense plea was a denunciation of the Suharto regime. While Subekti was not forthcoming about what transpired at Halim air base that morning, his assertion that he was present seems true. Heru Atmodjo has also claimed that he learned from other political prisoners that Subekti was at Halim (Sembiring and Sutedjo, *Gerakan 30 September*, 128–29).

17. Atmodjo interview, December 14, 2002, Jakarta.

18. According to Dani, the officers present at the meeting were Commodores Dewanto, Andoko, and Wattimena, Vice Marshal Makki Perdanakusuma, and Dani himself. The meeting was held in Dani's office at Wisma Angkasa (Katoppo, *Menyingkap Kabut Halim 1965*, 225).

19. Sukarno initiated a campaign against Malaysia in September 1963 that he called Konfrontasi (Confrontation). The Indonesian military stationed troops in Sumatra and Kalimantan for a possible invasion and occasionally

sent small groups of troops into Malaysian territory. The original name of the military command established to wage Confrontation was Koga. Sukarno reorganized this command in October 1964 and renamed it Kolaga: Komando Mandala Siaga (Mandala Vigilance Command). Dani was the commander of Kolaga. His vice commander after January 1, 1965, was Suharto. The commander of the Kolaga troops in Kalimantan was Supardjo.

20. Dani has said that he spent the night at Halim air base because he expected to learn more the next day about what was afoot. He slept in the air base's central command building instead of returning home or going to his own office in downtown Jakarta. It does not appear to be true, as Anderson and McVey surmised, that Dani was "picked up by AURI [air force] personnel and taken out to Halim [at 3 A.M.] to seal the conspirators' control of the bases by his 'authoritative' presence'" (*Preliminary Analysis*, 19).

21. Atmodjo interview, June 11, 2000.

22. Dani has explained that he wrote the "Order of the Day" sometime between 7:15 and 8 A.M. after hearing the movement's first announcement over the radio at Halim air base. He put the statement aside once he learned at 8 A.M. that Sukarno was coming to Halim. Dani considered what he had written to be a draft that he might revise after learning the president's position on the movement. The vice marshal had already sent the draft to Commodore Dewanto at air force headquarters to get his opinion. Apparently, because of a miscommunication, this draft was then issued as a finished document from the downtown headquarters at 9:30 A.M., before Dani could revise it (Katoppo, *Menyingkap Kabut Halim*, 238–39).

23. The involvement of individuals from the paratroop unit and the military police is based on oral interviews with former military personnel who participated in the movement, Subowo and Mujiyono (both are pseudonyms).

24. The number of people in the PKI-affiliated militias is not known for certain. Untung, during his Mahmillub trial, claimed that about two thousand civilians participated in the movement's action on October 1, 1965 (*"Gerakan 30 September" Dihadapan Mahmillub di Djakarta, Perkara Untung*, 40).

25. Anderson and McVey cited a newspaper report quoting Major General Umar Wirahadikusumah, the commander of Kodam Jaya (the Jakarta command), as claiming that his troops totaled sixty thousand (*Preliminary Analysis*, 66n13). I think the figure is too high, but I have not seen any other figure for the Kodam's troop strength.

26. Wirahadikusumah, *Dari Peristiwa ke Peristiwa*, 182–86.

27. The Suharto regime's own accounts contain no information about the participation of Sunardi and Anwas in the movement. See Notosusanto and Saleh, *Coup Attempt*, State Secretariat, *September 30th Movement*. Both men were later tried by a military tribunal, convicted despite the lack of evidence against them, and imprisoned until the late 1970s.

28. *"Gerakan 30 September" Dihadapan Mahmillub, Perkara Untung*, 77.

29. Ibid., 75.

30. Sembiring and Sutedjo, *Gerakan 30 September 1965,* 125–29.

31. Mahmillub transcript, Supardjo trial, defense plea *(pleidooi dari tertu-duh),* 6, 11.

32. The CIA report claims that Decree no. 1 was first broadcast at noon and decisions 1 and 2 at 1 P.M. (see *Indonesia—1965,* 25–26). The journal *Indonesia,* in publishing translations of the documents, claimed that all three announcements were read over the air at 2 P.M. ("Selected Documents," 137–39).

33. *"Gerakan 30 September" Dihadapan Mahmillub, Perkara Untung,* photographs between pages 8 and 9.

34. The radio station broadcast Omar Dani's "Order of the Day" sometime in the afternoon, although it had been released (by mistake, according to Dani) at 9:30 A.M. Dani based his statement on the information in the first broadcast (the movement as the protector of Sukarno) rather than the afternoon broadcasts (the movement as the usurper of Sukarno). The editors of *Indonesia* claim that Dani's statement was broadcast at 3:30 P.M. ("Selected Documents," 143). Dani himself has stated that it was broadcast at 1 P.M. (Katoppo, *Menyingkap Kabut Halim,* 239).

35. Sukarno used the term *Panca Azimat Revolusi,* the Five Charms of the Revolution, to refer to Nasakom, Pancasila, Manipol-Usdek, Trisakti, and Berdikari. Nasakom was the principle of combining the nationalist, religious, and Communist political tendencies into a single functioning nation-state. Pancasila consists of the five general principles that provide a basis for unity among Indonesians. The five are, roughly, a belief in one god, humanity, nationalism, democracy, and social justice. Manipol was Sukarno's Political Manifesto of 1959, which the government adopted as its guiding principle. Usdek was his acronym for five terms: the Constitution of 1945, Indonesian-style socialism, Guided Democracy, Guided Economy, and Indonesian self-identity. Trisakti referred to three principles: complete national sovereignty, self-sufficient economy, and national self-identity in culture. Berdikari, or standing on one's own feet *(berdiri di atas kaki sendiri),* was Sukarno's principle of national economic self-sufficiency.

36. *"Gerakan 30 September" Dihadapan Mahmillub, Perkara Untung,* 60.

37. Mahmillub transcript, Supardjo trial, 3rd session, February 24, 1967, 16–17. The official army version is that Sukarno patted Supardjo on the back and said, "Good job" (CIA, *Indonesia—1965,* 31). This appears to be a bowdlerization of Supardjo's testimony. Sukarno did not congratulate him for kidnapping the generals: he patted him on the back while threatening to punish him if he did not stop the movement. Sukarno did not know Supardjo very well, but he had met him on a number of occasions and had developed a great respect for him. At Halim Sukarno appears to have gotten along nicely with him. An intimacy was established by joking, backslapping, and speaking in Sundanese (the language of West Java). Neither was Sundanese—Supardjo was Javanese as the

o at the end of his name suggests—but both had spent enough time in West Java to speak the language fluently.

38. Surodjo and Soeparno, *Tuhan, Pergunakanlah Hati, Pikiran, and Tanganku,* 70.

39. The aides with Sukarno at Halim air base were Vice Admiral R. Eddy Martadinata, Inspector General Sutjipto Judodihardjo, Brigadier General Sabur, and Brigadier General Soetardio.

40. Surodjo and Soeparno, *Tuhan, Pergunakanlah Hati, Pikiran, and Tanganku,* 71.

41. Atmodjo interview, December 14, 2002. The CIA report claims that Supardjo shuttled between the Operations Command Center and Sergeant Sujatno's house four times that morning (9:30, 10:15, 11:15, and 11:45). The report does not cite the source of this information. See CIA, *Indonesia—1965,* diagram between pages 22 and 23. The diagram does not appear to be accurate because other reports indicate that Supardjo did not meet Sukarno at the Air Base Command Center until about 10 A.M. and that Sukarno had shifted to Commodore Soesanto's house at 11 A.M. The CIA's diagram does not show that Supardjo also shuttled between Soesanto's house and Sujatno's house.

42. According to the CIA's published report, "Supardjo asked that he be given an opportunity to consult with his 'comrades' on the matter. The President answered, 'Yes, all right, but return immediately.' . . . After conferring, they [the movement leaders] decided to recommend to Sukarno that he appoint Major General Pranoto" (CIA, *Indonesia—1965,* 32). According to Supardjo's account (see my chap. 3 and appendix 1), the movement recommended three names: Rukman's, Pranoto's, and Rachmat's.

43. On the reputations of Rukman and Rachmat, see Sundhaussen, *Road to Power,* 171–72.

44. Setiyono and Triyana, *Revolusi Belum Selesai,* 1:73.

45. Yogyakarta was not under the civil administration of Central Java. It was a special region (Daerah Istimewa). However, the Yogyakarta Special Region was integrated into the army's command structure that covered Central Java (the Diponegoro command).

46. For the events in Central Java I largely follow the account in Anderson and McVey, *Preliminary Analysis,* 46–53. The authors based their account on stories that appeared in local newspapers from October to December 1965.

47. One example is the passivity of the pro-PKI military officers in West Sumatra (A. Kahin, *Rebellion to Integration,* 240–41).

48. Formed in 1960, Kostrad was the army's first effort at creating a central reserve of troops. Although its troops were still on loan from the regional commands, Kostrad was designed to give the army commander (Yani from June 1962) battalions under his own command (Lowry, *Armed Forces of Indonesia,* 89).

49. Wirahadikusumah, *Dari Peristiwa ke Peristiwa,* 186.

50. Reksosamodra, *Memoar,* 246.

51. Nasution recalls that he arrived at 7:30 P.M. (Nasution, *Memenuhi Panggilan Tugas,* 6:241). Suharto recalls that Nasution arrived at about 5:30 P.M. (Soeharto, *My Thoughts, Words and Deeds,* 105).

52. "Selected Documents," 167.

53. *Tapol Bulletin,* no. 90 (December 1988), 20–21, citing *Indonesia Reports, Politics Supplement,* no. 25, August 1988. This information originally appeared in an anonymous Indonesian-language document titled "The Role of President Suharto in the 30 September Movement." The document appended a facsimile of the radiogram that Suharto had sent to the three battalions on September 21, 1965, ordering them to Jakarta for the Armed Forces Day parade.

54. When they arrived at Halim, these troops were refused entry to the base by air force officers. Confused, they loitered on the road south of the base (Katoppo, *Menyingkap Kabut Halim 1965,* 129).

55. The time of 6 P.M. is reported in Dinas Sejarah Militer TNI–Angkatan Darat, *Cuplikan Sejarah Perjuangan TNI–Angkatan Darat,* 496.

56. Juwono interview. Juwono (a pseudonym) was a member of the PKI's youth organization, Pemuda Rakjat, and he had been instructed by his superiors to occupy the telecommunications building.

57. Reksosamodra, *Memoar,* 247–48.

58. Hughes, *End of Sukarno,* 82.

59. The most detailed account of the events of the morning of October 2 in and around Halim is Katoppo, *Menyingkap Kabut Halim 1965,* 149–80.

2. Interpretations of the Movement

1. I will ignore three other interpretations, those by Dake, Holtzappel, and Fic. Dake has argued, on the basis of unreliable evidence, that President Sukarno was the mastermind of the movement (Dake, *In the Spirit of the Red Banteng*). Dake's sole piece of evidence is the transcript of the interrogation of President Sukarno's adjutant, Captain Bambang Widjanarko, by Kopkamtib (Operations Command to Restore Order and Security) personnel. Dake also has written the introduction to this transcript's original Indonesian text and English translation (Karni, *Devious Dalang*). For a gentle critique of Dake's far-fetched thesis, see Crouch, *Army and Politics in Indonesia,* 119–21. For a more trenchant critique see Ernst Utrecht's review of Dake's and Karni's books in "An Attempt to Corrupt Indonesian History." Holtzappel has argued, on the basis of wild misinterpretations of testimonies before the Mahmillub, that the air force officers, especially Major Soejono, were the real leaders of the movement (Holtzappel, "30 September Movement"). His article is too ill-informed to merit rebuttal. Fic has contended that Mao Zedong suggested to Aidit that the PKI kill the right-wing generals and that Aidit then gained Sukarno's assent to this plan. Fic has spun this tale out of his own imagination

(Fic, *Anatomy of the Jakarta Coup*, 94–105). Only solid evidence can outweigh the many reasons for believing that Sukarno and China had nothing to do with the plotting for the movement.

2. Soeharto, *My Thoughts, Words and Deeds*, 100. Alimin had not been a "PKI boss" since Aidit's generation displaced him in 1951.

3. Sugama, *Memori Jenderal Yoga*, 148, 152–53.

4. Brigadier General Sucipto was the assistant on the Koti staff in charge of political affairs. Koti, the Supreme Operations Command, was formed in 1963 by Sukarno so that he could better control the military and reduce Nasution's influence. Sukarno put many of his allies, even civilians, into it. But anti-Communist officers, like Sucipto, still found a place. On Subchan's role see A. M. Mandan, "Subchan Z. E.," 54.

5. Pusat Penerangan Angkatan Darat, *Fakta-fakta Persoalan Sekitar "Gerakan 30 September," Penerbitan Chusus no. 1*, October 5, 1965, 15–18. The army made this publication a monthly series and issued at least two more books, dated November 5, 1965, and December 5, 1965.

6. CIA Report No. 22 from U.S. embassy in Jakarta to White House, October 8, 1965, cited in Robinson, *Dark Side of Paradise*, 283.

7. Many of the PKI's buildings became government property. Under Suharto the party headquarters (the Secretariat of the Central Committee) became the office for the Ministry of Tourism.

8. Hughes, *End of Sukarno*, 141.

9. An Australian military intelligence report of December 1965 argued that "evidence of actual PKI involvement — that is of prior planning by the Central Committee — is largely circumstantial" (quoted in Easter, "'Keep the Indonesian Pot Boiling,'" 59–60).

10. Pusat Penerangan Angkatan Darat, *Fakta-fakta Persoalan Sekitar "Gerakan 30 September," Penerbitan Chusus no. 2*, November 5, 1965, 4.

11. "Berita Atjara Pemeriksaan," Latief interrogation report, October 25, 1965, Latief trial, Mahmillub documents. The interrogator was Captain Hasan Rany of the military police. On the state of Latief's health during the interrogation, see Latief, *Pledoi Kol. A. Latief*, 54–59. Many former political prisoners held in Salemba prison recall that Latief's cell emitted the noxious odor of rotting flesh. The wound in his leg left him with a permanent limp.

12. Untung claimed that he had no connection with the PKI and that he and Latief had originated the movement (*"Gerakan 30 September" Dihadapan Mahmillub, Perkara Untung*, 35–37).

13. Anderson and McVey reprinted and commented upon the Njono confession in *Preliminary Analysis*, 157–62. Hughes reprinted Aidit's confession and suggested that it was probably a forgery (see *End of Sukarno*, 177–82). Aidit had been the deputy chair of one chamber of the legislature (Majelis Permusyawaratan Rakyat, the People's Consultative Assembly, called the MPR) and a minister in Sukarno's cabinet. Aidit would not have composed an explanation

of the movement in front of midranking military personnel in rural Java immediately after his capture. He would have waited until he was produced before the public and President Sukarno. If he had so desired, he could have issued such an explanation any time before his capture on November 22. The text itself reads like a generic chronicle. The emphasis is on times and dates. Nothing indicates that Aidit himself wrote it. One sign that the confession is a forgery lies in its statement that the PKI planned to eliminate Pancasila after the coup. The idea that the PKI was anti-Pancasila was one of the army's standard slanders. (In fact, the party had supported making Pancasila the basic ideology of the state in the constitution-making body, the Konstituante, which met from November 1957 to July 1959.) It is absurd to think that Aidit would have denounced Pancasila, especially at that moment of crisis, when he had never denounced it before. Also, the confession has Aidit admitting to meeting Sukarno at Halim. Sukarno was surrounded by other people while at Halim. No one has ever claimed the two met there.

14. Anderson, "How Did the Generals Die?"

15. The U.S. ambassador to Indonesia in 1965, Marshall Green, has followed the Suharto regime's line in depicting the military officers such as Untung as "PKI pawns" (Green, *Indonesia*, 53).

16. *"Gerakan 30 September" Dihadapan Mahmillub, Perkara Untung,* 35, 38, 54.

17. Ibid., 55.

18. Ibid., 51.

19. Testimony of Major Soejono on February 16, 1966, in *"Gerakan 30 September" Dihadapan Mahmillub, Perkara Njono,* 208. By itself, Soejono's claim that Sjam was the leader cannot be taken seriously. Soejono's testimony was full of oddities and inconsistencies. He appeared to be engaged in a desperate attempt to shift blame from himself. His testimony is important because it contained one of the first, if not the first, mentions of Sjam's name in a public forum.

20. Hughes wrote in early 1967, "The mysterious 'Sjam,' it is now believed, was actually Tjugito" (*End of Sukarno*, 35).

21. Ibid., 35–36, 78.

22. Justus van der Kroef once claimed that the Cornell report "ignores the operations of the Biro Chusus." He did not mention that the Cornell report was written in January 1966, more than a year before the term *Biro Chusus* became known (Van der Kroef, "Origins of the 1965 Coup in Indonesia," 284).

23. Published only in English, the book was meant to convince foreign scholars, journalists, and diplomats that the Anderson and McVey report was wrong (Notosusanto and Saleh, *Coup Attempt of the "September 30 Movement"*). It was not translated into Indonesian until twenty years later: *Tragedi Nasional: Percobaan Kup G 30 S/PKI di Indonesia.*

24. The white book to which I refer is State Secretariat of the Republic of Indonesia, *September 30th Movement.*

25. Ibid., 63–70.

26. Njono, Supardjo, and Latief, for instance, rejected the validity of their interrogation reports when testifying at their trials. Untung did not explicitly reject his interrogation report, but his testimony contradicted it.

27. CIA, *Indonesia—1965*, 312. An ex-CIA agent specializing in Southeast Asia, Ralph McGehee, has claimed that this published report was meant to mislead. The agency "concocted a false account of what happened" for public consumption. Meanwhile, for internal purposes the CIA "composed a secret study of what really happened." The passage in McGehee's book about these two reports was partially censored when the CIA vetted his manuscript. Some details known to McGehee remain suppressed (see *Deadly Deceits*, 58).

28. Anderson and McVey, *Preliminary Analysis*, 92.

29. Van der Kroef, "Gestapu in Indonesia"; "Indonesia"; "Sukarno's Fall"; "Indonesian Communism since the 1965 Coup"; *Indonesia after Sukarno*, chap. 1; "Interpretations of the 1965 Coup in Indonesia"; "Origins of the 1965 Coup in Indonesia."

30. Pauker, *Rise and Fall of the Communist Party of Indonesia.*

31. Brackman, *Communist Collapse in Indonesia* and *Indonesia: The Gestapu Affair.*

32. The PKI's Politburo consisted of twelve men. Of these, four or five were chosen to function as members of its Working Committee, what was known as the Dewan Harian (or, literally, the Daily Council). According to Sudisman, this committee had four members in 1965: Aidit, Lukman, Njoto, and Sudisman himself. Sudisman corrected Sjam's statement that the Working Committee had consisted of five individuals (see transcript of Sudisman's Mahmillub trial, July 7, 1967). Subekti, in the confidential 1986 account that he wrote for a small group of surviving party loyalists, recalled that the Working Committee consisted of five men, the aforementioned four and Oloan Huta-pea (Subekti, "G-30-S Bukan Buatan PKI," 3). I trust Subekti on this point be-cause his account, although written much later than Sudisman's statement, was addressed to an internal party audience. Sudisman might have wished to deny that Hutapea, who was still at large in 1967, was such a high-ranking leader.

33. Anderson and McVey, "What Happened in Indonesia?" 40–42.

34. Anderson, "Petrus Dadi Ratu," 14. The Indonesian version of this essay was published in *Tempo*, April 10–16, 2000.

35. Aidit was executed somewhere near Boyolali, Central Java. The jour-nalist John Hughes noted in 1967 that "Aidit's death is unrecorded in any of-ficial document available to the public" (*End of Sukarno*, 175). In 1980 an army officer, Yasir Hadibroto, claimed responsibility for the murder. In late 1965 Hadibroto was a colonel who commanded Kostrad troops dispatched to Cen-tral Java to "destroy" the PKI. He claimed that he and his men killed Aidit without receiving a direct order from Suharto (see "Menangkap Maling den-gan Menggunakan Maling," *Kompas*, October 5, 1980; an English translation

appears in *Tapol Bulletin,* no. 41–42 [September–October 1980]: 11–14). Given Aidit's stature, it is unlikely that a colonel would have acted without direct orders from Suharto.

36. Anderson and McVey, *Preliminary Analysis,* 95.

37. Ibid., 95.

38. Ibid., 89.

39. Wertheim, "Whose Plot?" 202.

40. Anderson and McVey, *Preliminary Analysis,* 1.

41. Ibid., 1, 18.

42. In analyzing the coup attempts in the post-Marcos Philippines, Alfred McCoy argues that the rebel officers (the infamous RAM Boys) had bonded while in the military academy (*Closer Than Brothers,* 259–98).

43. Anderson and McVey, *Preliminary Analysis,* 38.

44. Anderson, "Petrus Dadi Ratu."

45. Anderson, "Tentang Pembunuhan Massal '65."

46. Crouch, *Army and Politics,* 116.

47. Crouch, "Another Look at the Indonesian 'Coup,'" 4.

48. Crouch, *Army and Politics,* 116–17.

49. Sudisman, *Analysis of Responsibility,* 4, 6–7.

50. Wertheim, "Suharto and the Untung Coup."

51. Wertheim does not cite the source for this story about Suharto's attending Untung's wedding. One of Suharto's subordinates in Kostrad, Kemal Idris, mentions in passing in his memoir that he attended Untung's wedding on behalf of Suharto. "I knew Untung from the time I received an order to represent Suharto at his wedding ceremony because he was a former subordinate of Suharto's" (Anwar et al., *Kemal Idris,* 180). Whether Suharto attended in person or sent Kemal Idris, he does appear to have been close to Untung.

52. Brackman, *Communist Collapse in Indonesia,* 100; *Der Spiegel,* June 27, 1970, p. 98.

53. Wertheim, "Suharto and the Untung Coup," 53.

54. Ibid., 54.

55. Ibid., 53.

56. Wertheim, "Whose Plot?" 205.

57. Ibid., 207.

58. Latief, *Pledoi Kol. A. Latief,* 129.

59. Ibid., 245.

60. Ibid., 279, 282.

61. Ibid., 282.

62. Ibid., 280.

63. Wertheim, "Whose Plot?" 204–5.

64. Peter Dale Scott has argued along similar lines: "Gestapu, Suharto's response, and the bloodbath were part of a single coherent scenario for a military

takeover." Suharto was the "principal conspirator in this scenario" (Scott, "United States and the Overthrow of Sukarno," 244–45).

65. Sukarno's vice prime minister, Soebandrio, has claimed that while he and Untung were in prison together, Untung told him that Suharto would ultimately rescue him. Untung believed that his death sentence was "just a show" *(hanya sandiwara)* and would not be carried out (Soebandrio, *Kesaksianku Tentang G-30-S,* 23). This information is not reliable. Heru Atmodjo, imprisoned with Untung and Soebandrio in Cimahi, is skeptical of it because Untung never spoke in a similar fashion to him (Atmodjo interview, December 14, 2002). Several other ex-political prisoners recall that in his later years in prison, Soebandrio had lost some of his sanity. By itself, his short book (written in 2000, after his release from prison) does not inspire much confidence. Despite the term *testimony* in the title, the book contains more speculation and second-hand information than eyewitness reporting and careful argumentation.

66. Wertheim, "Indonesia's Hidden History," 299.

67. According to the Suharto regime's version, Supardjo recommended Pranoto and Rukman (State Secretariat of the Republic of Indonesia, *Gerakan 30 September,* 145). According to Supardjo himself, he recommended Pranoto, Rukman, and Basuki Rachmat. See appendix 1.

68. While sitting in Commodore Soesanto's house at Halim air base, Sukarno discussed the appointment with Supardjo in front of at least seven other ministers and military officers. None of them later claimed that Supardjo proposed Suharto's name.

69. Wertheim, "Indonesia's Hidden History," 305.

70. Latief, *Pledoi Kol. A. Latief,* 279.

3. The Supardjo Document

1. Kolaga, the multiservice command, had two fronts for combat with Malaysia: one based in Medan (headed by Kemal Idris) and the other based in West Kalimantan (headed by Supardjo). According to most sources, these were named, respectively, the Second and Fourth Combat Commands. However, there appears to have been some confusion at the time as to whether they were named, in more sensible fashion, the First and Second Combat Commands. Mahmillub prosecutors identified Supardjo as the commander of the Second Combat Command. Another source of confusion is the role of Kostrad, the army reserves, in Kolaga. The commander of Kolaga was, from its start in May 1964 (when it was named Koga), Vice Marshal Omar Dani. The vice commander from January 1, 1965, onward was Suharto, who was simultaneously Kostrad commander. Suharto, in charge of Kolaga's troop deployments, insisted that all troops borrowed from the regional commands for Kolaga be transferred to Kostrad first (Crouch, *Army and Politics in Indonesia,* 70–71).

Supardjo, however, did not thereby become a subordinate of Suharto's or a Kostrad officer. For decisions about military operations, even as Supardjo was commanding Kostrad troops, he remained directly under Dani. It is inaccurate to describe Supardjo, as John Hughes does, as commander of the Fourth Combat Command of Kostrad (Hughes, *End of Sukarno*, 31). The former first deputy prime minister, Soebandrio, has confused the situation even further by claiming that Supardjo was "brought by Suharto into Kostrad and posted as Commander of the Second Combat Command" (Soebandrio, *Kesaksianku Tentang G-30-S*, 27). Supardjo was not brought into Kostrad, and Suharto was not responsible for his appointment to Kalimantan. Supardjo's appointment to Kolaga came in late 1964, before Suharto's appointment as vice commander. Another writer, accepting Soebandrio's false claim and raising it to a higher level of error, has described Supardjo as Suharto's *anak buah* (a personal follower, or loyal subordinate) (Harsutejo, *G-30-S*, 167).

2. Green, *Indonesia*, 53. Green incorrectly identifies Supardjo as a former military aide to Sukarno.

3. Soeharto, *My Thoughts, Words and Deeds*, 110.

4. Rey, "Dossier of the Indonesian Drama," 30; Anderson and McVey, *Preliminary Analysis*, 11.

5. *"Gerakan 30 September" Dihadapan Mahmillub, Perkara Untung*, 229–30.

6. Some have speculated that Supardjo may have been in league with Suharto in designing the movement since Supardjo met Suharto in West Kalimantan in the weeks before the action. As the vice commander of the forces for Confrontation, Suharto inspected the troops in West Kalimantan around mid-August 1965. A photo of the two men together on that occasion appears in Nurdin A. S.'s pamphlet, *Supardjo Direnggut Kalong*, 16. Wertheim mentioned this "joint excursion" as a fact worth pondering, although he acknowledged that "in itself this fact does not provide a strong basis for more concrete suspicions" (Wertheim, "Suharto and the Untung Coup," 54–55). Supardjo also met Yani, a victim of the movement, in the weeks before the action so the mere fact of an earlier meeting proves nothing.

7. The Mahmillub prosecutors contended that Supardjo and the movement had agreed beforehand that the signal for him to come to Jakarta would be the message that his child was sick. Supardjo's widow, in a conversation with me, rejected this allegation of a coded message. She asserted that her child was indeed seriously ill (Ibu Supardjo interview).

8. Mahmillub transcript, Supardjo trial, February–March 1967, defense plea *(pleidooi dari tertuduh)*, 5.

9. Supardjo recounted this story in court (Mahmillub transcript, Supardjo trial, defense plea [*pleidooi dari tertuduh*], 42).

10. Sugiarto (Supardjo's son) interview.

11. While living underground in Jakarta, Sudisman was the primary author of the self-criticism that was issued under the name of the Politburo in

September 1966. Supardjo may have written his analysis after reading the Politburo's document. Fic argues that Supardjo wrote his analysis in mid-October 1966, but Fic's source, the prosecutor at Supardjo's Mahmillub trial, cannot be relied upon for this information since he had no way of knowing (Fic, *Anatomy of the Jakarta Coup,* 330n1). Fic calls the document Supardjo's *otokritik*—a word he inexplicably puts in bold capital letters throughout his book. The term *otokritik,* meaning self-criticism, appears nowhere in the document itself. Fic does not mention that it is his own term for the document.

12. Mahmillub transcript, Supardjo trial, fourth session, February 25, 1967, 49, 55. In his defense plea Supardjo again rejected authorship of the document (defense plea [*pleidooi dari tertuduh*], 23).

13. Mahmillub transcript, Supardjo trial, fifth session, February 26, 1967, 2.

14. State Secretariat of the Republic of Indonesia, *September 30th Movement.*

15. Mahmillub transcript, Sudisman trial, Sjam's testimony, July 7, 1967. The section containing Sjam's testimony is not paginated.

16. Mahmillub transcript, Supardjo trial, third session, February 24, 1967, 48–50.

17. It is not clear to which officer Supardjo was referring. At least two officers pulled out of the planning meetings well before the action began: Major Agus Sigit and Captain Wahyudi, both from the army's Jakarta garrison. According to Heru Atmodjo, Sigit pulled out because he did not think the plan would succeed. Atmodjo met Sigit in prison in the late 1960s. Although Sigit had not joined the movement, in the military's eyes his attendance at a planning meeting was enough to warrant imprisonment (Atmodjo interview, December 19, 2004). Manai Sophiaan claims, based on second- and thirdhand information, that some officers had pulled out of the plot because of doubts of its success (Sophiaan, *Kehormatan Bagi Yang Berhak,* 89).

18. Mahmillub transcript, Supardjo trial, fourth session, February 25, 1967, 18.

19. Atmodjo interview, December 14, 2002.

20. Rewang interview.

21. Mahmillub transcript, Supardjo trial, third session, February 24, 1967, 2.

22. Sophiaan, *Kehormatan Bagi Yang Berhak,* 171–77; Saelan, *Dari Revolusi '45 Sampai Kudeta '66,* 305–6; G. Kahin, *Southeast Asia,* 156–57.

23. Although it was widely believed in Indonesia that Green had a hand in Park's coup, he probably did not. After reviewing the declassified records, Bruce Cumings believes that the State Department did not have advance knowledge of the coup (Cumings, *Korea's Place in the Sun,* 348).

24. Subekti, the former note taker for the PKI Politburo, noted in his 1986 analysis of the movement that Pono, who was imprisoned with Subekti in Cipinang, described Sjam as someone who intimidated and threatened those who disagreed with him in the planning meetings for the movement (Subekti, "G-30-S Bukan Buatan PKI," 11).

25. Sjam testimony, Mahmillub transcript, Sudisman trial, July 8, 1967.

26. Bungkus interview. Also see his comments in Anderson, "World of Sergeant-Major Bungkus," 24–25.

27. *"Gerakan 30 September" Dihadapan Mahmillub, Perkara Njono*, 55–56.

28. Captain Soeradi, a subordinate of Colonel Latief's, also claimed in his Mahmillub testimony that the number of sectors was six. Soeradi stated that he had been briefed on the movement's plan by Major Soejono on September 23. The following day Soejono introduced him to the commanders of the six sectors. He believed these six men were from the PKI. On September 25 he went to Lubang Buaya to plan the work of the sectors and delineate subsectors (*"Gerakan 30 September" Dihadapan Mahmillub, Perkara Untung*, 82–83). This issue of the sectors is another case where I rely upon the testimonies at the Mahmillub. From more solid evidence—the Supardjo document and the Juwono interview, which I describe later—it is clear that the movement had sectors for the militiamen. Because both Njono and Soeradi, on separate occasions, claimed it was six, it is safe to rely on their figure rather than Supardjo's.

29. Njono testimony, *"Gerakan 30 September" Dihadapan Mahmillub, Perkara Njono*, 87–98.

30. Juwono interview. Juwono is a pseudonym.

31. A Sukarno loyalist, Manai Sophiaan, learned about the plan for these kitchens *(dapur umum)* when speaking with former PKI members years later; see Sophiaan, *Kehormatan Bagi Yang Berhak*, 92.

32. Wieringa, *Sexual Politics in Indonesia*, 292.

33. Ibid., 294. The badges were meant to distinguish troops participating in the action from those who were not.

34. Oey Hay Djoen interview, January 24, 2002, Jakarta.

35. Peris Pardede testimony, *"Gerakan 30 September" Dihadapan Mahmillub, Perkara Njono*, 134. Because of the information Pardede provided to the army after his capture, Sudisman considered him to be a traitor to the PKI (Tan Swie Ling interview). Tan sheltered Sudisman in his Jakarta home in 1966.

36. Njono testimony, *"Gerakan 30 September" Dihadapan Mahmillub, Perkara Njono*, 87–88.

37. Mahmillub transcript, Sudisman trial, July 7, 1967. According to Supardjo's analysis, Sjam did not unilaterally decide to retreat. The movement leaders never made such a clear-cut decision. Manai Sophiaan claims that Sjam thought the PKI masses would stage demonstrations once the movement was underway (Sophiaan, *Kehormatan Bagi Yang Berhak*, 81, 89).

38. CIA, *Indonesia—1965*, i.

39. State Secretariat of the Republic of Indonesia, *September 30th Movement*, 116.

40. Mahmillub transcript, Supardjo trial, defense plea *(pleidooi dari tertuduh)*, 6, 11. As I noted in chapter 1, the original document of Decree no. 1 does not exist, so it is impossible to determine who signed it.

41. Mahmillub transcript, Supardjo trial, third session, February 24, 1967, 37.

42. Crouch, *Army and Politics in Indonesia,* 134. *Guided Democracy* was President Sukarno's term for the form of government he began in 1959. He dismissed the assembly that was drafting a new constitution (the Konstituante); restored the country's first constitution, which had been hurriedly written in 1945; canceled national elections; and reshuffled the members of parliament.

43. Major General Pranoto Reksosamodra was imprisoned on February 16, 1966, accused of being involved in the movement. He was released after less than a month and then kept under house arrest. He was imprisoned again in 1969 and not released until 1981 (Reksosamodra, *Memoar,* 250–51).

44. Mahmillub transcript, Supardjo trial, second session, February 23, 1967, 51.

45. In his memoir Suharto mentions that he abandoned Kostrad headquarters but does not specify the time (Soeharto, *My Thoughts, Words and Deeds,* 107).

46. Dani has denied Supardjo's allegation that he supported a bombing raid on Kostrad (Katoppo, *Menyingkap Kabut Halim 1965,* 255). At his trial Supardjo claimed that Dani had not supported the bombing run (Mahmillub transcript, Supardjo trial, second session, February 23, 1967, 55).

47. Atmodjo interview, December 14, 2002.

48. Ibid.

49. Department of State to the U.S. embassy in Jakarta, October 13, 1965, in Department of State, *FRUS 1964–1968,* 26:320.

50. U.S. embassy in Indonesia to Department of State, November 4, 1965, in Department of State, *FRUS 1964–1968,* 26:354.

51. Omar Dani testified at his Mahmillub trial that Sukarno rejected Suharto as temporary caretaker because he was "too stubborn" (quoted in Crouch, *Army and Politics in Indonesia,* 128).

52. On Suharto's premature transfer from his post as division commander in 1959, see Crouch, *Army and Politics in Indonesia,* 40, 124–25.

53. Benjamin, *Reflections,* 206.

4. Sjam and the Special Bureau

1. Sjam testimony, Mahmillub transcript, Sudisman trial, July 7, 1967. Pono (short for Supono) similarly testified that the Special Bureau was created in 1963–64 (Mahmillub transcript, Supono [Pono] trial, third session, January 1972).

2. The Communist Party launched an anticolonial revolt in 1926–27. The Dutch colonial government suppressed the revolt, then arrested thousands of Communists and nationalists and exiled them to Boven Digul, an internment camp in what is now West Papua.

3. All quotes and information attributed to Hasan in this chapter come from my recorded interview with him.

4. Sucipto and Sukrisno interviews. The latter is a pseudonym.

5. Siauw Giok Tjhan, "Berbagai Catatan," 9.

6. Oey Hay Djoen interview.

7. Subekti, "Kata Pendahuluan," 2.

8. A former army colonel, Muhammad Sidik Kardi, claimed that the Socialist Party of Indonesia began its own formal network of military officers after the party's failure in the 1955 elections. The party's strategy was to forsake a mass membership and instead build a party of well-educated cadre highly placed in the government and military. One officer who was widely known as a PSI partisan was Colonel Suwarto, the deputy director of the army's training center in Bandung (Kardi interview). I Ketut Reti, a prominent PSI figure in Denpasar, confirmed that the party had its own version of the Special Bureau (I Ketut Reti interview).

9. Lev, *Transition to Guided Democracy*, 5.

10. Siauw Giok Tjhan, "Berbagai Catatan," 9.

11. All references to Sukrisno's statements in the paragraphs that follow are from an unrecorded interview with him in Jakarta on July 14, 2005. Sukrisno is a pseudonym.

12. On Sjam's being part of the Pathuk group, see Elson, *Suharto*, 13, 317n3. About the Pathuk group itself and one of its leaders, Djohan Sjahrouza, see Legge, *Intellectuals and Nationalism*, 60–66, 126–29, and Moehamad, *Memoar Seorang Sosialis*, 348–57.

13. Oemiyah interview.

14. Benedict Anderson to author, January 3, 2002.

15. Sukrisno recalls meeting or hearing about the other more famous members of the Community Party of the Netherlands who had returned to Indonesia: Suripno, Setiadjit, and Abdulmadjid Djojoadiningrat. For more about these men, see Soerjono, "On Musso's Return."

16. At least four of the five became leading figures in the party. By 1965 Munir was a member of the PKI Politburo, Hartoyo was a leader of the BTI, Sukrisno taught in one of the party's schools, and Sjam, of course, was the leader of the Special Bureau.

17. The late Jacques Leclerc, a specialist in the history of the Indonesian left, argued that Aidit and Lukman's resurfacing from an underground existence in Jakarta was staged as a return from China and Vietnam (Leclerc, "Aidit dan Partai Pada Tahun 1950," 64). Also see Siauw Giok Tjhan, "Berbagai Catatan," 8.

18. Supardjo testimony, Mahmillub transcript, Supardjo trial, second session, February 23, 1967, 3–4.

19. The Suharto regime's 1994 white book is correct at least about the identity of the five men in the Special Bureau Center (State Secretariat of the Republic of Indonesia, *September 30th Movement*, 39–40).

20. Aleida interview.

21. Sucipto interview.

22. Rusyana interview. Rusyana is a pseudonym for a former member of the PKI's leadership for the province of West Java.

23. Sukrisno confirmed that Sjam married a Sundanese woman in 1951 and that she died of an illness before 1965 (Sukrisno interview).

24. Mahmillub transcript, Sudisman trial, Sjam testimony, July 8, 1967.

25. Subekti, "G-30-S Bukan Buatan PKI," 10.

26. It is possible that Parman knew of Sjam but did not receive adequate intelligence information about his activities. Perhaps Parman's agents were incompetent. Or perhaps they were complicit in the movement. Perhaps Suharto promised Parman that he and his Kostrad agents would keep track of Sjam and keep him informed. The possibilities are numerous.

27. Katoppo, *Menyingkap Kabut Halim 1965*, 237.

28. The U.S. embassy in Jakarta also received many reports. A former official in the embassy, Frances Galbraith, recalled, "We had rumors and reports almost every day of some kind of coup and this became such a flood of things it was very hard to separate the truth from the fiction, and most of it was fiction" (quoted in Brands, "Limits of Manipulation," 801).

29. In his global analysis of coups d'état, Edward Luttwak noted that preparations by coup plotters (contacting potential recruits, holding meetings, and the like) generate intelligence information for their opponents. But the precoup organizing also generates "an equal or greater amount of 'noise.'" The opponents have difficulty separating the hard, accurate data from the false or misleading data (the noise); they cannot always "identify the nature of the threat, since their capacity for processing information is not unlimited" (Luttwak, *Coup d'État*, 157).

30. The writers who have depicted Sjam as an army intelligence agent who was infiltrating the Communist Party usually point to his army identity card as proof. But the card itself proves nothing. The possession of such a card is consistent with the idea that he was a PKI loyalist who was infiltrating the army.

31. Mahmillub transcript, Sudisman trial, Sjam testimony, July 8, 1967.

32. On the Chairul Saleh allegation against Aidit, see Mortimer, *Indonesian Communism under Sukarno*, 377.

33. Van Dijk, *Rebellion under the Banner of Islam*, 124–25.

34. I met one former PKI supporter in Tasikmalaya who recalled that DII/TII insurgents descended from their hideouts in the mountains one night, entered the outskirts of the city, burned down his house, and murdered his father. As a fatherless teenager, he eagerly joined the "fence of legs" operation (Haryatna interview; Haryatna is a pseudonym).

35. Feith, *Decline of Constitutional Democracy in Indonesia*, 529–31.

36. Bismar interview. The late Bismar lived in exile from 1965 onward, first in China and then in Germany. Joesoef Isak, who was a close friend of

Bismar's, recalled that before 1965 he was aware that Bismar knew Abdul Latief (Isak interview).

37. The opinion of the former director of the intelligence agency BPI (Badan Pusat Intelijen), Brigadier General Soetarto (of the police), might be taken as representative of that of many pro-Sukarno officials. He acknowledged at his Mahmillub trial in 1973 that he had great respect for the PKI. Perhaps he believed that he was going to be sentenced to death (which he was) and therefore felt no need to be circumspect: "I saw that in the PKI's struggle, its struggle for the people's interest, and also, in my opinion, its values of hard work, it did not prioritize its own interests. The members sacrificed for the public interest and the interest of the party. What I can also say is that, for instance, the automobiles given by the government to those PKI members who were representatives in parliament did not become the personal property of the legislators themselves. They were handed over to the party's common pool. The party then decided who could use them" (Mahmillub transcript, R. Soegeng Soetarto trial, third session, 1973, 98–99). Soetarto, who was working under the first deputy prime minister, Soebandrio, was a bête noire of the Suharto clique. Soetarto was arrested in January 1966. He was granted a stay of execution and survived prison to be released in the mid-1990s.

38. Manai Sophiaan claims that Sjam received military training in China in the 1950s. Sophiaan based this claim on anonymous PKI sources (Sophiaan, *Kehormatan Bagi Yang Berhak,* 73). I trust Hasan on this matter because he had spent time in China himself and knew Sjam well.

39. Subekti, "G-30-S Bukan Buatan PKI," 15.

40. Heru Atmodjo recalls that Supardjo was impressed by the story he had heard of the physical abilities of Mao's guerrilla army during the pre-1949 fighting in China. The guerrillas were trained to run an entire day without stopping. This enabled them to outwit the enemy forces who did not calculate that the guerrillas could shift their position so quickly. Taking this story to heart, Supardjo persuaded his fellow prisoners at Cimahi—Atmodjo, Untung, and several others—to run around the inner courtyard of the prison and gradually build up their physical endurance. He had learned from his Chinese hosts that if one could run at a steady pace for forty minutes without stopping, one could run the entire day. And so the prisoners practiced running. Supardjo had a practical goal in mind: he planned that they would escape from the prison and then run nonstop for an entire night, thereby putting themselves outside the area in which the authorities would search for them (Atmodjo interview, December 14, 2002).

41. Sucipto interview.

42. Anderson to author.

43. In his July 1967 testimony Sjam named "Colonel Sidik" as a "progressive officer" who used to meet with the Special Bureau. At the time Colonel Muhammad Sidik Kardi was a prosecutor for the Mahmillub. He was arrested

only weeks later, in August 1967, and imprisoned for twelve years. I happened to interview Colonel Sidik in 2000 before I read Sjam's testimony. Sidik attributed his arrest to his refusal to cooperate in the effort to bring charges against President Sukarno. Sidik did not mention Sjam's accusation (Kardi interview). However, it must have been a factor behind his arrest. Unfortunately, Sidik died before I could interview him again.

44. Subekti, "Kata Pendahuluan," 3.

45. At the Mahmillub trial for Pono, Sjam stated that he had already served as a witness in about ten trials (Sjam testimony, Mahmillub transcript, Supono [Pono] trial, January 1972).

46. Siauw Giok Tjhan, "Berbagai Catatan," 9.

47. I noted Pradigdo and Pardede's betrayals earlier. The former revealed information that resulted in the arrest of many party leaders and members. On Suwarto, Kusnan, and Komalasakti see Siauw Giok Tjhan, "Berbagai Catatan," 9, 15–16. These men became interrogators and torturers for the military. Martin Aleida mentioned that Komalasakti became an assistant of the army in Jakarta to hunt down his erstwhile comrades (Aleida interview). An unflattering description of Komalasakti also appears in an autobiographical essay by another former political prisoner, Munadi, "Yang Tak Terlupakan," 5–6.

5. Aidit, the PKI, and the Movement

1. Sudisman, *Analysis of Responsibility*, 4.

2. Sudisman was also the main author of a document that was issued in September 1966 under the name of the Politburo: *Tegakkan PKI jang Marxis-Leninis untuk Memimpin Revolusi Demokrasi Rakjat Indonesia: Otokritik Politbiro CC-PKI* (Uphold a Marxist-Leninist PKI to Lead the Indonesian Democratic People's Revolution: The Self-Criticism of the Politburo of the PKI Central Committee). This document has recently been republished in combination with Sudisman's 1967 defense plea (his *pledoi*): Sudisman, *Pledoi Sudisman*.

3. Sudisman, *Analysis of Responsibility*, 4, 7.

4. Ibid., 7.

5. Ibid.

6. Ibid.

7. Ibid., 5.

8. Ibid.

9. Ibid.

10. Ibid., 7.

11. Ibid., 10–11.

12. Ibid., 10.

13. Ibid., 12.

14. Ibid., 18.

15. Ibid., 7.

16. Ibid., 18. By overthrowing the monarchy propped up by the British, the Qasim coup prompted a popular upsurge. There were large street demonstrations, union organizing efforts, and many new publications. The Iraqi Communist Party (ICP) welcomed the coup and acquired the freedom to operate in the open. The coup makers in the army, however, quickly suppressed the popular upsurge and became preoccupied with their own rivalries (Tripp, *History of Iraq*, 148–92). For a detailed account of the 1958 coup and the ICP's relationship to it, see Batatu, *Old Social Classes*, 789–807.

17. "Walaupun saya sendiri tidak mengatahui tapi itu dilakukan oleh kawan saksi Sjam atas instruksi kawan Aidit dan sayapun melakukan instruksi dari kawan Aidit, maka dari segi tanggung djawab saya ambil oper tanggung djawab itu semua" (Mahmillub transcript, Sudisman trial, session of July 8, 1967).

18. At his trial Sudisman referred to Supardjo as a clear example of a progressive army officer who was antagonistic to the army high command. He cited Supardjo's statements in court (in Supardjo's Mahmillub trial) as proof that the movement was an affair internal to the military (Sudisman, *Analysis of Responsibility*, 12). Sudisman could not have cited Supardjo's secret analysis (see appendix 1) to prove that point. That analysis, which Sudisman had probably read, argued that the movement was not internal to the military.

19. See appendix 2.

20. Hasan, "Autobiografi," 32.

21. *"Gerakan 30 September" Dihadapan Mahmillub, Perkara Njono.*

22. Subekti, "Jalan Pembebasan Rakyat Indonesia," 9.

23. In his 1972 defense plea Subekti stated that the date of the meeting was August 28 ("Jalan Pembebasan Rakyat Indonesia," 8). But in his 1986 analysis of the movement, he stated that the date was August 27 ("G-30-S Bukan Buatan PKI," 3). Munir, in his 1973 defense plea, stated that the meeting was either August 27 or 28 (Munir, "Membela Kemerdekaan, Demokrasi, dan Keadilan," 13–15).

24. Subekti, "Jalan Pembebasan Rakyat Indonesia," 11.

25. Ibid., 9.

26. This document was obtained by Hersri Setiawan from Jusuf Ajitorop in Beijing. It is now available in the collection of documents titled "Indonesian Exiles of the Left," deposited by Setiawan at the archive of the International Institute of Social History in Amsterdam. The untitled document consists of six sections that are individually titled. I draw upon only two sections: the first, entitled "G-30-S Bukan Buatan PKI," and the fourth section, entitled "Kata Pendahuluan."

27. Subekti, "Kata Pendahuluan," 1.

28. Subekti, "G-30-S Bukan Buatan PKI," 2.

29. Ibid., 12.

30. Ibid.

31. Oey Hay Djoen interview, January 24, 2002. A privately published booklet issued in 1979 in the name of the PKI's Central Committee similarly contended that Aidit had largely shut himself off from other party leaders in the weeks before the movement: "Comrade D. N. Aidit and several other comrades in the Politburo Working Committee, who agreed with and supported the actions, limited themselves to their own group" (Comite Central PKI, *Jawaban PKI Kepada Kopkamtib,* 9). The "several other comrades" named were Njono, Subekti, and Hutapea. The booklet was slightly inaccurate in identifying their positions in the party: only Hutapea was on the Politburo Working Committee, although Subekti, as the note taker for the committee, could be considered a member. Njono was in the Politburo, not on its Working Committee. I do not know who among the surviving PKI leaders spoke in the name of the essentially defunct Central Committee in the late 1970s. The anonymous author or authors adopted a pro-Soviet Union line and condemned the movement as the result of the Maoist tendencies of Aidit and his inner circle. Subekti mentioned in passing in his 1986 confidential document that Ruslan Wijayasastra, a fellow inmate at Cipinang prison, was the head of the Central Committee. Subekti was certainly not the author since his 1986 document critiqued Aidit from a Maoist perspective. The booklet also alleged, without evidence, that Sukarno had designed the movement and had invited Aidit to help carry it out. Much of the booklet's argumentation can be dismissed as speculation designed to fit a predetermined dogmatic conclusion. However, it might be correct on certain points that can be confirmed by other sources, such as Aidit's use of his own trusted confidantes in the weeks before the movement.

32. Friend, *Indonesian Destinies,* 102. Friend's information comes from Colonel George Benson, assistant to the U.S. ambassador in Jakarta for a U.S. program that encouraged Indonesian army officers to be active in civilian affairs.

33. Subekti, "G-30-S Bukan Buatan PKI," 13.

34. Ibid., 12.

35. Ibid., 15.

36. Subekti, "Jalan Pembebasan Rakyat Indonesia," 45–46.

37. Subekti's analysis can be criticized for its self-serving character. He denounced Aidit for acting on his own and denounced nearly every other member of the Politburo for not resisting. But he did not criticize his own lack of resistance. As he admitted in his courtroom defense plea, he was a kind of faithful servant to Aidit before the movement. Subekti acquiesced to Aidit's strategy of militarily preempting the Council of Generals. The awful errors that Subekti and other Politburo leaders identified after the movement's defeat were not apparent to them beforehand.

38. Tan Swie Ling interview.

39. The former Politburo member Peris Pardede claimed that Aidit told the Politburo in August, in the course of explaining that some progressive officers

wanted to act against the Council of Generals, that the strategy of preemption had advantages and disadvantages. Asked whether it was better to wait for the Council of Generals to act or to preempt them, Aidit responded: "About the costs and benefits, both options have their costs and their benefits" (Pardede testimony, *G-30-S Dihadapan Mahmillub, Perkara Njono*, 132). This claim seems accurate. One has to presume that Aidit was weighing his options.

40. Yani, *Profil Seorang Prajurit TNI*, 178; Soebandrio, *Kesaksianku Tentang G-30-S*, 12.

41. Mortimer, *Indonesian Communism under Sukarno*, 394.

42. The office was in a building, Wisma Warta, that included offices and hostels for other foreign journalists. It was located on the corner occupied today by Plaza Indonesia and the Hyatt.

43. Nursuhud was named a Central Committee member at the party's sixth national congress of 1959 (Partai Komunis Indonesia, *40 Tahun PKI*, 98). He wrote an account of the PKI's resistance to the 1957–58 PRRI rebellion in his home region of West Sumatra, *Menjingkap Tabir "Dewan Banteng."*

44. Sudisman, *Analysis of Responsibility*, 11. Sudisman criticized himself and other party leaders for overestimating the revolutionary character of the political situation in mid-1965. In the Politburo's self-criticism he wrote that the demonstrations and actions of that time, such as those against the U.S. government, were "still within the framework of partial and reformist demands." The party leaders, flush with success and carried away by the militancy of the time, convinced themselves that the revolution was at hand and dismissed dissenting reports: "The party leaders were not happy if the district committees and other party bodies reported the reality that the stage of growth of the mass actions was not as high as they had already concluded" (Sudisman, *Pledoi Sudisman; Kritik-Otokritik*, 117–18).

45. Isak interview. Saleh's office faced the Ciliwung River in downtown Jakarta.

46. Lev, "Indonesia 1965," 105.

47. Mahmillub transcript, Sudisman trial, Sjam testimony, July 8, 1967.

48. Sudisman, *Analysis of Responsibility*, 11. The term *safe-stellen* is a combination of English and Dutch.

49. Setiyono and Triyana, *Revolusi Belum Selesai*, 2:440. Sukarno also blamed the movement on the "adventurism of neocolonial powers" and "on some person [*oknum*] who wasn't honest [*benar*]" (Setiyono and Triyana, *Revolusi Belum Selesai*, 2:440). He did not elaborate on this enigmatic, ambiguous analysis.

50. Oey Hay Djoen interview.

51. Sophiaan, "Inspirasi dari Aljazair [Inspiration from Algeria]," chap. 2 in *Kehormatan Bagi Yang Berhak*.

52. For accounts of the coup see Humbaraci, *Algeria*, 217–46, and Quandt, *Revolution and Political Leadership*, 237–43. The account by the hagiographers

of Boumedienne (Francos and Sereni, *Un Algérien nommé Boumediene*, 161–79) is not without value.

53. Karim D. P., "Tiga Faktor Penyebab G-30-S."

54. Vergès cowrote a book about a woman who was one of the defendants in the case. See Arnaud and Vergès, *Pour Djamila Bouhired*.

55. For biographical information see Fejto, "Maoist in France" and Marnham, "One Man and His Monsters." Vergès was born in Thailand in 1925 of a French father and Vietnamese mother. He grew up in the French colony of La Réunion, fought for the French during World War II, and studied law in Paris in the late 1940s and early 1950s. He remains famous, or notorious, for serving since the 1980s as a lawyer for Nazis, war criminals, and ex-dictators. Among his clients have been Klaus Barbie, Slobodan Milosevic, and Tariq Aziz. He has offered to defend Saddam Hussein. The television program *60 Minutes* profiled Vergès on April 25, 2004.

56. Hindley's article, "The Indonesian Communist Party," offers a careful analysis of the PKI's position on the Sino-Soviet split.

57. Fejto, "Maoist in France," 122.

58. Quoted in Humbaraci, *Algeria*, 242.

59. Ibid., 241–42.

60. I have not been able to confirm that Aidit traveled to Algeria. The rest of the Indonesian delegation did not. Karim D. P. mentions only that Aidit met with Algerian Communists in Paris.

61. Isak interview.

62. First, *Power in Africa*, 449. First's parents were founding members of the South African Communist Party. Born in 1925, she was involved in the party from the time she was a youth. She married Joe Slovo, who later became the chairman of the party. The South African security forces assassinated her by a letter bomb while she was living in exile in neighboring Mozambique in 1982.

63. Ibid., 450.

64. Munir did not explain the time and context of Aidit's remark. It had to be sometime in August or September 1965 (Munir, "Membela Kemerdekaan, Demokrasi, dan Keadilan," 40). This is another example of a courtroom statement that can be given some credence since it accords with what is known from other sources.

65. Sudisman, *Analysis of Responsibility*, 7.

66. On the united front strategy see Hindley, *Communist Party of Indonesia*, 29–59, and Mortimer, *Indonesian Communism under Sukarno*, chap. 1.

67. Aidit participated in a large-scale PKI-organized research project in 1964 that investigated agrarian economic conditions. In the published results of that research he identified the "seven village devils" as *tuantanah djahat, lintah darat, tukang-idjon, kapitalis birokrat, tengkulak djahat, bandit desa, penguasa djahat* (Aidit, *Kaum Tani Mengganjang Setan2 Desa*, 27). The historian Hilmar

Farid has suggested that the party distinguished between good and bad members of a particular class according to their political affiliation: a good landlord was one who supported the PKI and/or Sukarno, while a bad landlord was one who supported political parties opposed to the PKI (Farid, "Class Question in Indonesian Social Sciences," 177).

68. This "dual aspect of the state" theory was denounced in the Politburo's self-criticism of 1966; see Sudisman, *Pledoi Sudisman; Kritik-Otokritik*, 102–9.

69. Oey Hay Djoen interview.

70. Quoted in Mortimer, *Indonesian Communism under Sukarno*, 380.

71. Anderson and McVey, *Preliminary Analysis*, 132–35.

72. Aleida interview.

6. Suharto, the Indonesian Army, and the United States

1. The following works, in emphasizing the limitations to U.S. power in Indonesian politics, wind up overlooking the ways in which the United States did exercise influence: Jones, *Indonesia;* Brands, "Limits of Manipulation"; Green, *Indonesia;* Gardner, *Shared Hopes, Separate Fears.*

2. Kolko, *Confronting the Third World;* Schmitz, *Thank God They're on Our Side;* Kinzer, *All the Shah's Men;* Immerman, *CIA in Guatemala;* Stevenson, *End of Nowhere.*

3. Assistant Secretary of State Walter Robertson, in a memo to J. F. Dulles, wrote that the PKI had an "absolute majority" of the votes in Java (quoted in Kahin and Kahin, *Subversion as Foreign Policy*, 95).

4. Quoted in Kahin and Kahin, *Subversion as Foreign Policy*, 86.

5. Ibid., 94.

6. "U.S. Policy on Indonesia," NSC 5901, January 16, 1959. The same words appear in the later revised document, "U.S. Policy on Indonesia," NSC 6023, December 19, 1960.

7. On the value of the aid see Kahin and Kahin, *Subversion as Foreign Policy*, 207.

8. Ibid., 211.

9. Ibid., 210.

10. Ibid., 211.

11. Quoted in Scott, "United States and the Overthrow of Sukarno," 246.

12. Jones, *Indonesia*, 362.

13. B. Evans, "Influence of the United States Army," 37, 40.

14. Rusk to President Johnson, July 17, 1964, memo cited in Peter Dale Scott, "U.S. and the Overthrow of Sukarno," 248n46.

15. Joint message from State Department, Agency for International Development, U.S. Information Agency, and Defense Department, July 12 1962, cited in Simpson, "Modernizing Indonesia, 115n28.

16. "Background to Plan of Action for Indonesia," NSC Action Memorandum 195, October 2, 1962, cited in Simpson, "Modernizing Indonesia," 129.

17. Sundhaussen, *Road to Power,* 173, 175–77.

18. B. Evans, "Influence of the United States Army," 28–29, 34–36.

19. Department of State, "Memorandum Prepared for the 303 Committee," February 23, 1965, in *FRUS 1964–1968,* 26:235n2.

20. Lev, "Political Role of the Army in Indonesia," 351. Lev noted that the army "held tenaciously to martial law" and ensured that it was extended long after the PRRI/Permesta rebellions had ended (353). Much to the army's displeasure, Sukarno ended martial law in May 1963.

21. Mackie, "Indonesia's Government Estates and Their Masters," 340–41, 344–45, 352–54.

22. See Nasution's own account of the army's social-political role during the Guided Democracy period, chap. 1 of *Kekaryaan ABRI.* Bourchier has termed Nasution's political thinking "corporatist." See his essay, "Conservative Political Ideology in Indonesia." Also see Reeve, "Corporatist State."

23. Quoted in Mrázek, *Sjahrir,* 455.

24. Pye, "Armies in the Process of Political Modernization," 76, 77, 80, 83, 89.

25. State Department Policy Planning Council, "Role of the Military in the Underdeveloped Areas," January 25, 1963, cited in Simpson, "Modernizing Indonesia," 115–16.

26. Pauker, "Role of the Military in Indonesia," 226.

27. Ibid., 225.

28. Ibid., 227.

29. Ransom, "Ford Country." Pauker brought Suwarto to Rand for a visit in 1962. Colonel Abdul Syukur, a former instructor at Seskoad, the Indonesian army's staff and command school, recalled that Pauker offered him the chance to go to the University of Pittsburgh, where Colonel Sukendro, a hard-line anti-Communist who had long favored a coup by the military, was studying (Syukur interview). Syukur, who was considered a Sukarnoist and a supporter of the movement's, was imprisoned by the Suharto regime from 1966 to 1981.

30. Sundhaussen, *Road to Power,* 165.

31. Glassburner, "Political Economy and the Suharto Regime," 33.

32. Ransom, "Ford Country"; Sadli, "Recollections of My Career."

33. Sundhaussen, *Road to Power,* 188.

34. Ibid., 187–88.

35. Omar Dani was not happy with Suharto's appointment (Surodjo and Soeparno, *Tuhan, Pergunakanlah Hati, Pikiran dan Tanganku,* 44–56).

36. Sundhaussen, *Road to Power,* 189. Supardjo stated at his Mahmillub trial that he felt that Yani's staff was deliberately sabotaging Confrontation

(Mahmillub transcript, Supardjo trial, second session, February 23, 1967). Mackie noted Supardjo's complaint in his book, *Confrontation*, 214.

37. Sugama, *Memori Jenderal Yoga*, 139; Pour, *Benny Moerdani*, 265–67. According to Sugama, Moertopo was also assigned to serve as an intelligence agent in the Second Combat Command in Sumatra. Moerdani, however, claims that it was called the First Combat Command.

38. Sugama, *Memori Jenderal Yoga*, 144; Pour, *Benny Moerdani*, 265–267.

39. Sugama, *Memori Jenderal Yoga*, 138.

40. Pour, *Benny Moerdani*, 256–57, 265–67. Pour is circumspect about Moerdani's role in Bangkok. He writes that Moerdani sent Indonesian infiltrators into Malaysia in accordance with the Confrontation strategy but also mentions that he and other army officers disagreed with Confrontation.

41. Sundhaussen, *Road to Power*, 188.

42. Ambassador Ellsworth Bunker to President Johnson, undated report [April 1965], "Indonesian-American Relations," in Department of State, *FRUS 1964–1968*, 26:256.

43. CIA, *Indonesia—1965*, 190–91.

44. On Sukendro's plots see Sundhaussen, *Road to Power*, chap. 4. In late 1965 Sukendro became the key liaison between the U.S. embassy and the army leadership of Suharto and Nasution. See the documents compiled in Department of State, *FRUS 1964–1968*, 26: 345–48, 351–53, 357–60, 363–66, 369–70. Sukendro soon fell out of Suharto's favor, perhaps for being too independent, and was imprisoned in 1967 for nine months. On Sukendro's later career see Jenkins, *Suharto and His Generals*, 70–73.

45. CIA, *Indonesia—1965*, 191. The former CIA station chief in Jakarta, B. Hugh Tovar, contradicted his employer's report when he wrote his retrospective account of the 1965 events. He claims that "the idea of the Generals' Council that has been bruited around for years is a myth. (I mean literally a myth.) . . . There was no generals' council separate from or independent of [Yani's general staff]." Tovar also denies that Yani and his generals were plotting against Sukarno (Tovar, "Indonesian Crisis of 1965–1966," 323). Given the existing evidence about the army high command's plotting against Sukarno, it is hard not to read Tovar's claim as mendacious.

46. U.S. embassy in Jakarta to Department of State, January 21, 1965, L. B. Johnson Library, National Security File, Indonesia, vol. 3, box 246, 91. Oddly enough, this important document is not included the *FRUS* volume pertaining to U.S. policy toward Indonesia in the mid-1960s. It is impossible to trust Tovar's statement that he "never had any indications whatsoever that the Indonesian Army officers were thinking about staging a coup" (Tovar, "Indonesian Crisis of 1965–1966," 322).

47. Bunker, "Indonesian-American Relations," 257.

48. "American-Indonesian Relations," presentation by Howard P. Jones at

Chiefs of Mission Conference, Baguio, Philippines, Howard P. Jones Papers, box 21, Hoover Institution Archives, 12.

49. Quoted in Subritzky, *Confronting Sukarno,* 126. Peck wrote this memo on November 27, 1964.

50. M. J. C. Templeton to Edward Peck, memo, December 19, 1964, cited in Simpson, "Modernizing Indonesia," 263n132.

51. Neville Maxwell, a British researcher, came across this document in the Pakistani archives. His letter about it was published in *Journal of Contemporary Asia* 9, no. 2 (1979): 251–52.

52. "The Succession Problem in Indonesia," DOS/INR Research Memo RFE-16, March 9, 1964, cited in Simpson, "Modernizing Indonesia," 126.

53. Ellsworth Bunker to President Johnson, "Indonesian-American Relations," n.d., in Department of State, *FRUS 1964–1968,* 26:257.

54. Department of State, "Memorandum Prepared for the 303 Committee," 234–37. Sukarno may well have been correct in alleging that the U.S. embassy gave an Indonesian person 150 million rupiah for conducting a propaganda campaign against him (speech before the cabinet, November 6, 1965, in Setiyono and Triyana, *Revolusi Belum Selesai,* 1:82).

55. Bunnell, "American 'Low Posture' Policy," 50.

56. Bunker, "Indonesian-American Relations," 256–57.

57. U.S. embassy in Jakarta to Department of State, telegram, August 23, 1965, in Department of State, *FRUS 1964-1968,* 26:286.

58. James C. Thompson Jr. of the National Security Council staff to President Johnson, memorandum, September 14, 1965, in Department of State, *FRUS 1964-1968,*26:299.

59. Benson, quoted in Friend, *Indonesian Destinies,* 102. Emphasis in original.

60. "Special Memorandum Prepared by the Director of the Office of National Estimates of the Central Intelligence Agency," January 26, 1965, in Department of State, *FRUS 1964-1968,* 26:219.

61. Bunnell, "American 'Low Posture' Policy," 59. Once again, Tovar's account appears to be mendacious. He wrote that the CIA "had no contingency plan for action of any kind" in case "the PKI did stage a coup" (Tovar, "Indonesian Crisis of 1965-1966," 322). From the declassified documents it is clear that the embassy, including Tovar and the CIA staff, had a contingency plan—it was to rely on the army to attack the PKI and to support the army once it did.

62. U.S. embassy in Jakarta to Department of State, March 6, 1964, *Declassified Documents Quarterly,* 1975, 117C.

63. U.S. embassy in Jakarta to Department of State, March 19, 1964, cited in Brands, "Limits of Manipulation," 794.

64. "American-Indonesian Relations," presentation by Jones, 12.

65. Indonesia Working Group Situation Report, October 4, 1965, quoted in Brands, "Limits of Manipulation," 802.

66. CIA Jakarta station cable to White House, October 5, 1965, quoted in Robinson, *Dark Side of Paradise*, 283n23.

67. Ibid.

68. CIA Report No. 22 (from Jakarta) to White House, October 8, 1965, quoted in Robinson, *Dark Side of Paradise*, 283.

69. U.S. embassy in Jakarta to Department of State, October 5, 1964; Department of State to the U.S. embassy in Jakarta, October 6, 1965, in Department of State, *FRUS 1964–1968*, 26: 309.

70. U.S. embassy in Jakarta to Department of State, October 14, 1964, in Department of State, *FRUS 1964–1968*, 26:321.

71. U.S. embassy in Jakarta to Department of State, telegram, November 4, 1965, in Department of State, *FRUS 1964–1968*, 26:354.

72. U.S. embassy in Jakarta to Department of State, October 20, 1965, cited in Simpson, "Modernizing Indonesia," 321.

73. On General Sukendro's urgent requests for communications equipment in November 1965 and U.S. provisioning of this equipment, see Department of State, *FRUS 1964–1968*, 26:364–66, 368–71, 440–43.

74. Kadane, letter to the editor, *New York Review of Books*, April 10, 1997, p. 64.

75. Kadane exposed Martens's lists in an article distributed by the States News Service in May 1990. Numerous newspapers picked up her story, including the *Washington Post* (May 21, 1990). Also see Kadane's follow-up comments in her letter to the editor of the *New York Review of Books*. The *New York Times* did not run Kadane's story but had one of its reporters review her findings (Michael Wines, "C.I.A. Tie Asserted in Indonesia Purge," July 12, 1990). Kadane deposited the transcripts of her interviews of former U.S. officials at the National Security Archive at George Washington University.

76. Robert Martens, letter to the editor, *Washington Post*, June 2, 1990. The Central Committee consisted of about eight-five people, and each of the roughly twenty provincial committees had about ten people. If one adds the leaders of the various affiliated organizations, such as trade unions, the total is about five hundred. Martens had to be listing district- and subdistrict-level party members. Note too that he might have provided more than "several thousand" names. Kadane put the total number at about five thousand. Martens's reassurances that the people listed were not "rank and file" is not of much comfort even if true. He provided the names over a six-month period during which he must have known that the individuals listed could well wind up murdered. As Ambassador Green noted in a memo, even the "smaller fry" were being executed.

77. U.S. embassy in Jakarta to Department of State, telegram, December 2, 1965, in Department of State, *FRUS 1964–1968*, 26:379–80. Once again Tovar

proves himself unreliable. In his 1994 article he dismissed allegations that the CIA had given money to student groups and denigrated his accusers as "people on the left, some sympathetic to either the PKI or Sukarno, and others merely anti-American." For Tovar only the unpatriotic could believe such rumors about the CIA. He blustered indignantly: "I don't mind being accused of something I did. But I hate to have something thrown at me that I didn't do" (Tovar, "Indonesian Crisis of 1965–1966," 336). The declassification of documents has not been kind to Tovar.

78. U.S. embassy in Jakarta to Department of State, telegram, November 4, 1965, in Department of State, *FRUS 1964–1968*, 26:355–56.

79. Ibid., 26:355.

80. U.S. embassy in Jakarta to Department of State, December 16, 1965, cited in Simpson, "Modernizing Indonesia," 343. Suharto put Saleh under house arrest on March 16, 1966, and then had him imprisoned one month later. Saleh died in suspicious circumstances at the Military Detention Center (Rumah Tahanan Militer) in Jakarta on February 8, 1967. The military's explanation, that he had a heart attack, was greeted with skepticism by his friends and relatives. He was forty-nine and in good health (Soewito, *Chairul Saleh*, 138–47).

81. Ambassador Green noted that the army would "be able in the long run to maintain its authority" only if it could "show concrete results in handling enormous economic and administrative problems" (U.S. embassy in Jakarta to Department of State, telegram, December 22, 1965, in Department of State, *FRUS 1964–1968*, 26:390).

82. U.S. embassy in Jakarta to Department of State, November 28, 1965, cited in Robinson, *Dark Side of Paradise*, 285. Also see Director of the Far Eastern Region (Blouin) to the Deputy Assistant Secretary of Defense for International Security Affairs (Friedman), memorandum, December 13, 1965, in Department of State, *FRUS 1964–1968*, 26:383–85.

83. Department of State, *FRUS 1964–1968*, 26:393n2, 401–2, 405, 407–9.

84. Ropa to Rostow, July 9, 1966, in Department of State, *FRUS 1964–1968*, 26:444, and Rusk to Johnson, August 1, 1966, 26:452.

85. On the role of these economists under the Suharto regime, see Winters, *Power in Motion*.

86. Toer and Prasetyo, *Memoar Oei Tjoe Tat*, 192.

87. Memorandum prepared in the Central Intelligence Agency, Washington, "Covert Assistance to the Indonesian Armed Forces Leaders," November 9, 1965, in Department of State, *FRUS 1964–1968*, 26:362.

88. Setiyono and Triyana, *Revolusi Belum Selesai*, 1:89.

89. Ibid., 44, 156.

90. Ibid., 163.

91. On this score I disagree with Robert Elson, who argues that Suharto, after becoming the caretaker army commander, had "no firm strategy on how

to proceed, nor towards what goal." Suharto proceeded "cautiously, carefully, and sensitively" over the months, "taking ground as it came to him" without being guided by "any grand vision or utopian scheming" (*Suharto*, 120–21). See my review of Elson's book in "Violence in the Suharto Regime's Wonderland."

92. Briefing Notes for President Johnson, February 15, 1966, in Department of State, *FRUS 1964-1968*, 26:403.

93. Setiyono and Triyana, *Revolusi Belum Selesai*, 2:184-85.

7. Assembling a New Narrative

1. Todorov, *Poetics of Prose*, 45.
2. Žižek, "Detective and the Analyst," 28.
3. Sheehan, "Simple Man in Pursuit of Power," 75.
4. Lev, "Indonesia 1965," 105.
5. On the Guided Democracy period Lev's book, *The Transition to Guided Democracy*, remains essential reading.
6. On the politics of Guided Democracy as a triangle, see Feith, "President Soekarno, the Army, and the Communists."
7. The most detailed account of the army's failed bid to repress the PKI in 1960 is van der Kroef, *Communist Party of Indonesia*, 227–40.
8. Legge, *Sukarno*, 421–22. For Soebandrio's version of the story about the telegram, see Soebandrio, *Kesaksianku Tentang G-30-S*, , 18–19. For the Suharto regime's version see State Secretariat of the Republic of Indonesia, *September 30th Movement*, 61–63.
9. On Sukarno and Hatta's abduction see Hering, *Soekarno*, 366–69.
10. Cribb and Brown, *Modern Indonesia*, 98. Sukarno and Hatta's prestige was not reduced by their kidnapping in 1945. Other examples include Sjahrir, kidnapped in Solo, June 1946; the resident and vice resident of Solo, kidnapped in November 1946; and the chief of the Yogyakarta police, Sudharsono, kidnapped in 1947.
11. Bungkus interview.
12. Hasworo, "Penangkapan dan Pembunuhan di Jawa Tengah."

Appendix 1. Some Factors That Influenced the Defeat of "the September 30th Movement"

1. I have no idea why these phrases are in quotes.
2. From the remainder of the document, it is clear that Supardjo means the leadership of the PKI. It is likely that Supardjo submitted this analysis to Sudisman, the surviving leader of the Politburo, who was preparing the party's self-criticism in mid-1966.
3. On the night of September 30, 1965, President Sukarno attended the closing ceremony of the National Technical Congress, at the Senayan Stadium.

Lieutenant Colonel Untung was part of the security detail for Sukarno's appearance there.

4. This officer might have been Major Bambang Supeno, the commander of the East Java Battalion 530. In his interrogation report (written by an army intelligence team), Supardjo is *alleged to have said* (this is an interrogation report that should be read with skepticism) that Sjam informed him on the morning of October 1 that he "still had some doubts" about Major Supeno (Departemen Angkatan Darat Team Optis-Perpu-Intel, "Laporan Interogasi Supardjo di RTM," January 19, 1967, 4; this document is within the Mahmillub trial records for Supardjo). Major Supeno's troops were the first to quit; they surrendered themselves to Kostrad, the army reserves, in the afternoon of October 1, though Major Supeno himself stayed at Halim air base with the rest of the plotters until the early morning of October 2. Major Supeno picked up the second in command of the battalion, Lieutenant Ngadimo, at the palace at around 2 P.M., as the troops began surrendering, and took him to Halim, according to Lieutenant Ngadimo's testimony at Untung's trial. The commander of Battalion 454, by contrast, tried to keep his troops at Merdeka Square; when he finally decided to abandon that position, he brought most of his men to Halim.

5. The text reads: "kita ber-revolusi pung-pung kita masih muda, kalau sudah tua buat apa." The term *pung-pung* must be a typographical error. It should be *mumpung* (while).

6. The main target was presumably General Nasution. The troops sent to kidnap him were led by a private.

7. Nato is Supardjo's clever abbreviation of *Na*sution and Suhar*to*.

8. The term in the original is *offensi-geest,* a combination of an Indonesian word *(offensi)* derived from Dutch *(offensief),* meaning offensive, and a Dutch word *(geest),* which means spirit.

9. The commanders of the four services—air force, navy, army, police—were simultaneously ministers in Sukarno's cabinet.

10. Suharto, not Nasution, forbade Pranoto to go to Halim.

11. Pak Djojo was the alias of Major Soejono of the air force, commander of the troops that guarded Halim air base. Supardjo might have used this alias in the document because he did not know Soejono's real name. That is a real possibility because Supardjo had joined the plotters only the day before and would have been introduced to the members when they were using their code names. The name Pak Djojo was also mentioned by Njono, the head of the PKI's Jakarta chapter, during his trial before the Mahmillub (Mahkamah Militer Luar Biasa, the Extraordinary Military Court). According to Njono, Pak Djojo was the pseudonym of a military officer who sought PKI volunteers for training at Lubang Buaya from June to September 1965 (*G-30-S Dihadapan Mahmillub, Perkara Njono,* 53–54, 64–65 79–82). Heru Atmodjo has confirmed in a conversation with me that Pak Djojo was the alias of Major Soejono.

12. Supardjo appears to be paraphrasing a passage from *Revolution and Counter-revolution in Germany* (1896), a compilation of newspaper articles originally published in 1852 under Marx's name but primarily written by Engels: "The defensive is the death of every armed rising; it is lost before it measures itself with its enemies. Surprise your antagonists while their forces are scattering, prepare new successes, however small, but daily; keep up the moral ascendancy which the first successful rising has given to you; rally those vacillating elements to your side which always follow the strongest impulse, and which always look out for the safer side; force your enemies to a retreat before they can collect their strength against you" (www.marxists.org/archive/marx/works/1852/germany/ch17.htm). Supardjo may not have read this text; it was a little-known title in the Marx and Engels oeuvre. Supardjo probably read Lenin's essay "Advice of an Onlooker" (written on October 21, 1917), which commented on this passage. Lenin's writings were more commonly read in pre-1965 Indonesia, no doubt because they were more easily understood and more relevant to a communist party preoccupied with day-to-day political strategizing.

13. The army command for West Java, called Siliwangi, had a reputation for anticommunism; its troops were used by the nationalist leadership to attack the PKI in East Java in 1948. The Siliwangi command was the home base of General Nasution.

14. This appears to be a criticism of the movement's radio announcement decommissioning Sukarno's cabinet.

15. I do not know to which brigades Supardjo was referring. Pranoto was Yani's assistant for personnel and did not have any troops under his direct command.

16. The identity of "Comrade Endang" is unknown.

17. This odd construction could be roughly translated as "a political strategy of surprise."

18. The use of the word *elements (unsur-unsur)* to refer to "democratic-revolutionary officers" is an oddity that I cannot explain.

19. The battalion from Central Java must refer to Battalion 454, which occupied Merdeka Square in the morning and then abandoned the position in the afternoon after receiving Suharto's order to surrender. Yet it is odd that Supardjo did not also fault the officers of Battalion 530 from East Java who surrendered to Kostrad. At least when the troops of Battalion 454 left the square, they avoided entering Kostrad. They fled to Halim.

20. Surjosumpeno was the army commander of the Central Java division. The officers of the September 30th Movement took over the division headquarters in Semarang on October 1 and placed him under arrest. Anderson and McVey noted that "Surjosumpeno was able to trick impressionable younger officers into leaving him alone long enough to allow him to make his escape" (*Preliminary Analysis,* 46). Supardjo was probably referring to this incident when criticizing the inability of junior officers to defy their superiors.

21. I have not been able to find the source of this quote.

22. Fic's translation of this document gives the number of battalions as thirteen. My version of the document clearly shows eighteen.

Appendix 2. The Testimony of Sjam

1. To my knowledge, the contents of Sjam's notebook were never made public.

2. The movement moved from Penas (the aerial survey division) to Sergeant Sujatno's house inside Halim air base in the morning, well before Battalion 530 surrendered to Kostrad in the afternoon.

Bibliography

Adam, Asvi Warman. "Dilema Megawati di Lubang Buaya." [Megawati's Dilemma at Lubang Buaya.] *Kompas,* October 8, 2003, www.kompas.com/kompas-cetak/0310/08/opini/611175.htm.

Agamben, Giorgio. *State of Exception.* Translated by Kevin Attell. Chicago: University of Chicago Press, 2005.

Aidit, D. N. *Kaum Tani Mengganjang Setan2 Desa.* [Peasants Crush the Village Devils.] Jakarta: Pembaruan, 1964.

Anderson, Benedict. "How Did the Generals Die?" *Indonesia* 43 (April 1987): 109–34.

———. "Petrus Dadi Ratu." *New Left Review* 3 (May–June 2000): 7–15.

———. "Tentang Pembunuhan Massal '65." [About the Mass Killings of 1965.] Interview with Ben Abel distributed on the Apakabar e-mail list, September 24, 1996, arus.kerjabudaya.org/htm/1965/1965/1965_Benson _Dalang.htm.

———. "The World of Sergeant-Major Bungkus: Two Interviews with Benedict Anderson and Arief Djati." *Indonesia* 78 (October 2004): 1–60.

Anderson, Benedict, and Ruth McVey. *A Preliminary Analysis of the October 1, 1965 Coup in Indonesia.* Ithaca, N.Y.: Cornell University Southeast Asia Program, 1971.

———. Letter to the editor. *New York Review of Books,* June 1, 1978, 40–42.

Anwar, H. Rosihan et al., eds. *Kemal Idris: Bertarung dalam Revolusi.* [Kemal Idris: Fighting in the Revolution.] Jakarta: Sinar Harapan, 1996.

Arnaud, Georges, and Jacques Vergès. *Pour Djamila Bouhired.* Paris: Minuit, 1957.

Badiou, Alain. *Ethics.* London: Verso, 2001.

Bartu, Peter. "The Militia, the Military, and the People of Bobonaro." In *Bitter Flowers, Sweet Flowers: East Timor, Indonesia, and the World Community,* edited by Richard Tanter, Mark Seldon, and Stephen Shalom. Lanham, Md.: Rowman and Littlefield, 2001.

Batatu, Hanna. *The Old Social Classes and the Revolutionary Movements of Iraq.* Princeton, N.J.: Princeton University Press, 1978.

Benjamin, Walter. *Reflections.* New York: Schocken, 1978.

Bourchier, David. "Conservative Political Ideology in Indonesia: A Fourth Wave?" In *Indonesia Today: Challenges of History,* edited by Grayson Lloyd and Shannon Smith. Singapore: Institute of Southeast Asian Studies, 2001.

Bourchier, David, and Vedi Hadiz, eds. *Indonesian Politics and Society: A Reader.* New York: RoutledgeCurzon, 2003.

Brackman, Arnold. *The Communist Collapse in Indonesia.* New York: Norton, 1969.

———. *Indonesia: The Gestapu Affair.* New York: American-Asian Educational Exchange, 1969.

Brands, H. W. "The Limits of Manipulation: How the United States Didn't Topple Sukarno." *Journal of American History* 76, no. 3 (December 1989): 785–808.

Budiawan. "When Memory Challenges History: Public Contestation of the Past on Post-Suharto Indonesia." *Southeast Asian Journal of Social Science* 28, no. 2 (2000): 35–57.

Bunnell, Frederick. "American 'Low Posture' Policy toward Indonesia in the Months Leading up to the 1965 'Coup.'" *Indonesia* 50 (October 1990): 29–60.

Central Intelligence Agency. *Indonesia—1965: The Coup That Backfired.* Washington, D.C.: CIA, 1968.

Chomsky, Noam. *Year 501: The Conquest Continues.* Boston: South End Press, 1993.

Chomsky, Noam, and Edward Herman. *The Washington Connection and Third World Fascism.* Vol. 1 of *The Political Economy of Human Rights.* Boston: South End Press, 1979.

Cohen, Stanley. *States of Denial: Knowing about Atrocities and Mass Suffering.* Cambridge, U.K.: Polity Press, 2001.

Comite Central PKI. *Jawaban PKI Kepada Kopkamtib: Pernyataan Comite Central PKI.* [PKI's Response to Kopkamtib: The Statement of the PKI Central Committee.] Jakarta, 1979. In the author's possession.

Coppel, Charles A. *Indonesian Chinese in Crisis.* New York: Oxford University Press, 1983.

Cribb, Robert, "Genocide in Indonesia, 1965–1966." *Journal of Genocide Research* 3, no. 2 (2001): 219–39.

———. "How Many Deaths? Problems in the Statistics of Massacre in Indonesia (1965–1966) and East Timor (1975–1980)." In *Violence in Indonesia,* edited by Ingrid Wessel and Georgia Wimhofer. Hamburg: Abera, 2001.

———, ed. *The Indonesian Killings of 1965–1966: Studies from Java and Bali.* Clayton, Victoria, Australia: Monash University Centre of Southeast Asian Studies, 1990.

Cribb, Robert, and Colin Brown. *Modern Indonesia: A History since 1945.* New York: Longman, 1995.

Crouch, Harold. "Another Look at the Indonesian 'Coup.'" *Indonesia* 15 (April 1973): 1–20.

———. *The Army and Politics in Indonesia.* Rev. ed. Ithaca, N.Y.: Cornell University Press, 1988.

Cumings, Bruce. *Korea's Place in the Sun: A Modern History.* New York: W. W. Norton, 1997.

Dake, A. C. A. *In the Spirit of the Red Banteng: Indonesian Communism between Moscow and Peking, 1959–1965.* The Hague: Mouton, 1973.

Darnton, Robert. "It Happened One Night." *New York Review of Books,* June 24, 2004, 60–64.

Departemen Pendidikan dan Kebudayaan. *Hakekat Pembangunan Monumen Pancasila Sakti.* [The Nature of the Development of the Pancasila Sakti Monument.] Jakarta: Departemen Pendidikan dan Kebudayaan, 1981.

Department of State. *Indonesia, Malaysia-Singapore, Philippines.* Vol. 26 of *Foreign Relations of the United States, 1964–1968.* Washington, D.C.: U.S. Government Printing Office, 2001.

Dinas Sejarah Militer TNI-Angkatan Darat. *Cuplikan Sejarah Perjuangan TNI-Angkatan Darat.* [Excerpts from the History of the Struggle of the Army.] Bandung, Indonesia: Mahjuma, 1972.

Dinuth, Alex. *Dokumen Terpilih Sekitar G-30-S/PKI.* [Selected Documents on the September 30th Movement/PKI.] Jakarta: Intermasa, 1997.

———. *Kewaspadaan Nasional dan Bahaya Laten Komunis.* [National Alertness and the Latent Danger of Communism.] Jakarta: Intermasa, 1997.

Easter, David. "'Keep the Indonesian Pot Boiling': Western Covert Intervention in Indonesia, October 1965–March 1966." *Cold War History* 5, no. 1 (February 2005): 55–73.

Elson, Robert. *Suharto: A Political Biography.* Cambridge: Cambridge University Press, 2001.

Evans, Bryan III. "The Influence of the United States Army on the Development of the Indonesian Army (1954–1964)." *Indonesia* 47 (April 1989): 25–48.

Evans, Richard J. *The Coming of the Third Reich.* London: Penguin, 2004.

Farid, Hilmar. "The Class Question in Indonesian Social Sciences." In *Social Science and Power in Indonesia,* edited by Vedi Hadiz and Daniel Dhakidae. Singapore: Institute of Southeast Asian Studies, 2005.

Fealy, Greg. *The Release of Indonesia's Political Prisoners: Domestic vs. Foreign Policy.* Clayton, Victoria, Australia: Monash University Centre of Southeast Asian Studies, 1995.

Feith, Herbert. *The Decline of Constitutional Democracy.* Ithaca, N.Y.: Cornell University Press, 1962.

———. "President Soekarno, the Army, and the Communists: The Triangle Changes Shape." *Asian Survey* 4, no. 8 (August 1964): 969–80.

Fejto, François. "A Maoist in France: Jacques Vergès and *Révolution.*" *China Quarterly* 19 (July–September 1964): 120–27.

Fic, Victor M. *Anatomy of the Jakarta Coup: October 1, 1965: The Collusion with China Which Destroyed the Army Command, President Sukarno and the Communist Party of Indonesia.* New Delhi: Abhinav, 2004.

First, Ruth. *Power in Africa: Political Power in Africa and the Coup d'État.* Harmondsworth, U.K.: Penguin, 1969.

Francos, Ania, and Jean-Pierre Sereni, *Un Algérien nommé Boumediene.* Paris: Stock, 1976.

Friend, Theodore. *Indonesian Destinies.* Cambridge, Mass.: Harvard University Press, 2003.

Gardner, Paul. *Shared Hopes, Separate Fears: Fifty Years of U.S.-Indonesian Relations.* Boulder, Colo.: Westview, 1997.

Geertz, Clifford. *After the Fact: Two Countries, Four Decades, One Anthropologist.* Cambridge, Mass.: Harvard University Press, 1995.

———. *Interpretation of Cultures: Selected Essays.* New York: Basic Books, 1973.

"Gerakan 30 September" Dihadapan Mahmillub, Perkara Njono. Jakarta: Pusat Pendidikan Kehakiman A.D., 1966.

"Gerakan 30 September" Dihadapan Mahmillub, Perkara Subandrio. 2 vols. Jakarta: Pusat Pendidikan Kehakiman A.D., 1966.

"Gerakan 30 September" Dihadapan Mahmillub, Perkara Untung. Jakarta: Pusat Pendidikan Kehakiman A.D., 1966.

Glassburner, Bruce. "Political Economy and the Suharto Regime." *Bulletin of Indonesian Economic Studies* 14, no. 3 (1978): 24–51.

Green, Marshall. *Indonesia: Crisis and Transformation, 1965–1968.* Washington, D.C.: Compass Press, 1990.

———. Interview for the CNN television series *The Cold War.* National Security Archives. www.gwu.edu/~nsarchiv/coldwar/interviews/episode-15/green6.html.

Hallward, Peter. *Badiou: A Subject to Truth.* Minneapolis: University of Minnesota Press, 2003.

Harsutejo. *G-30-S: Sejarah yang Digelapkan.* [September 30th Movement: The History That Has Been Concealed.] Jakarta: Hasta Mitra, 2003.

Hasan (pseudonym). "Autobiografi." [Autobiography.] Sixty-one-page typescript, 1998. In the author's possession.

Hasworo, Rinto Tri. "Penangkapan dan Pembunuhan di Jawa Tengah Setelah G-30-S." [The Arrests and Killings in Central Java after the September 30th Movement.] In *Tahun yang Tak Pernah Berakhir,* edited by John Roosa, Ayu Ratih, and Hilmar Farid. Jakarta: Elsam, 2004.

Hering, Bob. *Soekarno: Founding Father of Indonesia, A Biography, 1901–1945.* Leiden, The Netherlands: KITLV, 2002.

Heryanto, Ariel. "Where Communism Never Dies: Violence, Trauma and Narration in the Last Cold War Capitalist Authoritarian State." *International Journal of Cultural Studies* 2, no. 2 (1999): 147–77.

Hindley, Donald. *The Communist Party of Indonesia, 1951–1963.* Berkeley: University of California Press, 1966.

———. "The Indonesian Communist Party and the Conflict in the International Communist Movement." *China Quarterly* 19 (July–September 1964): 99–119.

Holtzappel, Coen. "The 30 September Movement: A Political Movement of the Armed Forces or an Intelligence Operation." *Journal of Contemporary Asia* 9, no. 2 (1979): 216-40.

Hughes, John. *The End of Sukarno: A Coup That Misfired, A Purge That Ran Wild.* 1967. Reprint, Singapore: Archipelago Press, 2002.

Humbaraci, Arslan. *Algeria: A Revolution That Failed.* London: Pall Mall Press, 1966.

Immerman, Richard. *The CIA in Guatemala: The Foreign Policy of Intervention.* Austin: University of Texas Press, 1982.

Ismail, Taufiq. *Katastrofi Mendunia: Marxisma, Leninisma, Stalinisma, Maoisma [sic], Narkoba.* [Globalized Catastrophe: Marxism, Leninism, Stalinism, Maoism, Narcotics.] Jakarta: Yayasan Titik Infinitum, 2004.

Jenkins, David. *Suharto and His Generals: Indonesian Military Politics, 1975–1983.* Ithaca, N.Y.: Cornell University Modern Indonesia Project, 1984.

Jones, Howard. *Indonesia: The Possible Dream.* New York: Harcourt Brace Jovanovich, 1971.

Kadane, Kathy. Letter to the editor. *New York Review of Books,* April 10, 1997.

Kahin, Audrey. *Rebellion to Integration: West Sumatra and the Indonesian Polity, 1926-1998.* Amsterdam: Amsterdam University Press, 1999.

Kahin, George McT. *Intervention: How the United States Became Involved in Vietnam.* New York: Alfred A. Knopf, 1986.

———. *Southeast Asia: A Testament.* London: RoutledgeCurzon, 2003.

Kahin, George, and Audrey Kahin. *Subversion as Foreign Policy: The Secret Eisenhower and Dulles Debacle in Indonesia.* New York: New Press, 1995.

Karim D. P., A. "Tiga Faktor Penyebab G-30-S." [Three Factors That Caused the September 30th Movement.] Text of speech delivered at a meeting in Jakarta, October 25, 1999.

Karni, Rahadi S., ed. and trans. *The Devious Dalang: Sukarno and the So-called Untung Putsch; Eye-witness Report by Bambang S. Widjanarko.* Introduction by Antonie C. A. Dake. The Hague: Interdoc, 1974.

Katoppo, Aristides, ed. *Menyingkap Kabut Halim 1965.* [Lifting the Fog over Halim Air Base, 1965.] Jakarta: Sinar Harapan, 1999.

Kinzer, Stephen. *All the Shah's Men: An American Coup and the Roots of Middle East Terror.* Hoboken, N.J.: John Wiley, 2003.

Kolko, Gabriel. *Confronting the Third World: United States Foreign Policy, 1945–1980.* New York: Pantheon, 1988.

Kopkamtib, *Himpunan Surat-Surat Keputusan/Perintah yang Berhubungan dengan Kopkamtib 1965-1969.* [A Compilation of Decrees/Orders Related to Kopkamtib, 1965-1969.] Jakarta, 1970.

Latief, Abdul. *Pledoi Kol. A. Latief, Soeharto Terlibat G30S.* [The Defense Statement of Col. A. Latief: Soeharto Was Involved in the September 30th Movement.] Jakarta: Institut Studi Arus Informasi, 2000.

———. "Serangan Umum 1 Maret 1949." [The All-Fronts Attack of March 1,

1949.] Manuscript written in Cipinang prison, Jakarta, in the late 1980s. In the author's possession.

Leclerc, Jacques. "Aidit dan Partai Pada Tahun 1950." [Aidit and the Party in 1950.] *Prisma* 11, no. 7 (July 1982): 61–78.

Legge, J. D. *Intellectuals and Nationalism in Indonesia: A Study of the Following Recruited by Sutan Sjahrir in Occupation Jakarta.* Ithaca, N.Y.: Cornell Modern Indonesia Project, 1988.

———. *Sukarno: A Political Biography.* 1972. Reprint, Singapore: Archipelago Press, 2003.

Lev, Daniel. "Indonesia 1965: The Year of the Coup." *Asian Survey* 6, no. 2 (February 1966): 103–10.

———. "The Political Role of the Army in Indonesia." *Pacific Affairs* 36 (Winter 1963–64): 349–64.

———. *The Transition to Guided Democracy: Indonesian Politics, 1957–1959.* Ithaca, N.Y.: Cornell University Southeast Asia Program, 1966.

Lowry, Robert. *The Armed Forces of Indonesia.* St. Leonards, New South Wales, Australia: Allen and Unwin, 1996.

Luttwak, Edward. *Coup d'État: A Practical Handbook.* New York: Fawcett, 1968.

McCormick, John P. "The Dilemmas of Dictatorship: Carl Schmitt and Constitutional Emergency Powers." In *Law as Politics: Carl Schmitt's Critique of Liberalism,* edited by David Dyzenhaus. Durham, N.C.: Duke University Press, 1998.

McCormick, Thomas. *America's Half-Century: United States Foreign Policy in the Cold War and After.* Baltimore: Johns Hopkins University Press, 1995.

McCoy, Alfred. *Closer Than Brothers: Manhood at the Philippine Military Academy.* New Haven, Conn.: Yale University Press, 1999.

McGregor, Katharine E. "Commemoration of 1 October, 'Hari Kesaktian Pancasila': A Post Mortem Analysis?" *Asian Studies Review* 26, no. 1 (March 2002): 39–72.

———. "Representing the Indonesian Past: The National Monument History Museum from Guided Democracy to the New Order." *Indonesia* 75 (April 2003): 91–122.

McGehee, Ralph. *Deadly Deceits: My 25 Years in the CIA.* New York: Sheridan Square, 1983.

Mackie, J. A. C. "Indonesia's Government Estates and Their Masters." *Pacific Affairs* 34 (Winter 1961–62): 337–60.

———. *Konfrontasi: The Indonesia-Malaysia Dispute, 1963–1966.* Kuala Lumpur: Oxford University Press, 1974.

McNamara, Robert. *In Retrospect: The Tragedy and Lessons of Vietnam.* With Brian VanDeMark. New York: Times Books, 1995.

Mandan, A. M., ed. *Subchan Z. E.: Sang Maestro, Politisi Intelektual dari Kalangan NU Modern.* [Subchan Z. E.: The Maestro, An Intellectual Politician from the Modern Nadhatul Ulama Circle.] Jakarta: Pustaka Indonesia Satu, 2001.

Marnham, Patrick. "One Man and His Monsters." *Sydney Morning Herald,* January 26, 2004.

Martinkus, John. *A Dirty Little War.* Sydney: Random House Australia, 2001.

Martowidjojo, Mangil. *Kesaksian Tentang Bung Karno 1945-1967.* [A Testimony about Bung Karno, 1945-1967.] Jakarta: Grasindo, 1999.

Maxwell, Neville. Letter to the editor. *Journal of Contemporary Asia* 9, no. 2 (1979): 251-52.

Moehamad, Djoeir. *Memoar Seorang Sosialis.* [Memoir of a Socialist.] Jakarta: Obor, 1997.

Mortimer, Rex. "Indonesia: Emigré Post-mortems on the PKI." *Australian Outlook* 28 (December 1968): 347-59.

———. *Indonesian Communism under Sukarno: Ideology and Politics, 1950-1965.* Ithaca, N.Y.: Cornell University Press, 1974.

Mrázek, Rudolf. *Sjahrir: Politics and Exile in Indonesia.* Ithaca, N.Y.: Cornell University Southeast Asia Program, 1994.

Mueller, John. "Reassessment of American Policy: 1965-1968." In *Vietnam Reconsidered,* edited by Harrison Salisbury. New York: Harper and Row, 1984.

Munadi. "Yang Tak Terlupakan." [What Is Not Forgotten.] Jakarta, 1999. Available online: www.geocities.com/cerita_kami/g30s/munadi.pdf.

Munir, Muhammad. "Membela Kemerdekaan, Demokrasi, dan Keadilan." [In Defense of Freedom, Democracy, and Justice.] Defense statement, Jakarta, March 2, 1973. International Institute of Social History, Suparna Sastra Diredja Papers, document 286.

Nasution, A. H. *Kekaryaan ABRI.* [The Military's Functionality.] Jakarta: Seruling Masa, 1971.

———. *Memenuhi Panggilan Tugas.* [Fulfilling the Call of Duty.] Vol. 6. Jakarta: Gunung Agung, 1987.

Newfield, Jack. *Robert Kennedy: A Memoir.* New York: E. P. Dutton, 1969.

Nixon, Richard M. "Asia after Vietnam." *Foreign Affairs* 46, no. 1 (October 1967): 111-25.

Notosusanto, Nugroho, and Ismail Saleh. *The Coup Attempt of the "September 30 Movement" in Indonesia.* Jakarta: Pembimbing Masa, 1968. Indonesian translation published as *Tragedi Nasional Percobaan Kup G30S/PKI di Indonesia.* Jakarta: Intermasa, 1993.

Nurdin A. S., M. *Supardjo Direnggut Kalong.* [Supardjo Nabbed by Operation Bat.] Jakarta: Varia, 1967.

Nursuhud. *Menjingkap Tabir "Dewan Banteng."* [Lifting the Veil of the "Banteng Council."] Jakarta: Pembaruan, 1958.

Partai Komunis Indonesia. *40 Tahun PKI.* [40 Years of the PKI.] Jakarta: Pembaruan, 1960.

Pascal, Blaise. *Pensées,* translated by A. J. Krailsheimer. London: Penguin, 1995.

Pauker, Guy. *The Rise and Fall of the Communist Party of Indonesia.* Santa Monica, Calif.: Rand, 1969.

——. "The Role of the Military in Indonesia." In *The Role of the Military in Underdeveloped Countries,* edited by John H. Johnson. Princeton, N.J.: Princeton University Press, 1962.

Porter, Gareth. *Perils of Dominance: Imbalance of Power and the Road to War in Vietnam.* Berkeley: University of California Press, 2005.

Pour, Julius. *Benny Moerdani: Profile of a Soldier Statesman.* Jakarta: Yayasan Kejuangan Sudirman, 1993.

Prunier, Gérard. *The Rwandan Crisis: History of a Genocide.* New York: Columbia University Press, 1995.

Pusat Penerangan Angkatan Darat. *Fakta-fakta Persoalan Sekitar "Gerakan 30 September," Penerbitan Chusus.* [Facts Regarding the September 30th Movement: A Special Publication.] Nos. 1–3, October–December 1965, Jakarta.

Pusat Sejarah dan Tradisi ABRI. *Bahaya Laten Komunisme di Indonesia.* [The Latent Danger of Communism in Indonesia.] 4 vols. Jakarta: Markas Besar ABRI, 1991.

——. *Buku Panduan Monumen Pancasila Sakti, Lubang Buaya.* [Guidebook to the Sacred Pancasila Monument, Lubang Buaya.] Jakarta: Pusat Sejarah dan Tradisi TNI, n.d., ca. 2000.

Pye, Lucien. "Armies in the Process of Political Modernization." In *The Role of the Military in Underdeveloped Countries,* edited by John H. Johnson. Princeton, N.J.: Princeton University Press, 1962.

Quandt, William. *Revolution and Political Leadership: Algeria, 1954–1968.* Cambridge, Mass.: MIT Press, 1969.

Ransom, David. "Ford Country: Building an Elite for Indonesia." In *The Trojan Horse: A Radical Look at Foreign Aid,* edited by Steve Weissman. Palo Alto, Calif.: Ramparts Press, 1975.

Reeve, David. "The Corporatist State: The Case of Golkar." In *State and Civil Society in Indonesia,* edited by Arief Budiman. Clayton, Victoria, Australia: Monash University Centre of Southeast Asian Studies, 1990.

Reksosamodra, Jenderal Raden Pranoto. *Memoar.* [Memoir.] Yogyakarta, Indonesia: Syarikat, 2002.

Rey, Lucien. "Dossier of the Indonesian Drama." *New Left Review* 36 (March–April 1966): 26–40.

Ricklefs, M. C. *A History of Modern Indonesia, c. 1300 to the Present.* Bloomington: Indiana University Press, 1981.

Ritchie, Donald, ed. *Rashomon.* New Brunswick, N.J.: Rutgers University Press, 1987.

Robinson, Geoffrey. *The Dark Side of Paradise: Political Violence in Bali.* Ithaca, N.Y.: Cornell University Press, 1995.

Roosa, John. "Violence and the Suharto Regime's Wonderland." Review of *Suharto: A Political Biography,* by Robert Elson, and *Violence and the State in*

Suharto's Indonesia, edited by Benedict Anderson. *Critical Asian Studies* 35 (2003): 315–23.

Roosa, John, Hilmar Farid, and Ayu Ratih, eds. *Tahun yang Tak Pernah Berakhir: Pengalaman Korban 1965: Esai-Esai Sejarah Lisan.* [The Year That Never Ended: The Experiences of the Victims of 1965; Oral History Essays.] Jakarta: Elsam, 2004.

Sadli, Muhammad. "Recollections of My Career." *Bulletin of Indonesian Economic Studies* 29, no. 1 (1993): 35–51.

Saelan, H. Maulwi. *Dari Revolusi '45 Sampai Kudeta '66.* [From the 1945 Revolution to the Coup d'État of 1966.] Jakarta: Yayasan Hak Bangsa, 2001.

Schmitt, Carl. *Political Theology: Four Chapters on the Concept of Sovereignty,* translated by G. Schwab. Cambridge, Mass.: MIT Press, 1985.

Schmitz, David. *Thank God They're on Our Side: The United States and Right-Wing Dictatorships, 1921–1965.* Chapel Hill: North Carolina University Press, 1999.

Scott, Peter Dale. *Coming to Jakarta: A Poem about Terror.* New York: New Directions, 1989.

———. *Deep Politics and the Death of JFK.* Berkeley: University of California Press, 1993.

———. "Exporting Military-Economic Development: America and the Overthrow of Sukarno." In *Ten Years' Military Terror in Indonesia,* edited by Malcolm Caldwell. Nottingham, U.K.: Spokesman Books, 1975.

———. "The United States and the Overthrow of Sukarno, 1965–67." *Pacific Affairs* 58 (Summer 1985): 239–64.

"Selected Documents Relating to the 'September 30th Movement' and Its Epilogue." *Indonesia* 1 (April 1966): 131–204.

Sembiring, Garda, and Harsono Sutedjo, eds. *Gerakan 30 September: Kesaksian Letkol (Pnb) Heru Atmodjo.* [The September 30th Movement: The Testimony of Lt. Col. (Air Force) Heru Atmodjo.] Jakarta: PEC, 2004.

Setiawan, Hersri. *Kamus Gestok* [Dictionary of the October 1 Movement]. Yogyakarta, Indonesia: Galang Press, 2003.

Setiyono, Budi, and Bonnie Triyana, eds. *Revolusi Belum Selesai: Kumpulan Pidato Presiden Sukarno 30 September 1965—Pelengkap Nawaksara.* [The Revolution Is Not Yet Finished: A Compilation of Speeches of President Sukarno, from 30 September 1965 to the Supplement to the "Nine Points" Speech.] 2 vols. Semarang, Indonesia: MESIASS, 2003.

Shaplen, Robert. *Time out of Hand: Revolution and Reaction in Southeast Asia.* New York: Harper and Row, 1969.

Sheehan, Neil. "A Simple Man in Pursuit of Power." *New York Times Magazine,* August 15, 1965.

Shoup, Laurence H., and William Minter. *Imperial Brain Trust: The Council on Foreign Relations and United States Policy.* New York: Monthly Review Press, 1977.

Siauw Giok Tjhan. "Berbagai Catatan dari Berbagai Macam Cerita yang Di-kumpulkan dalam Percakapan2 dengan Berbagai Teman Tahanan di Sa-lemba, Rumah Tahanan Chusus, dan Nirbaya." [Some Notes from Various Stories Collected from Conversations with Some Fellow Prisoners at Sa-lemba Prison, the Special Detention House, and Nirbaya Prison.] Jakarta, typescript, not dated, ca. late 1970s. In the author's possession.

———. (Under the pseudonym of Sigit). "The Smiling General Harus Ditun-tut ke Mahkamah." [The Smiling General Must be Put on Trial.] 1979. Privately printed and circulated, 1996. In the author's possession.

Siauw Tiong Djin. *Siauw Giok Tjhan.* Jakarta: Hasta Mitra, 1999.

Simpson, Brad. "Modernizing Indonesia: United States—Indonesian Rela-tions, 1961-1967." Ph.D. diss., Northwestern University, Chicago, 2003.

Soebandrio, H. *Kesaksianku Tentang G-30-S.* [My Testimony about the Sep-tember 30th Movement.] Jakarta: Forum Pendukung Reformasi Total, 2001.

Soeharto. *My Thoughts, Words and Deeds: An Autobiography.* Jakarta: Citra Lamtoro Gung Persada, 1991.

Soe Hok Gie. *Catatan Seorang Demonstran.* [Notes of a Demonstrator.] Ja-karta: LP3ES, 1989.

———. *Zaman Peralihan.* [The Time of Transition.] Yogyakarta: Bentang Bu-daya, 1995.

Soekarno. *Nationalism, Islam and Marxism,* translated by K. Warouw and P. D. Weldon. Ithaca, N.Y.: Modern Indonesia Project, 1970.

Soerjono. "On Musso's Return." *Indonesia* 29 (April 1980): 59-90.

Soewito, Irna. *Chairul Saleh: Tokoh Kontroversial.* [Chairul Saleh: A Contro-versial Figure.] Jakarta: Mutiara Rachmat, 1993.

Sophiaan, Manai. *Kehormatan Bagi Yang Berhak: Bung Karno Tidak Terlibat G30S/PKI.* [Honor for Those Who Deserve It: Bung Karno Was Not In-volved in the September 30th Movement/PKI.] Jakarta: Yayasan Mencer-daskan Kehidupan Bangsa, 1994.

Southwood, Julie, and Patrick Flanagan. *Indonesia: Law, Propaganda and Ter-ror.* London: Zed, 1983.

State Secretariat of the Republic of Indonesia. *The September 30th Movement: The Attempted Coup by the Indonesian Communist Party: Its Background, Ac-tions, and Eradication.* Jakarta, 1994. Indonesian version published as *Gera-kan 30 September: Pemberontakan Partai Komunis Indonesia: Latar Belakang, Aksi, dan Penumpasannya.* Jakarta, 1994.

Stevenson, Charles. *The End of Nowhere: American Policy toward Laos since 1954.* Boston: Beacon, 1972.

Subekti, Iskandar. "G-30-S Bukan Buatan PKI." [The September 30th Move-ment Was Not a Creation of the PKI.] 1986. Indonesian Exiles of the Left Collection. International Institute of Social History, Amsterdam.

———. "Jalan Pembebasan Rakyat Indonesia." [The Indonesian People's Path of Liberation.] Defense plea. December 16, 1972. In the author's possession.

———. "Kata Pendahuluan." [Introductory Note.] 1986. Indonesian Exiles of the Left Collection. International Institute of Social History, Amsterdam.

Subritzky, John. *Confronting Sukarno: British, American, Australian and New Zealand Diplomacy in the Malaysian-Indonesian Confrontation, 1961-1965.* New York: St. Martin's, 2000.

Sudisman. *Analysis of Responsibility*, translated by Benedict Anderson. Melbourne: Works Cooperative, 1975.

———. *Pledoi Sudisman; Kritik-Oto-kritik Seorang Politburo CC PKI.* [Defense Statement of Sudisman: Criticism-Self-criticism of a Member of the Politburo of the PKI's Central Committee.] Jakarta: Teplok Press, 2000.

Sugama, Yoga. *Memori Jenderal Yoga.* [The Memories of General Yoga.] Jakarta: Bina Rena Pariwara, 1990.

"Suharto's Role in the G30S." *Tapol Bulletin*, no. 90 (December 1988): 19-22.

Sujatmiko, Iwan Gardono. "Kehancuran PKI Tahun 1965-1966." [The Destruction of the PKI, 1965-1966.] *Sejarah* 9 (ca. 2001). *Sejarah* is a serial journal published in Jakarta by Masyarakat Sejarawan Indonesia.

Sulistyo, Hermawan. *Palu Arit di Ladang Tebu: Sejarah Pembantaian Massal yang Terlupakan 1965-1966.* [The Hammer and Sickle in the Sugarcane Fields: The History of a Forgotten Massacre, 1965-1966.] Jakarta: KPG, 2000.

Sundhaussen, Ulf. *The Road to Power: Indonesian Military Politics, 1945-1967.* Oxford: Oxford University Press, 1982.

Surodjo, B. A., and J. M. V. Soeparno. *Tuhan Pergunakanlah Hati, Pikiran dan Tanganku: Pledoi Omar Dani.* [God, May You Use My Heart, Mind, and Hands: The Defense Statement of Omar Dani.] Jakarta: Institut Studi Arus Informasi, 2002.

Sutley, Stewart. "The Indonesian 'New Order' as New Sovereign Space: Its Creation and Narrative of Self-concealment." *Space and Polity* 4, no. 2 (2000): 131-52.

Suyitno, L. S. *Pemasyarakatan Bahaya Laten Komunis dalam Rangka Meningkatkan Kewaspadaan Nasional.* [Socialization of the Latent Danger of Communism in the Framework of Increasing National Alertness.] Jakarta: Departemen Pertahanan Keamanan, Lembaga Ketahanan Nasional, 1997.

Taylor, Charles. *Philosophy and the Human Sciences: Philosophical Papers 2.* Cambridge: Cambridge University Press, 1985.

Todorov, Tzvetan. *The Poetics of Prose.* Ithaca, N.Y.: Cornell University Press, 1977.

Toer, Pramoedya Ananta, and S. A. Prasetyo, eds. *Memoar Oei Tjoe Tat.* [The Memoir of Oei Tjoe Tat.] Jakarta: Hasta Mitra, 1995.

Tovar, B. Hugh. "The Indonesian Crisis of 1965-1966: A Retrospective." *International Journal of Intelligence and Counterintelligence* 7, no. 3 (Fall 1994): 313-38.

"The Trial of D. N. Aidit." *Tapol Bulletin*, no. 41-42 (September-October 1980): 11-14.

Tripp, Charles. *A History of Iraq*. Cambridge: Cambridge University Press, 2000.

Trouillot, Michel-Ralph. *Silencing the Past: Power and the Production of History*. Boston: Beacon, 1995.

Utrecht, Ernst. "An Attempt to Corrupt Indonesian History." Review of *In the Spirit of the Red Banteng* by Antonie C.A. Dake, and *Devious Dalang*, edited and translated by Rahadi S. Karni. *Journal of Contemporary Asia* 5, no. 1 (1975): 99–102.

Van der Kroef, Justus. *The Communist Party of Indonesia: Its History, Program and Tactics*. Vancouver: University of British Columbia, 1965.

———. "Gestapu in Indonesia." *Orbis* 10 (Summer 1966): 458–87.

———. *Indonesia after Sukarno*. Vancouver: University of British Columbia Press, 1971.

———. "Indonesian Communism since the 1965 Coup." *Pacific Affairs* 43 (Spring 1970): 34–60.

———. "Indonesia: The Battle of the 'Old' and the 'New Order.'" *Australian Outlook* 21 (April 1967): 18–43.

———. "Interpretations of the 1965 Coup in Indonesia." *Pacific Affairs* 43(Winter 1970–71): 557–77.

———. "Origins of the 1965 Coup in Indonesia: Probabilities and Alternatives." *Journal of Southeast Asian Studies* 3, no. 2 (1972): 277–98.

———. "Sukarno's Fall." *Orbis* 11 (Summer 1967): 491–531.

van Dijk, C. *Rebellion under the Banner of Islam: The Darul Islam Movement in Indonesia*. The Hague: Martinus Nijhoff, 1981.

van Klinken, Gerry. "The Battle for History after Suharto." *Critical Asian Studies* 33 (2001): 323–50.

Wertheim, W. F. "Indonesia before and after the Untung Coup." *Pacific Affairs* 39, nos. 1–2 (Spring-Summer 1966): 115–27.

———. "Indonesia's Hidden History." In *Pramoedya Ananta Toer 70 Tahun: Essays to Honour Pramoedya Ananta Toer's 70th Year*, edited by Bob Hering. N.p.: Yayasan Kabar Seberang, 1995.

———. "Suharto and the Untung Coup—The Missing Link." *Journal of Contemporary Asia* 1, no. 1 (1970): 50–57.

———. "Whose Plot?—New Light on the 1965 Events." *Journal of Contemporary Asia* 9, no. 2 (1979): 197–215.

Wieringa, Saskia. *Sexual Politics in Indonesia*. New York: Palgrave/Macmillan, 2002.

Winters, Jeffrey. *Power in Motion: Capital Mobility and the Indonesian State*. Ithaca, N.Y.: Cornell University Press, 1996.

Wirahadikusumah, Umar. *Dari Peristiwa ke Peristiwa*. [From Event to Event.] Jakarta: Yayasan Kesejahteraan Jayakarta, 1983.

Yani, Amelia. *Profil Seorang Prajurit TNI*. [Profile of a TNI Soldier.] Jakarta: Sinar Harapan, 1988.

Žižek, Slavoj. "The Detective and the Analyst." *Literature and Psychology* 36, no. 4 (1990): 27–46.

——. "What Rumsfeld Doesn't Know That He Knows about Abu Ghraib." *In These Times,* May 21, 2004, www.inthesetimes.com/site/main/article/ 747/.

Mahmillub Records

Unpublished Trial Transcripts Consulted at the TNI Museum Satria Mandala, Documentation Division, Jakarta

Colonel Abdul Latief trial, 1978.
R. Soegeng Soetarto trial, 1973.
Sudisman trial, 1967.
Brigadier General M. A. Supardjo trial, 1967.
Supono [Pono] trial, 1972.

Archives

Hoover Institution Archives, Stanford University, California
    Guy Pauker Papers
    Howard P. Jones Papers
International Institute of Social History, Amsterdam
    Indonesian Exiles of the Left Collection
    Suparna Sastra Diredja Papers

Interviews

Unless otherwise noted, I conducted the interviews and recorded them, and the names of the interviewees are their real names. The transcripts and recordings of the recorded interviews are archived at the Institute of Indonesian Social History in Jakarta. The asterisked interviews were not recorded.

Aleida, Martin. August 8, 2004. Jakarta.
Atmodjo, Heru. June 11, 2000; December 14, 2002; December 19, 2004. Jakarta.
Bismar. April 1, 2001. Jakarta.
Bungkus. May 12, 2001. Besuki.
Dana, I Wayan. January 6, 2001. Denpasar.
Djayadi (pseudonym). April 1, 2001. Tasikmalaya.
Haryatna (pseudonym). April 4, 2001. Tasikmalaya.
Isak, Joesoef. December 20, 2003. Jakarta.
Juwono (pseudonym). Interview by Rahadian Permadi. June 19, 2000. Jakarta.
Kardi, Muhammad Sidik. May 29, 2000. Jakarta.
Mujiyono (pseudonym). June 16, 2000. Jakarta.

Oemiyah, Ibu. July 24, 2005. Yogyakarta.
Oey Hay Djoen. July 14, 2001. Jakarta; January 24, 2002, Jakarta.
Poniti. August 24, 2000. Kapal.
Pugeg. September 3, 2000. Denpasar.
Puger, Ibu. January 11, 2001. Denpasar.
Reti, I Ketut. January 7, 2001. Denpasar.
Rewang. June 27, 2001. Solo.
Rusyana (pseudonym). July 11, 2001. Jakarta.
Slamet. Interview by Razif. January 28, 2003. Jakarta.
Subowo (pseudonym). January 26, 2002. Jakarta.
Sucipto. September 4, 2003. Jakarta.
Sugiarto. 2001. Jakarta.
Sukrisno (pseudonym). July 14, 2005. Jakarta.
Supardjo, Ibu. February 2001. Jakarta
Suwira, Kompiyang. September 2, 2000. Denpasar.
Syukur, Abdul. Interview by Razif. May 22, 2000. Bandung.
Tan Swie Ling. March 16, 2001. Jakarta.
Tiara, Ibu (pseudonym). August 15, 2000. Denpasar.
Wayan (pseudonym). August 5, 2004. Ubud.

Index

Aceh, 225
Action Front for Crushing the September 30th Movement (Kap-Gestapu), 63, 196
Adjie, Ibrahim, 211, 215, 237-38
Agamben, Giorgio, 263n22
Aidit, Dipa Nusantara: as cabinet minister, 207; as director of Special Bureau, 41, 66-67, 82, 90, 93, 117, 121, 125-27, 131, 135-36, 138, 139-40, 143-46, 150-52, 159-60, 174-75, 203-4, 209, 212, 216, 247, 254-55; execution of, 69, 74, 140, 279n35; faked confession of, 65, 88, 277n13; falling into army's trap, 176-77, 193, 214; flight to Yogyakarta, 222-23, 258-59; at Halim airbase, 32, 42-43, 50, 60, 64, 81, 90, 152, 175, 219, 258-60; as leader of PKI, 21, 118, 120, 140, 147-54, 167, 174-75, 213, 215, 223, 260; reappearance in 1950, 125, 286n17; response to Algerian coup, 161-66; and revolution councils, 151, 166-67, 175, 213, 218-20, 252, 256; statements about movement to PKI leaders, 142-43, 147, 150, 213; and united front policy, 167-68, 170; weighing options, 142, 155-60, 209-11, 249-50, 291n39
air force, Indonesian (AURI), 19, 44-45, 48, 59, 99, 101, 112, 126, 130, 160, 181, 208, 210, 222, 230, 233, 235; Pasukan Pembela Pangkalan (Airbase Defense Troops), 256
Ajitorop, Jusuf, 147, 149, 290n23
Akutagawa, Ryunosuke, 20
Aleida, Martin, 126, 173, 289n47
Algeria, 161-65, 204
Algiers, 161, 163

Aliarcham Academy, 127, 168
Alimin, 62
Allison, John, 179
Anderson, Benedict, 22, 62, 65, 68-74, 81, 122, 135, 172-73, 203, 265n43, 273n20, 273n25
Angkatan Bersenjata, 184
Antara, 24
Anwas, 48, 109, 273n27
Arabian Nights, 137
Arbenz, Jacobo, 178
army, Indonesian: anticommunism of, 181-83, 186, 188, 205-7, 249, 300n7; Brawijaya division (East Java), 71; civic action, 183-84, 186-87, 192, 194; Diponegoro division (Central Java), 70-71, 84, 114, 214, 242; Information Department, 64; intelligence, 129-30, 214; Kodam Jaya (Jakarta garrison), 41, 45-47, 56, 101, 130, 215; and martial law, 184-85, 295n20; overthrowing Sukarno, 196-201; propaganda about the movement, 6, 24-25, 28-29, 62-69, 80-81, 88, 106-7, 175, 198-200, 224; repression of PKI, 4, 15-16, 22, 24, 193-96, 203; sabotaging Confrontation, 187-88; Seskoad (Sekolah Staf Komando Angkatan Darat), 186, 295n29; Siliwangi division (West Java), 71, 84, 95, 193, 215, 234, 237, 302n13; as state within a state, 177-78, 185-87; territorial warfare, 184; and U.S. aid, 182-84; waiting for a pretext, 176-78, 188-93, 208-9, 214. *See also* Battalion 328; Battalion 434; Battalion 530; Cakrabirawa; Kostrad; RPKAD

Army Strategic Reserve Command. *See* Kostrad

Ashari (Lieutenant Colonel), 55

Asia-Africa Conference, 134, 156, 161–62, 165, 178

Asia-Africa Journalists Association (Persatuan Wartawan Asia-Afrika; PWAA), 156–57, 162

Asmu, 147

Atmodjo, Heru, 18, 38–42, 44–45, 48, 50, 88, 92, 109, 112–13, 134, 218, 227, 272n16, 281n65, 283n17, 301n11

Badiou, Alain, 11–12

Baghdad Pact, 142

Bakorstanas (Badan Koordinasi Bantuan Pemantapan Stabilitas Nasional), 12

Ball, George, 15

Bandung, 46, 95, 134, 156, 186, 211, 228, 231, 234, 238

Bangkok, 188

Banjarmasin, 120

Banten, 122

Baperki (Badan Permusyawaratan Kewarganegaraan Indonesia), 18, 265n48

Barlian (Lieutenant Colonel), 179

Battalion 328, 57, 221

Battalion 454, 35, 37, 45, 56–57, 59–60, 65, 70, 100–101, 113–14, 222, 229, 231–32, 235, 239, 242, 251–52, 256–57, 302n19

Battalion 530, 35, 37, 45, 56–57, 65, 100–101, 111, 114, 229–32, 235, 238, 240, 251–52, 256–57, 302n19

Ben Bella, Ahmed, 161, 163–66

Benjamin, Walter, 263n22

Benson, George, 184, 192, 291n31

Berita Yudha, 184

Biro Chusus. *See* Special Bureau

Bismar, 287n36

Body for the Promotion of Sukarnoism, 206

Bono (Walujo), 42, 90, 121, 126, 128–30, 149–50, 152, 247, 250, 254

Borobudur, 8

Boumedienne (Colonel), 161–66, 175, 204, 213

Bourchier, David, 295n22

Boven Digul, 119, 285n2

BPI (Badan Pusat Intelijens), 129

Brackman, Arnold, 68

Brecht, Bertold, 114

Britain, 94, 142, 145, 187, 190, 194, 197, 209, 211

Brown, Colin, 7, 212

BTI (Barisan Tani Indonesia), 103, 119, 127

Bukittinggi, 181

Bundy, McGeorge, 264n34

Bundy, William, 15

Bungkus (Sergeant Major), 99, 272n13

Bunker, Ellsworth, 190–91

Bunnell, Frederick, 192

Cakrabirawa (palace guard), 35, 38, 41, 45, 52, 103, 170, 214, 216, 229, 232, 256, 271n7

Caltex, 197

Central Intelligence Agency (CIA), 63, 94, 171, 178; backing of PRRI/Permesta revolts, 168, 180–81; Jakarta station operations, 191–95, 198; report on the movement, 67–68, 189, 279n27

Chang Myon, 94

Chiang Kai-sek, 233

China, 13, 29, 125, 134–35, 163–65, 179, 198, 277n1

Chomsky, Noam, 16

CIA. *See* Central Intelligence Agency

Ciliwung River, 157

Cimahi prison, 134, 281n65, 288n40

Cipinang prison, 136, 149

Clark Air Base, 195

cold war, 16, 178

Communist Party of Algeria, 162–63, 165

Communist Party of France, 162–63

Communist Party of Germany, 31–32

Communist Party of Indonesia (PKI), 14, 18, 117–75 passim; alleged as movement mastermind, 4–8, 28–29, 62–69, 90–91, 115–16, 198–201, 221, 241,

255–56; alleged as not movement mastermind, 70–81, 142; and anticolonial struggle, 119, 152, 262nn13–14, 285n2; Central Committee, 67, 74, 90, 116, 119, 128–29, 147–50, 152, 154, 156, 168, 173–74, 213; Control Committee, 137; democratic centralism, 139, 153–54, 236, 253; destruction of, 15–16, 21–31, 63, 193–96, 223–24, 231, 239; dual aspect of the state theory, 168, 170, 294n68; and elections, 179, 206–7; Military Section, 118–21, 125; Organizational Department, 118, 125, 128, 246, 248, 258; participation in movement, 32, 45, 60, 64, 69, 97, 101–5, 141–43, 146, 149, 159, 174–75, 203–4, 213, 224; Politburo, 19, 64, 67, 86–88, 90–91, 93–94, 102, 104, 116, 120, 128, 141–43, 146, 147–50, 152–54, 166, 168, 174, 213, 223–24, 245, 291n31; Politburo Working Committee, 69, 75, 147–48, 151, 174, 259–60, 279n32, 291n31; popularity of, 181, 205–7, 216; populism of, 167–68, 170, 175; provincial committees, 127, 253; rivalry with army high command, 155–60, 176–78, 181–84, 186, 188–93, 205–10, 214, 221, 249–50; Section Committee, 104; self-criticism document, 153, 282n11, 289n2, 292n44; support to progressive officers, 141–42, 146–48, 150, 158–59, 174; Verification Committee, 137; as villain in Suharto regime propaganda, 10–12, 21, 33, 40. *See also* Aidit, Dipa Nusantara; Aliarcham Academy; *Harian Rakjat;* Pemuda Rakjat; Sjam; Special Bureau; Sudisman
Communist Party of Iraq, 290n16
Communist Party of North Korea, 168
Communist Party of South Africa, 165
Communist Party of the Netherlands, 123–24
Confrontation (Konfrontasi), 44, 114, 133–34, 168, 187–89, 194, 207, 211, 272n19
Cornell University, 22
Council of Generals (Dewan Jenderal), 35–36, 38, 44, 47, 52, 76, 80, 85, 94, 103, 106, 141–42, 144, 146–47, 150–51, 155, 158–59, 162, 166, 170–71, 174, 176, 189, 211–12, 214, 216, 224, 249–52, 254
coup d'état, 47, 71, 106, 142, 145, 155, 158, 160–65, 170, 176, 185, 189–90, 200–201, 208, 213–16, 222
Cribb, Robert, 7, 24, 30, 212
Crouch, Harold, 62, 73–74, 81, 106, 109, 115, 203, 265n43, 276n1
Cumings, Bruce, 283n23

Dahono, 173
Daino, 122
Dake, A. C. A., 276n1
Dani, Omar, 19, 129; as commander of Kolaga, 85, 187, 272n19, 281n1, 295n35; describing Sukarno's discussions with Suparjdo, 51–52; and the movement, 39–40, 44–45, 60, 90, 112, 222, 230, 235, 237, 272n18, 273n20, 273n22, 285n46, 285n51; and Supardjo, 94, 218
Darnton, Robert, 19–20
Darul Islam (DI), 86, 132–34, 198
deep politics, 17
detective stories, 20, 202–3, 266n57
Dewanto (Commodore), 59, 272n18, 273n22
Dewi Sukarno, 38
Diponegoro division. *See* army, Indonesian
DI/TII (Darul Islam/Tentara Islam Indonesia). *See* Darul Islam
Djajengminardo, Wisnoe, 44, 51
Djuanda, 198
Djuhartono (Brigadier General), 254
domino theory, 14–15, 264n34
Dulles, Allen, 178–80
Dulles, John Foster, 178–79

East Timor, 225, 268n93
Edie, Sarwo, 59
Elson, Robert, 299n91

Farid, Hilmar, 293n67
Fic, Victor, 17, 265n44, 276n1, 283n11
First, Ruth, 165
Flanagan, Patrick, 263n19

FLN (Front de Libération Nationale), 163, 165
Ford Foundation, 186
Formless Organization (Organisasi Tanpa Bentuk), 12
Fort Bragg, 183
Fort Leavenworth, 183, 186
Frankel, Max, 16
Friend, Theodore, 28

Galbraith, Frances, 287n28
Garut, 133
Geertz, Clifford, 28
Generation of 1966, 270n107
Germany, 197
Gerwani (Gerakan Wanita Indonesia), 40, 103, 198
Gestapu (Gerakan Tiga Puluh September), 29, 32, 200, 268n82
Gestok (Gerakan Satu Oktober), 32
Glassburner, Bruce, 186
Golkar (Golongan Karya), 184
Gramscian strategy, 184
Green, Marshall, 13, 85, 94, 113, 192, 194–96, 278n15, 282n2, 283n23, 299n81
Guided Democracy, 109, 206, 208, 285n42

Halim Air Force Base, 19, 32, 37–42, 44–45, 48, 50–54, 57–60, 64–66, 81–84, 90–91, 100–101, 109, 112–13, 146, 152, 174, 203, 219, 221–22, 230, 235, 237, 258; map of, 43
Halmana, 77
Hamim, 126–27
Harian Rakjat, 64, 70, 140, 148, 169–74
Harjati, 38–39
Hartoyo, 123
Haryono, Mas Tirtodarmo, 36, 40, 189
Hasan, 18, 21, 118–22, 126–28, 130–39, 144–46, 151, 159
Hatta, Mohammad, 4, 125, 167, 179, 212
Herman, Edward, 16
Heryanto, Ariel, 13
Hitler, Adolph, 31–32
Holmes, Sherlock, 20
Holtzappel, Coen, 276n1

Hughes, John, 66, 112, 278n20
Hunter, Helen-Louise, 68
Husein, Ahmad, 179–80
Hutapea, Oloan, 74, 147, 150, 279n32

Idris (Lieutenant Colonel), 55
Idris, Kemal (Colonel), 187, 280n51, 281n1
I Ketut Reti, 286n8
India, 140
Indochina, 14–15
Indonesian Journalists Association (Persatuan Wartawan Indonesia), 161
Indonesian Revolution Council. *See under* September 30th Movement
intelligence noise, 130, 214, 287n29
Iran, 178
Iraq, 142, 165, 204
Isak, Joesoef, 156–57, 162–66, 288n36
Iskandar (Major), 55
Islamabad, 190
Ismail, Taufiq, 269n99

Japan, 14, 120, 122, 145, 197, 246
Johnson, Alexis, 16
Johnson, Lyndon B., 15
Jones, Howard, 182, 189–93
Juwono, 102–3, 276n56

Kadane, Kathy, 195, 298n75
Kahin, George, 264n34
Kalimantan, 37, 85–86, 97, 114
Kapal (village), 29
Kardi, Muhammad Sidik (Colonel), 254, 286n8, 288n43
Karim D. P., 161–62, 261n1
Karnow, Stanley, 25–26
Karto, 118–22, 125, 209
Katamso (Colonel), 54
Kennedy, John F., 15, 17
Kennedy, Robert F., 26
KGB, 69
King, Seth, 25
Kolaga (Komando Mandala Siaga), 44, 84, 187, 273n19, 281n1
Kolko, Gabriel, 14
Komalasakti, Burhan, 137, 289n47
Kompas, 25, 199

Kopkamtib (Komando Operasi Pemulihan Keamanan dan Ketertiban), 12,
201, 263n19
Korea, 179
Kostrad (Army Strategic Reserve Command), 35, 45, 56–59, 62–63, 75–76, 78,
80, 101, 111, 113–14, 129, 187–88, 195,
214, 220–22, 229–30, 235, 252, 281n1;
formation of, 275n48
Koti (Komando Operasi Tertinggi), 129,
277n4
Kurosawa, Akira, 20
Kusnan, 137
Kusno, 42, 152, 259

laskar, 119
Latief, Abdul: as brigade commander,
46, 95, 97, 101; as Central Javanese
officer, 70–71, 84, 214; connection to
PKI, 133; as core leader of movement,
41, 45, 48–50, 60, 83, 89–92, 111, 115,
117, 144, 175, 203–4, 212, 237, 250, 255,
261nn5–6; defense plea, 6, 261n6; in-
forms Suharto of the movement, 5–
6, 75–78, 80, 113; interrogation of,
64–65, 68, 277n11; willing to call off
movement, 108, 218, 221
Leclerc, Jacques, 125, 286n17
Leibniz, Gottfried Wilhem, 107
Leimena, Johannes, 37, 52
Lenin, V. I., 123, 205, 302n12
Lesser Sundas, 179
Lev, Daniel, 121, 157, 184, 206
Life (magazine), 27
London, 190, 209
Lubang Buaya (Crocodile Hole): ceremony at, 10, 266n59, 270n105; killings
at, 3, 40, 225; movement personnel
gathered at, 36–37, 42, 58–60, 97, 99,
102–3, 217, 229–30, 233, 239–40; myth
of orgy and mutilation at, 8–10, 12,
40, 65, 81, 198, 200; as sacred space, 7,
10; use of, arranged by Soejono, 44
Lubis, Zulfiki, 198
Lukman, 74, 125, 140, 147, 150–51, 223, 260,
286n17
Luttwak, Edward, 287n29

Machiavelli, Niccolo, 136
Madiun affair, 8, 123, 125, 155, 193, 206
Mahabharata, 140
Mahmillub (Mahkamah Militer Luar
Biasa), 73, 118; establishment of, 201;
Njono trial, 66, 102, 104, 146; reli-
ability of testimonies at, 6, 61, 138,
271n5; as show trials, 6; Sjam's testi-
mony at, 61, 67, 69, 126, 135–36; Su-
disman trial, 69, 140–41, 143, 153;
Supardjo trial, 17, 48, 51, 87–88, 108;
Untung trial, 23, 61
Mahmud, Amir, 49
Makassar, 179
Malaysia, 37, 44, 84, 90, 103, 114, 133–34,
168, 187–88, 194, 207, 211
Malik, Adam, 196
Maluku, 179
Manikebu (Manifesto Kebudayaan), 184
Mao Zedong, 135, 163, 233, 276n1
Martens, Robert, 195, 298nn75–76
Martowidjojo, Mangil, 271n7, 272n12
Marx, Karl, 136, 205, 233, 302n12
Massachusetts Institute of Technology,
185
massacres of 1965–66, 4–5, 7, 12, 15–16,
21–28, 225; in Bali, 26–30; in Cen-
tral Java, 25, 29; and Chinese Indo-
nesians, 269n97; in East Java, 26, 28;
foreign reporting on, 25–28; social
memory of, 225, 269n99, 270n105; in
West Java, 29
Maxwell, Neville, 297n51
McCoy, Alfred, 280n42
McGehee, Ralph, 279n27
McNamara, Robert, 15
McVey, Ruth, 22, 62, 65, 68–74, 81, 172–
73, 273n20, 273n25
Medan, 120, 179
Megawati Soekarnoputri, 33
Menado, 134, 181
Menteng, 36–37, 56, 152
Merdeka Square, 35–36, 271n2
Message of the People's Suffering, 50
military, Indonesian. *See* air force, Indo-
nesian; army, Indonesian; Cakrabi-
rawa; Kolaga; Kopkamtib; Kostrad;

military, Indonesian *(continued)*
  Koti; navy, Indonesian; police, Indonesian; RPKAD
Military Assistance Group (MILTAG), 194
Moerdani, Benny, 188, 296n37, 296n40
Moertopo, Ali, 114, 188, 214, 296n37
Mortimer, Rex, 155–56
Moscow, 162, 178
Moser, Don, 27
Mossadegh, Mohammad, 178
Muljono (Major), 54
Munir, Muhammad, 19, 123, 147, 166, 174, 290n23
Murba Party, 131, 207
Mursid (Major General), 37, 238
Museum of PKI Treason (Museum Pengkhianatan PKI), 10
Mustafa (Colonel), 254

Nahdatul Ulama, 63
Nasakom (nasionalis, agama, komunis), 11, 104, 145, 159, 166–67, 213, 252–53, 267n61, 274n35
Nasution, Abdul H., 25, 93, 189; alliance with Suharto, 107, 109, 111, 113–14, 200–201, 222, 230–31, 235, 238–40, 242; as anticommunist, 116, 181–84, 193–94, 206, 214; arrival at Kostrad, 111, 276n51; attempted abduction of, 36–37, 99, 212, 217, 229, 233; as defense minister, 129, 183, 211; on the military's political role, 177–78, 184–86, 196, 209, 295n22; quoting of Supardjo document, 17
nationalization, 13, 185, 197, 208
National Monument History Museum, 262n14
navy, Indonesian, 48, 52, 129–30, 160, 208, 210
nekolim (neokolonialisme, kolonialisme, imperialisme), 207
Netherlands, 132, 145
New Yorker, 27
New York Times, 16, 25, 27, 205
New Zealand, 190

Nirbaya prison, 76
Nixon, Richard, 15
Njono: faked confession of, 88, 277n13, 301n11; as head of PKI Jakarta chapter, 102; as organizer of militia, 102, 104, 146, 174, 213, 220, 284n28; as Politburo member, 102, 147–48; trial of, 64–66
Njoto, 74, 140, 147, 150, 207, 223, 260
North Atlantic Treaty Organization (NATO), 190
North Sumatra, 180
Notosusanto, Nugroho, 67–68, 106, 262n14, 278n23
Nursuhud, 156–57, 292n43
Nusatenggara, 238

Oei Tjoe Tat, 261n4
Oemiyah, 122
Oey Hay Djoen, 119, 150, 160
Organisasi Perlawanan Rakyat, 132

Padang, 120
Pakistan, 190
palace guard. *See* Cakrabirawa
Palembang, 96, 179, 231
Panca Azimat Revolusi (Five Charms of the Revolution), 50, 169, 199
Pancasila, 10–11, 50, 262n11, 270n105, 274n35, 278n13
Panjaitan, Donald Ishak, 37, 40, 266n59
Papua New Guinea, 41
Pardede, Peris, 104, 137, 147, 284n35, 291n39
Park Chung Hee, 94
Parman (Captain), 55
Parman, S. (Major General), 37, 40, 114, 129, 150–51, 187, 189, 192, 214–15
Pasar Baru, 126
Pasha, Machmud (Colonel), 254
Pasundan, 124
Pathuk group, 122–25
Pauker, Guy, 68, 185–86, 295n29
Peace Corps, 208
peaceful coexistence, 163–64
Peck, Edward, 190

Pekalongan, 127
Pemuda Rakjat, 45, 64, 102–3, 173, 213, 223
Penas (Pemetaan Nasional), 42, 44, 252
Permesta (Perjuangan Semesta Alam),
132, 134, 168, 179–80, 184, 188, 198
Philippines, 181, 195
Phouma, Souvanna, 178
Pintu Besar Selatan, 172
PKI (Partai Komunis Indonesia). *See*
Communist Party of Indonesia
Poirot, Hercule, 20
police, Indonesian, 48, 52, 208, 210
politicide, 224
Pono (Supono Marsudidjojo), 41, 48, 50,
65–66, 73, 83, 89–90, 92, 121, 126–30,
144, 149–50, 203, 247, 250, 254, 261n5,
283n24
Pope, Allen, 181
Port Workers and Sailors Trade Union
(Serikat Buruh Pelabuhan dan Pe-
layaran), 124
Pradigdo, Soejono, 66, 87, 137, 289n47
Pramoedya Ananta Toer, 262n16
Pranoto Reksosamodra, 53, 56, 58–59, 79,
109–10, 113, 155, 221, 230, 238–39,
275n42, 285n43
PRRI (Pemerintah Revolusioner Repub-
lik Indonesia), 132–34, 168, 180–81,
184, 188, 198
Prunier, Gérard, 268n97
Puger, I Gde, 29
PWAA (Persatuan Wartawan Asia-
Afrika; Asia-Africa Journalists As-
sociation), 156–57, 162
Pye, Lucien, 185
Pyongyang, 168

Qasim (Colonel), 142, 165, 175, 204,
290n16

Rachmat, Basuki, 53, 79, 238
Rais, Amien, 33
Ramelan, Utomo, 55
Rand Corporation, 68, 185
Rashomon, 20
Reichstag fire, 31–32

Reston, James, 16
Révolution, 163
Revolution Council, Indonesian. *See
under* September 30th Movement
revolution councils. *See under* Septem-
ber 30th Movement
Rewang, 93, 147, 150
Riau, 120
Ricklefs, Merle, 7
Robertson, Walter, 294n3
Rostow, Walt, 185
RPKAD (Resimen Para Komando Ang-
katan Darat): attacking movement,
58–60, 113, 221–23, 230, 239, 267n81;
and the massacres, 29–30; stationed
near Jakarta, 46
RRI (Radio Republik Indonesia), 3, 34,
58, 142, 171, 219, 230, 235
Rubik's cube, 80
Rukman, U., 53, 79, 155, 238
Rumah Tahanan Militer (Military De-
tention Center), 76, 93, 153
Rumsfeld, Donald, 20, 266n56
Runturambi, F., 147
Rusk, Dean, 113, 183
Rwandan genocide, 30–31, 268n97

Sabur, M., 238, 271n7
Sacred Pancasila Monument (Monumen
Pancasila Sakti), 7–10, 23, 33
Sadli, Muhammad, 186
Saelan, H. Maulwi, 38–39, 271nn7–8
Sakirman, 140, 147, 150
Salatiga, 25, 55
Saleh, Chairul, 131, 157, 197, 207, 212,
299n80
Saleh, Ismail, 67–68, 106, 278n23
Sanusi, Anwar, 260
Scheherazade, 137
Schmitt, Carl, 12, 263n22
Scott, Peter Dale, 264n41, 280n64
Semarang, 54–55, 173, 186, 223
Senayan stadium, 38, 59
September 30th Movement: in Central
Java, 3, 54–55, 70–71, 83, 174, 220,
222–23, 238, 275n46; civilian militias

September 30th Movement *(continued)*
within, 45–46, 54–55, 64, 66, 70, 97,
101–5, 115, 174, 213, 220, 240, 273n24;
core leaders of, 6, 37, 39, 41–44, 65,
83, 101, 106–7, 109, 115, 116–17, 222,
261n5; defeat of, 3–4, 57–60, 70, 101,
112–13, 174, 204, 222, 239–41, 243–44,
252; delegation to Sukarno, 37–39,
42, 85, 217; kidnapping raids, 3, 36–
37, 98–99, 212, 217, 229, 231, 252,
301n6; killings by, 22, 40, 252, 266n59,
272n13; lack of contingency planning,
97–98, 234; lack of single leader, 89–
92, 106–7, 115, 204, 233–34, 236–37;
military strength of, 45–47, 95–97,
100–101, 215, 232, 243, 251, 256–57; as
mystery, 5–7, 16–17, 20–21, 80–82; occupying Merdeka Square, 3, 35–36,
45, 56–58, 75, 101, 220, 229–30, 232,
235, 302n19; planning meetings, 250,
272n14, 283n17; as a pretext for army
takeover, 4, 7, 21–22, 31–32, 193–94,
200–201, 214; proposal to attack Kostrad, 111–13, 222, 230, 235; radio announcements, 3, 5–6, 34–35, 38, 47–
50, 71–73, 84, 100–101, 106, 108–9,
217–20, 274n32, 274n34; Revolution
Council, Indonesian, 35, 47–50, 54–
55, 66, 72, 104, 108, 142, 144, 151, 166–
67, 175, 219, 221, 251–53, 255–56, 259;
revolution councils, 35, 61, 64, 72,
104, 107, 109, 212–13, 218–20; sectors
in Jakarta, 101–2, 104, 220, 230, 234,
284n28; in West Sumatra, 275n47
Seskoad (Sekolah Staf Komando Angkatan Darat). *See* army, Indonesian
Setiawan, Hersri, 290n26
Shaplen, Robert, 27
Shipworkers and Sailors Trade Union
(Serikat Buruh Kapal dan Pelayaran),
124
Siauw Giok Tjhan, 18, 119, 137
Sigit, Agus (Major), 144, 250, 283n17
Simbolon (Colonel), 179–80
Singapore, 188
Sino-Soviet conflict, 140, 163, 168

Sjahrir, 122, 185, 300n10
Sjahrouza, Djohan, 122
Sjam (Kamaruzaman): as Aidit's subordinate, 125, 128, 131, 135–36, 139–40,
143, 150–51, 159–60, 203, 209, 216,
247, 250–51, 254–56, 260; as alleged
army agent, 62, 69, 75–76, 78–79, 81,
137, 287n30; altering plan for revolution councils, 107–9, 219–20, 222;
background of, 41, 118, 122–25, 134–
35, 245–46, 259; betraying former
comrades, 136–37, 254, 288n43; capture of, 67; choosing deputy commanders, 92–93, 109, 219; as a core
leader of movement, 41, 48, 50, 53,
60, 65–66, 73, 83, 89–94, 104, 115,
139, 144–46, 233–34, 236–37, 240,
261n5; courtroom testimony of, 67–
69, 82, 91, 97, 125–26, 130–31, 137–
38, 143–44, 224, 245–60, 289n45; disguised as businessman, 126–29; execution of, 137, 149; initiating movement, 90–94, 115, 139, 144–45, 150–52,
203–4, 211–12, 215, 250–52; as intimidating and arrogant, 93, 95, 98, 115,
121, 135, 216, 229, 231–32, 283n24;
as the leader of Special Bureau, 21,
66, 69, 90, 115–17, 121–22, 124–38,
246–53; as link between Aidit and
movement officers, 150–51, 159, 174–
75, 204, 212; refusing to call off movement, 107–9, 218–19, 221–22, 238
SOBSI (Sentral Organisasi Buruh Seluruh Indonesia), 103, 166
Socialist Party, 122–24
Socialist Party of Indonesia (PSI), 121–
24, 286n8
Soebandrio, 19, 129, 209, 265n49, 281n65
Soeharto. *See* Suharto
Soe Hok Gie, 33, 270n107
Soejono (Major): alias Pak Djojo, 233,
301n11; brings Aidit to Halim, 258; as
commander of airbase troops, 41, 44–
45, 65, 71, 97, 101; as a core leader of
movement, 41–42, 48, 50, 83, 89–90,
117, 204, 212, 237, 255, 261n5, 276n1;

courtroom testimony of, 66, 278n19, 284n28; following Sjam's lead, 92, 115, 144, 250; interrogation of, 68; willing to call off movement, 218, 221

Soejono, Joko, 154

Soekarno. *See* Sukarno

Soeparto, 39

Soeradi (Captain), 284n28

Soesanto (Commodore), 52–53

Soetarto (Brigadier General), 288n37

Soetojo Siswomihardjo, 37, 40

SOKSI (Sentral Organisasi Karyawan Sosialis Indonesia), 184

Solo, 55, 77, 118, 120

Sophiaan, Manai, 161, 165, 283n17, 284n31, 284n37, 288n38

South Korea, 94

Southwood, Julie, 263n19

Soviet Union, 13, 16, 119, 142, 161, 165

Special Bureau (Biro Chusus): cell structure of, 126, 133–34; as clandestine organization, 18, 41, 126–29, 214; contacting officers, 121, 130–35, 209, 248–49; first public mention of, 66; leadership of, 126–27, 247, 253; origins of, 118–22, 257; position within PKI, 66–67, 115–18, 121, 126–29, 139, 150–51, 154, 246–47, 253; role within the movement, 73–74, 81, 90, 95–96, 105, 115, 144–46, 177, 211, 218, 249–52

Special Forces. *See* RPKAD

Stalin, Joseph, 135

Stanvac, 197

Subagiyo, 76

Subchan Z. E., 63

Subekti, Iskandar, 19, 42, 121, 128, 135–36, 138, 146–52, 155, 166, 174, 219, 272n16, 279n32, 283n24, 291n31, 291n37

Sucipto (Brigadier General), 63, 277n4

Sucipto Munandar, 127, 147

Sudisman: analysis of the movement, 74, 81, 140–43, 146, 153–55, 157, 159, 166, 174–75, 217, 223–24, 260, 290n18, 292n44; as main author of Politburo self-criticism, 86–87, 282n11, 289n2, 300n2; opinion of Pardede, 281n35,

292n44; as Politburo Working Committee member, 69, 74, 147, 259–60, 279n32; role in movement, 104, 141, 143, 150–52

Sugama, Yoga, 62, 68, 114, 188, 214, 296n37

Suganda (Major), 254

Sugiarto, 88, 227

Sugijono (Lieutenant Colonel), 54

Sugiman (Lieutenant Colonel), 55

Sugiono, 168

Suharto: alleged involvement in movement, 75–80, 82, 177, 203–4; attacking the movement, 4, 22–31, 56–60, 62–63, 105, 112–13, 221–24, 229–31, 234–35, 238–40, 242, 268n96, 279n35; as commander of Kostrad, 56–57, 76, 111–14, 214; coup d'état by, 4, 12–13, 22, 32–33, 196–201, 221, 224–25; economic strategy of, 196–97; friendship with Untung and Latief, 5, 75–78, 111, 203, 214, 280n51; and massacres, 23–24, 26–31, 224–25; sabotaging Confrontation, 114, 187–88; at Seskoad, 186–87; and Sukarno, 58–59, 109, 221; and Supardjo, 85, 282n6; suppressing autopsy report, 265n43; taking command of army, 4, 56–59, 110; as vice-commander of Kolaga, 114, 273n19, 281n1

Suharto, Ezy (Lieutenant Colonel), 55

Suharto, Sigit Harjojudanto, 77

Suharto regime: anticommunism of, 7–13, 33, 88; emergency law of, 12–13; fall of, 5, 19; fetishizing of the movement, 7–13, 22, 69, 81, 203; official version of the movement, 5–7, 21, 65–69, 75, 81, 88, 106–7, 116–17, 203, 286n19, 300n8

Suherman, 126

Suherman (Colonel), 49, 54, 70–71

Sujatmiko, Iwan Gardono, 269n99

Sujatno, Anis (Sergeant), 40, 42, 53

Sukardi (Colonel), 55

Sukarno: abducted in 1945, 212; alleged involvement in the movement,

Sukarno *(continued)*
276n1, 291n31; anti-imperialism of, 13, 33, 178, 197, 207; canceling elections, 182, 206, 285n42; decision on army caretaker, 53, 109-10, 220, 230, 238-39; discussions with Supardjo, 50-54, 79, 106, 218, 220, 274n37, 281n68; doctrines, 10-11, 33, 50, 267n61, 274n35; as figurehead, 201; and massacres, 25, 261n4; and the military, 35, 155-56, 186-89, 198-200, 206-11, 277n4, 295n20; movements on October 1 morning, 38-39, 50-54, 217; opposition to anti-PKI campaign, 22, 32, 198, 200; and the PKI, 159-60, 179, 188, 196, 205-8, 267n61; popularity of, 4, 22, 176, 186, 190, 208; refusal to support the movement, 51-52, 107, 109, 115, 167, 218, 221, 230-31, 237-38, 252; relations with the U.S., 191-92, 297n54; response to regional rebellions, 180; sickness of, 144-45, 188; and Suharto, 33, 200-201, 269n104, 285n51; view of the movement, 50-54, 198, 220, 261n2, 292n49; wives of, 38-39, 271n6; worried about potential coup, 94, 106, 155

Sukatno, 174, 213, 220

Sukendro, 189, 200, 206, 295n29; and U.S. embassy, 296n44

Sukirno (Captain), 37-38, 51, 57, 65, 85

Sukito, Wiratmo, 184

Sukrisno, 122-24, 129, 287n23

Sulawesi, 120-21, 167, 179, 181, 198

Sulzberger, C. L., 27

Sumatra, 96, 121, 133, 167, 179-81, 187, 198, 208

Sumitro (Major General), 26

Sumual (Lieutenant Colonel), 179

Sunardi, 48, 109, 273n27

Sundhaussen, Ulf, 186

Supardjo, M. A.: advocating resistance to Suharto, 111-13, 222, 235; analysis of the movement, 17-18, 82-116 passim, 117, 139, 144, 203, 227-44, 211-12, 215, 290n18; arrival in Jakarta, 83, 85,

282n7; authenticity of document, 17, 88, 227; capture of, 18; as commander in Kolaga, 84-86, 97, 114, 281n1; courtroom testimony of, 87-88, 91-92, 94, 125, 290n18; discussions with Sukarno, 50-54, 58, 79, 85, 106-7, 218, 274n37, 275nn41-42, 281n68; interrogation of, 68, 301n4; military career of, 86, 133; in prison, 93, 288n40; as putative deputy commander of movement, 17, 47-48, 84, 92; role within the movement, 37-42, 44, 60, 71, 83-86, 142, 222, 271n4; and Sjam, 85, 90-91, 133, 215, 254, 259, 301n4; and Sudisman, 86-87; and Suharto, 11, 113-14, 282n6; as supporter of PKI, 91-92, 116, 134-35, 215; view of Revolution Council, 48, 108-9

Supeno, Bambang (Major), 37-38, 51, 57, 65, 86, 301n4

Suprapto, R., 37, 40, 99, 189

Surabaya, 77, 122, 246

Suryasumpeno (Brigadier General), 54, 242, 302n20

Sutley, Stewart, 263n21

Suwadi, 42

Suwarno (Captain), 271n8

Suwarto (Colonel), 186-87, 196, 295n29

Suwarto, Sampir, 137

Syukur, Abdul, 295n29

Tanjung Karang, 96, 231

Tanjung Priok, 124-25

Tan Ling Djie, 120

Tan Swie Ling, 154

telecommunications building, 35, 40, 42, 57, 103, 173

Tendean, Pierre, 40

territorial warfare doctrine, 184, 186

Tien, Ibu, 77

Time (magazine), 16, 27

Tjugito, 66

Todorov, Tzvetan, 202

Topping, Seymour, 25-26

Tovar, B. Hugh, 194, 296nn45-46, 297n61, 298n77

Treason of the September 30th Movement/ PKI, The (film), 10, 23, 98
Trikora campaign, 77–78
Trouillot, Michel-Ralph, 30
Tuban, 122
Turkey, 142

United Nations, 188
United States government: alleged aid to Darul Islam, 132; Eisenhower administration, 14, 178–82; embassy in Jakarta, 13, 19, 35, 113, 176–77, 184, 189, 191–96, 201, 208–9; and Indonesia's natural resources, 13–15; Johnson administration, 19, 26, 182–83, 192; Joint Chiefs of Staff, 183; Kennedy administration, 182, 184–85; low posture policy, 191–92; National Security Agency (NSA), 195; National Security Council (NSC), 14, 180–82, 184, 190–91; State Department, 15, 19, 178, 185, 191, 193–94; supplied list of PKI names, 298nn75–76; support for Indonesian army, 94, 145, 181–87, 297n61; support for regional rebellions, 179–81; support for Suharto's takeover of power, 15–16, 26–27, 193–97; Truman administration, 14; waiting for pretext, 176–78, 190–93
University of California–Berkeley, 185–86
University of Indonesia, 186
University of Pittsburgh, 189
Untung (Lieutenant Colonel): capture of, 64; as a commander of the palace guard, 38–39, 45, 65, 97; as a core leader of movement, 41, 43, 53, 60, 82–83, 89–90, 92, 113, 117, 142, 203–4, 212, 216–17, 228, 230, 233–34, 236–37, 239–40, 251, 255, 261n5; courtroom testimony of, 65; following Sjam's lead, 92, 115, 144, 213, 250; friendship with Suharto, 62, 75–78, 80, 111, 175, 281n65; interrogation of, 64, 68; military career, 41, 64, 70, 215; on PKI's

role in movement, 65–66; as putative commander of movement, 3, 17, 34–35, 47, 63, 170, 174, 214–15, 219, 259; signing decrees, 48–50; willing to call off movement, 108–9, 115, 218–19, 221
USSR (Union of Soviet Socialist Republics). *See* Soviet Union
Utoyo, Hadiono Kusuma, 123
Utrecht, Ernst, 276n1

van der Kroef, Justus M., 68, 278n22
Vergès, Jacques, 163–64, 293n55
Vietnam, 15–16, 125, 134–35, 179, 264n34

Wahab, Bakri, 55
Wahyudi, 173
Wahyudi (Captain), 144, 250, 283n17
Walujo. *See* Bono
Wandi, 126
Washington Post, 25, 195
Wertheim, W. F., 62, 70, 73, 75–76, 78–79, 81, 137, 203, 220, 280n51, 282n6
West Kalimantan, 84
West New Guinea, 134
West Papua (Irian Jaya), 41, 77, 168, 214, 225
West Sumatra, 179–80
Widjanarko, Bambang, 276n1
Widoyo, 123
Wieringa, Saskia, 103
Wijayasastra, Ruslan, 147, 291n31
Wirahadikusumah, Umar, 56, 171, 211, 215, 221, 229–30, 273n25

Yani, Achmad, 3, 36, 40, 51, 53, 56, 58, 71, 78–79, 93, 99, 110, 114, 129, 155–56, 160, 176–77, 181, 183–84, 186–89, 192, 196, 206, 209–10, 212, 214, 217, 220
Yoga Sugama. *See* Sugama, Yoga
Yogyakarta, 54–55, 76, 80, 105, 120, 122–24, 223, 246, 258–59, 275n45

Žižek, Slavoj, 202

NEW PERSPECTIVES IN
SOUTHEAST ASIAN STUDIES

Pretext for Mass Murder: The September 30th Movement and Suharto's Coup d'État in Indonesia
John Roosa

Viêt Nam: Borderless Histories
Edited by Nhung Tuyet Tran and Anthony J. S. Reid